RESPONSES TO CHANGE
society, culture, and personality

Edited by
George A. DeVos
University of California, Berkeley

D. VAN NOSTRAND COMPANY
New York/Cincinnati/Toronto/London/Melbourne

HN
16
.R47
1976

D. Van Nostrand Company Regional Offices:
New York   Cincinnati   Millbrae

D. Van Nostrand Company International Offices:
London   Toronto   Melbourne

Copyright © 1976 by Litton Educational Publishing, Inc.

Library of Congress Catalog Card Number 74–17617
ISBN: 0–442–22094–4

All rights reserved. No part of this work covered by the copyright
hereon may be reproduced or used in any form or by any means—graphic,
electronic, or mechanical, including photocopying, recording, taping,
or information storage and retrieval systems—without written permission of
the publisher. Manufactured in the United States of America.

Published by D. Van Nostrand Company
450 West 33rd Street, New York, N. Y. 10001

Published simultaneously in Canada by
Van Nostrand Reinhold Ltd.

10   9   8   7   6   5   4   3   2   1

Preface

Responses to Change brings together the thought and research of thirteen eminent scholars concerned with assessing contemporary cultural and social change. In selecting the materials, dividing the book into parts, and providing introductory and concluding statements, the editor has sought to set forth the larger issues with which the articles are concerned, so that students of social change are provided with a framework for understanding and discussing the chapters. The introductions to the parts include definitions and distinctions which are explicitly illustrated in the chapters.

The book uses a number of methodological approaches indicating the range in which social science currently observes and analyzes change in culture, society, and personality. Represented are scholars from the fields of anthropology, sociology, and psychology, who discuss a variety of cultural areas: East and Southeast Asia, the Mediterranean world, the Arab world, India, Africa, Oceania, and the United States. The introductions to the parts, the introductory and concluding statements, and the chapters themselves include discussion of other areas and groups.

Part One focuses on cultural persistence in the face of social change in societies where social structures have changed radically while what is termed the ethos of a culture continues to exhibit some degree of functional autonomy. Part Two examines psychocultural reactions to acculturative forces in large geographic areas united by cultural similarity. Part Three considers the interrelationship of urbanization and adjustment and offers some surprising conclusions. Part Four turns to the problems of minority or subordinate status in situations of change.

The impetus for the present volume came from a conference and subsequent colloquium held in Japan several years ago in conjunction with the VIIIth International Congress of Anthropological and Ethnological Sciences. In addition to the works of some of those who attended the discussions at Hakone, Japan, the editor has been able to include the research reports of others writing about related topics. Edward Bruner, William Caudill, Morton Fried, Nathan Glazer, Theodore Graves, Akira Hoshino, John Gulick, Francis Hsu, Alex Inkeles, Robert Levy, Theodore Schwartz, Takao Sofue, and Melford Spiro attended the original meeting. Kenneth Abbott, Gerald Berreman, Robert LeVine, and Cynthia Nelson provided subsequent chapters for this book.

The exigencies of publishing have compelled the editor to summarize and truncate individual chapters, sacrificing some reporting of research methods in favor of conclusions and interpretations. A number of the topics can profit by expansion. The overall purpose of bringing them together in an integrated fashion could be achieved only by limiting the number of papers devoted to any given problem. There remain a good number of unresolved issues. Here and there the editor was able to preserve some of the stimulating differences of approach and opinion that characterize the contributors. Scholars find it quite possible to argue vehemently, in good will, while preserving basic respect and regard for the integrity of those with whom they differ. The editor is responsible for the final structure of the volume.

We would like to acknowledge our gratitude for the sponsorship afforded by the Institute of International Studies of the University of California and by the Wenner-Gren Foundation of Anthropological Research, which made the conference possible, and the extreme graciousness of Mr. Tominaga and his family, our hosts in Japan, who accommodated us at the Hoen-So Inn in Yumoto near Hakone. Professor Akita Hoshimo acted as our recorder and provided valuable editorial assistance. I am particularly grateful to Theodore Schwartz, who offered a number of suggestions and criticisms that helped to improve the clarity of the introductory and concluding discussions.

George DeVos
Berkeley, California 1975

Contents

Preface   iii

Introduction: Change as a Social Science Problem   1
   George A. DeVos

PART 1. PSYCHOCULTURAL PERSISTENCE AND SOCIAL CHANGE   13

1. Social Change and Cultural Continuity in Modern Japan   18
     William A. Caudill
2. Chinese Culture, Society, and Personality in Transition   45
     Morton H. Fried
3. Culture Change and the Persistence of the Chinese Personality   74
     Kenneth A. Abbott

PART 2. PATTERNS OF CHANGE: THE ETHOS OF AREAL CULTURES   105

4. Patterns of Personality in Africa   112
     Robert A. LeVine
5. The Ethos of Insecurity in Middle Eastern Culture   137
     John Gulick
6. The Cargo Cult: A Melanesian Type-Response to Change   157
     Theodore Schwartz

PART 3. URBANIZATION: ADAPTATION AND ADJUSTMENT   207

7. Personal Adjustment and Modernization   214
     Alex Inkeles and *David H. Smith*
8. Tradition and Modernization in Batak Society   234
     Edward M. Bruner
9. Psychological Problems of Japanese Urbanization   253
     Takao Sofue

PART 4. MINORITY OR SUBORDINATE STATUS AND CHANGE 269

10. American Ethnic Groups: Identity, Cultural Change, and Competence 278
    Nathan Glazer
11. Social Mobility and Change in India's Caste Society 294
    Gerald D. Berreman
12. Social Change and Sexual Identity in Contemporary Egypt 323
    Cynthia Nelson

Conclusion. Responses to Change: Recurrent Patterns 342
George A. DeVos

Index 361

Contributors 373

Introduction: Change as a Social Science Problem

George DeVos

In this volume the editor attempts to synthesize the thought and approach of representative contemporary social scientists—the sociologists, anthropologists, psychologists, and psychiatrists who met together in Hakone, Japan, in 1968. We did not return to the debates which engaged an earlier generation of social scientists. There was, for example, no concern with older problems that engaged anthropologists—whether patterns of change in culture are due to processes whereby there is an external diffusion of traits or to processes that cause periodic internal responses to the stimulus of invention. Those emphasizing *diffusion* suggested that change most often comes about by borrowing or "acculturation." They suggested that most human invention occurs once and spreads outward from its point of origin. Those emphasizing *independent invention* contended that conditions arise in which innovations of a material nature—such as the wheel—or of a conceptual nature—such as the calendar—have been invented independently many times in human evolution. Invasion and economic surplus have led to the formation of states with hierarchal social organizations.

Our purpose for meeting at Hakone to discuss cultural responses to change was not to arrive at a single, overarching explanatory principle. In the formulation of general theory, many determinants must be considered. Yet even today, much debate involves adherence to the superiority of one explanatory approach over another. At Hakone partisanship was not our purpose. We did seek to emphasize the importance, even the necessity, of a variety of approaches, including a psychological one. The express emphasis in this volume on psychological processes is not to minimize other possible approaches, but to point up issues that are sometimes ignored in social theory. The need to approach change "psychoculturally" is especially apparent to those represented in our volume who have concerned themselves in depth with processes of acculturation occurring in the individuals they have contacted personally in a number of different present-day cultures.

ACCULTURATION IN THE INDIVIDUAL AND IN SOCIETY

It is not surprising that social scientists today have shifted their emphasis from evolutionary concerns toward a more systematic and intense study of ongoing change within both simple and complex contemporary cultures. In previous work anthropologists frequently, in describing present or former cultures, have attempted to arrive at a picture of society that suggests stability in organization rather than change. If one considers only a recreated past, the idea that preliterate groups, unlike Western literate groups, do not change frequently appears to be supported. Assumptions about the stability of more technologically simple groups can easily be maintained if the groups' continuing history is ignored, and the people contacted are not overtly conscious that the behavior of their group has changed. The group may, indeed, appear to live life according to a pattern which has remained the same for many centuries. This may not be true. Today, however, when even the most remote peoples have been in contact with modern technology, there are very few groups which can maintain the illusion that their culture has not been changed, or at least been influenced, by the cultures of others. Members of nearly all extant cultures are self-consciously aware that contacts with the outside are causing them to change and to adapt to new possibilities, that is, to "acculturate."

As we use it in this book, *acculturation* is the process of diffusion—the spread of traits from one group to another—but so speeded up that one can observe and analyze the mechanisms determining change operating within given individuals. The influence of one group on another and the subsequent impact of change on the society can be directly observed in group social adaptation; change also influences the internal psychological processes which determine personality. Today, social science describes and records not only the group's *social behavior,* but also the *subjective experiences* of individuals within the group. It examines the psychological effects of the process of rapid culture change.

In the acculturative situation, the individual is presented with many possible new ways of behaving and perceiving, ways which may be quite different from those dictated by his culture's traditional norms and beliefs. Often, however, the social scientist can only observe the change in traits, such as the substitution of handshaking for elaborate formal greeting ceremonies, or in artifacts, such as the change from traditional forms of music-making to radio-listening. It is more difficult to observe the mediating psychodynamic processes which determine the relative ease or difficulty or the degree of selectivity involved when an individual or group is deciding what to accept or reject during the process of acculturation. That is, it is more difficult to know what the individual has "felt like" when he has given up, say, formal greetings and taken up handshaking and to know how painful the change has been for him or her.

The term *acculturation* refers to taking on from another culture both material traits and ways of interacting socially. A person acculturates or becomes acculturated when he borrows behavior characteristic of another culture. Acculturation implies that the borrowing groups' members are conscious of what is taking place, and further, that they have a conscious position about the advisability of change. It further implies that, in addition to conscious awareness, there are unconscious social-structural and personality variables that facilitate or impede both desired and undesired changes.

In psychocultural analysis, one studies acculturative behavior on three levels. The first is the *emic* level, the analysis of the human experience of a culture through the language and the perceptions shared by the participants themselves. There are also *etic* levels of analysis, understanding a culture in terms of and from the perspective of an outside observer. There are two kinds of etic analysis: analysis of social-structural dynamics and analysis of the unconscious psychological processes that affect the pattern of acculturation. These three levels are vantage points from which to observe the specifics of any particular patterning of acculturation in a given group.

In acculturation the stimulus to change comes from outside the group. In this sense, most culture change is acculturative. Nevertheless, no culture is without some form of indigenous, internally stimulated innovation. In this volume, however, we will focus primarily on what happens to groups experiencing change from outside sources.

Acculturation and Ethnic Identity

In situations of gradual culture contact, one can envision a slow diffusion of traits between two cultures over generations; one group eventually is assimilated into the culture of another without much individual awareness. But acculturation is a more rapid process, and it influences and modifies the sense of ethnic identity of groups and of the individuals within a group (DeVos and Romanucci-Ross 1975). In the situations described in this volume the group is aware that the acculturative process they are undergoing is related to a collective sense of group identity, and that it can challenge or alter that collective sense.

Two cultures that are in contact rarely acculturate reciprocally. More often, the politically subordinate or technologically inferior group adapts culture traits from the dominant group. Status enhancement is usually the inducement to accept new ideas or artifacts. Members of a group which is deemed "inferior" feel that by taking on the characteristics of a "superior" group they will, in turn, also become superior and receive the same respect that is granted to members of the superior group. In more evenly balanced situations, where neither group is clearly "superior," there may be a stand-off in the mutual adoption of traits, allowing each group to retain its self-conscious integrity.

The consideration of how status influences acculturation brings up vital questions with psychocultural ramifications: What is the relationship between processes of acculturation and the formation of social self-identity among members of donor and recipient groups in situations of contact? Ethnic identity is a crucial differentiator determining the modes of social adaptation and personal adjustment in a number of acculturative situations. How identity problems relate to acculturation is a recurrent subject touched upon in a number of different contexts in this volume.

THE DISTINCTION BETWEEN ADJUSTMENT AND ADAPTATION

For the most part "adjustment" and "adaptation" are loosely used as equivalent terms throughout the social sciences. They can refer both to the internal structures of personality and to processes of human communication and interaction that occur in social role relationships. More generally, they are used interchangeably as concepts of man's response to his environment. Their negative converses, maladjustment and maladaptation, can refer to some internal deficiency, to an incapacity for response in an individual, or to a response that is inadequate for physical or psychological survival.

The term *adjustment,* as used in this volume, refers to an ideal progression of maturation which is potential for all human beings. It is not culturally or situationally relative, but it is important to remember that the realization of this adjustment may be culturally fostered or deformed.

It is often said today that to be "well adjusted" in a "bad environment" could be pathological. This is not the proper use of the term adjustment in the sense intended here. Indeed, people can be deformed developmentally or by their culture in such a way that they adapt well to situations of human brutality. One cannot assume that they are at the same time internally well adjusted in the psychodynamic sense. They will be, in the sense we use the word here, much more likely to be maladjusted. An internally well adjusted person may survive in or adapt to a bad environment; however, one assumes he will attempt to effect changes in the environment. In the same situation a person who is internally maladjusted may be too rigid and poorly equipped to bring about ameliorative change. Adjustment, therefore, refers to maturational or developmental variables rather than to behavioral maneuvers in a social context. It is most helpful to maintain a clear distinction between the internal structuring of personality related to the concept of adjustment and those social, behavioral responses which can be seen as adaptive or maladaptive to the individual within his social nexus. Adjustment refers to personality; adaptation, to social structure.

This distinction was elucidated by Clyde Kluckhohn in his publication on Navaho witchcraft (1944). Kluckhohn distinguished between adaptation, which he defined as the relationship of the individual to society, and adjustment, the operation of the personality variables underlying behavior. Witchcraft, according to Kluckhohn, was functionally adaptive in deflecting aggressive feelings out of the group onto more distant outsiders. At the same time, witchcraft beliefs were internally adjustive for the individual who held them in that they acted as an outlet for aggressions which could otherwise have been disruptive of his personality. These adaptive and adjustive witchcraft functions could also be seen as relatively maladaptive to the social group in that a more well adapted group would not have needed to deflect aggressive feelings, or they could be seen as evidence of the relative maladjustment in one person compared with another person, who manifested less personal need to have recourse to witchcraft, because he could handle relationships more directly.

Kluckhohn's use of adjustment and adaptation was ahistorical: that is, he investigated a relatively static society in which no social-structural change was occurring. But we are concerned in this book on responses to change with a further application of these terms—with the adaptive and adjustive requirements in the changing situation of acculturation. In this type of situation, historical change itself can cause new external-adaptive institutions to come into being and can make new demands of change on the internal-adjustive mechanisms.

When investigators are attempting to determine whether specific changes are adaptive or maladaptive, they must examine several factors. The investigator is presented with a problem like the traditional psychiatric problem of distinguishing between structural-organic problems and functional-adjustment problems. For example, if his patient's psychiatric problem is alcoholism, the psychiatrist must first determine if the patient's individual bodily chemistry is affected abnormally by alcohol, and thus primarily a structural-organic problem, or if the alcoholism is a personality problem, indicating a maladjustive response to such pressures as loss of a job or marital tensions.

The social psychiatrist has a different, but related, problem. His task is not so much to determine the source of relatively debilitating or painful personal adjustments or maladjustments, but to determine whether these adjustments are socially adaptive or maladaptive *within a given cultural context*. In Japan, for example, a heavy drinker may continue working well on the job and thus evidence no social alcoholic maladaptation.

Psychiatrists and psychologists are primarily interested in mental health. When most Western psychiatrists and psychologists use the term "mental health," they are referring to mechanisms of psychological adjustment viewed from within Western culture. Their definitions of mental health reflect a consensus about what constitutes normal, "healthy," behavior within a particular cultural value system. This cultural orientation can result in ethnocentric value judgments governing the diagnosis and treatment of psychiatric illness. Thus within the Western cultural context, such practices as the lengthy swaddling or late breastfeeding of young children might be considered maladaptive, a possible sign of the mother's mental disorder and liable also to be detrimental to the child's development. However, the same behavior, viewed in a different cultural context, might be considered highly adaptive, in that it is seen as helping to protect the infant from the high risk of illness or accident. A Western psychiatrist who did not take the cultural context into consideration might be inclined to describe the Japanese practice of a child's sleeping in its parents' bed as injurious to mental health; such a culturally centered judgment would be a mistake.

Social scientists, in turn, focus primarily on patterns of social adaptation; that is, whether the individual remains in, or how he remains, or how he is brought into, or excluded from, social participation. They may tend to consider concern with personality or problems of adjustment extraneous, and thus be subject from the other side to the same kind of errors in judgment which characterized our hypothetical Western psychiatrist.

Caudill's (1959) work suggests that comprehension of the working relationship among anthropology, sociology, and psychology requires that we include culture as a crucial concept, along with the concepts of personality structure or personality functioning or social structure and social organization, if we are to understand the motivations of human behavior. He further cautions that we must avoid the tendency to reduce our explanation of behavior solely to social structural, or cultural, or personality theories. We must understand behavior as reflecting the interactive nature of culture, society, and personality, if we are to understand it fully.

A psychologist's knowledge of malfunctioning by itself—when malfunction is not based on an organic problem—may not help in the treatment of problem behavior, unless therapist and patient share the same beliefs and symbol systems in treatment. To this degree, treatment is irreducibly symbolic, in the literal sense of the word. For example, a Japanese patient may believe that he must honor his parents in certain ways and feel guilt for not having done so. If he goes to relieve his feeling of guilt to an American psychologist who thinks that belief in family responsibility to the point of self-sacrifice is in itself a sign of ill health, then the psychologist will not be able to help the Japanese unless and until there is more comprehension of the Japanese culture's family system. What we earlier defined as emic understanding is necessary to communication, regardless of one's scientific, etic (external) view of either social structure or personality adjustment. Some social or transcultural psychiatrists, in extending or reinterpreting the causes of mental health or illness have, therefore, found it necessary to differentiate between a culture's definitions of healthy behavior and their own imposed external concepts. If no attention is paid to indigenous perceptions of the meaning of particular forms of mental illness— or indeed, even to the perception of healthy behavior—within a culture, there can be no therapeutic process. An American Indian might more readily be helped by a medicine man who shares his own beliefs, than by a psychiatrist insensitive to the Indian's culture.

Similarly, for the social scientist, who often notes what might be considered in some settings as deviant behavior, it is essential to determine whether behavior is or is not integrative and socially adaptive within its own cultural setting. The cultural definitions given the behavior can alter its meaning for the individual, allowing him to remain socially integrated within his group. For example, Europeans now define behavior as hysteric or neurotic which was emically defined in a previous age as saintly or religious.

Certain forms of internal maladjustment in some cultural contexts may be interpreted not as requiring treatment but as signs that the individual has potential for a special vocation, such as that of shaman. A special way of life may be proposed for the sufferer, who can then adapt socially and relieve his internal pressures. Thus, apparently deviant behavior may become controllable, even socially useful. The personality structure may remain the same, but a positive social climate can foster adaptation rather than alienation.

Whether we are examining individual behavior from two points of view or similar behavior by different individuals in different contexts, the relationship between adaptation and adjustment is complex. In Chapter 6, Theodore Schwartz introduces his innovative concept, "pathomimetic behavior." This is a form of socially adaptive behavior in which, for purposes of strengthening group and individual religious belief, there is unconscious as well as conscious mimicry of forms of behavior which might in other circumstances indicate maladjustment or organic pathology. A shaman may exhibit his "possession" in seizures like those of epileptics. In native medicine, epileptic seizure is usually explained as the intrusion of an alien force, often a deity, into the body. In the case of the true epileptic, the behavior is maladjustive in the personality structure sense. Schwartz's position is that in the Melanesian shaman, whatever his state of consciousness or self-hypnosis, the behavior is not due to an underlying structural problem. Shamen manufacture their seizures at will and use them adaptively as part of religious ecstasy. In this pathomimetic behavior, the possessed individuals have somehow learned to manifest convulsions as a positive sign that a spirit has entered their bodies, so that communication with the supernatural becomes possible.

We shall try in this volume to distinguish between adjustive or maladjustive consequences of societal and cultural change (which influence the deeper integrative structure of personality organization) and those behavioral responses which are socially adaptive or maladaptive.

In many instances, problems of maladjustment only become clear when their maladaptive consequences are revealed. In other instances, the witnessed maladaptation is situational, due to ignorance of alternatives and not to personality rigidities. In the latter case, the problems may be readily resolved by altered circumstances, as is the case when severe political oppression causes temporary difficulty for a given people. In other cases (like that of the Arab world discussed by Gulick and by Nelson in this book) external political or social circumstances are made more difficult through the influence of negative, rigid adjustment patterns of some individuals in the culture itself. These negative patterns can be the result of childhood socialization which is reinforced in adult roles.

THE DISTINCTION BETWEEN CULTURE CHANGE AND SOCIAL CHANGE

Like adjustment and adaptation, "culture change" and "social change" are often used almost interchangeably in sociological and anthropological literature. In this volume, we try to make an explicit differentiation between these two concepts. *Social change* has been defined by Wilbert E. Moore as a change in human behavior resulting from changes in one or several of man's social institutions. Moore says, "Social change is the significant alteration of the social structures and manifestations of such structures embodied in norms (rules of conduct), values, and cultural products and symbols" (Moore 1968, p. 366). Social changes are changes in social behavior brought about by technological innovation, conquest, governmental reorganization, etc. The concept of *culture,* for him, is reserved for such traditional patterns as language, dress, and formal religious systems. Some of these patterns have high degrees of functional autonomy that may assure their persistence in spite of radical changes elsewhere in the social structure. For example, a country may build modern factories, but the people who work in those factories may continue to wear traditional dress and to worship in traditional ways.

Some social scientists, however, think that social structures are, in effect, cultural structures that govern the social arrangements and normative role expectations among groups and individuals. Such arrangements are cultural artifacts or institutions. All such institutions or cultural structures have social aspects in that they involve interpersonal and intergroup relations. It is useful to talk about social structure and social change as foci for study as long as these are not set in opposition to culture and culture change of which they are a part.

There are obvious problems in maintaining a logical exclusiveness between the concepts of culture and society. They tend to overlap, for instance, when one conceptualizes the family as a basic social institution within Moore's definition. Yet we know that socialization within the family can continue to pass on cultural traditions in spite of radical shifts in political and social organization that alter the structure of society. These patterned sets of behavior can persist in spite of deliberate attempts at change in some instances, while in other instances acculturation can occur in one generation causing radical shifts in child rearing.

We can maintain at least a partial distinction between social change and culture change in that we can distinguish a unique cultural "ethos" persisting in two different cultures that have modernized in quite similar ways. The *ethos* of a culture is the characteristic spirit or prevalent tone or sentiment of a people, institution, or system. As introduced by Gregory Bateson (1936) into anthropological terminology, ethos is, in effect, the emotional patterns reflected in cultural behavior. In situations of change, patternings in the emotional tone or implicit feelings underlying behavior may persist in spite of revision of legal or other externally sanctioned behavioral forms. Business executives from France, England, and the United States may, for example, all work in Western-style industries, wear similar clothes, drive similar cars, play golf, have cocktails at six, send their children to similar kinds of schools, and still be distinctly identifiable as French, English, or American because of the persisting patterns of emotional relationships found in their primary families or in their relations to women generally. This difference in emotional tone is even more evident in comparing Japanese business executives to their American or European counterparts.

Caudill, in describing Japan in Chapter 1, delineates this distinction between cultural persistence in continuing ethnological relationships, such as the family, and social change related to law and technology. He suggests we should distinguish between society and culture. A converse point of view is that both cultural persistence and social change are relative and partial. That social change *is* cultural change in some aspects of a culture can be compatible with the persistence of other aspects of the culture.

Caudill's absolute distinction between cultural persistence and social change ultimately breaks down; yet we can find it of value in examining particular processes occurring in a given society. When the resistance to change in the emotional patterns or "ethos" of a culture conflicts with rapid changes in social structure, it produces many of the observable tensions and disequilibria in all areas of the world. In many societies, the socialization of the young does not prepare them for the rapid changes they will experience in adult roles.

RESPONSES TO CHANGE

Everywhere change has become central to people's awareness: technological change; the continual appearance of innovative social behavior, both from within the culture and outside it; demographic change; rapid ecological change; change induced by internal incongruities in economic and political patterns and by conflicting ideologies. In previous epochs, most of the world's people were only dimly aware that forces such as these were inducing changes that influenced their society and, in turn, their individual lives. But people now have a new sense of history marked by a consciousness of change. The chapters which follow examine societies' responses to change.

In this text, consideration of change is organized around four major recurring issues:

The articles in Part One focus on the interplay of cultural persistence and social change. The studies of Chinese and Japanese cultures and societies illustrate how some social structures may have changed radically in these ancient, literate, politically united cultures, while the ethos of their peoples continues to exhibit some degree of functional autonomy.

Part Two examines psychocultural reactions to acculturative forces in large geographic areas united by cultural similarity rather than by political or social cohesion. In these chapters, an areal culture concept is helpful in understanding the persistent similarities of responses to change in the culturally related, but politically or socially isolated, geographic areas of black Africa, the Arab world, and the Pacific region of Melanesian Oceania.

The chapters in Part Three focus on the interrelationship of urbanization and psychocultural patterns of adjustment and adaptation. Surprisingly, the authors of these chapters find that, contrary to much that is implied in American sociological theory, urbanization very often relieves stress more than it induces stress for those who migrate to the city.

The papers in Part Four examine problems of minority or subordinate status in acculturation and change. In this last section, we also examine different responses to change found in some given ethnic groups, classes, castes, or sexual segments of complex cultures. Change does not affect all social segments at the same rate or in the same way. Change can therefore lead to conflict and a need to realign the various parts of complex societies—be they economic, ethnic, or sexual.

REFERENCES

Bateson, G. 1936. *Naven.* London: Cambridge University Press.
DeVos, G. and Romanucci-Ross, L. 1975. *Ethnic Identity.* Palo Alto: Mayfield Publications.
Kluckhohn, C. 1944. *Navaho Witchcraft.* Boston: Beacon Press.
Moore, W. 1968. *International Encyclopedia of Social Sciences,* vol. 14. New York: Macmillan.

PART 1

Psychocultural Persistence and Social Change

In this first series of contributions, we examine several theoretical approaches to persistence and change specifically within the Chinese and Japanese cultures, which have been unified politically and socially for most of the last thousand years.

CULTURE CONTINUITIES DESPITE MODERNIZATION

In Chapter 1, "Cultural Continuity in Modern Japan," William Caudill discusses changes occurring with modernization in Japan and spells out a distinction between social structure and culture. During the conference preceding this publication, Theodore Schwartz denied this distinction and suggested that the concept of culture itself is sufficient. He thinks Caudill's usage of social structure only singles out some types of social structure as not changing as rapidly as others. Role systems or family structure, according to Schwartz, should be seen as parts of a social structure which are less quickly affected by change. What is called culture and social structure for Schwartz are basically two sides of the same coin. With technology, the development of such aspects of society as a social class system has inevitable effects upon the living styles of people within these various social segments. Schwartz would rather, therefore, suggest in his terminology that "operative" culture and society can be changed without causing a consequent immediate change in "intimate" society and culture. Both Schwartz and Caudill agree, however, that the *ethos*—the emotional, interpersonal climate of a culture—can persist in spite of rapid, large-scale changes brought about by industrialization and the migration of populations into the urban environment. Their disagreement is terminological, not operational.

It might help in resolving the difference between Schwartz and Caudill to consider that the terms culture and social structure *do* in fact suggest differences in approach to be found among social scientists. Caudill emphasizes that those who use the term "social structure" prefer an ahistorical, functional approach in perceiving the society; in effect, a form of structural-functional analysis. This point of view de-emphasizes the effects of specific historical change and concentrates on the present-day operations of institutions within the society. In contrast with this approach, those who use the concept of "culture" emphasize the influence of historical continuity. They think that deposited in the layered behavior of individuals, without their conscious awareness, are residual manifestations of social-structural interactions of the past, as well as behavior determined by the present structures of society. "Culture" refers, then, to the continuity of learned forms of behavior inherited from the unique histories of particular peoples, as well as to ongoing functions.

One might make an analogy to two approaches to personality found in psychology. There are personality theorists, principally within the Gestalt school, who say that one can understand personality, without going into the individual's history simply by an acute observation of personality functioning in the present. The psychoanalytic school, on the other hand, stresses that personality is a product of the past experience of the individual at various developmental stages, and thus, that all of his past experience is relevant to understanding the individual's present situation. In terms of culture, therefore, one would argue that particular cultural traditions have within themselves manifestations of previous stages of technology, religion, and modalities of social interaction, and, furthermore, that these past events color the perceptions of individuals presently being socialized within a given cultural situation.

What Caudill's chapter indicates is the persistence of what may be termed Japanese national character in spite of the radical changes occurring with modernization. He also points out that the Japanese attempted deliberately and self-consciously, for some period at least, to retard some forms of social change while at the same time they permitted an advanced technological change. By social change, Caudill refers here to the maintenance of legal institutions and patterns of sanctioning of ways of behavior principally in relation to family structure.

In Japan today, even with the legal impediments to social change removed, one still notices the persistence of cultural patterns that have psychological viability such as arranged marriage, and social patterns such as the force of hierarchical organization in industry. One may argue with the terms used, but the differential rates of change in some features of Japanese culture, compared with persistences in others, are very well demonstrated in Caudill's chapter.

Not raised in any of our papers, unfortunately, is a discussion of the complex interaction of external social sanctions and the earlier internalization of social sanctions in rapidly changing cultures. Caudill's paper only alludes to such problems.

COMPLEXITY AND VARIABILITY VERSUS PERSONALITY SIMILARITIES

Morton Fried takes on the recognizably impossible task of considering complexities of social and cultural change in China. The total legal restructuring of Chinese society in the post-Communist period raises the basic questions of the effect of radical social change on the persistence of psychocultural traditions. Fried himself, not a specialist in the field of culture and personality, brings to his approach a healthy skepticism concerning the various previous attempts made to delineate a unitary Chinese national character. His own concentration has been on the interrelationship of social and political structures within Chinese society. He is not hostile to the concepts of psychological anthropology, but rather offers us a challenging skepticism as to what has been already accomplished. He acknowledges the need for further research rather than deriding its objectives. He acknowledges that there are uniquely "Chinese" psychological ideas to be found pervading Chinese thought and action, while he recognizes also the difficulties inherent in epitomizing the main features of such a highly complex culture as the Chinese; he recognizes there are thematic persistences carrying on through time and history. He finds equally that there are some generalized patterns that are seemingly related to personality modalities underlying Chinese behavior.

That there are considerable differences between the Chinese and the Japanese is quickly observable by anyone coming in contact with them. The reason for such differences has been explored in part by Francis Hsu in some of his writings.[1] Other issues, however, have not been explored in a way that is satisfying and so need further explicit detailed delineation. Distinctions between Chinese and non-Chinese, for example, are

---

[1]Hsu, Francis L. K., *Clan, Caste and Club*, Princeton, N.J.: Van Nostrand, 1963; "Eros, Affect, and Pao" in Francis Hsu (ed.), *Kinship and Culture,* Chicago: Aldine Publishing Co., 1971; *Under the Ancestor's Shadow,* New York: Columbia University Press, 1948; "Chinese Kinship and Chinese Behavior" in Ping-ti Ho and Tang Tsou (eds.), *China in Crisis: China's Heritage and the Communist Political System,* Chicago: University of Chicago Press, 1968.

not an issue in Chinese thought; not that they do not exist, but they are taken for granted in a way quite different from that experienced by the Japanese in thinking about foreigners.

Fried points out that to say something about adaptation or adjustment for an entire people without regard to regional and intragroup structural differences vastly oversimplifies. He stresses that social class in China has been an important variable from the past into the present, and that we should not impute generalizations about the gentry to the vast number of Chinese peasants. Fried's paper includes a brief but cogent consideration of the modern political scene and the relationship of cultural continuity and psychological factors to the Chinese "cultural revolution."

In Chapter 3, "Persistence of Chinese Personality at Home and Abroad," we reverse the approach to the question of adaptation and adjustment within changing Chinese society and start out empirically by examining the results of a test battery collected from overseas Chinese in San Francisco and in Taipei. This chapter by Kenneth Abbott complements Morton Fried's. It offers concrete test data which affirm the highly similar nature of Chinese responses from two such dissimilar migrant Chinese groups as the Cantonese of San Francisco and the Fukienese of Taipei. The San Franciscan Chinese are a small minority who have only recently immigrated to the United States, but the Taiwanese are a majority group who have been on the island for three hundred years. The two migrant groups also found very different political and linguistic systems. Thus, they have integrated very differently into their host cultures, aboriginal Taiwan and industrialized America. Yet even in these two very different social climates their test responses to items of a social-interactional nature remain dramatically similar.

Abbott attempts to single out some of the key internal adjustive mechanisms common to many Chinese. He emphasizes above all *intragroup* dependency and self-restraint. Secondly, associated with a strong tendency toward maintaining harmony in human and natural functioning, is a basic inclination to see phenomena as wholes rather than in constituent parts. Abbott then suggests that certain key defense mechanisms tend to characterize the Chinese response to the environment. What Western psychologists identify as projection and displacement are very common among the Chinese, as among other peoples. One sees especially in Chinese women, according to Abbott's data, a considerable amount of somatization, the body becoming the focus of displacements of interpersonal tensions and difficulties.

Abbott cautions that interpretations of Chinese character which cite passivity and dependence as characteristic of the Chinese are made from a Western viewpoint; for the Chinese themselves, such socialization is adaptive to the cultural imperatives to be harmonious and collectivistic in behavior. Mechanisms which emphasize "passivity" and "dependency" are not only adjustive within the Chinese personality system, but are socially adaptive to a society that emphasizes harmony and collectivity of behavior. Relative dominance or an individualistic achievement orientation are undesirable for an individual Chinese who must remain concerned with the opinions of others and equal sensitivity to social relations and group norms.

Chapter 1

Social Change and Cultural Continuity in Modern Japan

William A. Caudill*

In this chapter I shall discuss the effects of social and cultural change on psychological adjustment and then apply that discussion to modern Japan. The first part of this paper sharpens the distinction between the concepts of social structure and culture and considers the meaning of these concepts for understanding the behavior of people in countries which are undergoing, or already have achieved, what is currently called modernization. The next task of the chapter is more difficult: the literature on Japan, especially since the end of World War II, is fairly adequate in its description of personality, social structure, and culture, but these concepts are usually considered singly rather than treated in interaction, and it is even less usual that any of them is viewed within a context of change over time. The second part of the paper, therefore, is based on a review of literature written in the last one hundred years on the topic of Japanese national character, and I attempt to summarize the psychological and behavioral characteristics of Japanese people that seem to me to have persisted from the past and that remain viable in modern Japa-

---

*William A. Caudill was on the staff of the National Institute of Health at the time of his death. This paper was extracted from a longer one presented at the Hakone symposium. It was published after Caudill's death in *Ethos* 1 (2). His widow kindly permitted the editors of *Ethos* and of this volume to make such alteration and selection of his essay as were necessary to bring the material into conformity with publication requirements. We sincerely hope and believe that in this editorial process we have done no violence to Caudill's intent.

nese life. These characteristics as reported in the literature tend to have a "timeless" quality. In the third part of the chapter I attempt to give them some historical depth and to view them within the context of recent change in Japan. The third part of this chapter is meant to be suggestive of leads for research that needs to be done in the near future.

OVERVIEW

A Westerner coming to Japan, particularly if he enters the country through Haneda Airport and is plunged into the gigantic city of Tokyo, is immediately struck with the tremendous vitality and modernity of Japan today, with the dense mass of modern buildings and elevated highways, with the abundance of industrial and consumer goods, and with the efficient and complex management of business and government. Such a visitor would be ill-advised, however, to conclude quickly that Tokyo "is just like New York" or that "there is nothing left of the older Japan."

As soon as a Western foreigner (a *gaijin*) stops being a tourist and tries to settle down to work in the country, he will begin to find that the physical arrangements of life, the paths toward meeting people important for him, interpersonal relations in general, and many aspects of behavior and emotional response are bewildering and sometimes incomprehensible. He is likely to feel physically crowded when walking in the central area of the city, riding on public transportation, or driving, and when servants intrude into what he feels to be his private space. He will probably come to feel that he can never be alone, often not even in the bedroom or the bath. This feeling comes not so much from a high density of people as from differences between the definition and meaning of comfortable spatial arrangements in Japanese and Western culture (see Hall 1968). He is also likely to find that he cannot, with any real degree of success, approach people directly in order to further his work; rather, it will be necessary to find and make skillful use of a complex network of other persons who will introduce him to those he wishes to reach. Once engaged in such a network he will have to learn that he is no longer entirely a free agent and that he has incurred a finely graded set of personal obligations that must be repaid if his work is to go forward smoothly. Relations that he initially interpreted as warm and friendly may well turn out later not to be so, and requests for direct answers to questions may be met with what he experiences as evasiveness and withdrawal. If after several months, in frustration, he says to himself, "I can't understand these people," then he will be on the way to recognizing that the very modern society in which he is attempting to work operates in terms of a culture with which he is most unfamiliar.

The initial difficulties of such a foreigner in Tokyo are not due to some inherently mysterious quality in Japanese life. A foreigner trying to work for the first time in New York, Rome, or Rio de Janeiro would be likely to encounter difficulties equal in intensity though varying in content. All of these cities are similarly modern, but each also has developed within a distinctive culture, and in this sense they are different.

This chapter, then, attempts to sort out the behavioral and psychological implications of the relations of tradition and modernity as these occur in general in any country, and to examine in particular the nature of these relations in Japan. Most of the writers referred to later in this paper pose this problem in one way or another. The literature is frequently confusing in that there are those who say there is nothing of the old Japan left and others who say there is quite a lot remaining.

Some of the confusion in the literature on modernization and its effects stems from an insufficiently long historical perspective on human behavior. For millions of years man lived as a hunter in simple societies, and this way of life must have had a profound effect on the development of the human personality (see Lorenz 1963; and also, Freud 1930; Norbeck, Price-Williams and McCord 1968). About 10,000 years ago, with the advent of agricultural life, societies became more complex and differentiated, and there was a development of distinctive cultural traditions that often persisted over several thousand years. In these long-enduring traditional societies there probably was a somewhat greater integration of social structure, culture, and psychological adjustment than in modern societies. I say "somewhat greater integration" advisedly because such integration is never complete, and there always is considerable variation in social and cultural expectations and psychological adjustment in any society at any point in time. In a world-wide sense, it is only in the last five hundred years—which is quite recently in terms of human history—that people living in these various traditional societies have been in meaningful contact. And it is merely in the last one hundred years, with the rapid development and application of scientific knowledge, that we have spoken about "modern" societies.

The application of scientific knowledge in modern life has had a profound effect upon social structure, although probably more so in the more public (occupational, political, etc.) than in the more private (familial, religious, etc.) aspects of living. Thus, modern social structure and traditional culture may be in some conflict, but underneath people are, psychologically, much as they have always been. I think we tend to overrate the intensity of the effect of modernization upon psychological adjustment and personality characteristics (in this regard, see Chapter 7).

By modernization we mean the similar changes in occupational and industrial structure which accompany technological advancement. This process usually stratifies a society into social classes (or levels of responsibility) closely tied to position in the occupational structure. In this sense, middle-class managerial personnel in England and France may have more in common than either group has with working-class machine operators in their own country. Yet such Englishmen and Frenchmen are different in their approach to work, politics, family life, or sexual activity. They are different in those historically derived and culturally patterned ways of thinking, feeling, and behaving that are passed on, often unknowingly, from one generation to the next and that are shared in considerable part by all members of a society. In short, they are different in ethos. Each of these dimensions—position in modern social structure, and continuity of historical culture—exerts a relatively independent influence on human behavior, and both dimensions need to be considered simultaneously in the investigation of the psychological characteristics of a people.

Social Change and Cultural Change

There is a fairly common tendency in scientific writing to blur the distinction between social and cultural dimensions of behavior by the use of such combined terms as "sociocultural." Anthropologists often subsume one dimension under the other by thinking of social structure solely as a part of culture; sociologists, on the other hand, frequently ignore the cultural dimension by concentrating on and emphasizing the effect of position on the social structure.

Many persons, of course, have pointed to the persistence of older cultural traits in a situation of social change. My contribution is to stress the relative separateness of these two dimensions of human life: considerable change can take place in the social dimension with the result that several countries do indeed come to be alike in important ways, while at the same time cultural differences persist, and each country remains quite distinctive.

My position differs somewhat from several others that have been taken in the literature. Obviously, the simple-minded position that a country becomes just like another country is never true. A more sophisticated approach, however, takes the position that as a country adopts Western ways of doing things, and develops a social structure that is congruent with the demands of modern technology, then that country does become more like the West. A good illustration of this tendency for countries to become alike is the similarity in the ratings of occupational prestige in modern countries (see Inkeles and Rossi 1956; Hodge, Treiman, and Rossi 1966; Ramsey and Smith 1960). There is considerable merit in such a position if it does not, at the same time, consider that the older culture is now merely of antiquated interest and will quickly waste away. Another position in the current literature is that modernization takes its own particular form in each country—as, for example, in the contrasts drawn by

Bendix (1967) between England, Germany, and Japan. This position has great merit, but it does tend to underplay the similarities brought about by the process of modernization.

Gusfield's (1967) position in an article on "Tradition and Modernity: Misplaced Polarities in the Study of Social Change" is close to that taken in this paper. He says: "The capacity of old and new cultures and structures to exist without conflict and even with mutual adaptations is a frequent phenomenon of social change; the old is not necessarily *replaced* by the new. . . . To conclude, the often too common practice of pitting tradition and modernity against each other as paired opposites tends to overlook the mixtures and blends which reality displays" (Gusfield 1967: 354, 362; see also, Eisenstadt 1964; Roos and Hadar 1968).

In this paper, I consider modern social structure and historically derived culture as separate systems or dimensions of human life, each dimension having a considerable effect on human behavior. In general, I think modern social structure produces similarities in behavior when one country is compared with another, but equally I think historically derived culture produces differences in behavior in the several countries. Empirically, the question boils down to the amount of variance accounted for by each of these independent variables in samples of human behavior.

There is considerable evidence in the literature to support this approach. For example, in a comparative study in Italy and the United States of parents' values concerning their children's behavior, Pearlin and Kohn (1966) demonstrate that middle-class parents in both countries are more likely to value the child's self-direction, and working-class parents in both countries place a greater emphasis on the child's conformity to external proscription. Equally, they show that *regardless of social class*, American parents are more likely than Italian parents to value happiness, popularity, and consideration, while Italian parents more than American parents tend to value manners, obedience, and seriousness. Thus, from the same body of data, we can see similarities in the social classes and differences in the cultures of the two countries.

Another example, in this case internal to a country but seen across time, comes from Japan. The social structure of Japan has certainly changed markedly since the Japanese adopted the Gregorian calendar in 1872. Yet there was a dramatic decrease in the birth rate in 1906 and in 1966 compared with that in contiguous years in both instances (see Azumi 1968). Each of these years marks the beginning of a cycle of the old lunar-solar calendar when, once in sixty years, the sign of the fire and the horse are in conjunction, and girls born in such a year (so the belief goes) will be of harsh temperament and invite misfortune. To avoid this, the Japanese apparently falsified the registration of the year of birth at the start of the earlier cycle and actually restricted the number of births at the start of the current cycle. The motivation, however, was the same in both instances, thus linking the feelings of parents across three generations of time and over the even wider gulf of two world wars and fantastic scientific progress and social change.

Over the years, George DeVos and I, both jointly and individually, in a series of essays and research reports dealing with Japanese Americans and Japanese in Japan, have argued for the separate consideration of the effects of modern social structure and historical culture on psychological adjustment (see Caudill and DeVos 1956; Caudill 1958; DeVos 1968). Thus, from work with Japanese Americans in Chicago in the late 1940s, it is clear that the Nisei in their overt behavior and achievement had successfully moved into the middle-class level of the general occupational structure, but in a more covert sense their values and personality characteristics were deeply influenced by the Japanese cultural expectations of their parents (Caudill and DeVos 1956). This earlier research led me into the study of values (Caudill and Scarr 1962) and patterns of emotions (Caudill 1962) in Japan, and it soon became clear that in these matters Japanese and Americans were closer to each other in occupational than in familial life. These findings are in line with the previously mentioned idea that modernization will have a greater effect upon the social structure of the more public than upon the more private aspects of life.

In the more narrow focus on family life, we can again see structural similarities and cultural differences. The structural similarities in the family across societies probably are not, however, very closely tied to the process of modernization but result from the fewer possibilities of variation in basic family structure than in larger social units such as occupational and political systems. The reasons for the relative lack of variation in basic family structure have often been credited to the infant's biological need for care and the role of the father in procreation and then as provider. This implies the persistence over time of the nuclear family regardless of the nature of the wider social structure in which it is found.

We have probably tried too hard in our thinking to force the structure of the family to fit the general nature of the wider social structure under examination. It seems likely that the basic structure of the family has been essentially the same from the beginning of human life. Nevertheless, despite the similarity in structure, the content of what is "taught" to the infant varies widely, and so again we have both the effects of structural similarities and cultural differences.

There is considerable evidence in the literature for these ideas. For example, Goode's (1963) thesis is that modernization is creating a "revolution" throughout the world, and that there are many similarities in family structure throughout the world, but that these two phenomena are by no means causally related. In his final chapter he concludes:

It cannot be assumed that merely because people say things are changing greatly that they have indeed changed much from the past. . . . The amount of work that needs to be done is great, and few sociologists in Europe and the United States have been properly trained for historical research. The importance of such research in this field cannot be overemphasized, simply because so many "facts" need to be corrected: ideal patterns of family behavior have been thought to be real ones, and a hypothetical harmony in past family relations has been assumed, rather than treated as an hypothesis to be tested. Even for the recent period we have pointed out various illustrations of incorrect assumptions about the past—for example, the supposed pattern of youthful marriage in Western family systems, or the frequency of extremely large families living under one roof in many cultures. . . .

We have also noted that some family behavior thought to be a recent change is, in fact, simply a continuation of older patterns. . . . It is almost certainly incorrect to assume that both society and family were relatively static prior to industrialization and that the recent changes have occurred only because the modern world has begun to share in a new technology. (Goode 1963: 366–370)

Burch (1967) also argued convincingly from a comparative analysis of census data that the variation in the size and structure of the family throughout the world is much less than it is usually thought to be. As Burch says:

A widely held generalization in the field of family sociology posits a close inverse relation between urbanization and industrialization on the one hand and the "extended family" on the other. Within societies, this is taken to mean that extended families are more prevalent in rural than in urban areas; cross-culturally, that extended families are more prevalent in underdeveloped than in developed societies. Over time, it is taken to mean that as a society develops the extended family tends to be replaced as a modal form by the independent nuclear (or conjugal) family of husband, wife, and their children (Burch 1967: 345).

As a theme for his counter-argument Burch then picks up a heretical statement of Marion J. Levy's: "The general outlines and nature of the actual family structures have been virtually identical in certain strategic respects in all known societies in world history for well over 50 per cent of the members of those societies" (cited in Burch 1967: 349). Burch goes on to analyze census data available through the United Nations and finds considerable support for Levy's statement over a very wide range of countries—large and small, urban and rural, developed and undeveloped. Burch concludes:

An analysis of selected census data for recent periods has shown that, among and within nations, the variation in average size of the private household or residential family is much smaller than is often believed to be the case. . . . It becomes clear also that since children comprise a large portion of the average family of residence, variation in average size of private households as reported in census data may have little to do with extended family structure, but reflect variations in the number of surviving children. . . . Finally, instances have been found in which the average number of other relatives per household is higher in urban than in rural areas. This finding points to the need for modification of the view that the extension of residential families stands in a simple inverse relationship to urbanization (Burch 1967: 363).

Specifically with reference to the American family, Furstenberg (1966) has cast doubt on how much change has taken place over the last two hundred years; and for the Japanese family, Smith's (1973) data indicate that the average size of urban households has not changed much since the eighteenth century. In our work with middle-class Japanese and American families we find very little difference in size or structure of the families in the two countries, but a great deal of difference in the culturally patterned behavior of family members. These and other matters concerning the Japanese family will be discussed more fully in the third part of this chapter.

So far, we have considered social structure and culture as independent variables in a broad sense, and have narrowed our focus to the family in terms of its structural and cultural characteristics. If we narrow our focus further still, and look at the effects on the individual of occupying a particular position within the structure of the family (for example, only child, first son, last daughter), then we approach one of the sources of individual psychological differences. We can narrow the focus even further and look at genetic and maturational differences in the individuals who occupy these particular positions in the family.

Inherent in the preceding line of thought is the idea of at least four interrelated, but still conceptually separate, dimensions of human behavior: social-structural, cultural, psychological, and biological. The amount of variance that can occur in terms of the effects of each of these dimensions on human behavior (or, in other words, the degree of "flexibility" in each dimension) is probably greatest in the social-structural dimension and becomes progressively less in the movement to the cultural, the psychological, and finally to the biological dimension. That each of these dimensions is separate enough to be considered as a system in its own right, and yet is still open enough to be interrelated with the other dimensions, helps to account for the often expressed idea that all human beings are somehow the same and yet somehow different. They are more the same in biological nature and psychological characteristics, and less alike in cultural identity and position in the social structure. On an empirical level, this sort of thinking argues for maintaining each of these dimensions as a separate independent variable in attempting to account for the variance found in samples of human behavior.

A concrete illustration of the preceding line of thought is provided in a recent observational study of the effects of cultural differences on infant and caretaker behavior in the home. We selected normal, first-born infants from urban middle-class families in Japan and the United States, and then controlled for the amount of variance due to the sex of the infant and to the position of the family in the social structure (in terms of whether the father's occupation was bureaucratic or entrepreneurial). Roughly speaking, about 25 percent of the variance in behavior proved to be due to cultural differences, and the accounting for this proportion of the variance is statistically highly significant. At the same time, however, it should be emphasized that a much larger proportion of the variance is not explained by any of our independent variables, and this unexplained variance might be due to a lot of things including basic similarities between our Japanese and American subjects (see Caudill and Weinstein 1969).

To date, the literature on national differences does not tend to report research results in the manner just illustrated. Rather, results are usually phrased in all or none terms; for example, statements are made that the Japanese are like this and the Americans are like that, when what is really meant is that Japanese are somewhat more like this and Americans are somewhat more like that, but there is a large area of overlap and similarity. For this reason I have reservations about the literature on Japanese national characteristics, and yet I think we can learn something, at least in the sense of hypotheses to be tested, from a review of such literature. In the third part of the paper I try to provide some perspective on these ideas about Japanese psychological and behavioral characteristics by making use of the general distinctions drawn in the preceding discussion between the effects that seem to be due more to the development of a modern social structure and those that seem to be due more to the historical continuity of the culture.

JAPANESE PSYCHOLOGICAL AND BEHAVIORAL CHARACTERISTICS

The literature on Japanese national character of the past hundred or so years reveals much similarity. This literature tends to assume that psychological characteristics have somehow become "homogenized" throughout the population. The persistence of ubiquitous characteristics may indeed be true, but we need to find out how to study national character objectively, with proper attention to variations in historical and structural variables.

The literature reviewed was written, roughly speaking, during four time periods: the first of these starts in the late nineteenth century and extends into the early twentieth century; the second period comprises the 1920s and 1930s; the third period includes the 1940s and the early 1950s; the most recent period extends from about 1955 to the present.

What follows is a list, with some commentary, of themes recurring over the years that I feel are important in the study of Japanese personality and character. The order of the items does not imply any order of importance or even of sharp separation between themes, as many of them are closely interrelated in ways that cannot be spelled out here.

A sense of the importance of the group. This emphasis on the importance of the group rather than of the individual is especially characteristic of the family, as well as of the school, place of employment, or any other long-enduring group to which one belongs. An individual in Japan, in a profound sense, exists only in terms of the groups to which he belongs, and there is little separate identity apart from such contexts. Scarr and I found that Japanese, more than Americans, emphasize the value of collaterality in familial and occupational areas of life (Caudill and Scarr 1962).

A sense of obligation and gratitude. It is still a virtue in modern Japan to acknowledge and repay personal obligations (to recognize one's *on* to others), and a person who does not do this is held in contempt. It is also still a virtue to have a strong sense of duty *(giri)* and loyalty to the various meaningful groups of which one is a member.

A sense of sympathy and compassion (ninjō) *for others.* This sense of human feeling can be very strong, but it is often expressed impulsively and fleetingly, and should not get in the way of duty although it is recognized that it sometimes does. This latter problem, of course, has long been a standard precipitator of interpersonal crises.

A sense of "we" versus "they." This is very pronounced within Japanese society in terms of "our group" versus the stranger or the outsider, and is equally strong when it is applied in terms of "we Japanese" versus the people of any other country. In some contexts there possibly is a closer feeling toward Chinese and other Asians than toward white or black people, but this is a very complicated matter and depends a great deal on the sense in which the comparison is being made. Although people from a different country are definitely placed as outsiders, there also is a great interest in them and curiosity about them.

This "we" versus "they" tendency is one that repeatedly occurs in the literature. Writing in 1904, Hearn complains that after some fourteen years of living in Japan he has not been able to make a close relationship with anyone. He says, "Perhaps in two or three cases out of a thousand he [the foreigner] may obtain something precious—a lasting and kindly esteem, based upon moral comprehension; but should he wish for more he must remain in the state of the Antarctic explorer, seeking, month after month, to no purpose, some inlet through endless cliffs of everlasting ice" (Hearn 1904: 472).

Hearn should have known better than to complain in this way and attribute his experience to being from another country. As Seidensticker (1961) points out some sixty years later:

> But while they seek physical proximity, the Japanese are short on comradeship. . . . A man's lifetime friends tend to be from his high school [or college] days. . . . For this brief period of springtime revelry, comradeship as equals is possible. If such comradeship may be described as a horizontal relationship, vertical relationships become common thereafter. These are the much stiffer and more restrained relations of junior to senior and inferior to superior, which exist within the closed hierarchy of a company, a university, or even a political party or philanthropic organization. . . . The tight faction, as suspicious of outsiders as one tomcat is of another, is at once a curse and a blessing. . . .

There is an air of disgruntlement in the writings of Hearn and Seidensticker, but Maruyama (1965) also writes in a similar but more scholarly way of the balance in Japanese life (during the years since the Meiji period) of the four concepts of individualization, democratization, privatization, and atomization. In his paper the modern Japanese individual is seen largely in terms of privatization and atomization. Maruyama's privatized individual has withdrawn into his small personal, familial, and occupational "we groups," and has largely turned his back on the wider world. This condition is not uncommon in other industrialized countries, but in Japan it is combined with the organization of life into many parallel vertical structures. It is not surprising, then, that interpersonal relations are usually perceived by Japanese as difficult to handle—whether with other Japanese or with foreigners.

An underlying emotionality and excitability which is controlled by compulsive attention to details, plans, and rules. This tendency to be excitable, and to rely on emotional feeling and intuition as much as on reason, is also a theme that recurs frequently in the literature. For example, at the beginning of the twentieth century we find Nitobe (1905: 109-10) saying, "Personally I believe it was our very excitability and sensitiveness which made it a necessity to recognize and enforce constant self-repression. . . ." Similarly in the late 1920s we find Watsuji (1961: 207) saying, "Even the Japanese . . . who seem to have liberated themselves so valiantly and heroically from the shackles of the traditions of their past still reveal their national character explicitly in their impatient excitability." And, in the late 1940s Nakamura (1964: 531), in writing about the effects on thought of a limited social nexus in Japan, says, "Upon this limited basis, there is little intention to make each man's understanding and expression universal or logical, so that, in general, the thinking of most Japanese tends to be intuitive and emotional." Finally, and from a somewhat different perspective, the unrest among Japanese college students, their excitability and factionalism as they have tried to give voice to their political feelings, was exceeded by none (Mehnert 1969).

A willingness to work hard and to persevere toward long-range goals. Despite all the emotionality that is always so close to the surface in Japanese life, if a person is treated in what he regards as a decent fashion he is willing to work very hard at his tasks. He also feels he can accomplish these tasks a good deal better if a highly detailed plan is laid out specifying what he is expected to do to achieve the long-range goal.

Devotion to parents, and especially a long-enduring tie to the mother. The image of the mother, as she appears in the minds of the majority of Japanese, is of a self-sacrificing, succoring, and enveloping being. This psychological image probably has greater intensity than the actual behavior of the mother would warrant, but such is often the fate of images. The role of the mother in Japanese culture deserves a full-scale historical and contemporary investigation in its own right.

An emphasis on self-effacement and a tendency to attribute responsibility to others rather than taking responsibility for one's own actions. This latter tendency is nicely illustrated in Niyekawa's (1968) work. She used stick-figure cartoons showing interpersonal conflicts with a negative outcome; responses to these cartoons were measured by a questionnaire completed by samples of Japanese, American, and German subjects. In her study, the Japanese subjects significantly attributed more responsibility to others than did the American or German subjects, who took more personal responsibility for unfortunate results.

An attitude of deference and politeness toward one's superiors and toward those with whom one has a tie, coupled with obliviousness toward those with whom one does not have a tie. In human terms, this means a sensitivity toward those who are within a personal network, and a reluctance to help or to become involved with those people who are not within such a network. In material terms, this means taking good care of things that belong to one's group, and taking little care of public property.

A tendency for understatement and an emphasis on nonverbal communication. Japanese seem to be more sensitive to, and make more conscious use of, many forms of nonverbal communication in human relations through the medium of gestures and physical proximity than Americans, who predominantly use verbal communication within a context of physical separateness. One example of this is provided by the difference in sleeping arrangements in Japan and America (see Caudill and Plath 1966), and another is provided by Fisher and Yoshida (1968) in an analysis of Japanese proverbs. In addition, there is the greater comfortableness that Japanese feel in expressing themselves in writing rather than in speaking, as in the *shi-shōsetsu* novel (Hibbett 1966). In this connection I found in my research that at six years of age the American children spoke more freely, but the Japanese children read and wrote more easily.

A strong feeling of fatalism and of the ephemeral nature of things. This tendency gives an apparent air of mild depression to actions and feelings in many areas of Japanese life. I suspect that this tinge of depression is connected with very deep feelings about the relation to the mother, but it is more obviously linked to Buddhistic thought.

A great pleasure in the simple things of life. Being in beautiful surroundings, playing with children, bathing, drinking, eating, and sex are taken by the majority of Japanese as simple pleasures to be enjoyed for the immediate satisfaction that they give; many Westerners have a great deal more trouble deriving pleasure from such relatively simple though important pasttimes (see Caudill 1962).

I could go on with such a list, but I think enough has been said to indicate a certain consistency in the ways in which Japanese personality and character have been seen over the years. If one had the skill, and the temerity, a more interesting job could probably be done through an analysis of Japanese novels and personal histories. Such analysis has, in part, already been done in the critical comment provided along with translations by such scholars as Ivan Morris, Donald Keene, Howard Hibbett, and Edward Seidensticker—especially in Seidensticker's excellent work (1965) on Nagai Kafū.

Most of the writers whom I investigated for the foregoing discussion arrived at their conclusions on a clinical or subjective basis, or through a consideration of historical materials. There certainly is nothing particularly wrong in reaching conclusions in these ways, but I feel strongly that we need to go beyond such methods and to find more empirical and testable approaches to the study of national character. Some attempts in this direction have appeared in the literature, for example, Abate and Berrien (1967), Tanaka (1967), and Triandis, Vassiliou, and Nassiakou (1968).

A second major criticism of the writings to date on Japanese national character is that they give little attention to the problem of variation: there is little concern with the changes that have surely taken place over time; there is almost no attempt to treat the differences that must exist by sex and age; and there has been no serious investigation of the effects of position in the social structure on personality characteristics either for the past or for the present. These are the areas in which we need further research.

PSYCHOLOGICAL IMPLICATIONS OF CHANGE AND CONTINUITY IN MODERN JAPAN

Personality does not just unfold from the inside as a person grows older, nor indeed is it only responsive to pressures from the family and peers; it is also affected in direct and indirect ways by broader changes taking place in the social structure and culture of a country. Such broader changes in Japan have been particularly prominent in the last twenty-five years. Specifically, I think we need to know much more about (a) historical trends, (b) the psychological implications in Japan of ecology (both natural and man-made), (c) social structure as interrelated with economic development, and (d) family life.

Historical Trends

In the last few decades many scholars have been engaged in the attempt to explain how Japan got to where it is at present, and the answers to this question certainly involve a psychological dimension which, as yet, remains to be defined from an analysis of historical materials. As Passin (1968) notes, the national unity of a country is of great importance as a precondition for modernization. Japan already had a strong national unity by 1868 and was a compact insular country with clearly defined and virtually unchallenged boundaries. It is true that over a period of several thousand years Japan has had contacts with Korea, China, and for some seventy years, during the latter part of the sixteenth and early part of the seventeenth centuries, with Europe. But looked at in the perspective of history Japan has, perhaps uniquely among countries in the world, sustained an isolation until the end of the nineteenth century. This long experience of isolation may have contributed to that special "national self-consciousness" that most foreign observers feel is characteristic of Japan, both as a nation and as a people (see Reischauer 1957).

By the end of the nineteenth century the Japanese had been ethnically united for a thousand years and were a highly homogeneous population—racially, linguistically, and culturally. Perhaps because of this fact, Japanese love to make much of small regional differences which delight folklorists, make for pleasant conversation, and allow persons on a trip to bring back small presents of local meaning to their families. So also with language—although Japanese has its dialects, the choice in 1868 at the beginning of the Meiji period of a modified Tokyo dialect for a national language presented few problems and left no alienated linguistic communities.

Toward the end of the nineteenth century when Japan made the decision to modernize, the task was carried out in a highly planned fashion by an already existing elite in close touch with the rest of the population. In a real sense, many of the values that existed in the premodern Tokugawa period in Japan (see Bellah 1957) were congruent with those needed in a modern society and served to smooth the transition to newer forms of bureaucracy, education, and economic development.

In general, over the last century Japan has worked toward rapid technological and institutional change, but has controlled or deliberately retarded social change (Bennett 1968). Change in Japan has largely been carried out from above, by the samurai and their leaders during the Meiji period, and by the American Occupation forces following World War II. The Japanese system of social relations has been a vehicle for action toward change, but not the object of change itself. This retention of the Japanese system of social relations has often worked against the type of democratic, public, rational social planning and spontaneous social reform familiar in many Western countries. In a gross sense, then, to many Western and Japanese social analysts, Japanese society presents a dual image: an essentially Western set of urban and industrial institutions on the one hand, and an essentially Eastern communal system of social relations on the other. The contrast between these two images has given rise to many of the problems of the social science analysis of Japanese modernization. The answers to these problems, of course, are offered along two lines. One set of answers says that the Japanese social system will wither away in the face of a modern technological economy. The other set of answers says that the Japanese social system, with some modifications due to modernization, works perfectly well and will persist. One cannot know with finality what the answer will be as Japanese society is in transition, but my prediction is that the resulting product will still be very Japanese. In any case, I agree with Bennett (1968: 42) when he says: "We have also suggested that conventional concepts of modernization or Westernization are not especially relevant as a frame of reference for the study of change in Japan. . . . [However,] sociological frames derived from the study of social mobility, social problems, migration, welfare, urbanization, alienation and mass culture are as meaningful and applicable as tools of analysis for Japan as in the West. This suggests that research on Japanese social change will benefit greatly from systematic comparisons with specific Western countries undergoing analogous experiences. This work has already begun."

Ecology

Despite the triteness of the subject, I do not know of anyone, with the exception of Watsuji Tetsuro in the late 1920s, who has seriously addressed himself to the human implications of the fact that Japan *is* a small insular country with the bulk of the population of about 100 million squeezed into roughly 24 percent of the land area. The urban population of Japan was only 9 percent in 1889, it rose to 18 percent by 1920, to 38 percent by 1940, to 68 percent by 1965, and to over 80 percent by 1970. Many of these urban-dwellers are poorly housed, lack adequate transportation, and do not have proper facilities for the disposal of their waste products. Numerous farmers living near cities now work in factories while the women till the land, and it is important to learn how children are reared under such conditions. At the same time, there has been available a great variety and abundance of consumer goods; ownership of major appliances and automobiles has increased tremendously, and mass communication is possibly better than in the United States. In short, life in major urban areas is very modern: it is crowded and hectic, expensive and frustrating, often unhealthy and dangerous, and very interesting and diverting. Such conditions are likely to have an effect on personality characteristics, which as yet we know very little about. (Takao Sofue further discusses aspects of urban and rural change in Japan in Chapter 9.)

Social Structure and Economic Development

One key aspect of modern social structure in Japan, having its roots deep in the past, is the strong tendency for consequential human relations to have a vertical structure (Nakane 1967). Almost any field of endeavor—business, government, academic life, or the arts—is composed of tight, vertically structured organizations that demand strict allegiance, self-sacrifice, and an extreme (to Western sensibilities) penetration of the organization into the private lives of its members. In return for such a commitment, the organization protects its members in many ways, and expects those directly above and below each other in rank to be personally solicitous and attentive to each other's needs. Between parallel organizations in the same field, cooperation and communication are severely restricted, and competition is fierce. One result of such a system is that within a single organization, let alone across organizations, it is very difficult to achieve satisfactory horizontal ties among equals. Indeed, as Passin (1966) points out, since relative status is so important, the greatest danger may come from those closest in standing; among persons who are close in rank, harmonious working relations based on mutual reliance can, at a moment's notice, become discordant and filled with resentment. It is no wonder, then, as Nakane (1967) notes, that within such a structure a person feels he must be in a personal and affective relationship with his senior.

This sensitivity to ranking and the need for an affective relation with superiors (and, concomitantly, the need of the superiors for personal attention from their juniors) sounds very much like Doi's discussion of the concept of *amaeru*—the wish to depend and presume upon another's benevolence—that he uses as an explanatory principle in his writings about Japanese personality (see, for example, Doi 1962). Doi has a very important point when he makes a concept out of the verb *amaeru*. At the same time it is clear that Japan could not have been rebuilt after World War II to its level of worldwide importance without the use of a great deal of adaptive aggression.

Combining the ideas of vertical structure in social organization and the wish to *amaeru* in human relations, I think one can understand something of both the "genius" and the "curse" of Japanese life. When things are going well in a tight vertical structure and the individual feels taken care of and secure, he can work very successfully and creatively as a member of his group, and a tremendous amount can be accomplished. Yet this system (as is true for any system) has its vulnerabilities, and these are all too obvious in the psychological effects on a person who has been rejected by his group and has nowhere to turn. We need much more empirical testing of both the positive and negative effects of this aspect of Japanese social life.

In the last one hundred years Japan has developed a modern occupational class structure of managers, white-collar workers, and skilled laborers. This class structure has been defined and described by Japanese sociologists, particularly in the excellent research by Odaka and his students which utilized careful sampling in the six largest cities of Japan (see Odaka 1964, and Odaka and Nishihira 1965), but as yet there has been little work that relates psychological characteristics to social class position and social mobility.

When objective criteria are used to determine social status (occupation, education, amount of income, and number of expensive consumer goods owned by the family), Odaka arrives at five social classes which are, in general, comparable to those defined by Hollingshead for the United States, but the proportionate distribution is different. Odaka's upper class contains about 3 percent of the total; then, while recognizing differences in the levels, Odaka combines the next three classes into a broad band of people representing 70 percent of the population which he calls middle class; this leaves about 28 percent occupying a working-class level composed of semi-skilled workers. Odaka is probably correct in his groupings, and in this sense the large proportion of people falling into a middle-class range does make Japan more homogeneous in class structure than most other countries. One would also expect to find a greater homogeneity in values, attitudes, and other psychological characteristics, but this remains to be established. Surprisingly, to date we have better reports on the psychological characteristics of deprived segments of the population (see the excellent book on *burakumin* by DeVos and Wagatsuma 1966, and the beginning study of an impoverished community by Taira 1969) than on the more representative middle classes.

The sharing of a similar social status probably does not serve to bind people together very strongly in Japan; for example, there is little sense of the solidarity of labor as a class against management as a class. Instead, as already discussed, a person's identification is more likely to be with a particular company or other organization—that is, his ties are more within a specific, vertical structure than within a general and horizontally extended one. Unions in Japan are not organized tightly across companies in a horizontal sense; rather, each large company tends to have its own union, and these unions are loosely grouped into several federations that are more active politically than in industry-wide collective bargaining. This state of affairs helps to account for the finding by Odaka (1964) that a dual allegiance to both company and union was the most common response in a study of workers in eight large companies.

Social mobility occurs from one generation to the next, or within a person's own lifetime. A large proportion of young adult Japanese at present are better educated and have better jobs than their fathers. At the same time, the increasing level of education in the general population makes the competition for jobs fiercer and the opportunities for rapid advancement less likely (see Sumiya 1967). It is somewhat ironic that the people most stuck with the more traditional "lifetime commitment" to their jobs are the so-called "new middle class" (see Vogel 1963), that is, the salarymen. In a study by Tominaga (1962), and in the employment survey for 1967 by the Ministry of Labor (Japan Information Service 1968), the people with the lowest rate of job changing are white-collar workers and salarymen, while managers and skilled labor change jobs more frequently, regardless of the size of business, though the rate of turnover is greater in small than in large establishments. Thus, there is a willingness to take "greater risks" on the part of managers and skilled labor, and on the part of employees in small businesses. It is scarcely any wonder, then, that a greater apathy about one's work is found among white-collar workers in large companies. For example, in an attitudinal survey of employees in two electric power companies which asked for an order of preference concerning work, recreation, and home life, 56 percent of the employees placed home life first, 30 percent placed recreation first, and only 8 percent placed their work first (Odaka 1963).

These facts about social mobility across and within generations in Japan fairly cry out for studies of psychological adjustment. To what extent does the better education of children contribute to difficulties in interpersonal relations with their less well educated parents? What effect does the excessive competition for entrance to high status schools and for more desirable jobs have on the personality characteristics of children and young adults? What is the meaning in human terms of increased apathy toward and lack of involvement in occupational success on the part of ordinary salarymen?

In the preceding discussion I have several times referred to a contrast between the ways of life of persons working in small versus large organizations in urban Japan. A substantial proportion of Japanese industry and trade is still carried out in tiny establishments, usually businesses run by the family aided by four or five outside workers who are brought in from the country or elsewhere and either live in the home with the family or reside nearby. The Japanese government has been complaining since the end of World War II about these small industries, but they will not go away. The actual number of such businesses tends to increase from year to year, even though the rate of bankruptcy among such businesses also increases, and wages are lower than those paid for comparable work in large companies. We are faced here with the same old problem: Are these small businesses in Japan going to wither away because they are not an "economically sound" part of the modern industrial structure, or are they going to persist? I think that the relative proportion of such businesses will decrease but that this way of life will still loom larger in Japan than in, for example, the United States because it is so deeply rooted in Japanese culture.

Psychologically, what is important about these small businesses is that in them work and family life are more intertwined than in the salaryman's family. Daily life in the small business family frequently appears bustling and gay; the shop is usually either in the home or only a few blocks from it. The father often is at home for lunch, and sees his children more frequently than does the salaryman father. The attention the mother gives the child in the small business family is equaled by the attention from other female members of the household, such as the grandmother or unmarried sisters. In contrast, there are usually fewer persons in the salaryman's household, and little or no connection between work and home life. The mother in the salaryman's family is often at home by herself doing housework or watching television. When her children are home from school they more frequently play inside the house and are less out in the neighborhood. The more exclusive attention of the mother to her child in the salaryman's family can make her presence a more hovering one than in the small business family. The distinction between these two types of families is not just an economic one but stands for somewhat different ways of life in Japan that are linked to the development of somewhat different personality characteristics.

I have been talking mainly about problems of social structure in relation to urban situations, but a word should be said about rural life. Both

Western and Japanese anthropologists and sociologists have spent so much of their time studying rural Japan that one might almost think that no cities existed in Japan.

The rural world and the urban world seem to be more closely linked in Japan than in western countries. Until after World War II a person's family records were kept in the place where he was born and not where he was living as an adult, family graveyards are frequently located in the ancestral village, and it is customary to travel back to the rural home several times a year for an extended family gathering. Migration from the villages to urban areas, which has so greatly increased in recent years, has never been a mad rush to the city, but rather represents a decision on the part of the family as to which of the children should go to the city and whom they should contact for help when they arrive (see Vogel 1967). Thus there is still a substantial movement back and forth between rural and urban life in Japan. This is due partly to the small size of the country, and partly to the strong familial and group ties.

In the years after World War II much has changed in rural life: the impact of land reform, the increased mechanization of agriculture, and the loosening of the formal rules for conducting family life (see Dore 1959). Yet the emphasis is still on the family and not on the individual.

The tremendous expansion of urban areas in Japan has put many farming communities next to cities. In families where the father and other adult male members often work during the week in nearby factories and leave the mother and children to care for the farm, the problem is to decide whether a family is a farming family or not. The father increases the family income, but his absence overburdens the mother and children and changes the nature of family life. As yet we know little about the psychological effects of this, and other, developments in rural areas.

Family Life

There are apparent misconceptions concerning family life in Japan, which need to be corrected. Personality is formed initially within the context of the family and, as indicated earlier, we now know that there are many more gross similarities in the size and structure of the family throughout the world than previously supposed. It is likely that these similarities in family life help to bring about those psychological similarities that make all of us more alike than different.

Smith (1960) has shown that the average size of urban households in Japan in the eighteenth century was about the same as it is now. This historical perspective is a useful addition to Koyama's (1965) emphasis on the decreasing size of urban households in recent years under the influences of modern life, the legalization of abortion, and the increasing age at time of marriage. What seems to have happened is that the urban household in Japan increased in size, perhaps under the influence of political pressure, from the end of the nineteenth century to the beginning of World War II, and then began to decrease. Koyama believes that there is a strong tendency for the traditional extended family (which perhaps never existed in large numbers except at certain stages in the family cycle) to separate into modern nuclear families. Koyama (1962) has also pointed out that we must be specific about the stage in the family cycle to which we are referring in our research. In Japan today it is very usual for a family to start out as a couple living in an apartment; to have children, incorporate one or two grandparents, and move to a house; and then to decrease in size and number of generations as the old folks die and the children are married, so that the parents end up as an old nuclear family waiting to see how they will be taken care of in their terminal years.

One reason for the great outpouring of writing on the Japanese family in recent years is the drastic legal changes that took place in the concept of the family after the end of World War II. The revised Civil Code of Japan abolished primogeniture and gave all offspring equal rights to inheritance. It also shifted the responsibility of caring for retired parents from the eldest son to all of the children. In addition, it greatly enhanced the status of the wife by emphasizing the rights of the individual and the equality of the sexes. Further investigation is needed of the changing proportion (now about equally balanced) between "arranged" and "love" marriages in response to the last of these changes.

We have probably never paid enough attention to the underlying psychological strength of the Japanese woman—whether as single individual, wife, or mother. Her status in society has risen and fallen during various periods in history, but she has never been as downtrodden or powerless as she is sometimes depicted by Western writers. The feminine ideal during the latter part of the feudal age (in the Edo period from about 1600 to the beginning of the Meiji period in 1867) can best be summed up as: ". . . service and self-effacement. Weakness was not desired. 'Tenderness is the means; resolution is the essence,' said the books of ethics" (Ackroyd 1959: 66).

It is conventional nowadays to point to the increasing power of the wife in the home and to the greater number of women who are employed in comparison to the period before World War II (see Koyama 1961). This increase in the status of women, however, is not a new thing in Japan if we take a long enough historical perspective. Ackroyd (1959: 31) opens her fascinating article on women in feudal Japan by saying: "During the feudal age in Japan (1185-1867), Japanese women suffered a serious decline in status. Although they were already laboring under social and legal restrictions when the period opened, at first they enjoyed a position of considerable strength under the law and had scope for independent action."

As feudalism progressed, the general status of women declined drastically, but there remained important distinctions between the position of women in the types of families most common in the military and their position in the peasant and developing merchant classes. The remnants of these distinctions can be found even today in the somewhat different structure of the family in the upper, middle, and lower classes in modern Japan. Such differences need to be studied for their psychological and interpersonal implications both in the earlier and later history of Japan.

In our earlier work on family life (Caudill and Plath 1966) we found that a person in modern, urban Japan can expect as a matter of preference rather than necessity to co-sleep in a two-generation group—first as a child, then as a parent, and later as a grandparent—over half of his life cycle. This finding has been confirmed for rural areas by Morioka (1968). Kuromaru has found the same sort of sleeping arrangements for families in another urban area, that of Ashiya. He finds no correlation between the development of psychiatric difficulties and such a sleeping pattern; rather, he believes that such sleeping arrangements do, in general, contribute to that aspect of the Japanese character which emphasizes communality over individuality in family life. In our data from the cities of Tokyo, Kyoto, and Matsumoto, we found no statistically significant variation in this group sleeping pattern by social class, or by occupational style of life—in salaryman or small business families. Thus, despite the real differences brought about by modernization, within the family in Japan as night falls and the family settles down for sleep, the overall pattern is one of cultural similarity in co-sleeping, and this Japanese pattern is in strong contrast to that found in Western countries at present.

In our longitudinal study of mothers and children, we have found areas both of similarity and of difference between three- to four-month-old infants in Japan and the United States (Caudill and Weinstein 1969). The similarities occur in the areas of biological needs and their care: mothers in both cultures spend equal amounts of time in feeding, diapering, and dressing their infants, and the infants spend the same amount of time in sleeping and eating. But the styles of care are different: American mothers do more positioning of, and chatting to, their infants, while Japanese mothers do more carrying, rocking, and lulling of their infants. Our data also show that, probably as a result of these differences in conditioning, the American infant is more physically active, more given to exploring his environment, and more vocal—especially more happily vocal. The Japanese infant, in contrast, is only greater in unhappy vocalization. It seems the American mother wants a happily vocal, active, and exploring baby, and the Japanese mother wants a quiet, inactive, and contented baby. Our data indicate that by three to four months of age infants in the two cultures have already learned to behave in culturally patterned ways, well before any development of the ability to use language. Thus, culture would appear to be "built into" the person, at least in nascent form, even by three months of age.

We were particularly puzzled as to why the Japanese baby should be greater in unhappy vocalization. Upon analysis of the data, it became clear that the Japanese mother took longer to respond to her infant's cries, and hence her infant had higher "unhappy vocal" scores (Caudill 1969). Perhaps the Japanese mother feels that since she is "part of the baby," she knows what is good for the baby, and she responds according to her feelings and not according to those of the baby. But the American mother seems to feel that the baby is separate from her, and that she needs the baby's signals to tell her what he wants, and particularly she responds more quickly to her baby's unhappy cries.

This greater consideration of the child as a separate individual seems apparent in our data from observations of the same children at two-and-a-half and at six years of age in both cultures. Our initial impression is in line with the findings on somewhat older children by Matsumoto and Smith (1961).

One further problem in the area of family life needs attention. Although it shows some signs of rising, the average age of retirement from a job in Japan is still fifty-five years, but the ordinary man's retirement income is not sufficient to support his family, and he receives virtually nothing from national or private pension plans. Here is a fertile field for questions of psychological adjustment. What happens to a man in the years between fifty-five and death? What happens to his wife and to children who are unable to support themselves? As Plath (1972) has vividly pointed out, the "after years" are anything but a pleasant time of leisure in Japan.

CONCLUSION

I believe that in this discussion sufficient evidence has been presented to indicate that modern social structure and historical culture should be treated as separate variables; both have fairly independent effects on behavior and psychological adjustment. As countries develop modern social structures in line with the requirements of increasing industrialization and technological advancement, they become more alike, but this does not mean that the traditional culture is lost; it persists in many important ways that deeply influence a person's way of thinking, emotional response, and behavior.

Specifically for Japan, the last hundred years have shown both great social change and cultural continuity. As yet, however, we know very little about the psychological effects of such combined change and continuity, and in this paper I have indicated many issues on which we need further work. I hope in the future we can be more comparative in our research on problems in Japanese life. At the same time, we should avoid concentrating on comparisons of Japan with the United States, and come more to include comparisons with other countries in the world, such as those in Southeast Asia and Europe. Japan may well have much in common with other countries on matters relating to family life, child rearing, and personality development, and these similarities would be lost in comparisons with the United States in which differences probably would be more prominent.

In the coming decades as some of us continue to try to bring about a more humanistic unity in the world we must keep clearly in mind not only the similarities in people's lives brought about by modern social structure, but also the very real cultural differences in thinking and behavior that add a zest to human life but which can also impede communication across national boundaries. In this period of, hopefully temporary, resurgent nationalism, it is only at our peril that we can ignore either in research or politics the existence of meaningful cultural differences. Such differences must be consciously recognized, studied, and made explicit so that they can be enjoyed as variations in human experience rather than serving as sources of misunderstanding.

REFERENCES

Abate, Mario, and Berrien, F.K. 1967. "Validation of Stereotyes: Japanese versus American students," *Journal of Personality and Social Psychology* 7:435–38.

Ackroyd, Joyce. 1959. "Women in Feudal Japan," *Transactions of the Asiatic Society of Japan,* 3rd series, 7:31–68.

Azumi, Koya. 1968. "The Mysterious Drop in Japan's Birth Rate," *Trans-action* 5:6 (May): 46–48.

Bellah, Robert N. 1957. *Tokugawa Religion.* Glencoe, Ill.: Free Press.

Bendix, Reinhard. 1967. "Preconditions of Development: A Comparison of Japan and Germany," in *Aspects of Social Change in Modern Japan,* edited by R. P. Dore. Princeton: Princeton University Press.

Bennett, John. 1968. "Tradition, Modernity and Communalism in Japan's Modernization," in *Tradition and Modernity: Conflict or Congruence,* edited by Joseph Gusfield. Entire issue of the *Journal of Social Issues,* 24:4:25–64.

Burch, Thomas K. 1967. "The Size and Structure of Families: A Comparative Analysis of Census Data," *American Sociological Review* 32:347–63.

Caudill, William. 1958. *Effects of Social and Cultural Systems in Reactions to Stress.* New York: Social Science Research Council, pamphlet number 14.

———. 1962. "Patterns of Emotion in Modern Japan," in *Japanese Culture: Its Development and Characteristics,* edited by Robert J. Smith and Richard K. Beardsley. Chicago: Aldine.

———. 1969. "Tiny Dramas: Vocal Communication between Mother and Infant in Japanese and American Families," paper presented at the second conference in the program on Culture and Mental Health in Asia and the Pacific, East-West Center, Honolulu, 17–21 March 1969.

Caudill, William, and DeVos, George. 1956. "Achievement, Culture and Personality: The Case of the Japanese Americans," *American Anthropologist* 58:1102–26.

Caudill, William, and Plath, David W. 1966. "Who Sleeps by Whom? Parent-Child Involvement in Urban Japanese Families," *Psychiatry* 29:344–66.

Caudill, William, and Scarr, Harry A. 1962. "Japanese Value Orientations and Culture Change," *Ethnology* 1:53–91.

Caudill, William, and Weinstein, Helen. 1969. "Maternal Care and Infant Behavior in Japan and America," *Psychiatry* 32:12–43.

DeVos, George A. 1968. "Achievement and Innovation in Culture and Personality," in *The study of personality: an interdisciplinary appraisal,* edited by Edward Norbeck et al. New York: Holt, Rinehart and Winston.

DeVos, George, and Wagatsuma, Hiroshi. 1966. *Japan's Invisible Race: Caste in Culture and Personality.* Berkeley: University of California Press.

Doi, L. Takeo. 1962. *"Amae:* A Key Concept for Understanding Japanese Personality Structure," in *Japanese Culture: Its Development and Characteristics,* edited by Robert J. Smith and Richard K. Beardsley. Chicago: Aldine.

Dore, R. P. 1959. *Land Reform in Japan.* London: Oxford University Press.

———. 1965. *Education in Tokugawa Japan.* London: Routledge and Kegan Paul.

Eisenstadt, S.N. 1964. "Breakdowns of Modernization," *Economic Development and Cultural Change* 12: 345–67.

Fisher, J.L., and Yoshida, Teigo. 1968. "The Nature of Speech According to Japanese Proverbs," *Journal of American Folklore* 81:34–43.

Freud, Sigmund. 1930. *Civilization and Its Discontents.* London: Hogarth Press.

Goode, William J. 1963. *World Revolution and Family Patterns.* New York: Free Press.

Gusfield, Joseph R. 1967. "Tradition and Modernity: Misplaced Polarities in the Study of Social Change." *American Journal of Sociology* 72:351–62.

Hall, Edward T. 1968. "Proxemics," *Current Anthropology* 9:83–108.

Hearn, Lafcadio. 1904. *Japan: An Attempt at Interpretation.* New York: Macmillan.

Hibbett, Howard. 1966. "Tradition and Trauma in the Contemporary Japanese Novel," *Daedalus* 95: 925–40. Issued as volume 95, number 4, of the Proceedings of the American Academy of Arts and Sciences.

Hodge, Robert W.; Treiman, Donald J.; and Rossi, Peter. 1966. "A Comparative Study of Occupational Prestige," in *Class, Status and Power,* 2nd ed., edited by Reinhard Bendix and Seymour Martin Lipset. New York: Free Press.

Inkeles, Alex, and Rossi, Peter. 1956. "National Comparisons of Occupational Prestige," *American Journal of Sociology* 61:329–39.

Japan Information Service. 1968. "Job-changing, A Growing Trend," *Japan Report* 14: 23:3–5.
Koyama, Takashi. 1961. *The Changing Social Position of Women in Japan.* Paris: United Nations Educational, Scientific and Cultural Organization.
———. 1962. "Changing Family Structure in Japan," in *Japanese Culture: Its Development and Characteristics,* edited by Robert J. Smith and Richard K. Beardsley. Chicago: Aldine.
———. 1965. "The Family in Post-War Japan," *Journal of Social and Political Ideas in Japan* 3:3:11–16.
Lorenz, Konrad. 1963. *On Aggression.* New York: Harcourt, Brace and World.
Maruyama, Masao. 1965. "Patterns of Individuation and the Case of Japan: A Conceptual Scheme," in *Changing Japanese Attitudes Toward Modernization,* edited by Marius B. Jansen. Princeton: Princeton University Press.
Matsumoto, Misao, and Smith, Henrietta T. 1961. "Japanese and American Children's Perception of Parents," *Journal of Genetic Psychology* 98:83–88.
Mehnert, Klaus. 1969. "Student Warriors: A Closer Look," *Atlas* 17:3:34–36.
Morioka, Kiyomi. 1968. *"Dare to dare ga issho ni neru ka"* [Who sleeps together?], *Seishin* [Mind] 1:2:18–23.
Nakamura, Hajime. 1964 (1947). *Ways of Thinking of Eastern Peoples: India, China, Tibet, Japan,* revised English translation edited by Philip P. Wiener. Honolulu: East-West Center Press.
Nakane, Chie. 1967. *"Tate shakai no ningen-kankei"* [Interpersonal relations in a vertical society]. Tokyo: Kōdansha.
Nitobe, Inazo. 1905. *Bushido: The Soul of Japan.* New York: G.P. Putnam's Sons.
Niyekawa, Agnes M. 1968. *A Study of Second Language Learning.* Honolulu: College of Education, University of Hawaii.
Norbeck, Edward. 1961. "Post-war Cultural Change and Continuity in Northeastern Japan," *American Anthropologist* 63: 297–321.
Norbeck, Edward; Price-Williams, Douglas; and McCord, William M., eds. 1968. *The Study of Personality: An Interdisciplinary Appraisal.* New York: Holt, Rinehart and Winston.
Odaka, Kunio. 1963. "Traditionalism, Democracy in Japanese Industry," *Industrial Relations* 3:95–103.
———. 1964. "Modern Man and His Occupation," *Journal of Social and Political Ideas in Japan* 22:46–50.
———. 1964–65. "The Middle Classes in Japan," *Contemporary Japan* 28:1:10–32 and 28:2:268–96.
Odaka, Kunio, and Nishihira, Shigeki. 1965. "Social Mobility in Japan: A Report on the 1955 Survey of Social Stratification and Social Mobility in Japan," *East Asian Cultural Studies* 4:83–126.
Okada, Yuzuru, ed. 1965. "Postwar Social Change." Entire issue of *Journal of Social and Political Ideas in Japan,* 3:3.
Passin, Herbert. 1966. "Socio-cultural Factors in Japan's Perception of Her Internatonal Role," paper presented to a conference at the Hudson Institute, October 1966.

Pearlin, Leonard I., and Kohn, Melvin L. 1966. "Social Class, Occupation, and Parental Values: A Cross-national Study," *American Sociological Review* 31:466–79.

Plath, David W. 1972. "Japan: The After Years," in *Aging and Modernization*, edited by Donald O. Cowgill and Lowell D. Holmes. New York: Appleton-Century-Crofts.

Ramsey, Charles E., and Smith, Robert J. 1960. "Japanese and American Perceptions of Occupations," *American Journal of Sociology* 65:475–82.

Reischauer, Edwin. 1957. *The United States and Japan* (revised edition). Cambridge, Mass.: Harvard University Press.

Roos, Leslie L., and Hadar, Josef. 1968. "Attitude Change and Turkish Modernization," *Behavioral Science* 13:433–44.

Seidensticker, Edward. 1961. *Japan.* New York: Time Inc.

———. 1965. *Kafū the Scribbler.* Stanford: Stanford University Press.

Smith, Robert J. 1960. "Pre-industrial Urbanism in Japan: A Consideration of Multiple Traditions in a Feudal Society," *Economic Development and Cultural Change* 9:241–57.

———. 1973. "Town and City in Pre-modern Japan: Small Families, Small Households, and Residential Instability," in *Urban Anthropology*, edited by Aidan Southall. London: Oxford University Press.

Taira, Koji. 1969. "Urban Poverty, Ragpickers, and the 'Ants' Villa' in Tokyo," *Economic Development and Cultural Change* 17:155–77.

Tanaka, Yasumasa. 1967. "Cross-cultural Compatibility of the Affective Meaning Systems (measured by means of multilingual semantic differentials)," *Journal of Social Issues* 23:27–46.

Tominaga, Ken'ichi. 1962. "Occupational Mobility in Japanese Society: Analysis of Labor Market in Japan," *Journal of Economic Behavior* 2:1–37.

Triandis, Harry C.; Vassiliou, Vasso; and Nassiakou, Maria. 1968. "Three Cross-cultural Studies of Subjective Culture," *Journal of Personality and Social Psychology*, 8: Monograph Supplement.

Vogel, Ezra F. 1963. *Japan's New Middle Class: The Salary Man and his Family in a Tokyo Suburb.* Berkeley: University of California Press.

———. 1967. "Kinship Structure, Migration to the City, and Modernization," in *Aspects of Social Change in Modern Japan*, edited by R. P. Dore. Princeton: Princeton University Press.

Watsuji, Tetsuro. 1961 (1935). *A Climate: A Philosophical Study* (translated by Geoffrey Bownas). Tokyo: Printing Bureau, Japanese Government. (originally published in Japanese in 1935 under the title of *Fūdo;* many of the chapters were published separately as articles in the late 1920s and early 1930s.)

Chapter 2

Chinese Culture, Society, and Personality in Transition

Morton H. Fried

There are at least two ways in which the question of the relationship between culture and personality can be raised, and each seems of very great significance in the Chinese milieu. One may begin with the cultural and societal end, for example, and ask how the seemingly vast changes in Chinese culture and society have affected the people of China. In this context we are primarily interested in the psychological consequences of the changes and a host of questions arise, such as the adjustments made by older members of the society who were reared under different personality-molding conditions. We might then move to consider the young—their education in, and their adaptation to a society that may regard the major upheaval of the cultural revolution as a way of life. It would also be of considerable interest to compare and contrast the psychological adaptations being made in the People's Republic of China (PRC) with those in the Republic of China (ROC), the remnant of the former Nationalist state in Taiwan. To conduct such investigations we have to face some exceptionally difficult methodological problems: paucity of basic research possibilities in the PRC, the very wide spread of base cultures there, and the difficulty of obtaining reliable information in the face of authoritarian governmental pressures, both overt and covert, on both sides of the Taiwan Straits, but especially in the PRC.

We might also proceed from the other end, inquiring into the possible effects of specific character structure on sociocultural events. One set of such questions has already inspired a good deal of speculation—how the personality of Mao Tse-tung has affected the course of events in China for the past fifty years or more. For example, Stuart Schram (who, it must be said, rejects the theory of psychological causality) notes that:

> The various indications of Mao's hostility to his father and his own statements on the "dialectical struggles" in his family, in which he sided with his mother and brother against the paternal "ruling power," might lead some to a psychoanalytic explanation of his revolutionary attitudes. (Schram 1969, p. 21.)

As early as the winter of 1917–18, when Mao was twenty-four, he was attacking China's "three bonds," the ties binding ruler and subject, father and son, and husband and wife, declaring that they had to be done away with for the salvation of China (p. 27). Although few scholars are tempted to attribute massive sociocultural movements to the peculiarities of a single character, there is an easier recourse to theories of national character. Thus, Mao's individually hostile relationship to his father is sometimes generalized as a typical element of Chinese social structure. This type of generalization only scratches the surface of an enormous problem: what is at stake is nothing less than the question of the motive forces of cultural process and particularly the question of the accessibility of that process to human direction and control.

The substantive and methodological problems attending the study of individual and mass psychological adjustments to social and cultural change in China are huge. Certainly an examination of this length, incorporating no original research, can have as its goal only the stimulation of some readers, hoping to move them to a broader and deeper exploration of the literature and perhaps to fresh research. That goal may also render somewhat more acceptable the fact that the remarks which follow are offered by a non-Chinese social scientist lacking credentials in the field of psychological anthropology.

BACKGROUND TO CHANGE: CHINESE CULTURE AND SOCIETY

To begin with, we must consider the problems confronting attempts to generate basic generalizations about Chinese culture and society. Such generalizations are essential as baselines against which changes can be measured. Let us begin with the common sense observation that Chinese culture—despite internal temporal, regional, and class variations—displays sufficient integrity and cohesiveness to be readily and consistently recognized as a whole and differentiated from comparable systems. This recognition occurs among those who carry the culture, whether they identify themselves physically (as *li-min*, "black-haired people") or culturally (as *Han-jen* or *Tong-yen*, "people of Han or T'ang"). It also occurs among peoples of other cultures, including those adjacent to the Chinese, such as the Koreans, Japanese, Burmese, and Vietnamese, and those physically encysted within China, such as Chuang, Minchia, and Lolo.

Even though there are innumerable instances of variation, the Chinese regard themselves as bearers of a common culture. Indeed, this identification extends far beyond the most freely interpreted boundaries of the Chinese political state and encompasses overseas Chinese, in every part of the world, even after generations of physical removal (see Chapter 3). Such clarity of cultural recognition is by no means unique to the Chinese, although the Chinese Empire has been termed "the major exception in the pre-modern world to what would appear to be the rule that units of territorial and demographic extent comparable to that of China are not stable entities over long periods of time" (Elvin 1973, p. 17). This ostensible coherence, unity, and boundedness of Chinese culture plays a major role in validating any notion of a generalized Chinese basic or modal personality structure or national character model.

The question of what, then, constitutes the basis for recognizing specific individuals as Chinese can only be answered by referring to cultural cues. Important as this matter is, it has received surprisingly little attention. The matter is of specific concern to our topic, for among the cues leading to identification could well be the complex of expected behavior summarized under a modal personality rubric. For example, a young person born overseas to parents of *Huach'iao* descent often grows up in total ignorance of the ancestral language, yet frequently develops the strongest identification with the culture of that remote homeland. Unquestionably, part of that identification arises from what is best summed up as the racist orientation of the new sociocultural milieu, experienced by the young Chinese as constricting their mobility because the prejudice against them prevents their free acceptance in the new society. Without minimizing such a factor, or the significance of physical type as a basis of group identity, one can still examine the weight of common personality in the development of group consciousness.

Various attempts have been made, by Chinese and non-Chinese scholars, to distill the essential traits of Chinese culture. We have space merely to suggest a few such schemes. Han Yu-shan and Derk Bodde both give first place in their considerations of the essentials in Chinese culture to the *theme of the harmonious interaction of humankind and nature* (Han 1946: 4–5; Bodde 1946, pp. 20–22). Various implications of this theme are relevant to our own inquiry. Although the Chinese are said to have characteristically sought accommodation with nature, they are now actively altering the environment on a scale beyond anything previously attempted in the culture. This alteration of the environment is sometimes seen as a parallel to the Maoist insistence upon active participation in the political process by as many individuals as can be aroused. There are implicit dangers in provoking such broad change, because the concept of the "mandate of heaven" provides that all natural disasters are unfavorable judgments upon those in power. Actually, the statement that the new changes go against the previously upheld cultural theme of harmonious interaction can only be controversial. According to the so-called hydraulic interpretation of Chinese society, what is known as the "Asiatic Mode of Production" requires massive reordering of the productive juxtaposition of land and water, plus derivative constructions. Such a view regards the changes under the People's Republic as primarily quantitative, not qualitative (see Wittfogel 1957, ch. 2; Wittfogel 1970).

The themes of man's harmonious interaction with nature and the mandate of heaven also ramify far beyond gross societal effects and encompass myriad local and familial consequences through beliefs in various linked systems of geomancy and astrology. Little or nothing has been heard of such beliefs in recent years, although the attacks leveled against them during the Red Guard upheavals of the first cultural revolution suggest persistence even under great pressure.

Another main feature of Chinese culture enumerated by Han Yu-shan (Han 1946, pp. 3–17) is the emphasis on social groups, especially domestic groupings, rather than on the individual. This is related to the centrality of the concept of filial piety and leads to the consequence that the physical, emotional, and financial security of the individual is insured by others, mainly by the family and other associations based on kinship. Bodde, too, emphasizes the concern for orderly social relations and the intensity of intergenerational bonds represented by genealogy, ancestor worship, and filial piety. He notes the crucial role of the family, with such concepts as *kuo-chia*, "nation," which combines the ideographs for country and family, and *min chih fu mu*, the appellation for the emperor, literally meaning "the people's father and mother."

Like Han, the eminent sinologist Balazs (1964), and most others who have offered similar analyses, Bodde finds a relatively high degree of social mobility, partially as a result of the merit examination system. He also discusses the generally held Chinese notions that the basic nature of man is good, that education is greatly esteemed, and that there is nothing in Chinese ideology that makes suffering a virtue or an inevitable and major part of life. Although Bodde became somewhat equivocal about the point in a later contribution (Bodde 1957, pp. 58–60), he originally identified a dislike for violence as an important element, however paradoxically linked to the concept of a "right of revolution." Finally, Bodde, again like many others, notes the institutional existence of graft and corruption, associating it with the chronic underpayment of officials at all levels.

While many other attempts have been made to distill the essential ingredients of Chinese civilization, most add nothing to the list already given, but gloss the points in subtly different ways. There is, of course, a group of contributions that come at the problem from another direction—the writings that approach China as an outstanding example of what has been called "Asiatic society," "hydraulic society," or even "oriental despotism." Starting long before Marx, this type of analysis has played a political as well as academic role in the history of ideas. Among those who have contributed along the lines of this theory in this century are Max Weber, Karl August Wittfogel, Chi Ch'ao-ting, Owen Lattimore, and others whose main expertise is in Chinese fields. To delve deeply into the theses of these writers, some of whom conduct bitter skirmishes against the others, would take this article astray. It should be sufficient to itemize the main ingredients added by these scholars to what we have already described.

These can be reduced, for the purposes of this paper, to three main points and a small number of corollaries. First, below the level of central government (brought into being and nourished by need for flood control, irrigation, drainage, and other tasks requiring massive, organized labor forces) society is "cellular," composed of many more or less identically structured local population units that are essentially self-sufficient, inward-oriented and hostile to the outside. Second, the ruling sector of the society, apart from the emperor, comprises the scholar-gentry-officials and constitutes a genuine social class with strong continuity and a distinctive ideology, manifested in a clearly defined life style. Third, the political structure is totalitarian, by which Balazs, for example, meant that "no private undertaking nor any aspect of public life could escape regulation" (Balazs 1964, p. 10). Since it is evident that there is a contradiction between this point and the assertion of the cellular nature of the countryside, certain corollaries are called for and may be found in concepts of the "law of diminishing administrative returns" and "beggars' democracy." Since imperial Chinese governments, handicapped by slow and inefficient means of communication, could not bring the full weight of government to bear on all localities, an alternate strategy developed—the selective use of terror as a political instrument. In the interstices grew a certain degree of local autonomy, although the domination of the gentry was rarely threatened.

Before leaving the topic of thematic analyses of Chinese culture, we must pay special attention to the contribution by Francis L. K. Hsu (1969). Following the methodological lead of E. A. Hoebel, Hsu responds to the problems of comparative analysis by providing a model of Chinese culture in the form of fourteen postulates and seventy-five corollaries and sub-corollaries. The first postulate concerns filial piety and the second includes the web of patrilineal kinship. These we have seen already. The third of Hsu's postulates raises a new dimension and has obvious significance for our main topic—it states flatly that women are inferior to men. The next five postulates lay out the hierarchical categories of both real and spiritual worlds. The tenth postulate specifies the behavioral aspects of the previously itemized hierarchical statuses. Eleven declares good and evil relative and eternal and the twelfth opts for non-violence and negotiation. Thirteen elevates reciprocity, but the corollaries make it clear that such reciprocity involves the concept of proper rather than identical or strictly equivalent responsive acts, thus conforming to the prior emphasis on status hierarchy. The final postulate is worth quoting in full:

> China is the oldest country in the world and the Chinese way of life is superior, but there are many Chinese who are ignorant and inferior (human beings are not equal), just as there are many non-Chinese peoples who do not share the Chinese ways (Hsu 1969, p. 71).

We have come full circle, returning through Hsu's postulates to the Chinese recognition that they bear a common and distinct culture. If we could easily accept generalizations, we would be well on the way to establishing a predictive model of Chinese basic personality. Of course, Hsu introduces his scheme with the warning that his postulates "are first approximations . . . subject to improvements," (p. 65) but he does not doubt, and has made amply clear in previous work, that he believes that a unitary set of statements can be constructed that will apply to all bearers of Chinese culture. Indeed, he asserts that "even in their present state, most of these postulates can already serve as guideposts for anticipating or even predicting future developments on a probability basis" (p. 65).

There is a great temptation here to launch into an extended criticism of the thematic approach to culture, particularly when applied to one of such huge dimensions as the Chinese. Such an approach can achieve its object only through selective neglect of history, compression of areal spread and regional differences, and by ironing out subcultural variations associated with class as if they were mere wrinkles in the social fabric. (For further discussion of these points see Fried, 1973, pp. 348–54.) Only if such defects are remembered, can we use this kind of thematic approach without creating more problems than we resolve.

SOME FORMULATIONS OF CHINESE BASIC PERSONALITY OR NATIONAL CHARACTER

Following Wallace's suggestion (1961: 106) we note the distinction between the terms "national character" and "basic personality," and agree that while the former might be more appropriate on grounds of the political sophistication of China, the latter is much better because

It merely refers to a structure of articulated personality characteristics and processes attributable, non-statistically, to almost all members of some culturally bounded population (p. 106).

The reference to the non-statistical aspect of basic personality is particularly welcome, since the information that has been gathered on this subject derives from something considerably less than 1/1000th of one percent of the current population.

According to Wallace, basic personality differs from "modal personality" in that the latter implies statistically valid central tendencies.

Basic personality is a non-statistical concept, emphasizing the importance of pattern and attempting to dispose of questions of frequency by excluding "deviants" and "peripheral" traits, thus leaving a core structure which is supposedly common to all members of a group (p. 109).

We must not forget that much of what is said in this field is based solidly on intuition or, at best, disciplined extrapolation from relatively tiny data bases. It is only fair to note, on the other hand, that some of the studies which include statements about Chinese personality are rather neatly performed, with some care taken to establish the significance of the sample and to exercise some control over the gathering of data.

Dependence and Orality

We can begin our survey on the highest level of generality with the predominant opinion that Chinese basic personality tends quite markedly to avoid change and cling to tradition. Take, for example, the study conducted in Taiwan by Godwin C. Chu, dealing with the "persuasibility" of Chinese subjects. Chu's experiments were calculated to reveal various differences with respect to the ease or reluctance with which subjects, representing different sectors of Chinese society, would change their opinions. Chu then compared his results with non-Chinese data. These experimental results were consistent with the conventionally assumed Chinese submission to authority of age, status, and traditional values. Chu extrapolates that this submissive attitude operates against the formation of commitments to "modern ideologies" such as freedom of speech or social progress (Chu 1967, pp. 286–87). Chu's experiments indicate one departure from stereotype that seems to have been something of a surprise to him. Female subjects showed definite and fairly regular negative reactions to and resentment of male authority. The significance of this finding is evident in the context of drives in the People's Republic for changes in women's status (see Young 1973; Sidel 1973; Wolf 1972).

Chu obtained evidence that a major factor reinforcing resistance to persuasion for his Chinese subjects was their ideological preset. All subjects, but males in particular, showed strong resistance to opinion shifts that went against previous ideological assumptions, the Chinese reaction in this respect differing from that of American subjects. (It must be mentioned that differences in real political environments exist and might well affect experimental results.) Chu's findings with respect to ideology seem at least partially parallel to those of the social psychologist Ai-li S. Chin in her discussion of the "model man" and "ideal local party secretary" in Chinese Communist society (A. S. Chen [sic] 1964). Chin concludes her study by recognizing that Communist China continues a long Chinese tradition of maintaining or changing ideology, "of inducing desirable behavior through moral teaching" based on the use of paragons.

Assertions of an easy dependence on exemplary authority leads us to a larger theory of Chinese basic personality as characteristically dependent. While not exclusive to the works of psychoanalytically inclined scholars, the most extensive discussions of this theme are psychoanalytic ones, such as those of John Weakland (1950, 1956), Warner Muensterberger (1951), and Hsien Rin (1966), to mention a few. Prominent in the theory of dependence is the contention that Chinese culture is conspicuously oral in its behavioral emphases.

Whatever its etiology, and however trite the observation, Chinese orality is frequently adduced from the obvious significance given food preparation and consumption. The Chinese commonly say, "Have you eaten?" when we would say hello. What is more, the pattern seems to be an ancient one. We are all familiar, of course, with the fact that the government of the People's Republic uses feasting as a tool of diplomatic intercourse. Food and its preparation has served Mao as a metaphor, as in his Yenan speech on February 1, 1942 (Schram 1969, pp. 176–77). Yet we are obviously in great danger of being superficial.

There is no gainsaying that mere maintenance of caloric subsistence has been and continues to be the major preoccupation as well as occupation of a vast portion of the Chinese population. The problematic nature of the food supply would seem to be cause enough for manifestations of food anxiety and fixation. Yet, evidently, other factors must be involved, for portions of the population which have not known hunger and have no reason to anticipate it nonetheless engage in many food-centered activities. To a far greater degree than in our culture, for instance, ritual activity is associated with food. There is also the common association of religious rites of various kinds with "sacrifice" (actually more usually displays) of food, carried out in the temples, at graves and shrines and in the house. This waste distresses the current governments of the PRC and of Taiwan, just as it did the ancient governments of China.

The question arises whether the prolonged exposure to famine and hunger has created or is associated with feelings of guilt and sin extending throughout the entire society. If this is the case, such feelings might assist us in understanding Chinese reactions to changes instituted by a government which has made the conquest of hunger a paramount goal. It would also throw light on the nature of "thought reform," and the significance of confession and self-criticism in the process.

Wolfram Eberhard (1967, p. 66) notes that the *Cheng-fa nien-ch'u ching*, a Buddhist text said to date from the sixth century, "emphasizes the punishment of persons who let others starve or do not let others participate in good food. Such persons are reincarnated as 'hungry spirits.'" Few categories of demon are as feared and abhorred as this. Whatever the contemporary situation on the mainland, in Taiwan the spirit category of "hungry spirit," *ngo kuei*, is still regarded as very potent. In city and countryside alike, shrines abound, some just recently constructed, that are commemorated to these anonymous and thoroughly dangerous lost souls who died without offspring and failed to make other arrangements for having sacrifices made to their memory. More recent Chinese Buddhist texts prescribe "severe and repeated punishments" for failure to treat food properly, wasting or mistreating it. Eberhard (1967, pp. 74-5) calls such maledictions "typically Chinese," and suggests that the general idea might reflect "constant threat of hunger." Such behavior is still regarded not only as sinful, but as cause for great shame and guilt. Eberhard notes a revealing incident in another Buddhist text: a pauper who once was rich is fed by monks who reveal to him that the rice he is eating is that thrown away by him in his wealthy days. Learning this, he commits suicide (p. 100).

Whatever the present regard in which theories of personality hold such concepts as orality, more has been associated with the term than attitudes toward food. There is a general dependency on others, who are viewed as parental, and particularly maternal, surrogates. Warner Muensterberger, for example, has suggested that, at least in southeastern China, the complex of dependency includes opium smoking and addictive gambling (Muensterberger 1951). Francis Hsu, however, points out that there are cultural and historical factors in drug addiction (Hsu 1953, pp. 56-61).

This orality is attributed to a number of interacting causes. Much is made of assertions that the Chinese infant experiences breastfeeding not merely on demand but almost continuously for prolonged sessions, beyond eighteen months or to the arrival of the next child. Unfortunately, although there may be clinical literature in medical records, the literature of ethnography is scanty on actually observed sequences of child rearing behavior. When the subject arises in ethnographic works, whether by Chinese or foreigners, observations tend to be impressionistic summaries or reminiscences.

One of the most extensively expressed theories of the orality of Chinese national character is that of Richard Solomon, who uses it to help explain some critical developments in the history of the People's Republic, particularly the Cultural Revolution. Solomon's theory and its exposition have had mixed reviews, to put it mildly. Some scholars think that he has offered insufficient evidence to assure his conclusions (DeVos 1974; Metzger 1972), but his ideas are nonetheless intriguing. Basic to Solomon's argument is the observation that Chinese child rearing patterns call for the reward of achievement by feeding (Solomon 1971) with concomitant withholding of food as a major punishment. In general, the dining table is "the place where more routine social disciplines are developed," hence a locus of anxiety (p. 43). "Authority becomes associated with who eats before or better than whom, and who can speak and who must listen" (p. 44).

Solomon argues that the complex of love, communicated mainly through oral indulgence, is coupled with strict external discipline and the discouragement of "explorations of autonomous behavior." The result is arrest at an oral stage and dependency on guidance and external discipline (pp. 66–67). Parental discipline, however, is often expressed in sudden sharp outbursts. The alternation of such flurries with interludes of indulgence are said by Solomon to have a parallel in a basic Chinese "social rhythm" of alternation between *ho-p'ing* and *hun-luan,* "the alternation between 'harmony' and the 'confusion' of vented aggression" (p. 80). Solomon applies this concept to the understanding of the Cultural Revolution, indicating that Mao had faith that *luan,* interpreted as "controlled political conflict," "was the answer to China's continuing struggle with 'revisionism' . . ." (p. 498).

Margery Wolf reports that mothers enhance their feeling of security by selectively, but steadily, undermining and minimizing the father's role in child rearing (Wolf 1970), but the same observer offers a variety of situations in which young children threaten mother with paternal interference. Mothers frequently respond by threatening to direct the father's wrath against the child. Mao Tse-tung describes his mother in a variant of this conduct:

> She pitied the poor and often gave them rice when they came to ask for it during famines. But she could not do so when my father was present. . . . We had many quarrels in my home over this question. There were two "parties" in the family. One was my father, the Ruling Power. The Opposition was made up of myself, my mother, my brother, and some-

times even the labourer. . . . The dialectical struggle in our family was constantly developing (Snow 1971, pp. 114–15).

Wolfram Eberhard who studied more than eight hundred dreams from Chinese subjects concludes that they show "the great emotional distance from their father" (Eberhard 1967, p. 77).

Weakland affirms that this orally-fixated dependency, the consequence of Chinese child rearing customs, is the major basis of the typical Chinese organization of action both on individual and institutional levels. He alleges that the mild form of limb binding in the child's first few months reduces tactile experience in favor of total concentration on sucking and other oral stimuli. He maintains that this form of dependence is not seen as weakness, but as the foundation of interactions that take one through life.

Sexuality and Orality

Another general view of Chinese character also asserts its arrest at an oral stage, but turns attention instead to allegedly consequential problems of genital sexuality. John Weakland in particular has attempted to develop this conception. He believes that the structure of Chinese culture requires sexual repression, because active manifestations of sexual desire through the satisfaction or attempted satisfaction of genital drives lead to parental disapproval in the form of threatened or actual withdrawal of love. Conversely, it is asserted that self-discipline in sexual behavior, demonstrated by restraint, if not abstinence, produces parental approval and overt manifestations of love (Weakland 1956, pp. 246–47). The psychiatrist Hsien Rin (1966, p. 12) supports this and offers the opinion that the maturing male is subdued by powerful threats of castration.

Whatever materials may exist in clinical records, the general study of sexual behavior in China is even more neglected than was the same subject matter in the West until recent years. R. H. van Gulik's (1961) study of the history of Chinese sexual practices, as revealed in literature and art, generally supports statements like those above. But there are important differences. An objection may be made that van Gulik's materials apply primarily to upper-class sections of society and throw little light on the behavior of common people. Nonetheless, it is worthwhile to examine some of van Gulik's insights.

A variety of textual sources provide a surprisingly rich, although often spotty, record of sexual ideals, beliefs, and customs going at least as far back as middle or late Chou times (2,500 years ago) and perhaps further. The function of intercourse was said to be twofold: for procreation and for strengthening the male. The latter belief involved the elaborate ties between human physique, physiology, and psychology, on the one hand, and the cosmos and nature on the other. In the grand scheme of things, females were classified as *yin,* along with darkness, secrecy, mystery, coldness, and negativity. Males were associated with the *yang* principle, light, clarity, heat, and positivity. As with most Chinese concepts of this kind, exclusiveness is explicitly denied: men also have varying degrees of *yin* essence, although always to a relatively small degree unless pathology is involved, and women display the converse. Chinese sexual literature describes semen as the male's "most precious possession, the source not only of his health but his very life" (van Gulik 1961, p. 47). It might be added that it also represented the treasury of his parents and all his ancestors to whom he owed the ineradicable obligation of continuing the line. Indeed, in the views of some commentators, all ejaculation was potentially harmful, but that which was experienced in the course of procreation could be viewed as a sacrifice to the ancestors.

Another view, quite possibly more popular, held that through proper performance of intercourse a man could stimulate an increase in his *yang* force through absorption of *yin* from the female. The situation was potentially dangerous, in either case, for a woman also stood to benefit physically and emotionally from draining the man of *yang* force. Thus she would attempt by all means to stimulate him to ejaculate, while he attempted to bring her to climax without ejaculating.

Another problem is the ways in which the sexual act is regarded by those who perform it. One encounters a theory of widespread fear of sexuality, especially in Chinese men (Heyer 1953). Ancient Chinese literary and philosophical materials present sexual energies in a cosmological way. Chinese medicine considers health and illness a matter of balance of forces, particularly with respect to *yang* and *yin;* abuse of balance, for example by excessive loss of semen, or encountering a female partner whose *yin* is overly powerful, or failing to schedule intercourse for appropriate astrological days or hours, can be debilitating or even fatal. The theme of *vagina dentata* is present in various guises, as in the well known novel *Chin P'ing Mei:* "A sweet girl of eighteen years/her breasts are soft and white/but below her waist she carries a sword/that will behead all foolish men./Although one does not see/their severed heads loll/imperceptibly she will drain your bones/of the last drops of marrow" (cited in van Gulik 1961, p. 288).

It is also clear from the literary materials that a favorite way of characterizing intercourse is in terms of struggle and warfare; victory in the battle goes "to him or her, who during sexual intercourse, succeeds in obtaining the other's vital essence. . ." (van Gulik 1961, p. 157).

The widespread theme of the danger of intercourse may help us understand the toleration of separations, which seems much greater than that manifest in our own culture. Of course, we cannot take the point too far. Travelling officials often brought concubines or female servants in their retinues, and prostitutes have been an invariable commodity in wine houses. Conversely, there are equally strong indications that a very ancient and continuous element in Chinese sexual attitudes has been the right of wives and concubines to the sexual attentions of their husbands, although not to the extent of his ejaculation.

Probably the most recurrent theme in Levy's (1974) collection of Chinese sex jokes is that portraying women as the primary instigators of sexual intercourse. Brides are shown as unbearably eager or fully experienced, and into old age the women are pictured as having much greater sexual appetite than men.

The status of women is a subject in its own right; here simply a comment on continuity and change. Van Gulik asserts that differences exist in the attitude toward women displayed by Confucianism and by Taoism. The former clearly asserted female inferiority; its prescription can be read in numerous ancient books. On the other hand, Taoism, particularly in its popular forms, emphasized the importance of the female principle in achieving harmony, and sometimes in its alchemical manifestations raised the concept of female essence to a very high degree. According to van Gulik, Buddhism, during its first millenium in China, also presented women in terms much closer to equality than was acceptable in Confucian ideology. The rise of neo-Confucianism is said to have begun to tip the balance against the Taoist and Buddhist view; the texts of the latter are said to have undergone drastic expurgation of sexual and related materials during this period. The same writer asserts (p. 246) that the completion of the theme was accomplished as a result of the Mongol conquest which he believes institutionalized the seclusion of women in the attempt to keep upper-class ladies from Mongol eyes. I cannot evaluate this theory, but it is interesting to note the words of Mao Tse-tung:

> Women, in addition to being dominated by these three systems of authority [state, clan, and religious], . . . are also dominated by the men (the authority of the husband). . . . As to the authority of the husband, this has always been weaker among the poor peasants because, out of economic necessity, their womenfolk have to do more manual labour than the women of the richer classes, and therefore have more say and greater power of decision in family matters (Mao, *Selected Works*, I [1964], pp. 44–45).

There are frequent assertions of Chinese puritanism and sexual repression. Van Gulik believes that a major shift in Chinese attitudes towards sex took place in the seventeenth century with the Manchu conquest, a previous view of sexual activity as natural and proper giving way to the notion that it was dirty and to be repressed. Eberhard disagrees, placing any such change in Sung times (960–1279). Others believe that the profound change came with the victory of Mao, charging that the preceding Nationalist government's war against prostitution, pornography, and dancing was ineffectual. Yet none of these views is quite satisfactory, since the historical phenomenon itself seems cyclical as well as showing variation along familiar fault-lines of region and class.

Dependency and Sociocultural Behavior

One interesting, but unpublished study of Chinese sociocultural organization, affirms the dependent nature of Chinese sociocultural behavior in terms of the formation of coalitions (Stover 1961). The concept of the dyad is as crucial to this view as the concept of the individual to some analyses of western culture and society. Stover points out that Chinese prefer to depend upon others rather than do things directly for themselves. Stover offers an explanation of the social structural consequences of this preference:

> It is because Chinese non-kin social relationships are indeed modeled after those originating in the family that many social groups at large are organized like closed, cellular primary-groups and that personal relations in them follow the hidden rules, implicit in the described family code, of exact status definition, hierarchical organization, ritualized formality, and, above all, the tendency of social status to persist unalterably through time (Stover 1961, p. xxiv).

Weakland proposes that this background results in a characteristic style of Chinese action in which activity is divided into two relatively unequal parts, a long preparatory period and a relatively short, rapid burst of accomplishment. Emphasis is on the former portion, particularly when the activity involves direct personal relations. When the activity involves things, as when a painting is made, the actor thinks everything through as carefully as possible, then does the actual painting very quickly, taking perhaps only a few minutes. When dealing with people, however, the complexities mount as the variables may continue to change even as they are employed. But the basic style is the same, as in Weakland's example of rural litigation in which great effort is put into plotting the event to its conclusion before anything "real" is done. My own observation of an election in immediately pre-Communist Ch'uhsien furnishes another case in point: it was agreed before the election that the winner would be an old man who craved the honor but who, upon winning, would decline it on the grounds of age, giving the office to his opponent (Fried 1953, pp. 215–16).

All of this, of course, is quite consistent with Hsu's analysis of Chinese society as *"situation centered,"* in which, as we saw earlier, "emphasis [is] . . . put upon an individual's appropriate place and behavior among his fellowmen" (Hsu 1953: 10). Hsu is aware of the implication of dependency, since in the same context he adds that, "Being more situation-centered, the Chinese is inclined to be socially or psychologically dependent on others. . ." (p. 10).

Considering the limited amount of rigorously gathered material on Chinese child rearing, assertions about general psychological coordinates of childhood personality and its formation must rest to a considerable extent on extrapolations from autobiographical recollections, and investigations involving the use of projective tests.

A carefully executed study in Taiwan administered Rorschach tests to 347 "normal" adults, all from north Taiwan and mainly from rural areas, selected to conform as far as possible with the proportion represented in the 1956 census with regard to sex, age, educational level, and occupation. The subjects were tested in various locales. The basic findings cite and confirm the earlier work of Abel and Hsu (1949) and can be summarized as follows:

> In China, from ancient days down to the present, rules of decorum have strictly governed people's behavior. Spontaneity and impulsivity are not encouraged. Feelings and emotions, even those between children and parents, should be controlled firmly and expressed only via proprieties and other formal ways. In short, one should keep a proper distance, both physical and psychological, from others. This formalism has long been an important element in the practices of Chinese child training and under it Chinese young people achieved their detached roles in interpersonal relationship and their lack of awareness of contacts with others (Yang Kuo-shu, et al. 1963, p. 184).

Scofield and Sun, in interviews with Chinese in the United States, found American Chinese child-rearing practices more severe and rigid than American practices in the same general behavioral areas—sphincter and bladder control, weaning age and means used to secure weaning. They reported that Chinese Americans place severe restrictions on sexual activity, including self-exploration and manipulation, from the time of birth. They further asserted evidence of severe restrictions on displays of behavioral independence in children. As a result, they predicted "that the modal personality of the Chinese Americans, when compared with the Americans, can be described as being more withdrawn, more shy, more emotionally insecure, more introverted, more sensitive, more suspicious, more cold and aloof" (Scofield and Sun 1960, p. 22).

Such studies present an auspicious beginning. However, we cannot overlook the fact that the total number of respondents is terribly small, that it is even smaller if Chinese born or living in the United States are set aside. Beyond this, with the exception of the Rorschach study by K. S. Yang and his associates, the predominance of students among the subjects is very high and likely to be skewing. Additionally, none of the available studies has any further ethnic breakdown, but tends to assume homogeneity on the part of the subject population. Finally, there is an unfortunate lack of direct coupling of projective test data and analysis with close behavioral observation and ethnographic accounting.

CONTINUITY AND CHANGE IN CHINESE CULTURE

Obviously culture change is a vast topic; it is also as controversial as anything in contemporary politics. Indeed, the disputation is part of the political scene. The Nationalists, clinging to their remnant Republic of China on Taiwan, denounce the Communists as total innovators having no significant links with China's cultural past. For different reasons, the Communist government on the mainland asserts its novelty, with certain reservations. Meanwhile institutional and individual behavioral patterns recognizable from the past, sometimes the remarkably distant past, crop up again in the People's Republic, often to the proclaimed despair of the people in power.

The concept of Chinese culture as stagnant through two thousand or more years has little to recommend or substantiate it. China has been continually affected by the diffusion of elements from the outside, and has undergone both continuous and intermittent changes as an internal process. Chinese did not have to change drastically to contemplate *change* itself. There was a considerable tradition of change and reaction to change on which to build. I do not wish to suggest that the tempo of change or the magnitude of changes remained constant. There is good reason to think otherwise—to believe that as early as the last century of Ming (1369–1644) and certainly by middle Ch'ing (about 1775) rates of change were accelerating as the result of at least three factors: soaring population, increased frequency of contact with societies of different and mechanically advanced technologies, and the physical spread of Chinese culture with attendant increase in the rate of encapsulation of non-Han cultures.

In taking a brief look at the most general things that can be said about cultural continuity and change in the context of our special concern for psychological adjustment, we begin with Taiwan and move on to the People's Republic.

Republic of China

For many reasons the version of Chinese culture being harbored on the island of Formosa should be different from that of the mainland. Taiwan is a fine case of regional cultural specialization. Whatever may be made of archaeological materials that seem to suggest the possibility of very early connections with the Chinese mainland, the beginnings of significant Chinese settlement go back about three hundred years. Immigrants displaced an aboriginal Malayo-Polynesian population that spoke several different languages. Its cultures varied more widely than might be expected in such a small area, but most resembled those of the northern Philippines. Although Chinese in every accepted meaning of the term, the immigrants were not representative of Chinese culture in general, but came from two major ethnic-linguistic enclaves and a particular social class. There was strong predominance of Minnan speakers from the nearest Chinese province, Fukien, and a smaller, but still large, population of Hakka, mainly from Kwangtung. For a long time those who came were mainly impoverished peasants; later, more successful rural elements, merchants, and some scholars came. In any event, the Chinese culture of Taiwan never epitomized China as a whole. Curiously, one way in which Formosa is sometimes said to have differed is in easier acceptance of technological and social change; during the decade prior to Japanese control, Taiwan was perhaps the most progressive of all Chinese provinces or territories in terms of the building of railroads and telegraph lines and even in the reform of relations of agricultural tenure and tenancy.

The Taiwanese have never been completely supine in dealing with governmental power; indeed, rebellious episodes going back two hundred years and more are still commemorated in active ceremonials. Resistance was put up against the Japanese, not to mention more recent events related to "retrocession," the Nationalist government's preferred term for the political treatment of Taiwan after the defeat of Japan. Nonetheless, Taiwan did not repel the influences of either the Japanese or the postretrocession mainlanders. Particularly with regard to the former, considering that the period of influence was a full fifty years (1895–1945), and considering that the cultural differences between Taiwanese and Japanese were of obviously greater magnitude than between Taiwanese and Chinese, we must ask, to what extent do the present cultures (subcultures?) of Taiwan—Minnan and Hakka—represent unique constellations?

This question points to the problem of methodology. When psychocultural research pertaining to Chinese is carried out with Taiwanese subjects, what provisions have to be made to avoid interpretive error arising from their unique cultural histories? Mere awareness of this feature, and an accompanying awareness that congruence between Minnan and Hakka Taiwanese should not be assumed, has not been adequately demonstrated in the work done so far.

Further sources of change affecting behavior and personality formation in contemporary Taiwan must be mentioned. Since 1948 there seem to have been considerable changes in diet, mainly in frequency and proportions of important foods and in preparation of cuisine. The main sources of change are Japanese and diverse mainland influences, although the effects of new food products from the United States have been increasingly conspicuous in the last decade. Many superficial aspects of culture show change: clothing styles, cosmetics and conceptions of physical beauty, house and building construction and furnishings, recreational styles and entertainments, travel, and the like. Other shifts seem to have occurred which suggest chains of changes, the ends often not in sight. Here one thinks of the great alterations in agriculture in terms not only of cultigens and technology, but also market relations, land tenure, credit and social relations (such as the effects of farmers' associations). Perhaps even deeper changes are improved physical health, reduced child mortality, and declining family size, especially in certain social sectors. Increasing exposure to education, enormous reduction of illiteracy, and new forms of employment are all capable of influencing personality formation in various ways, not least by subtly altering intergenerational and intersexual relationships and other significant elements of child rearing.

Yet for all of these changes and variations, the most obvious empirical fact is that the culture of Taiwan is visibly Chinese. It displays some heterodox features but has never, to my knowledge, been taken for anything but Chinese. Even the most separatist of those in the Formosan independence movement, who emphasize that Formosan culture is a synthesis of at least four discrete traditions, Chinese, aboriginal, Japanese, and European, admit the dominance of the Chinese contribution.

People's Republic of China

When the Ch'ing dynasty ended in 1911, pigtails were cut and feet, if not untied, were bound with rapidly declining frequency. Other changes came, but much more gradually, and most were well foreshadowed in events which had taken place decades earlier. When the Communist government came to power, there were probably even fewer instances of immediate change. Even twenty-five years later the question of the extent and profundity of change brings no certain answer. This must seem paradoxical, because the Chinese Communist Revolution is often described as the most sweeping social upheaval in human history, with Maoism holding out an image of change dwarfing all previous political, social, and cultural revolutions.

Yet Mao Tse-tung himself has repeatedly warned of the limited nature of the changes that have accompanied the progress of his revolution. Actually, Mao's development of this theme has grown in importance in recent times. Thirty years ago, before achieving widespread power, he heavily emphasized the total changes to be brought about by communism. More recently he has emphasized that substantial changes in Chinese society and culture have occurred but are of uncertain durability in the short range of history. According to the overarching theory, the triumph of such changes in the long run cannot be questioned but they are in constant danger of attack and even reversal.

Political Changes

In 1969, a major theme of PRC propaganda was an assertion of the "triumph," as a consequence of the Cultural Revolution, of the lower and middle peasants and the proletariat in "seizing control of the superstructure." Essentially, this concept declares that politics is in command; hence masses of people who by certain standards should be the passive victims of an unfavorable technological and economic status, are defying such standards by raising ideological demands and maintaining a social system far in advance of that which might otherwise be expected. This theme is central to understanding contemporary mainland China, for it illuminates the staggering contradiction between China's claim to worldwide ideological preeminence and the reality of her limited technology and total economy. This problem is exacerbated by a lingering Marxist requirement for a materialist approach. But the Maoists have long since gotten rid of "vulgar materialism" and other "vulgar determinisms" in favor of their own unique dialectics. This means that extreme pressures for change are repeatedly exerted by higher authority in this tough state structure. Furthermore, the changes that are demanded often appear to be greatly in excess of the capabilities of those asked to make them. The twenty-five-year history of the Chinese Communist state presents to some observers a record at least as freighted with failure to change as with successful transformation.

Several major changes have been attempted. Let us offer some suggestions. I would agree with those identifying the key change as that which has been sought in the relations between the whole population and the means of economic production. But, greatly weakened and jeopardized as it may be, private property has not been abolished in China. Quite apart from the household plots that have several times been abolished, only to reappear as a means of increasing food production, and quite apart from the fact that most housing throughout China is owned by its main occupants, usually its builders, there are much larger privately owned enterprises. Even where ownership is not private, major differences exist in productivity, salaries, and perquisites. Important elements of the "national bourgeoisie" still exist, maintaining privileged economic roles. Never in Chinese history has private wealth and property been so insecure, but the change is capable of presentation in quantitative terms, since such property has been weak throughout Chinese history (Wittfogel 1957, p. 289–300). The matter is further complicated by the numerous changes of policy that have been made during these two decades of Mao's rule and by our knowledge of local variation. Whether the functioning units have been individual families, APCs, teams, brigades, or communes, inequality has existed and been recognized by higher Communist authority. In the cities as well, what Maoism condemns as "economism," essentially the demand for rewards commensurate with different quantities and qualities of work, repeatedly rears its head. The implicit tie between economism and inequality does not really bother the Maoists; they long ago denounced equalitarianism as a peasant form of left wing deviation. Most bothersome are the links between economism and specialist expertise on the one hand, and greater concern for oneself and one's family, rather than for society, on the other.

Changes in the Family

Although the family has been hyperbolized by some of the analysts of Chinese society, even those who see it more realistically grant its enormous importance in the organization of Chinese society for milleniums. A widely held assumption has been that the individual's main significance derived from the fact that he linked generations yet to come with their ancestors. This notion played a key role in shaping sexual concepts, ideas of interpersonal relationship, status and hierarchy, and thereby set the stage for crucial events and conceptions of the child rearing process, helping to produce certain uniformities in personality, which coalesce in the construct known as Chinese national character. Chinese Communism, Maoism in particular, seeks to change this drastically. Contrary to some politically motivated charges, there has been little, if any, direct assault on the small family as such, although larger kin groups such as extended families and lineages have been given a hard time. The latter, seemingly at the point of extinction, nonetheless show possibilities of reemergence if the "capitalist roaders" should become more successful. The economic base upon which extended families and lineages thrived has been almost completely destroyed, but the economic base upon which the nuclear family thrives is probably enhanced.

This can be gathered from a variety of materials published in the Mainland: official documents condemning practices that favor individuals' household economies, propaganda urging change, Red Guard newspapers baring the details of life of party officials high and low, cadres, and even ordinary citizens with proper class backgrounds. Such information presents us with a picture of nuclear families functioning in the division of labor much as peasant families have been described in the community study literature and, what is more, continuing to function as centers of orientation and security for the young, albeit more and more often sharing the former function with state organized creches and nursery schools. Although we have been told proudly that a favorite song in these nurseries continues to be *"Yeh ch'in, niang ch'in, pu ju Mao Chuhsi ch'in* (Daddy is dear/ mommy is dear/ but not so dear/ as Chairman Mao)," we also read editorial remarks such as these which appeared in *People's Daily* (Peking):

> However, the home continues to be a position for educating the younger generation because parents shoulder a very important responsibility for teaching their children. In the present drive to resume classes while carrying on revolution, how to make good use of the home and to mobilize students' parents . . . is an important link in making a success. . . . Once parents are armed with the thought of Mao Tse-tung they . . . can . . . play the proper role of teaching their children by words and deeds (*Jenmin Jihpao*, 12 July 1967, as translated in *Survey of the China Mainland Press*, 3986, 24 July 1967, pp. 13–15).

Despite the depredations of Red Guards and threats of barracks life in People's Communes, the evidence indicates that the family remains a major unit in the fabric of Chinese society.

Changes in Class and Status

It is not possible to go into even such limited detail with regard to other areas of greatest asserted or demonstrated change in Chinese culture under the Communist government; I shall merely enumerate some of the most important. Following our earlier mention of class as a source of subcultural variation, a word must be said about changes in class structure. In theory, China now exalts three classes—the poor and middle peasants in the countryside and the proletariat in the cities. Yet, one of the manifest reasons for launching the Cultural Revolution was fear that persons of higher class origins or those who had themselves mounted the class ladder, even under the Communist regime (by taking advantage of their bureaucratic positions, their technical expertise, or their command of party ideology), were on the point of taking over the revolution. The Maoists see the crux of the matter inside the individual conscience. The operative slogans have been "draw proper boundaries" and "serve the people." The former demands that those of bad class background divide themselves from relatives who continue to act superior to the revolution and its goals; the latter suggests forms of behavior consonant with proper class status. Work and location assignments, sometimes apparently involuntary, assist toward this end.

Probably the greatest pressure has been directed against the aggregate classified loosely, but conventionally, as intellectuals. Professors and teachers, artists, writers, practitioners of western medicine, and the like have undergone severe repression; the knowledge of this is so widespread as to require no elaboration here.

Changes are asserted and have been observed in the roles and statuses of women and the relations between youth and age. Actually, it is very difficult to make clear determination of the real conditions. Anecdotal material suggests that the general position of women has, indeed, improved in various ways. Yet, as we already saw in a remark made by Mao over forty years ago, the position of lower-class women, relative to males of their class, was more equivalent than that found in higher classes. On the other hand, I have no intention of minimizing the fact that females are no longer sold into servitude or prostitution. But women do not seem, at least yet, to have had conspicuous success in finding places of state power; the few who have seem to have done so through their association with husbands or male relatives. In this context it is interesting to note that one of the early victims of the Cultural Revolution was a woman, Tung Pien, who had been editor of the influential *Chung-kuo Fu-nu* (Women of China). She was sent into disgrace in mid-1966 on the grounds that she had "opposed the red flag by raising the red flag," (i.e., had subtly undermined Maoism by using it incorrectly). As revealed in the pages of her own magazine:

> In the name of helping women cadres and women workers handle contradictions between house-keeping and children and revolutionary work, she freely publicized such bourgeois revisionist absurdities as that women live for the sake of revolution, also for the sake of husbands and children, that a warm, small family is happiness, that giving birth to and raising children is the natural duty of women, and that the spouse one chooses must "share one's feelings and tastes" (*Chung-kuo Fu-nu*, August 1966, as translated in *Survey of China Mainland Magazines*, 548, 31 October 1966, p. 24).

I cannot refrain from commenting that the quoted passage neatly mingles hoary attitudes with some novelties. The latter clearly involves the downgrading of the significance of having and raising children. There is nothing new in the separation of the interests of the husband and the wife or in the mockery of the "warm, small family." Both of these negative views are characteristic attributes of the traditional gentry, who emphasized the primary obligations of the wife to her parents-in-law. The ideal wife in Communist China is socialized for society; the ideal wife in Confucian China was domesticated for the extended family. In neither case are romantic ties to the husband of any great importance; indeed, they can be a nuisance or a threat. Even on this matter, however, there is constant vacillation. Recently, for example, accounts of life in the small family were usually quite glowing. Describing a visit to a factory in Shenyang, a writer for *Peking Review*

> called on a young couple living in one of the factory's residential areas. The husband, Ma Cheng-chiang, is a technician and likes playing stringed instruments. Shao Pei-yen, his wife, is an electric welder in the machinery workshop who loves singing. They often met during rehearsals at the theatres and fell in love. A year later, in 1966, they got married and have a boy who goes to the factory nursery during the daytime. They usually eat in the factory's canteen, but sometimes when they are free in the evening they eat supper at home.
>
> Ma Cheng-chiang told me: "We help each other politically and in family life. When she's busy with some other work after knocking off, I go to the nursery to pick up our boy and cook supper . . . we study together and sometimes sing songs. We often go to visit our parents on weekends."
>
> This couple married late, in response to the call of the government. Ma was 27 and Shao 25. They have only one child (*Peking Review*, No. 20, 18 May 1973, p. 12).

Changes in the Roles of Youth

The analysis of changes in the standing of youth in contemporary Mainland Chinese society is similar in many ways to the foregoing discussion of the role of women. The regime places great weight on proper training of children, but how does this differ from what we see in Taiwan, or, for that matter, in earlier periods of Chinese history? Obviously, the near universality of literacy differentiates both contemporary Chinese states from their predecessors, but the abstract conception of youth as requiring proper detailed indoctrination goes back into the remote past. If we turn, then, to the actual roles played by youth, we encounter a confused picture. In some circumstances and at certain times youth quite obviously play a more active role in Chinese societal decision making than ever before. But such instances are limited and not general; for the most part the major roles and decisions are in the hands of adults, often the aged—consider the present leaders of the People's Republic of China. Indeed, what we know about the conditions of youth suggests that the young remain subject to the didactic manipulations of their seniors.

The role of youth is one of the most prominent in current actions and propaganda of the Chinese Communist regime."Youth should stand in the forefront of the revolutionary ranks." "Young people of the whole country bestir yourselves!" These are slogans of the day. As in years past, the problems are manifold. In exhorting the youth, the propagandists must not lose sight of the revolutionary priority of peasants and workers; indeed, a main thrust of the campaign is to move the young from city to country and integrate them with the masses. The words of Mao are repeatedly recalled:

> We must help our young people to understand that ours is still a very poor country, that we cannot change this situation radically in a short time, and that only through the united efforts of our younger generation and all our people, working with their own hands, can China be made strong and prosperous within a period of several decades (*Peking Review,* 18 May 1973, pp. 8–9, translating *Hongqi,* 5, 1973).

There is, of course, another side to Mao's thinking about youth. It is the side revealed in his Yenan speech of May 4, 1939, on "The Orientation of the Youth Movement" in which he speaks of a major anti-revolutionary counter-current in the youth movement which is unwilling or reluctant "to integrate . . . with the broad masses of workers and peasants" (Mao 1965, Vol. II, p. 246). Even more pessimistic are the remarks reported by Edgar Snow in a paraphrase of an interview with Mao. The question was, what might the young do with this revolution?

> He . . . could not know, he said. He doubted that anyone could be sure. There were two possibilities. There could be continued development of the Revolution toward Communism, the other possibility was that youth could negate the Revolution. . . . Of course he did not hope for counter-revolution. But future events would be decided by future generations and in accordance with conditions we could not foresee. . . . The youth of today and those to come after them would assess the work of the Revolution in accordance with values of their own. Mao's voice dropped away, and he half closed his eyes. Man's condition on this earth was changing with ever increasing rapidity. A thousand years from now all of them, he said, even Marx, Engels, and Lenin, would possibly appear rather ridiculous (Snow 1971, pp. 374–75).

Clearly related to the foregoing is a further question that concerns whatever projections may be attempted of the stability of the Communist regime and especially the endurance of some of its great successes in change. As has already been implied, there is a somewhat exceptional "on and off" quality to even the most ordinary lives in the PRC since 1949. Nowhere else, so far as I know, have such drastic shifts in public orientation occurred so frequently. Nowhere else have the physical effects of such shifts been so pervasive, reaching all levels of the population and the remotest corners of the state. Involved are such things as *hsia-fang,* the sending down of officials and office holders to do manual work for a month or two and the temporary or permanent demotion of military officers. There are movements of contention and criticism like that of the "hundred flowers" and the grim reaping that followed that brief bloom. After the passing of the first Cultural Revolution came another and more serious wave of population transfers, emphasizing the movement of students to the countryside and to pioneer areas. With the advent of a second Cultural Revolution, albeit one that does not display any of the energy or experimentation of the first, there is concrete evidence that major forces in the Chinese Communist Party regard continual reversals as a viable political technique. To some it appears that such systems run the risk of a loss of confidence among the citizenry. Yet the spectre of aborted careers still seems the lesser menace in a China that has so long known the ineffable continuity of bureaucratic elitism. It is perhaps comparable to the long history of business failure of all sizes and scopes, yet capitalism has never been threatened in a bourgeois country by a lack of fresh recruits. Robert Lifton considered this problem and suggests that its pivot is "the special malleability of the young." Even though youth is probably less malleable than assumed to be by fervent Maoists, there is a "periodic emergence of large numbers of young adults who have as yet experienced neither revolutionary exultation nor disillusionment and who can be drawn anew into national programs of development or revitalization" (Lifton 1968, pp. 158–59).

Mental Health in the PRC

This raises a final question, too big for more than a fleeting glance, but one that requires some mention. What has this environment of political, economic and social change meant in terms of what is loosely called "mental health"? Unfortunately, it is exceptionally difficult to provide arguments based on hard data relating to this matter. Just before the coming to power of the Communists in China, the World Health Organization of the United Nations sent Professor Karl M. Bowman on a mission to China. He surveyed conditions relating to neuropsychiatric illnesses and treatment and reported on his findings at the APA meetings. He said that he found no reason to believe that Chinese differed in any fundamental way from Americans in their basic psychological nature. Indeed he remarked that he had "the impression that the mental diseases [of China] were essentially the same as in the United States" (Bermann 1970, p. 228).

It is not known with any certainty how many hospital beds were allocated to psychiatric patients on the eve of the Communist takeover; some sources speak of one or two thousand, some mention six thousand.

Since subsequent figures are given in terms of percentage increases, the possibilities of error are great. This is further complicated by Chinese attitudes toward mental illness, neatly summed up by psychiatrist Lin Tsung-yi:

> The concept of 'normal' in the particular culture, and the threshold of tolerance of the community or family, influence the diagnosis of psychopathic personality. The comparatively higher tolerance of deviant behavior in Chinese families may partly explain the relatively low incidence of psychopathic personality. At the same time, the leading principle of Chinese life—filial piety—which results in conformity to authority or traditional social pattern, may limit the diagnosis of psychopathic personality (Lin 1953, p. 333).

Of course, the "leading principle" of filial piety is no longer quite so highly regarded, particularly at this time of writing when the main thrust in the PRC is against Confucius and his latter-day cohorts, Lin Piao, Liu Shao-ch'i and the Soviet power-holders (sic). On the other hand, there may be new reasons why Chinese rates of mental illness continue to seem low:

> In some Communist countries the overall incidence of mental disorder is asserted to be lower than in the Western World. This lower incidence is attributed to the people's unity in the common purpose of building up Communist societies, to the slower tempo of life, to the fact that individuals have fewer decisions to make, and to a group life which involves the mental and emotional therapy of sharing one another's problems and affairs (Kiev 1968, p. 14).

One western psychiatrist who has visited the People's Republic of China a few times during the past two decades finds that a sound program for mental health has been developed:

> China has jumped one or more difficult and costly stages . . . by swiftly passing through custodial psychiatry and on to the therapeutic community. China today is a gigantic therapeutic community. . . . Thanks to its revolution it has moved from a sociopathological state directly to a state of social health (Bermann 1968, p. 259).

Just as academic ventures into statements about Chinese national character are largely conjectural and intuitive, so the nonacademic propaganda emphasizes goals and dreams and prefers reality only when it mirrors those desires. As yet, the PRC has not permitted any deep penetration of Chinese society by social scientists, whether Chinese or alien. In a trip of a few weeks some remarkable impressions and much valuable information may be gained, but we cannot begin to find answers for the truly deep questions. Until such fieldwork is possible, and it could come quite quickly, we will have to regard all speculation on Chinese psychological reaction to cultural change with strong reservations.

REFERENCES

Abel, Theodora, and Hsu, Francis L. K. 1949. "Some Aspects of Personality of Chinese as Revealed by the Rorschach Test," *Journal of Projective Techniques* 13:285–301.
Balazs, Etienne. 1964. *Chinese Civilization and Bureaucracy*. Translated by H.M. Wright; edited by Arthur F. Wright. New Haven: Yale University Press.
Bermann, Gregorio. 1968. "Mental Health in China," in *Psychiatry in the Communist World*, edited by Ari Kiev. New York: Science House.
Bodde, Derk. 1946. "Dominant Ideas," in *China*, edited by Hailey F. MacNair. Berkeley: University of California Press.
———. 1957. *China's Cultural Tradition: What and Whether*. New York: Rinehart.
Chen, A.S. [Ai-li S. Chin]. 1964. "The Ideal Local Party Secretary and the 'Model' Man," *The China Quarterly* 17:229–40.
Chu, Goodwin C. 1967. "Sex Differences in Persuasability Factors Among Chinese," *International Journal of Psychology* 2:283–88.
DeVos, George A. 1974. "Mao's Revolution on the Couch?" *Modern Asian Studies* 8:113–44.
Eberhard, Wolfram. 1967. *Guilt and Sin in Traditional China*. Berkeley: University of California Press.
Elvin, Mark. 1973. *The Pattern of the Chinese Past*. London: Eyre Methuen.
Fried, Morton H. 1953. *Fabric of Chinese Society*. New York: Praeger.
———. 1973. "China: An Anthropological Overview," in *An Introduction to Chinese Civilization*, edited by John Meskill. New York: Columbia University Press.
Han, Yu-shan. 1946. "Moulding Forces," in *China*, edited by Harley F. MacNair. Berkeley: University of California Press.
Heyer, Virginia. 1953. "Relations Between Men and Women in Chinese Stories," in *The Study of Culture at a Distance*, edited by Margaret Mead and Rhoda Metraux. Chicago: University of Chicago Press.
Hsu, Francis L.K. 1953. *American and Chinese*. New York: Henry Schuman.
———. 1969. *The Study of Literate Civilizations*. New York: Holt, Rinehart and Winston.
Kiev, Ari. 1968. "Introduction," in *Psychiatry in the Communist World*, edited by Ari Kiev. New York: Science House.
LaBarre, Weston. 1946. "Some Observations on Character Structure in the Orient: II. The Chinese," *Psychiatry* 9:215–37, 375–95.
Levy, Howard S. 1974. *Chinese Sex Jokes in Traditional Times*. Taipei: The Orient Cultural Service, Asian Folklore and Social Life Monograph, vol. 58.
Lifton, Robert J. 1968. *Revolutionary Immortality: Mao Tse-tung and the Chinese Cultural Revolution*. New York: Random House.

Lin, Tsung-yi. 1953. "A Study of the Incidence of Mental Disorders in Chinese and Other Cultures," *Psychiatry* 16:313–36.
Mao Tse-tung. 1961–65. *Selected Works.* 4 vols. Peking: Foreign Languages Press.
Metzger, Thomas. 1972. "On Chinese Political Culture," *Journal of Asian Studies* 32:101–5.
Muensterberger, Warner. 1951. "Orality and Dependence: Characteristics of Southern Chinese," *Psychoanalysis and the Social Sciences* 3:37–69.
Rin, Hsien. 1963. "Koro: A Consideration on Chinese Concepts of Illness and Case Illustrations," *Transcultural Psychiatric Research* 15:23–30.
———. 1966. "Two Forms of Vital Deficiency Syndrome Among Chinese Male Mental Patients," *Transcultural Psychiatric Research* 3:19–21, 1966.
Schram, Stuart. 1969. *The Political Thought of Mao Tse-tung*, 2nd ed. revised. New York: Praeger.
Scofield, Robert W., and Sun, Chin-wan. 1960. "A Comparative Study of the Differential Effects upon Personality of Chinese and American Child Training Practices," *Journal of Social Psychology* 52: 221–24.
Sidel, Ruth. 1973. *Women and Child Care in China.* Baltimore: Penguin.
Skinner, G.W. 1966. "Filial Sons and Their Sisters: Configuration and Culture in Chinese Families," paper prepared for the Conference on Kinship in Chinese Society, September 1966, Greystone House, Riverdale, New York.
Snow, Edgar. 1971. "Interview With Mao," in *The China Reader,* vol. 3, Communist China, edited by Franz Schurmann and Orvell Schell. New York: Random House.
Solomon, Richard. 1971. *Mao's Revolution and the Chinese Political Culture.* Berkeley: University of California Press.
Stover, Leon. 1964. "'Face' and Verbal Analogues of Interaction in Chinese Culture: A Theory of Formalized Social Behavior Based upon Participant-Observation of an Upper Class Chinese Household, Together with a Biographical Study of the Primary Informant." Ph.D. dissertation, Columbia University. Ann Arbor: University Microfilms.
van Gulick, Robert H. 1961. *Sexual Life in Ancient China.* Leiden: Brill.
Wallace, Anthony F.C. 1961. *Culture and Personality.* New York: Random House.
Weakland, John. 1950. "The Organization of Action in Chinese Culture," *Psychiatry* 13:361–70.
———. 1956. "Orality in Chinese Conceptions of Male Genital Sexuality," *Psychiatry* 19:237–47.
Wittfogel, Karl A. 1957. *Oriental Despotism.* New Haven: Yale University Press.
———. 1970. *Agriculture: A Key to the Understanding of Chinese Society, Past and Present.* George Ernest Morrison Lectures in Ethnology, No. 31. Canberra: Australia National University.
Wolf, Margery. 1970. "Child Training and the Chinese Family," in *Family and Kinship in Chinese Society,* edited by Maurice Freedman. Stanford: Stanford University Press.
———. 1972. *Women and the Family in Rural Taiwan.* Stanford: Stanford University Press.

Yang, Kuo-shu; Tzuo, H.Y.; and Wu, C.Y. 1963. "Rorschach Responses of Normal Chinese Adults: III, The Popular Responses," *Journal of Social Psychology* 60:175–86.
Young, Marilyn (ed.). 1973. *Women in China*. Ann Arbor: Center for Chinese Studies, University of Michigan Press.

Chapter 3

Culture Change and the Persistence of the Chinese Personality

Kenneth A. Abbott

This chapter assumes that human beings of various national, racial, and cultural groups are born with approximately the same potential range of personality development and expression but that each group demonstrates selectivity in the personality traits it develops. Some particularly "Chinese" personality components, identified in an analysis of responses to the California Psychological Inventory (CPI) collected in the Chinese Family Life Study in San Francisco and Taipei, illustrate this selectivity in personality formation. These personality components, or modalities, are directly involved in the processes of adaptation and adjustment to social and cultural change observed in Chinese communities in the disparate settings of San Francisco and Taipei. By comparing data from two Chinese subgroups with established American norms, we will attempt to sketch some high-frequency personality patterns found in Chinese society.

We are concerned with how social institutions in a Chinese community, principally the family, affect the socialization of children to become "Chinese," whether in the United States or in Taiwan. We shall examine some of the supporting cultural values that influence this socialization and, in turn, are sustained by succeeding generations.

Chinese communities include a wide range of groups, both inside and outside of political China. Outside of China, whole areas such as Singapore have become primarily Chinese in culture; millions of Chinese live in smaller enclaves throughout Southeast Asia and elsewhere. Within this world community of Chinese, several variant groups, all considered to be Chinese (such as those represented by the various provinces or by dialect groups—Cantonese, Fukienese, Wu, Hakka, Mandarin), form distinct subethnic stereotypes. These regional and subethnic differences exist both in China and overseas.

The CPI data utilized here were collected in the late 1960s from two major regional groups: Cantonese (mostly Toysanese) in the United States and Fukienese (Min-nan) in Taiwan. Conclusions based upon this data are tested against conclusions drawn from data reported in the earlier literature referring to the Chinese in a wide variety of places and including the other two main subgroups, Mandarin and Wu. While regional differences are important and can be significant, we will make a case for communalities that transcend them.

Cultures change, as do social processes, modal personality features, and even the physical environment. For example, the modern European is physically too large to wear a medieval knight's suit of armor. On a social level, the Westerner's political status is so changed that he is not likely to give a medieval oath of fealty. Philosophically, his modern understanding of child development and human rights provide him with a vantage point quite different from anything known in the Middle Ages. Historical social change is equally evident and momentous in the Chinese world. Change, be it technological (such as the introduction of a new strain of rice or the completion of the Grand Canal), cultural (such as the introduction of Buddhism or the evolution of Taoism), or political (such as the conquest by the Manchus or the emergence of the Ming) has always been present in China, as in other parts of the world. It has frequently affected accepted limits and expressions of personality.

However, there have been notable continuities. These relatively unchanging constants in personality (over time and among subgroups) permit an attempt to delineate the features of a modal personality configuration unique to Chinese society. In this chapter, persisting personality components in Chinese society are examined for their possible sociocultural origins and explored for their psycho-sociocultural consequences.

Westerners approaching the Chinese value system are usually saddled with their own culturally derived concepts; Chinese actions are based upon different assumptions and are ordered by different priorities. These assumptions and priorities are associated with corresponding socialization processes and personality dynamics and configurations. The uniqueness of these personality configurations is indicated by the CPI data we are presenting, by other cited psychological data, and by statements of insightful commentators both inside and outside Chinese culture (Abegg 1952; Dawson 1967).

THE CHINESE FAMILY LIFE STUDY DATA

A preliminary presentation and discussion of CPI data collected in San Francisco and Taipei provides an outline of the three principal personality components we are concerned with in this paper: intragroup dependency and self-restraint, total gestalt or global perception, and somatization and projection as key defenses.

TABLE 3.1. Some Components of Personality in Chinese Society, Their Socio-Cultural Origins, and the Psycho-Socio-Cultural Consequences as Related to CPI Scales.*

Sociocultural Origins	Personality Components	Psycho-Socio-Cultural Consequences
Philosophical concepts and/or mores	Intragroup dependency and self-restraint (Sc, Do, Cs, Sy, Sp, Sa, Re, Sc)	Collectivity in family and society (Ac, Ai)
Child-rearing and socialization	Total gestalt or global perception (Ie, Fx, To)	The indirect approach and "face" (Sp, Gi, Fe)
	Somatization and projection as key defenses (Wb, To)	

*For an explanation of the abbreviations, see Table 3.2.

The CPI, a personality assessment instrument with 480 items, is divided into the eighteen individual scales listed in Table 3.2. Extensive reliability and validity tests have been conducted and are cited in the test manual (Gough 1969).

TABLE 3.2. Scales of the California Psychological Inventory

Class I. Measures of Poise, Ascendancy, and Self-Assurance

1. Do Dominance
2. Cs Capacity-for-status
3. Sy Sociability
4. Sp Social-presence
5. Sa Self-acceptance
6. Wb Sense of well-being

Class II. Measures of Socialization, Maturity, and Responsibility

7. Re   Responsibility
8. So   Socialization
9. Sc   Self-control
10. To Tolerance
11. Gi Good-impression
12. Cm Communality

Class III. Measures of Achievement Potential and Intellectual Efficiency

13. Ac Achievement-via-conformance
14. Ai Achievement-via-independence
15. Ie Intellectual-efficiency

Class IV. Measures of Intellectual and Interest Modes

16. Py Psychological-mindedness
17. Fx Flexibility
18. Fe Femininity

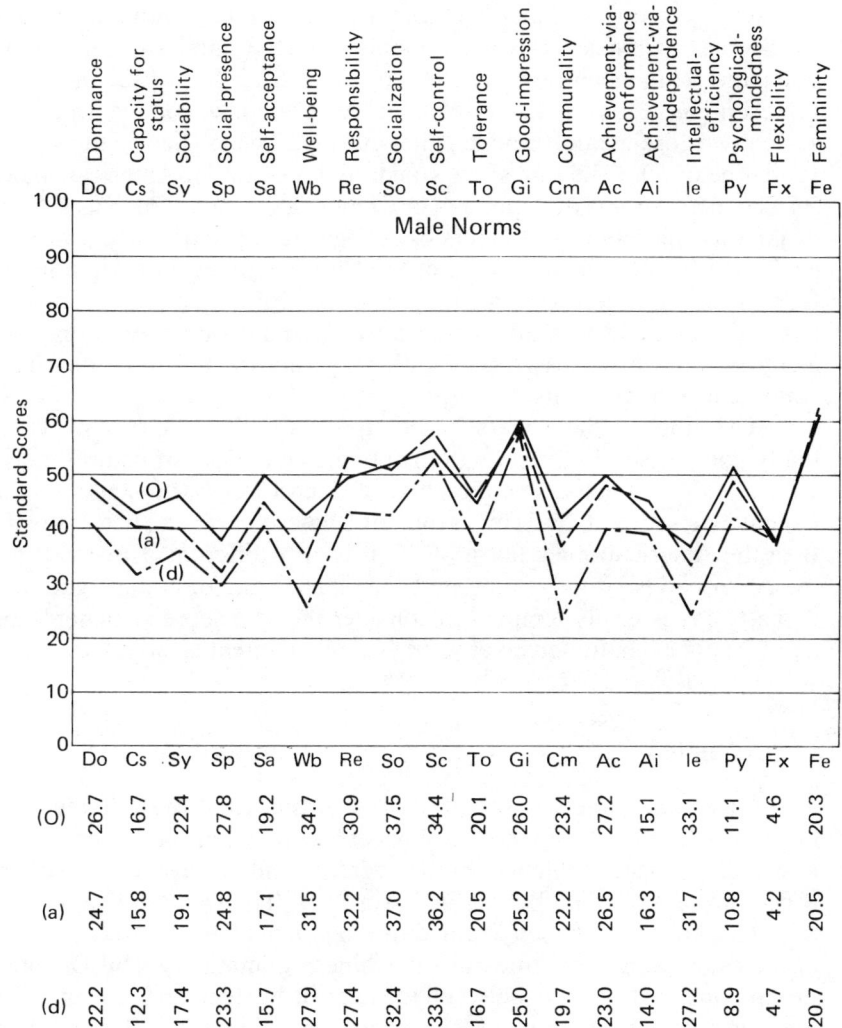

FIGURE 3.1.

(0) Sample. San Francisco Cantonese fathers (sons with positive high school performance): N = 30.
(a) Sample. Taipei fathers (some college education): N = 26.
(d) Sample. Taipei fathers (illiterate): N = 23.

Mean CPI scores of Taipei Min-nan fathers (a) Sample and (d) Sample and of San Francisco Cantonese fathers (0) Sample. The American norm is 50. Numbers below the graph indicate raw scores.

Raw scores are converted into standard scores by using a standard profile sheet reproduced in Figure 3.1. (Since the profile sheet is constructed according to American norms, error in representing mean standard scores of Chinese is always possible.) For the standardizing American population, the mean raw score on any given scale lies on the median line representing a standardized score of 50. For instance, the Dominance scale raw score mean for male Americans is 27 which lies on the standard score line of 50. (The raw score standard deviation for American males is 5.) The mean scores of American or Chinese subgroups (such as salesmen or janitors, high school students or college students) produce a variety of profiles. When the *mean scores* of the Chinese groups consistently differ from those of Americans—as they do—this difference then becomes the basis for comparative study. Characteristic Chinese configurations can be analyzed both in terms of their internal structure and in comparison to American configurations.

Utilizing profile sheets based upon American norms provides a ready comparison but results in the obvious handicap of using American values and perspectives as the point of departure. For instance, a mean Dominance score of 25.5 for a group of Chinese men is no better or worse than the American male norm of 27; it is only different. However, given the American positive valuation of Dominance and of being higher up on a chart, one is easily tempted to consider the 25.5 score as being "not as good" as 27 even though no absolute value judgment is intended.

Samples

The San Francisco sample tested in this study was divided as indicated in Table 3.3. Each family was chosen according to the status of one of its teenage members. Both the father and mother were also tested if they were available, but siblings were not. The Outstanding (O) group of teenagers was chosen from those nominated by a cross-section of agencies, groups, and clubs in the Chinese community The Delinquent group consisted of boys between the ages of thirteen and seventeen who were on formal probation in San Francisco between June 1966 and August 1967 and who were willing to participate in the study. The Nondelinquent (N) group, selected by a randomized process and matched by age and location to the Delinquent (D) group, consisted of boys in the public school classes of some of the delinquents, boys involved in a publicly sponsored Summer Youth Program, and youth members of three social agencies and two churches. The three groups of youth were equivalent in age, length of time lived in the United States, and residence in San Francisco.

TABLE 3.3. Number of Family Members in the San Francisco CPI Sample by Status of Teenager

Subsample	Fathers	Mothers	Sons
Outstanding (O)	20	22	22
Nondelinquent (N)	24	29	30
Delinquent (D)	29	29	34
Total	73	80	86

The Taipei sample was divided into four equal stratified random subsamples according to the education of the father as recorded in the Kuting District Office. The father, mother, and all teenagers between thirteen and seventeen in Min-nan families with both parents available were interviewed. (Min-nan intact families whose names were drawn but who could not be interviewed showed no particular pattern.) Subsamples are unequal in size because of a few invalid tests and because a few families stopped after only one member had completed testing.

TABLE 3.4. Number of Family Members in the Taipei Sample by Education of Father

Subsample	Fathers	Mothers	Sons	Daughters
Some college (a)	26	26	24	19
Some high school (b)	27	26	16	26
Some grammar school (c)	25	26	20	25
Illiterate (d)	23	25	22	16
Total	101	103	82	86

The three profiles in Figure 3.1 represent the mean scores of the San Francisco O group fathers, the Taipei a-group fathers, and the Taipei d-group fathers. The first two groups had similar mean ages and with few exceptions, were men from the middle, upper middle, and upper socioeconomic classes. The San Francisco group, men of Cantonese origin either born in the United States or resident there, included natives or descendants of people of the Canton City area, the Toysan area, and the Chungsan area—all districts within one hundred and fifty miles of Canton City. The Taipei a-group were all Min-nan men living in the Kuting district, most of whom had migrated from other parts of Taiwan.

Preliminary Discussion

When we inspect the general shape of the a- and O-group CPI profiles, as seen in Figure 3.1, we find that a "Chinese" profile is evident whether the records are obtained in California or in Taiwan. This profile includes high scores on the Self-control, Good-impression, and Femininity scales. When compared to American subsamples, the entire section representing measures of Poise, Ascendancy, and Self-assurance is lower (with Social-presence and Well-being scores being the lowest) for a group of Chinese men with similar education and social status. Other low mean scores are recorded on the Tolerance, Communality, Intellectual-efficiency, and Flexibility scales. The Achievement scores (Achievement-via-conformance and Achievement-via-independence) are in the middle of the total range but are significantly lower than for a comparable group of American men. Moreover, the slope is from Ac down to Ai, whereas American group mean scores tend to slope from Ac up to Ai.

These profiles, according to an ordinary interpretation of CPI configurations in the United States, would indicate personality attributes that place a high value on how the individual appears to others and impose a high degree of self-control on the individual's behavior. The individual does not overtly express his desire for dominance and tends to be reserved in his face-to-face relationships and participation in groups, where he feels somewhat ill at ease. There is a general tendency, shown in the low Well-being score, to somatize (express through bodily symptoms) emotional problems. This tendency is most dramatically apparent on the profiles of individuals in the lower classes, that is, the d-group fathers in Figure 3.1, and it is even more marked among lower-class women. The Tolerance, Flexibility, and Intellectual-efficiency scores interpreted together seem to indicate a pattern of seeing conditions or relations as a single gestalt and staying persistently with this "whole picture."

THE CHINESE VALUE SYSTEM

We have briefly summarized only some of our empirical data that graphically demonstrate the similarity of modal personality in different Chinese subgroups residing in vastly differing geographical and social environments. However, we need first to examine some basic Chinese values and childhood socialization patterns that may interact in personality development to create these modalities.

Philosophical Concepts and Social Mores

The Chinese view the world as being in constant movement, but this movement is not seen as progressive or developmental in the Western sense; it either oscillates between two rather indistinctly defined poles or is cyclical, with an inevitable return to a starting point (Bodde 1953). All forces in the world are relative and connected. Men and supernatural forces such as T'ien (Heaven), lesser "gods" like the T'u ti shen (local earth divinities), or even Kuei (ghosts) are part of a cyclical process extending through time (Yang 1961). People go to the "other world" and return to earth through rebirth. A god, a spirit, an emperor, and a common man are all subject to this process and do not control it. An individual has led many lives and possesses several souls. Since one cannot escape from this process, harmony within it becomes quite important, and Ho (harmony) is the key concept in all relationships between god(s) and man and between man and man.

The Chinese grows up in an ordered world. His brothers and sisters are numbered by their position in the family and addressed by him in kinship terms indicating whether he is older or younger and sometimes his ordinal position in the family. Aunts and uncles are clearly denoted as paternal or maternal. A child starts school by writing Chinese characters one by one, each in its own box on a practice sheet. Characters are written in one of a few prescribed styles, and form is certainly as important as content. Memorization is a major study technique. The Western ideas of creativity and individualism are not accented and must be held within accepted norms.

When he graduates from school, the Chinese does not go out to win his fortune; he stays home with his family (Hsu 1967). From there, he goes into business, professional life, or government service. Harmony is with the past as well as the present and future. Yet within this context of continuing harmony, the mainland Chinese are carrying out one of the most extensive revolutions of all time; the Republic of China's use of modern technology is rapidly bringing Taiwan to second position in the Far East in individual output, per capita income, and general education, and in Singapore and Hawaii Chinese entrepreneurs are joining the world giants of commerce and construction by utilizing technical and scientific innovation. Harmony does not prevent the status quo from changing. Kan Yu-wei in the Ch'ing dynasty advocated revolutionary change, as had many before him, but always within the Confucian system. Chiang Kai-shek was clearly within this system, and even Mao Tse-tung is more a part of the system than he would probably acknowledge (Bodde 1953).

In human affairs, the concepts of Jen (human-heartedness or benevolence) and I (righteousness) are crucial. Jen is perhaps best expressed in Western thought as agape or unselfish love and concern for one's fellow man. Jen's essential meaning is goodness, particularly goodness of personal relationships. But Jen is not merely an attitude toward someone as exhibited in Hsiao (filial piety); it is, as developed in the Confucian analects, "the ideal psychological state for a human individual in which there is minimal anxiety or irrational hostility [and] marked increase in the ability to empathize with other people and to be genuinely concerned with their welfare" (Lin 1939, p. 476). Thus Jen becomes the quintessence of Ho (harmony) in human relations.

But to be truly harmonious, a relationship must be "right": *i*, or righteousness, "means the 'oughtness' of a situation; it is a categorical imperative" (Dai 1966, p. 99). The moral component of harmony can be compared to the Western concept of conscience or superego. When an individual follows this imperative (as embodied in the classics, folklore, and art, from which he memorizes, absorbs, and internalizes it) he expresses and feels Ch'eng (sincerity). To be insincere is a serious matter, for the individual has offended I and has upset harmonious relationship.

The Wu-lun, or Five Social Dyads, are the relationships of Chin (affection) between parent and child, I (righteousness) between ruler and subject, Pien (distinction) between husband and wife, Hsu (order) between old and young, and Shin (sincerity) between friends. These relationships, if practiced appropriately, result in harmonious and smoothly functioning families and communities that make up an entire nation. Relationships where Li is followed enable I, Jen, and Ho to come into being, and "it was and is the Li that made a Chinese a Chinese" (Ruey 1967: 53).

This schema has developed over more than two thousand years of Chinese history. Confucius, Mencius, Hsun-tzu, Chu Hsi, and many others have added to, subtracted from, and refined it. It has been changed here and adjusted there, but it is still the frame of reference (with allowances for regional and personal variations) used by all Chinese who consider themselves Chinese. It is perpetuated by song-singing, story-telling, and associated folkways. Millions still study the Classics inside and outside of mainland China. There is good reason to believe that the Confucian system is alive and well—and an important influence on personality formation and functioning (Tseng 1973). Evidence to this end is presented by a Western-oriented scholar, William T. Liu (1966), who used an adaptation of the Kluckhohn-Strodtbeck scale to establish that, while there are significant value differences according to age, education, and social status, strong vestiges of the Confucian heritage persist to the present day. Working in Hong Kong with three samples of adolescent students (parents included in two samples) which represented a group heavily influenced by the West, a group less influenced by the West, and a group of recent refugees, he finds a marked consensus between the teenagers and their parents in each group. Although he sees a trend toward individualism and future orientation, it is clear that traditional views continue to have substantial support.

These received values support the perception that an individual is subordinate to the whole. A high value is placed upon the proper procedure. In this setting, the individual represses noticeable independent striving and achieves on behalf of the group, always responsive to the supreme value of harmony.

Value systems may be codified and learned abstractly in school, but the learner has been prepared for his schooling by his early experience at home. Socialization in the early childhood years and subsequent family life make the formal value system operative. Although the Chinese family literature is voluminous, until recently there has not been much attention paid to early socialization. The next section will present a few salient features of child rearing in Chinese society.

Early Childhood Socialization

Socialization of children in Chinese society has been conditioned, above all, by a strong consideration of the family as a unit. Although actual socialization may vary by class and education (Mitchell and Tsang 1969) and the size or structure of the family may vary in different sectors of society (Yang 1967), the family retains its function of inculcating values (O'Hara 1967) and is seen—both in Taiwan and on the mainland (Chin 1960)—as the basic unit of national society.

Attention to the welfare of the family as a unit rather than to the welfare of children as individuals has been discussed at length by Francis Hsu (1955), with numerous examples illustrating that children are but small parts of the whole family and that the oldest members of the living unit, parents or grandparents, occupy its privileged roles. Focus on the performance of the family as a unit tends to define the status of each member and his role performance primarily in terms of his contribution to the larger unit. Only secondary concern is shown for his psychological development.

This focus on family-unit functioning rather than on individual child development does not lessen the emotional investment of family members in the child. In fact, since the parents as well as the child are responsible for his role performance, the child may be subject to more intense object relations than in a less structured family organization. Through the child, a wife becomes a mother and a husband a father—important changes in a society placing high priority on continuity of the family. If the new child is not the first, he creates the statuses of older and younger siblings—an occurrence that has social and psychological significance for him and his siblings since age, birth order, and sex all set limits to his social functioning and personality development.

"The backbone of the family in traditional China is the father-son relationship," begins a well-known statement on the classical family (Hsu 1959). Francis Hsu goes on to point out that, although the ideal is glorification of the father-son relationship and estrangement of the sexes, this ideal is usually compromised. Morton Fried's (1959) assessment of the effect of the first ten years of Communist rule on the family in mainland China points out that, while male and female roles and the roles of parents and adults were being drastically altered through new freedom in marriage choice and divorce, the practice of Hsiao (filial piety) by children (even after they became adults) is still a "virtue of socialist youth."

Ai-li Chin (1966) has produced the most extensive recent analysis of family relationships in both Taiwan and mainland China. Analyzing a substantial sample of short stories written in both countries in the early 1960s, she compares them with data from the 1920s and 1950s. In the 1920s, a general revolt of women against men, and youth against age, took place. Ideas of individuality and self-determination were advanced against the collectivity of the family and a life prearranged and controlled by elders. Of course, the extent of the previous control and the success of the revolt varied widely by family, social class, and geographical region. The Republican marriage code of 1931, the marriage code of 1950, increased urbanization, and influences from Japan and the West all promoted the status of women, circumscribed the functions of the extended family, and enhanced the personal rights of the individual. Salaff's (1973) more recent work reports considerable movement in the cities and among the party elite towards self-selection of mates and nuclear family residency. However, the masses in the countryside, while dropping bride prices and involving the youth more, follow patterns more similar to the past.

While the large family ideal was a focus in the early 1950s, there has been something of a return to the ideal of the Yen father as long as he is a good socialist. There is ambivalence about the preferred virtues of a wife. Value is placed both upon the old-fashioned wifely virtues and upon excelling in the production unit, but the old wifely virtues seem to be winning. Actually, the family has not been destroyed by urbanization in Taiwan or by ideology on the mainland. Strong, centralized governments with strong leaders, schooled in the old dictum that strong families make a strong state, are not likely to undercut a relationship that they feel supports their own position. Mao has replaced the extended family with the production unit (often they are the same) and in effect has made himself the clan head of each clan. Chiang had a similarly remote but powerful position in Taiwan.

The CPI data from the Chinese Family Life Study indicates that relatively weak fathers (as indicated by their Dominance scores) are much more common in the families of delinquent boys than in the families of the control group. This relatively low dominance of men in the father role in a culture that expects fathers to be dominant may interfere in the father-son identification process and stimulate acting-out against authority by the boys (Abbott 1968). Although both the Delinquent sample and its control group were distributed across a wide socioeconomic range, greater poverty is associated with a diminished authority role for the father.

There is an enormous literature, written mostly by foreigners, on the status of women in China and its change. This literature resoundingly makes the point that over the centuries, women in China, as elsewhere in the world, have been subjugated and have had little opportunity to develop as individuals except when they have had a kind father or husband. Women's lower CPI scores in Achievement, Dominance, and Social Ascendancy scales support this view. Often the only emotional escape route for women has been somatization and physical complaints, as is indicated by extremely low Well-being scores. An item analysis of this scale reveals women with almost unbelievably negative self-appraisals of their physical condition who continue to function in day-to-day living.

The status and attitudes of women are important considerations in childhood socialization. Chinese boys saw their mothers as repressed and passive. They observed the indirect methods frequently used by their mothers to attain an object. They learned that a distant power, regardless of its virtue, controlled others. If the Yen father concept was operative, it is small wonder that male children integrated personality components of the person they were emotionally closest to—passivity, indirectness, nonaggression. Later, when the boys became Yen fathers, fear of failure and emotional needs for displacement kept them well within the socially accepted father role. The submissive, subjugated mother may have been an extremely important factor in the development of personality in Chinese culture. An exhaustive current study of child socialization patterns in Chinese society by Richard Wilson (1974) indicates that the old values of a stern father and loving mother continue to be held, even within the social reality of much weaker fathers and stronger mothers.

When families move to urban living units containing only nuclear or stem families, when individualism is more accepted, and when women approach a more equal status, several important changes seem to appear in family structure and functioning. Husbands and wives expand their communication and are emotionally closer, fathers are more accessible to their children, and children—especially boys—become more aggressive and assertive. Mitchell and Lo (1968), in a pilot study of preschool children in Hong Kong, rated ten submissive children and ten assertive children (in a nursery for working-class people) by two independent procedures and followed up with interviews of their mothers. They found that permissive (but not submissive) rather than restrictive mothers were associated with assertive children. Furthermore, it is probable that assertive boys also had meaningfully close relations with their fathers. Clear distinctions were seen between parental treatment of boys and girls. Girls obtained their assertiveness by a route not studied or described in the study.

A Chinese mother makes an effort to restrain her child through constant care and attention in the first three years of his life. This practice is attested to by Muensterberger's (1951) interview data which record that babies were swaddled, always carried by someone, and usually slept with someone. Nursing continues to two years of age or longer, and toilet training starts at almost two, although mothers in Taipei can be seen holding even smaller children over the street gutters. At about the age of three, the child enters a relatively free period, not necessarily with parental approval, until age five or six. As Solomon (1966) and Wolf (1970) have indicated, on the basis of a large number of interviews and actual observations respectively, parents make the assumption that children do not have good judgment in the first five or so years of life and that their needs must be anticipated. This anticipation, the constant companionship of his mother, siblings, or cousins, and extensive inclusion in family life (little separation for early bedtime or from the work scene) all socialize the child as a member of a collectivity—a member who is assumed to need instruction, who has little responsibility for his own behavior, who has no special rights, and who is subject to constant teaching and supervision.

At school age, the child enters a new world. He is now held responsible for his own behavior. After age six, the child's father becomes more remote, although a girl may retain her close relationship with him. The behavior of adults toward the child is less indulgent and may even be harsh as they direct his highly controlled participation in learning the intellectual concepts of Hsiao, Li, and Ho. Aggression at any age is not permitted (Sollenberger 1968). Children are taught not to hurt others or themselves, not to be reckless, and to avoid injury.

SOME "CHINESE" PERSONALITY COMPONENTS

Intragroup Dependency and Self-restraint

Western commentators on China have frequently and erroneously characterized the Chinese as being a people "of eternal standstill" and "generally passive." The apparent passivity in Chinese society has been described in psychological jargon as psychological dependency or orality, presumably brought about by the overindulgence of children and by lack of early emphasis upon toilet training, and is said to be evidenced later in life by an excessive concern with food. Wilson (1974) traces passivity to certain patterns of child rearing in which the mother withholds love. However, taking action within the context of a group rather than as an individual should not be confused with dependency, and choosing indirect rather than direct action should not be mistaken for passivity.

Both Taiwanese (Min-nan) a-group and American (Cantonese) O-group fathers score on or below the standard score mean on the first six scales, which might be described collectively as a measure of apparent passivity. Taiwanese fathers consistently score lower on each of these scales than Cantonese fathers. Therefore, since these two groups are roughly equivalent in age, education, and socioeconomic class, one can speculate that modal personality patterns dictated by culture are responsible for these configurations and their parallel differences from American group profiles. While these two Chinese groups were selected by different criteria, they probably occupy similar social positions. The Cantonese fathers in San Francisco were chosen because their sons were judged outstanding and the Min-nan fathers because they had completed a year or more of college. Actually, since all the Min-nan fathers had some college and some of the San Francisco fathers had not attended college at all, we could have expected the mean scores of the Min-nan fathers to be higher. (College student CPI profiles in the United States are generally higher than those of high school students.)

In Taiwan, people with more education generally have higher scores. While only profiles of fathers with some college education (a) and illiterates (d) are shown in Figure 3.1, two other groups were also tested: fathers with some high school (b) and some grammar school (c). The b and c profiles tended to fall between the a and d profiles. The overall similarity of profiles seems clearly to result from a general Chinese culture shared by both Min-nan and Cantonese. Both groups have been viewed as outgoing and aggressive when compared to most other Chinese, but there is little evidence of this aggressiveness in published personality studies.

An adaptation of the Cornell Medical Index used in Taiwan with 100 college students revealed that while 50 percent of the men indicated they get irritated easily and 24 percent said they might hate as a result, only 10 percent said they would quarrel. In a comparable group of Chinese neurotics, 74 percent said they would easily get irritated but only 24 percent would quarrel. Obviously, strong cultural controls are operating to impose self-restraint (Rin et al. 1951). An initial survey of P-F test ("picture frustration" test) results administered to a Taipei sample of the Chinese Family Life Study reveals the same tendency to contain oneself. Another study in Taiwan to establish Rorschach norms found that it was important for Chinese individuals to keep proper physical and psychological distances from each other. As an affect of child rearing, this formalism enables Chinese young people to achieve detached roles in interpersonal relationships (Yang et al. 1963).

As for Cantonese, a Rorschach study of adolescents in Hawaii found them to be "typically cautious, constricted and conventional when faced with a new and threatening situation," and "conspicuously lacking in oppositional tendencies or in feelings of self-assertiveness" (Hsu et al. 1961). Abel and Hsu (1949), also working with Rorschach responses (mostly from Cantonese) declare that they fit into a Chinese cultural pattern of controlling impulses and maintaining a pliant but to some degree distanced role in interpersonal relationships.

The psychological data presented above clearly provide a basis for the common Western assumption that Chinese are "passive" and "dependent." Before going on to probable causes, we should point out again that these attributes receive different valuation in Chinese and American cultures. Chien-hou Hwang (1967), in an analysis of Edwards Personal Preference Schedule scores, notes that in Edward's terms, his sample of students from two universities in Taiwan score low on Exhibition, Dominance, Change, and Aggressiveness scales and high on Abasement, Deference, Endurance, and Order. But, quoting the Lun-yu, Hwang points out that the latter four qualities, when seen as "humility, gentleness, restraint, and living by rite are highly desirable traits in Chinese culture."

Muensterberger (1951) attributes this "passivity" and "dependency" to oral indulgence and failure of the individual to learn oral renunciation. However, Weakland uses the same evidence of a cultural accent on food to speculate that oral indulgence in early childhood is not wholehearted. It is surrounded by anxiety, since the mother is performing before the critical audience of her husband's family. Actually, the mother feeds to control or inhibit motor activity of the child and may resent the child, since her status is dependent upon him. The possible effect of unstable food supplies in parts of Chinese society is touched upon in Eberhard's (1970) comparison of dreams of Chinese residents in San Francisco and Taipei. The dreams of respondents in San Francisco showed dramatically less concern with food. (For another discussion of Chinese orality and dependency, see Chapter 2.)

Actually, both terms—passivity and dependency—are Western terms, important to people who value assertiveness and individuality. By contrast, a very sick man under psychiatric treatment in Peking was characterized by "directness of manner, love of dominating, and a high degree of competitiveness" (Dai 1944). In the United States, this description would fit a successful businessman. If *ho* (harmony) and collectivity (family) are the supreme values of the culture, then obviously assertiveness and individuality cannot be maximized. The individual can function only in the context of the group and in the most cooperative way possible.

Thus hostile and aggressive impulses are quashed or smothered in Chinese children and hostile impulses toward elders are even more severely condemned. In a comparative study of the early 1950s, the relative unacceptableness of resistance is indicated in the responses to Thematic Apperception Test card 1, a picture of a boy sitting at a table and looking at a violin on the table. In an American student group 68 percent projected resistance into their responses to the picture, but in Hsu's testing (1953) in Taiwan and Hong Kong, only 37 percent of the students in Taiwan and 30 percent of the students in Hong Kong did so. (Our work with the T.A.T. in the late 1950s confirms the continuity of relatively few stories of resistance given to this card in a sample taken fifteen years later.) Early motor activity such as clutching is discouraged in Chinese infants, and babies are carried as long as possible. Later they are discouraged from running, jumping, and exercising. While the classic large Chinese family is not frequently found, families with more than a set of parents and their children are common. Therefore, the child is rarely alone. Nowhere is his individuality emphasized, and everywhere harmony is stressed.

We have documented the usual Western contention that Chinese are passive and dependent and have set forth the argument that this is a Western *interpretation* of behaviors that are performed in response to Chinese cultural imperatives to be harmonious and collectivistic. Finally, we introduced CPI data to indicate that a Chinese can be assertive but not in an individualistic manner. Any relatively dominant, achievement-oriented, and extroverted behavior must be compensated by an equally great concern for the opinion of others, social relations, and group norms in order to comply with the cultural standard of harmony. Our work in the late 1960s confirms the continuity of such patterns.

Holistic Perception

Associated with the strong tendency of the Chinese toward harmony in human and natural functioning is a more basic perceptual inclination to see phenomena as wholes rather than in parts. The data from several Rorschach studies point to a Chinese tendency to perceive stimuli in this way, whereas Westerners tend to the reverse. As Chinese become socialized into Western patterns, whether in China or in the United States, they seem to move away from strong emphasis on global responses (Hellersberg 1953).

Related to holistic perception is the use of rote memory in learning and difficulty in reasoning by analogue. We can speculate that people who see a whole memorize what they see as a total model rather than as a sum of parts. They tend to describe or discuss parts as they relate to the whole rather than to perceive the whole as developing from its combined parts (Goodnow 1961). Since the intellectual efficiency (Ie) scale of the CPI is designed to test the degree of personal and intellectual efficiency achieved by the individual, according to Western concepts of progressive intellectual thinking, we could expect the performance of Chinese on this scale to run counter to American norms and in accordance with the Chinese emphasis on perception of the whole. Those tested who have been exposed to Western-style conceptual thinking, either at home or in school, tend to have higher Ie scores than those without such exposure. Unfortunately, none of the tests reviewed here have directly tested ability to see relationships within the whole, a test to which one might suspect the Chinese would respond very well.

The CPI manual reports that American college men score a standard deviation higher on Ie (intellectual efficiency) than high school boys. Similarly, American research scientists and graduate students in psychology, who are specialists in logical thought that starts with small phenomena or propositions and builds toward a whole or a larger-scale theory, have mean scores a standard deviation above the mean for all American males. When we look at Figure 3.1, we see that all the groups of Chinese men fall well below the standard mean on this scale.

When examining the mean profiles of the sons of the a- and O-groups of men (not shown here), we find that the Min-nan boys' score of 31.2 is slightly lower than the 31.7 score of their fathers and that the San Francisco boys' score of 34.4 exceeds their fathers' score of 33.4. If their scores followed the American pattern, both groups of boys might score substantially lower than their fathers. The Taiwan high school youth are sons of college men; thus, we can guess that they are exposed to Western-style conceptual thinking, both at home and in school and that this exposure influences them. The San Francisco boys, educated mainly in the Western system, already exceed their fathers, most of whom were educated entirely or partly in the Chinese system. Finally, sons of the Taipei fathers in the two lowest educational groups scored 29.6 and 29.1, substantially lower than the other Taipei boys, perhaps reflecting their lack of contact with a Western conceptual system which would have prepared them for higher scoring on the Ie scale. Nevertheless, their scores were higher than those of their fathers, which perhaps reflects their greater exposure to education of any sort.

Two other CPI scales, tolerance (To) and Flexibility (Fx), also may reflect this Chinese proclivity to perceive and conceptualize in wholes. All the subgroups in San Francisco and Taipei tended to score low on these scales. While this scoring may be related to a tendency to be wary of other individuals and groups and to project psychologically, it also may reflect the difficulty of individuals who perceive phenomena as wholes in interchanging or manipulating components of knowledge or social situations.

The tendency to see things holistically may start when the child sees the family rather than himself as a whole. Later the Chinese child learns many more models as wholes: ceremonies, painting, writing, and so on. As he repeats and copies them they become part of him.

TWO KEY DEFENSES IN CHINESE PERSONALITY

Although the number of "defenses" (coping or feedback mechanisms that pattern the response of the individual to action in his environment) such as projection, displacement, and identification, are limited, their possible combinations are infinite and may vary from culture to culture. Moreover, their rate of use by an individual or group can be quite selective. Therefore, if we assume that personality modalities are shaped by the interaction of persons with their cultural, social, and physical environments, we may conclude that the defenses having the highest frequency of use will be those most consistent with cultural values or social norms, although the whole range of psychological defenses may be available to each ethnic group and practiced to some extent by some people in each group. Research indicates that somatization and projection are frequently used and salient defenses within Chinese society. Of course, it is recognized that projection is a frequent defense in most societies. Other coping mechanisms such as sublimation, displacement, and identification are also in common use. When a social system places high value on harmony and sees a group (family) with defined roles as the basic unit of the system, direct within-group confrontation is nearly impossible. Acting out, or displacement within the group, can be threatening to group roles (statuses) and thus to the group itself. Therefore its members may tend to project negative characteristics outside the group or may defend against the conscious acknowledgement of negative feelings through somatization.

Correct behavior for a Chinese lies in seeking help and in responding to a need made evident by others, not in individual initiative and effort directed toward one's own ends (Weakland 1950). One finds, therefore, that projection, or attributing initiative to another, is deeply embedded in the social dynamics of Chinese society. If there is a cultural pattern of expecting action from without and restrictions upon direct action within, then projection of hostility, aggression, and other negative feelings that arise daily in human activity are not only to be expected but are almost ensured. Other patterns of behavior compatible to a high-frequency use of projection are obsessive-compulsive behavior, such as fanatic loyalty or preoccupation with symmetry, and passive-aggressive defense systems represented by ambivalence toward authority (Dai 1957).

Finney makes a good case for reaction-formation as a major defense in Chinese society (1969). He defines it as "systematically doing the opposite of one's impulse" while answering the question "How can I deal with the demands that people make on me, the rules and regulations that people impose upon me?" Working with students in Hawaii in carefully controlled work, he determined that Chinese ranked first in "reaction-forming qualities" among eleven ethnic groups, making them able to restrain their feelings and impulses, be thrifty, and work hard toward a distant goal. Our CPI data with its low mean scores on the Fx and To scales supports Finney's contentions.

Somatization

A careful study done under the supervision of Hsien Rin, Hong-min Chu, and Tsung-yi Lin (1966) with an age-stratified random sample of 488 men and women in Taiwan provides a wealth of data on psychophysiological reactions. Of the total sample, 42 percent reported such reactions. Only 54 percent of the sample reported psychiatric problems of any kind, so that psychophysiological disorders represent 75 percent of the total. Chinese coming from the mainland and Taiwanese-born have roughly the same proportion of disorders. Individuals with a high commitment to traditional Chinese values but also a high involvement in modern life patterns had the lowest rate (30.3 percent), while people with the lowest commitment to traditional values and the least contact with modern life had the highest rate (82.4 percent). Youngest daughters had the highest rate in siblingships, whether they were the youngest child (72 percent) or the youngest girl (64 percent). Men and women in general had about the same rate in the sample of 102 men and 104 women.

In our CPI data, the Well-being scale has a number of items that indicate a tendency to somatize psychosocial problems. An inspection of Figure 3.1 quickly reveals that the Taipei groups fall from one to two standard deviations below the standard score mean. The mean score (34.7) of San Francisco O fathers is higher but is still nearly a standard deviation from the American norm. A cursory item analysis of the Well-being scale revealed that Chinese respondents to the test frequently answered questions on the scale dealing with health in such a way as to lower their scores. For instance, more than three-fourths of the San Francisco O fathers indicated that they had one or more physical problems such as sensitive skin, vomiting, or a stiff neck, or that they had sometimes pretended to be ill in order to avoid something.

Projection

If we assume that projection is a psychological defense mechanism whose overuse results in paranoia, then the incidence of paranoia in its various manifestations tells us something about the general use of projection as a defense in everyday life. Cameron and Torgerson (1962), working with Chinese military men, reported that the incidence of paranoia symptomatology was significantly higher than in a similar American military population. Twenty-one of the sixty-three patients they studied had paranoid features, a fact they attributed to parental rejection and little leeway for socially acceptable expressions of hostility. In a comparative study using the 16 P-F Test with Chinese and American students of the University of Oklahoma, Scofield (1960) found that the greatest difference between the two groups was in the "paranoid" factor. Most of the forty students in the Chinese sample had been born in China and had been in the United States for less than two years.

On the mainland, of the patients admitted to the Peking Municipal Psychopathic Hospital from 1933 to 1938, 22.2 percent were schizophrenic and 5.4 percent were paranoid or in a paranoid state (Dai 1941). Cerny (1965) indicates that schizophrenia accounts for 50 percent of all hospitalized mental cases and 40 percent of all psychoses on the mainland. In a sample of 2000 schizophrenics in Shanghai over 46 percent were listed as paranoid. In nine cases that Dai presents from his Peking material, eight used paranoid projection as a major defense mechanism. For instance, a Kuei (ghost) seized an elderly woman and jumped on her stomach, and another Kuei ruthlessly pursued a twenty-year-old high school student, who went to the police for protection. Yeh (1969), after reviewing a study of forty students who had returned to Taiwan from overseas because of mental illness and finding thirty-four of them exhibiting paranoia as a major feature, comments on the cultural acceptance of this extreme form of projection by saying, "Paranoid patterns of behavior, then, may be easily regarded as 'average' or 'non-psychotic' in current Chinese society unless they are overtly disturbing."

Attempts at wish-fulfillment, working through guilt conflicts, and manipulation of significant others through projection onto a Kuei who inhabits or possesses the individual have been dealt with in some detail by Yap in Hong Kong (1960). The patients he described were usually women with little or no education. Lin (1953) also discusses nine cases with similar seizures (Hsieh-ping) by Kuei, most of them in uneducated females of hysteric personality, at the bottom of the social ladder. Psychophysiological reactions may have been impractical and projecting blame or fears upon others may not have been effectively heard, and so they resorted to the supernatural. The other alternative open to women is suicide, or more likely—as Yap (1958) indicates—attempted suicide. More than twice as many women as men attempted suicide in the critical years between 16 and 30—the years in which a woman is getting married, having her first children, and getting used to a new family.

A number of writers have indicated that depression is not common in Chinese society as a psychopathological factor. Ratnavale (1973) reports its absence in a large psychiatric facility in Shanghai. Tseng and Hsu (1970) point out that the word *depression* does not even exist in Chinese and cite a low incidence in Taiwan. However, Marsella et al. (1973) in their review of the literature find differing reports concerning its incidence. Their own empirical research relates depression in their Chinese-American respondents to somatic complaints.

SOME CONCLUSIONS ABOUT ADAPTATION AND ADJUSTMENT IN CHINESE PERSONALITY

Earlier in this chapter, we made some effort to establish the fact that Chinese society is neither changeless nor rigidly stable. In fact, some aspects of change are provided for ideologically, illustrated in family socialization patterns, and evidenced in personality modalities. Before examining some specific aspects of change, we should consider whether Confucianism as the major custodian of Chinese cultural values possesses the capacity for change.

While the term "Confucian thought" can be construed to mean only the Confucian canon and its direct commentary, it is often taken to have a much wider meaning, as the repository of the works of Confucius, Mencius, and Chu Hsi and as a framework for Taoism, Chinese Buddhism, practical political thought, and folkloristic aphorisms. While the major thrust of Confucian thought has been conservative and has dwelt on the Wu-lun, "in this century, Liang Shu-ming, Chen Li-fu and others have interpreted Confucianism largely as a philosophy of evolutionary change and continual adaptation" (Roy 1963). This provision for social change is not exactly new, since the I Ching *(Book of Changes)* fully incorporated into the Confucian tradition during the Han Dynasty, provides for change within the system rather than a change of systems.

Stoodley (1967), working with a random sample of Hong Kong Chinese students in 1963, found that 62 percent of his respondents accepted Confucian teaching outright or considered it the best guide to social behavior, with some adaptation. Only 5.6 percent completely rejected Confucian teachings. This was in a British crown colony where many students were considering going to the West. Even on the mainland, Communist ideology must wage a continual fight to maintain its identity and not to be incorporated and adapted into the Confucian state. If we assume that Confucian thought is an institution with the capacity to adapt and change, we can see change in Chinese society in a somewhat different light (Cole 1965). Rather than seeing a conflict between old Chinese philosophy and new Western thinking, we can see change as the incorporation and adaptation of the results of technology, science, and urbanization into a system of thought that has maintained its vitality through the incursion of three major religions (Buddhism, Islam, and Christianity), a continual influx of new peoples, complete defeat by two military forces (Mongols and Manchus), and partition and overrule by foreigners (Japan and the West). Viewing social change from within the Confucian system puts into different perspective the relatively small role played by the entering Western values that accompany urbanization and technological change. We can then see more clearly both structural and functional change, since we are not focusing on a conflict.

Collectivity vs. Individuality

Ch'en Li-fu states the Confucian position well when he defines the isolated individual as an abstraction. For when the five relationships are properly observed to the full and extended to all created things, then man's life and that of the universe become one, and the universe becomes a moral universe. The individual's life interpenetrates the life of the whole as he is always a member of a family or group (Singh et al. 1962).

The Chinese family is not disappearing overnight, but it is adapting to new social situations both within China and overseas. The joint family has maintained itself in the United States, the very citadel of individualism (Barnett 1960). The classical Chinese rural joint family—living, cooking, and working together—has been replaced, but relatives continue to work together and own businesses jointly. It is common practice for apartment houses to be owned and lived in jointly by Chinese-American sons and their families, and numerous community and family occasions are celebrated together around a common banquet table. The extended family of uncles and cousins is very real in business, in times of celebrations, and at times of crisis.

Students of the Chinese family have often equated family solidarity with subordination of the individual, but the Chinese themselves have not always seen family structure as so confining. Writing about changes in the Chinese way of life under the Communists, Chen (1953) complains that in the place of the old individualism, collectivism is now being promoted. His attack against forced attendance at outside meetings highlights the fact that life inside the family, at least for men, was seen as relatively uncontrolled. In a study of stereotypes in Hawaii including several ethnic student groups, considerable numbers of each of seven other groups saw the Chinese as having a "close-knit family." None of the Chinese students saw themselves this way (Vinacke 1949). Rather, Chinese have subjectively defined themselves in terms of family loyalties. Even family members suffering from severe emotional problems retained their loyalty to each other. They simply could not see themselves apart from their families.

Some empirical reports do suggest change in adjustment and possibly in social adaptation patterns. Family influences on adjustment as affected by the changing concept of the individual have been investigated in two recent field-work studies in Hong Kong. Mitchell and Lo (1969) tentatively established that in personal adjustment the more assertive children had mothers who treated them permissively, gave them more freedom, involved them in the adult world of conversation, and punished them less harshly than the mothers of dependent children. All these changes in mother-child relationships may have been brought about by greater cohesiveness of nuclear family units (though they may still function in a joint family to some degree), greater equality of husband and wife, and a deeper affective relationship between spouses brought about by more association with each other rather than with same-sexed members of the extended family. Liu (1966a), working in Hong Kong with two small samples of nine families each, one of local families and the other of refugees, notes that the local families have a more stable set of interpersonal relationships, with the father as a warm and congenial leader, the mother as a supporter of his role, and the son relating more affectively to his mother but in communication with both parents. The refugee family has an equally strong father; the son tends to agree readily with him but with almost a lack of personal identification. If we see the refugee families as being more traditional, there seems to be movement in the local families toward a more affective family unit with less emphasis on status, greater acceptance of disagreement, and more capacity for individual development. In other work Liu has established that individualism has become an increasingly prominent aspect of the value orientation of Hong Kong's Chinese (1966b).

Chinese youth and their parents are in a gradual process of adaptation and change, as illustrated by their attitude toward Hsiao (filial piety) and arranged marriage and by distribution of authority in the family. The Stoodley (1967) study in Hong Kong, which is supported by the Podmore and Chaney (1974) study in the same area, indicates that while the concept of obedience to the father is still very strong, utter obedience to him is out of the question. The limits of Hsiao are changing, not the concept; respect is still an absolute, while obedience is subject to negotiation. Gallin (1967) points out that rather than lose a fight to maintain the "no longer functional institution" of arranged marriage, Taiwanese parents have compromised by giving the young people a voice but have kept much of the form. The form also preserves the value of Hsiao. From questionnaires returned by 938 college and high school students in Taiwan, Lung and Chang (1967) found that 41.5 percent of their respondents came from families tending toward egalitarian or democratic decision making with participation of all family members. Another 39.4 percent leaned toward a patriarchal type and 17.5 percent toward a matriarchal type, with 1.5 percent unclassified. On the basis of their findings, they could say that the Chinese family has changed from the traditional centralized to the modern decentralized type. Of course, while the inclusion of high school students broadened the basis of their sample, it is probable that a large part of the more traditionally oriented population was not represented in this sample based upon student families. Furthermore, the 39.4 percent of this sample still tending toward patriarchal structure indicates that although a change in family structure may be in process, it is far from being complete. More recent work in Taiwan (Chu 1974) indicates considerable contribution of the extended family on an economic basis and an increase in the number of families that see themselves as extended families on the basis of close residence and constant interaction.

Our CPI data have indicated that Chinese generally do not tend to be direct, socially assertive individuals. This is illustrated by their relatively low Social Ascendancy scales and relatively high scores on such scales as Responsibility, Socialization, Self-control, and Good-impression, which reveal great concern with integration into a larger social unit. The relative positions of the Ac and Ai scales—achievement through cooperation versus individual achievement—further indicate individualistic nonassertiveness. It should be noted that the Ai scale was constructed for Americans, who associate individual achievement directly with competition. Achievement-oriented behavior by individuals in Chinese society is not uncommon (McClelland 1963); however, it is on the behalf of the group (family), and the element of competition often is not individualized. Desire for advancement is just as evident, but the stress in China is on cultivation of one's mind and character through study (Chin 1948). Except for specialized groups, American norms favor higher Ai scores.

Of all the subgroups in Taipei and San Francisco, no adult group of parents, male or female of any class, has an Ai mean score in excess of its Ac mean score, but the San Francisco Outstanding boys and two groups of Taipei girls, (c) and (d), have Ai scores slightly in excess of Ac scores. It appears that many Chinese-American boys have internalized the values of the American culture. Whether the impetus of change to individual achievement comes from within the family structure or from cultural pressure exerted in the American school and community, change has occurred. Most of the youth in the O sample had attended some Chinese school but were still more assertive than their parents.

The Taipei girls who scored relatively high on Ai were from the two groups, (c) and (d), whose fathers had little or no education. As lower-class girls in an urban setting, they had less to gain by conforming and more to win through independent achievement. Modern urban life, with its opportunities for individual employment, had made the choice of independence a real option. Lower-class family units may be smaller, so that the changed family structure and more affective relationships hinted at by Liu may also be a factor. On the other hand, adaptive processes may be working quite differently for girls (Li 1974). Chinese-American high school senior girls in Hawaii, tested with the Edwards Personal Preference schedule, had markedly higher mean scores on the Dominance and Achievement scales than a comparable group of Caucasian girls. In the same research, Chinese-American boys tested about the same as the girls, but significantly lower than Caucasian boys (Fenz and Arkoff 1962).

The Indirect Approach

The use of intermediaries (go-betweens), extensive negotiation prior to decision making, and the indirect approach have been developed to a high degree in Chinese society. Restriction of primary relationships largely to the family made dealing with other groups a procedure to be handled with great care. Failure to anticipate the motives and actions of the outside person or group would affect a significant number of relatives, and therefore transactions with people outside the family were to be worried about, conducted through go-betweens, and by all means done indirectly.

Much of the control of emotion involved in relations with people outside the family or even within the family has been institutionalized in the concept of *mien-tzu* (face). Hu's (1944) classic discussion of *mien-tzu* starts by reporting that while the concept is represented differently in different parts of China, the function of the institution seems to be uniform throughout the culture. Hu describes more than twenty different ways in which *mien-tzu* is used to regulate interpersonal relations.

Reliance upon go-betweens continues outside of China. Lucy Huang (1956) describes how students from China in the United States pressed married students into service to perform the traditional roles of matchmaking and introduction. Chinese men who had migrated to Liverpool, even though many eventually married English wives, similarly pressed friends into service. This behavior is probably a product of a personality configuration that mitigates against one's acting directly on his own behalf. Anxiety about the possible response of the outside world, which in part induces the indirect approach, is clearly shown in Kuhlen's (1945) application of the Pressey Interest-Attitude Test to Chinese and Japanese adolescents whose families had recently migrated to Hawaii. This test presents 360 items, 90 of which are arranged in each of four subtests classified as disapprovals, worries, interests, and admirations. There was little difference from other American adolescents in the mean scores on the subtests for interests and admirations. However, the Chinese and Japanese showed much greater capacities than other American youth for disapproving and for worrying. Kuhlen speculated that the Chinese tendency to be twice as worried as non-Asian Americans about events originating in society and outside the self was largely due to the fact that the students were going through the process of cross-cultural change that accompanies migration.

When we look at the CPI data presented earlier in this paper in reference to indirection in approach, our attention is drawn to three scales: Social-presence (Sp), Good-impression (Gi), and Femininity (Fe). Examination of Figure 3.1 reveals that Sp is one of the low points on all the profiles presented. A low Sp score indicates relative uneasiness about functioning in groups outside one's own. While the Sp scores are lowest in the Taipei groups, even San Francisco O fathers present this as one of their three lowest mean scores and the lowest of any of their Social-ascendancy scores. Heavy reliance on the family as a primary group seems to make functioning in outside groups in Chinese society an uncomfortable process even for people who have an overall healthy ego-structure (high Self-acceptance, Well-being, and Capacity-for-status) and who enjoy associating with others (high Sociability).

Just as the Sp scale indicates the comfortableness of an individual's personal functioning within a group of "others," the Good-impression (Gi) scale indicates a person's concern for the opinions of others. The highest, or one of the highest, peaks of the profiles we have seen is that formed by the Gi scale. All the adult groups in both San Francisco and Taipei tend to have high mean Gi scores, but some of the youth subgroups have significantly lower mean scores. In San Francisco, all three groups of youth (D, N, O) have lower scores than their parents. The O group mean score is similar to the American norm for adolescents, the D group considerably below it, and the N group in-between. The Taiwanese adolescents, both boys and girls, tend to have lower mean scores than their parents. The children of fathers with the most education score the lowest on the Gi scale. Those relatively low mean scores in Taipei are nearly the same as the American norm for adolescents. Traditional cultural norms in social functioning and modal personality appear to be altering under the influence of modern education.

Finally, the profiles in Figure 3.1 show high scores for these samples of men on the femininity scale. Even the two men with the highest Dominance scores are near the standard mean. Although the Fe scale can be used cross-culturally to discriminate between sexes, it measures psychological dispositions traditionally called "masculine" or "feminine," rather than physiological sex-linked attributes. The CPI manual describes people who score in a masculine direction as "outgoing, hard-headed, ambitious, blunt and direct in thinking and action." People who score in a feminine direction are "appreciative, patient, helpful, respectful and accepting of others." Therefore it is easy to see that the Chinese in these groups who have low Social-ascendancy scores and high Good-impression scores also might have high Femininity scores. Although the Fe scale clearly distinguishes between Chinese men and women, in a society where indirectness, consideration of others' opinions, and restraint are highly valued and practiced, the men's and women's mean scores are close to each other, with the mean score for Chinese men being higher than that of American men (Fong and Peskin 1969). These data are supported by the generally observed Chinese tendency to depend upon particularistic relationships with primary groups, to construct relations around Hsiao (filial piety), and to use indirect approaches to goals.

SUMMARY

An examination of some measurements of psychosocial functioning has revealed that the mean profiles of two quite different groups of Chinese—in Taiwan and San Francisco—are remarkably similar when age and sex are controlled. One point which emerged strongly was that the emphasis in Chinese culture on the family unit rather than on the individual, and on harmony as the highest good, seems to curtail individual aggressiveness. There are indications that adaptive system change is an interactive process involving the cultural system, the personality system, the structure of the family, and the larger social system. Thus technology, part of the culture, may change the involvement of the individual in the labor market. This occupational change, by restructuring residential patterns and stability, may alter the size and structure of the family. The child, grown to adulthood with an adapted personality, influences the continual reshaping of family functioning and the structuring of social institutions. However, this general change process is a result of interactions within and among cultural, social, and personality systems and generally develops gradually—with much of the old culture system continuing in the changed society.

REFERENCES

Abbott, Kenneth A. 1968. "The Use of the California Psychological Inventory in an Intensive Study of Family Systems," *Psychology and Education* (Taipei) 2: 49–60.

Abegg, Lily. 1952. *The Mind of East Asia*. London: Thames and Hudson.

Abel, Theodore M., and Hsu, Francis L.K. 1949. "Some Aspects of Personality of Chinese as Revealed by the Rorschach Test," *Journal of Projective Techniques* 13:3: 68–72.

Barnett, Milton L. 1960. "Kinship as a Factor Affecting Cantonese Economic Adaptation in the United States," *Human Organization* 19:40–46.

Bodde, Derk. 1953. "Harmony and Conflict in Chinese Philosophy," in *Studies in Chinese Thought,* edited by Arthur F. Wright. Chicago: University of Chicago Press.

Cameron, Richard R., and Torgerson, Fernando G. 1962. "Cultural Considerations in the Teaching of American Psychiatry to the Chinese" *Mental Hygiene* 46:229–47.

Cerny, Jan. 1965. "Chinese Psychiatry," *The International Journal of Psychiatry* 1:2:229–47.

Chen, Theodore Hsi-en. 1953. "The Marxist Remolding of Chinese Society," *The Journal of Sociology,* 58:340–46.

Chin, Ai-li S. 1948. "Some Problems of Chinese Youth in Transition," *American Journal of Sociology* 51:1–9.

———. 1966. *Modern Chinese Fiction and Family Relations.* Center for International Studies. Cambridge, Mass.: Massachusetts Institute of Technology.

Chu, Solomon S. 1974. "Some Aspects of Extended Kinship in a Chinese Community," *Journal of Marriage and the Family* 36:3: 628–33.

Cole, Allan B. 1965. "Contrasting Modernization in China and Japan," *Chung Chi Journal* (Hong Kong) 4:2:99–138.

Dai, Bingham. 1941. "Divided Loyalty in War," *Psychiatry* 7:4:327–40.

———. 1944. "Personality Problems in Chinese Culture," *American Sociological Review* 6:5:688–96.

———.1957. "Obsessive-Compulsive Disorders in Chinese Culture," *Social Problems* 4:4:313–21.

Dawson, Raymond. 1967. *The Chinese Chameleon.* London: Oxford University Press, 1967.

Eberhard, Wolfram. 1970. "A Comparison of Dreams of San Francisco's Chinese-Americans with Dreams of Taiwanese," in *Collected Essays,* vol. 2. Hong Kong: Hong Kong University Press.

Fenz, Walter D., and Arkoff, Abe. 1962. "Comparative Need Patterns of Five Ancestry Groups in Hawaii," *Journal of Social Psychology* 58:67–89.

Finney, Joseph C. 1969. "Intercultural Differences in Personality," in *Culture Change, Mental Health, and Poverty,* edited by J.C. Finney. Lexington: University of Kentucky Press.

Fong, Stanley L.M., and Peskin, Harvey. 1969. "Sex-role Strain and Personality Adjustment of China-born Students in America: A Pilot Study," *Journal of Abnormal Psychology* 74:5:563–67.

Freedman, Maurice. 1966. *Chinese Lineage and Society: Fukien and Kwangtung.* New York: Athlone Press.

Fried, Morton H. 1959. "The Family in China: The People's Republic," in *The Family: Its Function and Destiny,* edited by Ruth Anshen. New York: Harper & Row.

Gallin, Bernard. 1967. "Emerging Individualism in Changing Rural Taiwan," *Journal of the China Society* 5:3–8.

Goodnow, Robert E. 1961. "Study of Chinese Personality," *July Report* pp. 33–35. Washington, D.C.: Human Ecology Fund.

Gough, Harrison G. 1969. *Manual for the California Psychological Inventory.* Palo Alto, Calif.: Consulting Psychologist's Press.

Hellersberg, Elizabeth F. 1953. "Visual Perception and Spatial Organization: A Study of Performance on the Horn-Hellersberg Test by Chinese Subjects," in *The Study of Culture at a Distance,* edited by Mead and Metraux. Chicago: University of Chicago Press.

Hsu, Francis L.K. 1953. "A Thematic Appercention Test Study of Chinese, Hindu, and American College Students," in *Class, Caste and Clan,* edited by F.L.K. Hsu. New York: D. Van Nostrand Co.

———. 1955. *Americans and Chinese.* London: Grosset Press.

———. 1959. "The Family in China: The Classical Form," in *The Family: Its Function and Destiny,* edited by Ruth Anshen. New York: Harper & Row.

———. 1967. "Family System and the Economy: China," in *Personalities and Cultures,* edited by Robert Hunt. Garden City, N.Y.: Natural History Press.

Hsu, Francis L.K.; Watrous, Blanche G.; and Lord, Edith M. 1961. "Culture Pattern and Adolescent Behavior," *International Journal of Social Psychiatry* 7:1:33-53.

Hu, Hsien-chin. 1944. "The Chinese Concepts of 'Face,'" *American Anthropologist* 46:1:45-64.

Huang, Lucy. 1956. "Dating and Courtship Innovations of Chinese Students in America," *Marriage and Family Living* 18:1:25-30.

Hwang, Chien-hou. 1967. "A Study of the Personal Preferences of Chinese University Students by Edwards Personal Preference Schedule," *Psychology and Education* (Taipei) 1:52-68.

Kuhlen, Raymond G. 1945. "The Interests and Attitudes of Japanese, Chinese and White Adolescents: A Study in Culture and Personality," *Journal of Social Psychology* 21:121-33.

Li, Anita King-fun. 1974. "Parental Attitudes, Test Anxiety, and Achievement Motivation: A Hong Kong Study," *Journal of Social Psychology* 93: 3-12.

Lin, Tsung-yi. 1953. "Study of the Incidence of Mental Disorder in Chinese and Other Cultures," *Psychiatry* 16:4:313-36.

Liu, William T. 1966. "Chinese Value Orientations in Hong Kong," *Sociological Analysis* 27:2:53-66.

———. 1966b. "Family Interactions Among Local and Refugee Families in Hong Kong," *Journal of Marriage and the Family* 28:3:314-23.

Lung, Kuan-hai, and Chang, Shiao-chun. 1967. "A Study of Chinese Family Organization," *Journal of Sociology* 3:117-36.

Marsella, A.J.; Kinzie, D.; and Gordon, P. 1973. "Ethnic Variations in the Expression of Depression," *Journal of Cross-cultural Psychology* 4:4:435-58.

McClelland, David C. 1963. "Motivational Patterns in Southeast Asia with Special Reference to the Chinese Case," *Journal of Social Issues* 19:6-19.

Mitchell, Robert E., and Lo, Irene. 1968. "Implications of Changes in Family Authority Relations for the Development of Assertiveness in Hong Kong Children," *Asian Survey* 8:309-22.

Mitchell, Robert E., and Tsang, Annie. 1969. *Family Life in Urban Hong Kong.* Hong Kong: Urban Family Life Survey.

Mitchell, Robert E., and Wong, Sophie. 1969. *Pupil, Parent, and School*. Hong Kong: Urban Family Life Survey.

Muensterberger, Warner. 1951. "Orality and Dependency: Characteristics of Southern Chinese," in *Social Sciences*, vol. 3. New York: International University Press.

O'Hara, Albert. 1967. "Some Indications of Changes in Functions of the Family in China," *Journal of Sociology* (Taipei) 3:59–84.

Podmore, David, and Chaney, David. 1974. "Family Norms in a Rapidly Industrializing Society: Hong Kong," *Journal of Marriage and the Family* 36:2:400–07.

Ratnavale, David N. 1973. "Psychiatry in Shanghai, China: Observations in 1973," *American Journal of Psychiatry* 130:10:1082–87.

Rin, Hsien; Shih, Ling-yu; Lee, Hong-sheng; and Ko, Yung-ho. 1951. "A Comparative Study of Psychiatric Symptoms Manifested by Neurotic Patients and College Students," *Acta Psychologica Taiwanica* 3:57–72.

Rin, Hsien; Chu, Hung-ming; and Lin, Tsung-yi. 1966. "Psychophysiological Reactions of a Rural and Suburban Population in Taiwan," *Acta Psychiatrica Scandinavia* 42: 410–73.

Roy, A.T. 1963. "Confucianism and Social Change," *Chung Chi Journal* 1: 88–104.

Ruey, Yih-fu. 1967. "The Five Social Dyads as a Means of Social Control," *Journal of Sociology* (Taipei) 3: 47–50.

Salaff, Janet W. 1973. "The Emerging Conjugal Relationship in the People's Republic of China," *Journal of Marriage and the Family* 35: 4: 705–17.

Scofield, Robert W. 1960. "A Comparative Study of the Differential Effect upon Personality of Chinese and American Child Training Practices," *Journal of Social Psychology* 52: 221–29.

Singh, Paras Nath; Huang, Sophia Chang; and Thompson, George G. 1962. "A Comparative Study of Selected Attitudes, Values and Personality Characteristics of American, Chinese, and Indian Students," *Journal of Social Psychology* 57: 123–32.

Sollenberger, Richard T. 1968. "Chinese-American Child-rearing Practices and Juvenile Delinquency," *Journal of Social Psychology* 74: 13–23.

Solomon, Richard H. 1966. "The Chinese Revolution and the Politics of Dependency." Doctoral dissertation. University of Michigan.

———. 1971. *Mao's Revolution and the Chinese Political Culture*. Berkeley and Los Angeles: University of California Press.

Stoodley, Bartlett H. 1967. "Normative Family Orientations of Chinese College Students in Hong Kong," *Journal of Marriage and the Family* 29: 4: 773–82.

Tseng, Wen-shing. 1973. "The Concept of Personality and Confucian Thought," *Psychiatry* 36:191–202.

Tseng, Wen-shing, and Hsu, Jing. 1970. "Chinese Culture, Personality Formation and Mental Illness," *International Journal of Social Psychiatry* 16:1:5–14.

Vinacke, W. Edgar. 1949. "Stereotyping Among National-Racial Groups in Hawaii: A Study in Ethnocentricism," *Journal of Social Psychology* 30:265–91.

Weakland, John H. 1950. "The Organization of Action in Chinese Culture," *Psychiatry* 13:361–70.
———. 1956. "Orality in Chinese Conceptions of Male Genital Sexuality," *Psychiatry* 19:237–47.
Wilson, Richard W. 1974. *The Moral State: A Study of the Political Socialization of Chinese and American Children.* New York: The Free Press.
Wolf, Margery. 1970. "Child Training and the Chinese Family," in *Family and Kinship in Chinese Society*, edited by Maurice Freedman. Stanford: Stanford University Press.
Yang, C. K. 1961. *Religion in Chinese Society.* Berkeley and Los Angeles: University of California Press.
Yang, Kuo-shu; Tzuo, Huan-yuan; and Wu, Ching-yi. 1963. "Rorschach Responses of Normal Chinese Adults: II, The Popular Responses," *Journal of Social Psychology* 60:175–86.
Yang, Martin, M.C. 1960. "The Possession Syndrome: A Comparison of Hong Kong and French Findings," *Journal of Mental Science* 106:442:114–37.
———. 1967. "Child Training and Child Behavior in Varying Family Patterns in a Changing Chinese Society," *Journal of Sociology* (Taipei) 3:77–83.
Yap, Pow-meng. 1958. *Suicide in Hong Kong, with Special Reference to Attempted-Suicide.* Hong Kong: Hong Kong University Press.
Yeh, Eng-kung. 1969. "Paranoid Manifestations Among the Chinese Students Studying Abroad: A Preliminary Report," paper presented at the Conference on Culture and Mental Health in Asia and the Pacific, Social Science Research Institute, University of Hawaii 17–21 March 1969.

PART 2

Patterns of Change: The Ethos of Areal Cultures

The chapters in this section deal with the nature of cultural-specific responses to external social and political pressures to change. We consider in each instance large geographic areas united by continuities in culture rather than by political or social cohesion—black Africa, the modern Arab world, and Melanesia. The authors independently affirm a major contention: the responses to change noted, either adaptive or maladaptive, are not only determined by previous cultural patterns, but also extend beyond specific socio-political units, over vast regions that have somehow remained similar in their "ethos," as Bateson termed it.

In his germinal work *Naven* (1936), Bateson made an intensive analysis of a singular ritual found among the Iatmul of New Guinea that demonstrated for him how integrative patterns of thought and emotion were internally consistent and penetrated every feature of Iatmul culture. There is a world view, or *eidos*, which manifests itself in forms and patterns of every cultural institution, from the legal to the familial. There is also the *ethos* of a culture which includes these patterned forms of behavior as well as patterns of emotional responses and of values. These emotional responses and values give behavior a distinctive quality and express the essential principles or the dominant characteristics of the entire culture.

The finding that broad areal cultures keep a similar ethos raises several issues relating the following chapters to one another. First, there is the general question whether we can actually speak of the existence of cultural and societal similarities that extend over large culture areas despite manifest differences between particular groups. Second, if such areal patterns exist, what are the peculiar culture-specific responses to change in each instance? What, for example, has been the effect of foreign domination or colonization? Third, can we find reasons for the stipulated psychocultural similarities for groups located within the same areal culture? Are there common features of their primary and secondary socialization? Fourth, are there ecological features, of community or kinship organization as well as of internal family dynamics, that determine, or reinforce, these common patterns of socialization which contribute to peculiarities of personality development?

PERSISTENT MODALITIES IN PERSONALITY RELATED TO CULTURE AREA

In the first chapter of this section Robert LeVine raises the issue of pan-African personality similarities. If such a concept has any validity, it is based upon the fact that there are cultural configurations of widespread commonality. Thus, we can expect average continuities in personality distribution somewhat unique to Africans. Without direct recourse to the concept of an African ethos, LeVine sees unifying patterns, despite the dispersion of Africans into a variety of cultures. These patterns relate to subsistence, the marriage relationship, and the structure of political organizations. Although specific features taken singly are not exclusively African, the particular *combination* of traits is distinctly African.

LeVine very carefully avoids stereotyping. He stresses that there is more variation at the level of individuals than at the level of societies. LeVine argues that demographic and environmental similarities themselves would tend to produce similarities in personality structure, since individuals over long spans of time have faced common adaptive problems. These adaptive problems work their way into the adjustive personality structures. LeVine would argue, however, that in the intermediate levels of personality structure, rather than at a deeper unconscious level, the characteristic effects of environmental-social adaptation over time would be most noted. That is to say, he would argue that there are universal human traits shared by all which go deeper than those characteristics that one considers "African." Nevertheless, he has identified certain configurations of behavioral characteristics which are more common in Africa than elsewhere.

In conclusion, LeVine emphasizes that these pan-African characteristics are modulated by specific social and cultural differences occurring among the pasturalists, the agriculturalists, and the new urban classes of educated Africans who are influenced by Western formal education. As LeVine has indicated in his own work, there are radical differences between tribal groups with variant cultures. His study in Nigeria contrasting the Ibo, Hausa, and Yorba attests to these variations. Yet LeVine has been impressed, as have been others, with the persistence of cultural continuities in given groups despite integration, close interpersonal contact, and great pressures toward modernization that influence Nigerians in general.

According to LeVine, one can generalize to a degree across the complex political and social divisions of black Africa. Theodore Schwartz in describing the cargo cults of Melanesia argues in a similar fashion that the widespread appearance of the cargo cult indicates the validity of an areal culture definition of Melanesia. This area spreads across wide ranges of ocean and difficult interior terrains. Similar responses to culture contact appear despite this wide geographic separation. On the other hand, these Melanesian traits are totally absent in relatively contiguous areas of Polynesia or Indonesia.

Similar cultural-specific generalizations are made by Gulick concerning the political-social patterns found throughout North Africa and the Middle East, an area which he feels can be united conceptually as the Arab world. Similarities do occur, despite many of the historical and social dissimilarities between such disparate states as present-day Syria, Egypt, and Morocco. Robert Levy, in a related paper presented at our conference, points up striking congruences in the reports of research done throughout the Polynesian and Micronesian island cultures. Each author refers to the relationship between early socialization, family composition, and lineage patterns which mediate socialization, and the value patterns institutionalized in basic economic and political organizations. Similarities in these basic institutions account for similarities of response within groups that are not united in any direct political or social organization.

THE INTERNAL SOCIAL AND POLITICAL RESPONSES TO EXTERNAL POLITICAL DOMINANCE

A second issue uniting the chapters of Part Two is the persistence of similarities in the response to external dominance. All of the areas considered have gone through some form of colonial domination in the past century. The nature of their responses to colonial dominance and to recent political independence is at least as much a function of the internal cultural and social patterns as of the policies or the circumstances of colonialism or political liberation.

Melford Spiro, in a paper which was included in our original conference, focuses on cultural persistence despite the very considerable changes wrought on Burmese society by British colonial domination. He finds that in the structuring of hostile affect in Burmese, there is little difference between the contemporary and the preconquest Burmese. In the area of emotions, the effect of the British colonial experience can be noted not in how hostility is generated within in the individual Burmese, but in how its expression has been institutionalized differently. His point is that socialization experiences within the household and in the immediate community have not been directly affected by external political dominance. What is "Burmese" in emotional structure has survived and has been transmitted in new forms of expression in modernizing, formal institutions.

In Chapter 5 John Gulick discusses the patterns of political and social distrust in the Arab world. He suggests that these patterns are not only a result of long experience with tyrannical, corrupt, and predatory rulers, both indigenous and external, but have also been equally determined by self-perpetuating mental sets that remain a chronic source of intrapersonal and social stress. The source of such maladaptive and maladjustive continuities is found in aspects of the kinship system and the sexual status system. Community ecology and the traditional relationships of individuals to the state also affect these patterns. Gulick sees a current attempt to revise these basic institutions in the light of modernized values, including a movement to change the position of women in Arab culture. He infers that such a movement will have decided repercussions, not only in family life, but also in the functioning of political institutions. These conclusions are in accordance with those reached by Nelson in Chapter 12 on the changing status of Egyptian women.

In Levy's examination of the diverse nature of colonial incursions in Oceania, not included here, he found considerable diversity in the degrees of maladaptive social disorganization resulting from foreign dominance. In some instances, the effects were highly similar to the situations of subordinate status, documented in Part Four. There was in some instances a drastic reduction of indigenous population as well as a moving-in of European groups, which reduced the native population to a minority status, whatever its relative numbers.

In other instances in Polynesia, syncretic blending of modern and traditional, European and native elements produced new patterns that were highly adaptive and even, in some instances, less stressful for the individual than the culture pattern of the past. Mead's conclusion in the particular instance of Samoa was that the newer syncretic culture had not increased problems of inner adjustment, but had actually diminished problems of external adaptation and was thus, in regard to individual stress, an improvement.

But the results of contact were not always so happy. In stark contrast to the Samoan situation was that of Raratonga and Aitutake. Some observers believe that depopulation of these islands was not due solely to disease, but to disease coupled with reactive forms of extreme apathy which lowered the "will to live" of the people of these islands. This apathy resulted from a disruptive missionary influence which had broken the old culture without fostering any restorative process.

Generally speaking, Levy and others characterize the whole Oceanic area as quickly amenable to changes in political form, social behavior and religious beliefs, because none of these levels of social interaction were part of the core personality. In fact, many of the changes were, as already indicated, stress reducing.

Theodore Schwartz's chapter, on the Melanesian cargo cults, relates areal similarity to the specific phenomena of cargo cults—an area-typical, religious, revivalist response to culture contact. To explain this phenomena, Schwartz argues for similarities in personality for all of Melanesia. He contends that a "paranoid ethos" characterizes the entire area. Patterns of suspicion and distrust are interrelated with a Melanesian concept of personal adequacy which can be realized only through the competitive acquisition of wealth as a means of enhancing status. The contrast between the personality variables described by Schwartz and those described by Levy indicates the different areal patterns of Melanesia and Polynesia. These psychocultural features help to account for the fact that this particular cargo cult phenomenon exists only in the Melanesian culture area and has never appeared in Polynesia, although Polynesian and Melanesian cultures both had similar contacts with European political and social colonization.

KINSHIP ORGANIZATION AND BASIC SOCIALIZATION

The effects of kinship organization on internal family dynamics and therefore on basic socialization is an issue that runs through the chapters on areal culture as well as those of other sections of this volume. Levine, in discussing the ultra-areal characteristics of black Africa, stressed the high incidence of polygamy and patrilocality in one hundred and sixteen diverse African cultures. It follows that these patterns influence the type of mother-father-child interaction that causes some of the overall similarities. Similarly, Gulick sees the relation between extended families and their component nuclear families as one of the chief sources of stress in Arab kinship patterning. This stress is caused by the impossibility of achieving the ideal male-superior pattern of family life that is nevertheless rigidly insisted upon. The rigid insistence on the maintenance of ideals against patently contrary realities contributes to quarrels and bickering. Psychological denial systems develop which result in chronic levels of intrapsychic stress and interpersonal conflict. Similarly, in Schwartz's general description of Melanesia, the in-marrying spouse from another, potentially hostile village is continually perceived as a potential spy, and the loyalties of lineage, which cut across villages and which divide the family itself, feed into the overall distrust that separates Melanesians. In contrast, the Polynesians and Micronesians as discussed by Levy are more relaxed about lineage considerations. The relative receptivity of Polynesians to some features of social change results from the interplay of their kinship system with socialization practices. For example, the casual adoption of children is widespread.

Reviewing the chapters in this volume one notes that much more systematic research is necessary on comparative approaches to kinship socialization. Many current studies of kinship only report the formal, often ideal, structure, ignoring the tensions that result from the impossibility of realizing that ideal. Attention should also be paid to the fact that the way kinship is used may be influenced by other interpersonal factors in socialization. Thus, the psychocultural *use* of the kinship structure may express tensions not inherent in the kinship system itself, but caused by the specific personality development and reaction to the system of the individual involved. There are numerous cases in which kinship problems are an arena for the expression of internal tensions, as well as cases in which kinship structures themselves produce conflicts. At any rate, more specific research needs to be done to clarify these dynamic relationships.

PATTERNS OF COGNITION AND THE AREAL CULTURE CONCEPT

The personality variables specific to a culture are not limited to emotional traits, but also include similarities in basic cognitive structures. Both in the case of Africa and that of Polynesia, there is a characteristic pattern of "concrete thinking." Such a form of cognition was suited to the requirements of the traditional culture; it is, however, less suited to a more modern environment. The acquisition of literacy and new patterns of adaptive cognition may proceed smoothly where their need is generally recognized. On the other hand, in some settings, the very act of compliance to the demands of formal education may threaten the social self-identity of minority groups. Thus, eagerness to acquire new cognitive skills is reported in Melanesia, New Guinea, and in some of the new states in Africa; but in some areas of Polynesia or among some ethnic minorities in the United States there are problems of non-learning or refusing to learn.

RELIGIOUS CULTS AS A REACTION TO CHANGE

Finally, a major issue in considering forms of adaptive and adjustive response to change is considered directly in Theodore Schwartz's article: the restructuring of religious beliefs as a response to change.

Schwartz's paper is a well thought out critique of a number of prevailing theories of psychocultural dynamics and religious phenomena. He considers and rejects as incomplete such popular theories as those that see revitalization movements as "religions of the oppressed"; "cognitive dissonance theory," popular in psychology; and theories attempting to relate a concept of intrapsychic stress to religious expressive phenomena. This paper is, in my judgment, the best brief examination of the issues involved in a psychocultural approach to religious cult behavior. Religious cults as responses to change exist worldwide. Nevertheless, the forms and the content taken by cult behavior are related to psycho-cultural patterns that distinguish groups from one another. In short, culture patterns determine in good part the direction taken and the forms of adaptation possible for given groups, whether they be religious or secular in nature.

Chapter 4

Patterns of Personality in Africa*

Robert A. LeVine

This chapter is neither a research report in the usual sense nor a documented review of the literature, but an attempt by a psychological anthropologist to extract from his experience of Africans preliminary answers to general questions that specialists rarely consider but cannot afford to ignore: are there distinctively African patterns of personality? What differences are there in behavior and personality between Africans and Westerners? How do the personality characteristics of Africans affect their social adaptation to changing conditions? This overview, going beyond empirical findings and using personal experience as well as scientific data as a source of generalization, is intended to stimulate systematic research and identify issues worthy of investigation.

The term "personality" is used here to refer to consistencies in the behavior of a human individual, consistencies that cannot be attributed to temporary states in his organism or temporary conditions in his environment but which endure over substantial periods of his life. I assume that personality characteristics vary widely among individuals in a given popu-

---

*An earlier version of this article appeared as "Personality and Change," in *The African Experience* (J. Paden and E. Soja, eds.), Vol. I, Northwestern University Press, 1970. I am grateful for the comments and criticism of Monica H. Wilson, who is of course not responsible for these contents. I am also indebted to the Center for Advanced Study in the Behavioral Sciences, where this final version was prepared. During the period of writing and revision the author was supported by a Research Scientist Development Award (KO2–MH–18,444–10) from the National Institute of Mental Health.

lation, just as do physical characteristics like height and weight. These distributions are not identical across all human populations; they differ in central tendency as well as other ways. Thus, though personality refers to consistencies of individuals, the individuals of a given population tend to show, when statistically aggregated, some central tendencies among themselves and average differences between themselves and some other populations. I assume that these average differences are caused primarily by differences in the social and cultural environments in which individuals of different populations grow up. If environmental conditions are similar in two populations, so should be the distribution of personality characteristics, according to this theory.

From this perspective, the question of an African personality takes us back to two prior questions: (1) Are there environmental differences among African populations of a quality and quantity to lead us to expect average differences in personality distributions? (2) How does environmental variation among African populations compare in magnitude with environmental differences between Africa and other parts of the world? In other words, are African societies and cultures, regardless of their differences from one another, distinguishable as a group from societies and cultures elsewhere? The available evidence indicates that they are. This is not to deny the major variations along lines of economy (hunting and gathering, pastoral, agricultural; presence versus absence of markets; amount of occupational differentiation), kinship (patrilineal, matrilineal, nonunilineal), social and political stratification, community structure (urban, clustered village, dispersed settlement), religion, and aesthetic tradition. It is simply to suggest that there are strong central tendencies of economy, social structure, and culture among African populations and that these are somewhat distinctive in a comparison of regions of the world. The relative homogeneity and distinctiveness of African sociocultural environments can be seen in Sawyer and Levine's (1966, p. 723) analysis of the cross-cultural data provided by Murdock (1957) on 565 ethnographically defined societies, of which 116 are from Africa south of the Sahara, and in Barry's (1968) analysis of the *Ethnographic Atlas* data on 863 societies, 238 of them African.

From these data, crude as they are, a distinctive African cultural profile begins to emerge. In economy, agriculture is overwhelmingly dominant over hunting and gathering and animal husbandry, but it is an agriculture in which men are less frequently involved than in any cultural region of the world. The association of animal husbandry with men, even where it is not a dominant subsistence activity, exceeds that of other regions. In family and kinship institutions, Africa leads the world in the incidence of polygynous societies, and the associated mother-child household is so widespread that Africa has the lowest frequency on two other household variables that are quite common in other regions. The tracing of the descent line through the father (patrilineality), the residence of a couple with the husband's family (patrilocality), and bride price prevail among African societies as they do almost nowhere else in the world, and bilateral descent has its lowest incidence there. Finally, indigenous slavery and hereditary succession to local office are considerably more frequent in Africa than in other regions. Lacking figures, I would nevertheless argue that aspects of indigenous religion, such as beliefs in ancestor spirits and in witchcraft and sorcery, have similar distributions.

These facts have two distinct types of implications. First, there is the indication of homogeneity in socioeconomic institutions in subSaharan Africa. Basic characteristics like agriculture, polygyny, patrilocality, patrilineality, bride price, and hereditary succession to local office are present in at least three-quarters of the societies there. Together with what social anthropologists know less formally about Africa, this suggests a common context of experience for Africans growing up in diverse parts of the continent. The second type of implication concerns the distinctiveness of these socioeconomic characteristics: none of them is in itself uniquely African, for they are all found elsewhere as well; but the *particular combinations* of traits may be distinctively African. There is not simply agriculture, but agriculture in which women supply a large proportion of the labor; not just polygyny but polygyny in which each wife and her children have a physically separate residential unit; not only patrilineality but patrilocality as well. The traits in themselves are not uniquely African, but the *profile of traits* appears to be. In other words, it is not the customs that are distinctive but the patterns or constellations of cultural characteristics. This suggests that the common context of experience shared by so many Africans is not widely shared by populations outside of Africa, even though many of the specific customs are.

Do these shared and distinctive environmental patterns produce similarly shared and distinctive personality distributions among the populations of Africa? The data to answer this question do not exist and are so far from being obtained that we are limited to discussing what form they might take if we had them. Speculating from a personality-trait perspective, I would argue that there will be no distinctively African personality traits, but possible profiles of traits, like the cultural profiles discussed above, that are more frequent in Africa than elsewhere. In other words, even if there is one, or more, profile of traits that distinguishes African populations from populations elsewhere in the world, this profile will not characterize all or even a majority of Africans, but just a larger proportion of Africans than non-Africans. Thus "the African personality" cannot be more than a matter of statistical tendency and is likely to show somewhat less uniformity across African populations than do patterns of culture.

From a different perspective, that of personality as a system with interdependent parts, the focus would be less on the parts in themselves and more on their organization, their relations to one another, and their contributions toward the functioning of the system. In the psychoanalytic view, for example, personality is seen as made up of a drive organization, a reality organization, and an organization of moral constraints, and their relative strengths and degrees of development and their characteristic ways of interacting constitute the individual's enduring patterns of reaction to events in his environment and in his physical organism. If we assume that environmental adaptation is a major goal for a functioning personality structure, and that environmental forces help create a structure that will be adaptive, then it seems likely that a population having faced common adaptive problems for many generations would tend to share structural solutions to them. Thus environmental similarities at the level of population or continent would tend to produce similarities in personality structure, just as they would tend to produce similarities in profiles of personality traits.

The degree to which we see population-wide or continent-wide commonalities in personality characteristics depends partly on the level of abstraction of our concepts rather than on what is really there. It is possible, for example, to conceptualize the fear of witches in three different ways: in its concrete cultural context, so that it is seen as specific to a single cultural group; as an instance of a general category of "witchfear," so that it is seen as characteristic of many African and non-African societies; or in terms of projection of hostility, so that it is applicable to all populations in some measure but in varying degrees and varying contexts. The arbitrariness of which conception one chooses cannot be dispelled until comparable data not only on behavior but on its *functions for the individual* are available on enough populations in Africa and elsewhere that scientific agreement on structural similarities and differences can be reached. Until then, characterizations of personality at the level of population, region, or continent must reflect the observer's range of experience and knowledge, the level of abstraction at which he chooses to operate, his ability to detect (accurately or mistakenly) psychological similarities in diverse contexts, and his guesses as to whether behavioral similarities indicate similarities in personality structure and function.

UNIFORMITIES AND VARIATIONS IN AFRICAN BEHAVIOR

Despite the skepticism of the foregoing section, I attempt here—based on my personal experience and observations in East and West Africa and on my reading of the ethnographic literature—to describe patterns of personality in Africa in terms of characteristics which are broadly shared across the continent.

Several qualifications are necessary concerning my outline of widespread African personality patterns. First, it is limited in scope to the agricultural peoples of subSaharan Africa and does not apply to primarily pastoral or hunting groups, to the modernized elites of the cities, or to North Africa and the East Horn. Second, it is limited in depth to the more observable, social personality characteristics; it is description close to the social surface of personality structure rather than to the underlying dynamics. The dynamics may show through, particularly toward the end of the outline, but I do not attempt depth interpretations. In fact, some of the tendencies dealt with are social expectations and might seem better described as properties of roles than of persons. I concede this to the point of using the term "behavior" rather than "personality" above but I would contend that, in order for large numbers of persons to internalize these role demands and social expectations, their personality structures must already be compatible. The reader may reach his own decision on this issue. I make no effort to portray personality as a functioning system of coordinated structures because this would be even more speculative than such portraits usually are; thus my account appears to be that of trait psychology, with the door left open to future structural analyses. Finally, it must be emphasized that this is a personal account in which I have allowed myself to generalize rather freely while hoping to remain objective. The point of view is that of the Western culture shared by this writer and his intended readership; contrasts between Western and African behavior and attitudes are explicit or implicit throughout.

The following are seven characteristics I believe to be widespread among the populations of subSaharan Africa:

Social Distance between Persons Differing in Age and Sex

African social life involves institutionalized restrictions on social contact between age and sex groups, and the arrangements of social activities in space and time tend to separate males from females and older from younger generations. Interaction between the sexes and generations tends to be highly prescribed by custom and often appears relatively formal and unspontaneous. What is most striking about these social distance patterns to a Western observer is that they apply to interpersonal relations within the family, which we are used to thinking of as a unit of relaxed informality; relations between husbands and wives, parents and their children (especially adult children), and junior siblings and co-wives are regulated in accordance with institutionalized restrictions, segregation patterns, and customary prescriptions. The evidence for this is vast and can be discussed in terms of avoidance, segregated activities, and formality of interaction.

The most institutionalized avoidance patterns have been documented by anthropologists, for example, the in-law avoidances of eastern Africa, which may mean that a man and his mother-in-law must never meet or see one another, or (as among the Zulu) that a young wife must carefully avoid mention of potentially sexual or aggressive topics in the presence of her senior in-laws. In western Kenya and other parts of East Africa, there is generational avoidance, in which young men and those whom they call "fathers," must avoid a wider range of personal contacts, from physical touching to discussing sexual topics or even jointly hearing them discussed. Relations between these generations tend to be stiff and restrained, with the younger generation especially inhibited in the presence of their elders. In the western Sudan, avoidance of the eldest son is especially common and takes a variety of institutionalized forms. Sometimes the eldest son of the father must be raised apart from the latter and must make efforts to avoid being seen by him; in other groups, avoidance between father and eldest son only becomes a social necessity when the son reaches maturity. Among the Hausa, the eldest child (of either sex) of each wife must avoid visible social contact with both parents; the avoidance is sometimes applied to the second child as well. These customs, and others like them, have meanings in their respective local contexts which anthropologists have taken pains to elucidate in terms of potentials for conflict that would be disruptive to the social structure if not regulated by avoidance. What is significant here, however, is that the members of these African societies are reported to experience the avoidance patterns as a satisfying way of life which is concordant with their own desires and fears, and that these institutionalized avoidances are but the most dramatic aspects of a much more general tendency.

The tendency for persons and groups distinguished by sex and age (or generation) to avoid one another is often concealed and made easier by segregated residential and other social arrangements that provide external barriers to their contact. Thus, no individual initiative or effort is necessary to maintain social distance. Houses and settlements and the explicit customs concerning their use provide structural arrangements for eating, sleeping, sexual activity, work, and recreation in which contact between the sexes and certain age groups is effectively minimized. Different age-sex categories are assigned their particular spaces for carrying out their activities, and they develop different activity schedules that limit interaction across social distance boundaries. The most massive forms of age segregation—the age villages of the Nyakyusa and the young warriors' settlements (manyatta) of the Masai—have perhaps received the most attention, but more subtle forms of age and sex segregation are pervasive in African societies. For example, houses are often laid out to provide husbands with space where they can (and do) eat and sleep separately from their wives and children; sexual contact between husband and wife is often confined to a brief segment of the night. Married women usually have their own distinctive routines and activity spaces that tend to unite groups of them and to separate them from other adults in the domestic group and neighborhood. The following description by an Acholi woman of life in her home community is typical:

> At meal time all the children eat with the mother, sitting on the kitchen floor, while the father eats alone. It is common in the villages to find a group of two or three families eating together, each woman having cooked two separate dishes, one for the men and one for the women and children. If there are a large number of children, one separate dish can be served to the children only. The two or three men, heads of the different families, will sit together near a fire outside or inside a house. (Apoko in Fox 1967, p. 53)

It is impossible in this brief summary to do justice to the rich variation in arrangements of this sort which have been described for the peoples of Africa. Suffice it to say that they share the characteristic of creating barriers to interaction between categories of persons whom Westerners feel belong together, particularly when they are members of the same family, and that Africans find this a satisfactory and desirable order of things. In fact, when men and women and young and old do participate jointly in a public event, they are likely to go and return separately and to cluster by age-sex groups at the event, thus spontaneously maintaining social distance (even between husbands and wives, parents and adult children) when the barriers are temporarily lowered.

Despite the limits set by avoidance and segregation customs, the sexes and generations do come into contact in African families and communities. When they do, their interaction is often highly institutionalized and includes safeguards against intrusions on privacy and explicitly prescribed greetings, conversational topics, and role obligations. Deviation from these prescribed norms is regarded as punishable or at least embarrassing if publicly revealed. Behavior among family members and other kinsmen often appears and is presented by informants as heavily standardized, allowing little leeway for voluntary idiosyncratic variation. There is a degree of social prescription and proscription in African families and other primary groups that we are accustomed to only in our "formal organizations," namely, bureaucratic settings. Furthermore, the adherence to institutionalized norms of behavior acts as a barrier to what Westerners regard as intimacy, such as the sharing of innermost thoughts and feelings, the giving and taking of emotional support, the private regression to childish means of expressing affection, and the experience of temporary union (loss of ego boundaries) with another person. It seems that intimacy in this sense, and the individualized relationships that accompany it, are of less importance to Africans than other goals of interpersonal relations described below. So the relative formality of behavior, like the customs of avoidance and segregation, maintains social and emotional distance between persons. Africans regard their greater formality as perfectly "natural" and "normal"; they do not experience their social boundaries as uncomfortable, isolating, or destructive to their individuality. Because they do experience as natural and comfortable types of role demands which we would experience so differently, the maintenance of social distance in African societies must be regarded as a *psychological* characteristic of the participating populations as well as a *structural* characteristic of their social systems.

Age and Sex Hierarchy

Turning to the content of prescribed interpersonal behavior among Africans differentiated by age and sex, no aspect is more evident than the giving and receiving of deference, respect, and precedence. Variations in rank, status, and power at every level tend to be given public emphasis, and each society has its distinctive hierarchy of social positions. African status hierarchies vary widely in differentiation, depth, distribution of decision-making functions, and ritual elaboration. But for all of them, in most aspects of social life, men are ranked higher than women, married persons are ranked higher than those who are socially immature, and men with adult children are ranked higher than their juniors. Much social interaction is accounted for by the deference and respect paid to men by women, to adults by children, and to elders by youths. The display of deference does not always signify the dominance of one person over another—indeed, sometimes the person deferring is quite autonomous—but it is nonetheless regarded as an indispensable feature of proper behavior. Deference is expressed in respectful terms of address, in appropriate greetings and blessings, in submissive gestures like bowing or prostration, in receiving a gift with two hands instead of one, and the like. The elaborate deference displayed daily in an ordinary Yoruba compound might find its nearest Western counterpart in a European royal court, and while the Yoruba are extreme among Africans in the flamboyance of the gestures used, they are not extreme in other aspects of their deference. Respect entails not only deferential behavior but also various kinds of restraint and avoidance. The latter was described above; perhaps the most widespread form of restraint is refraining from disagreeing with a status superior to his face. Thus one rarely sees open arguments across the most important age and sex boundaries, and when they occur they are regarded as serious if not downright scandalous.

In the distribution of leisure and other conspicuous advantages the African age-sex hierarchies contrast most sharply with Western values. This can be seen clearly in a contemporary African home that has Western-type chairs but not enough to go around. An honored guest is always given precedence in seating, but immediately thereafter come the senior men of the house or neighborhood. If the seating of the senior men means that women and children must stand, that is quite appropriate, for they are regarded as marginal to a gathering of men and in any event should yield to someone higher in the age-sex hierarchy. A similar situation obtains for the distribution of meat, which is a rare delicacy for most Africans: the senior men often have it first, women are allowed to have what is left over, and children may receive none. The frequent exclusion of children from meat-eating occurs even among relatively affluent urban families, and in western Nigeria we found that one of the most typical childhood memories of punishment reported by adolescent pupils was being beaten for sneaking meat out of the cooking pot. From the other side of the continent, Kenya, comes this recollection by a man from the Idakho area of the Luhya people:

> I once helped myself to *shihango*, the roasted meat that is kept for emergency cases, without the permission of my mother. When she came home and discovered that the hidden treasure had been removed and eaten, she did not wait to report me to my father. She gave me a thorough beating then and there, threatening to cut off my hands, these being the limbs I had used for stealing! (Lijembe in Fox 1967, p. 7)

The basic principle is: in any public or semipublic situation, those of higher rank must be served or relieved of burdens by those lower in the hierarchy, and the former must be granted precedence in the use or consumption of any valued good. Thus wives must carry heavy loads for the husband while he walks unencumbered; children are constantly sent to fetch and carry and convey messages around the home and community. The same principle holds among senior and junior siblings and co-wives and other kin, and has been applied to bureaucratic relationships such as that between schoolteacher and pupil or high and low ranking civil servant. Thus the allocation of work, and especially menial, burdensome, or servile tasks reflects the distribution of status: the higher one's status, the less work visibly performed and the greater the tendency to delegate tasks to inferiors. Giving orders and discussing whether or not they have been carried out, like deference and respect behavior, account for much of the content of social interactions between unequal persons in African societies.

Emphasis on Material Transaction in Interpersonal Relations

In considering the content of socially prescribed interpersonal behavior, we have seen that much of African behavior is hierarchically ordered, and that this order involves the giving and receiving of deference, respect, commands, and tribute between persons occupying unequal social positions. There is another dimension of content, however, that Africans emphasize when describing relationships of equality or inequality, namely, obligations to give and receive material goods—food, gifts, financial help, property, and offspring. Relationships are frequently characterized by Africans primarily in terms of the type of material transaction involved: who gives what to whom under what conditions. Even premarital sexual liaisons and courtship are discussed in these terms. In contrast with the Western attitude (genuine or hypocritical) that the emotional component in interpersonal relations is more important than any transfer of material goods involved (the latter being thought of as something incidental), Africans are frankly and directly concerned with the material transfer itself as indicative of the quality of the relationship. This is best illustrated with respect to food and feeding. Volumes could be written on the social and cultural meanings of food and feeding in African societies. Family relationships are often described in terms of feeding or providing food. Visitors are accepted, honored, or rejected in terms of the food and drink provided for them (e.g., the amount and quality), and they in turn show their friendliness and trust by accepting food and drink. Husbands reject their wives and neighbors express suspicious hostility by refusing food when offered, something that invariably creates alarm and tension. The sharing of food at an ordinary meal or a sacrifice to the spirits creates important bonds between persons. As Audrey Richards (1932) pointed out many years ago, African chiefs feed their followers in time of famine, thus providing a reserve food supply for the group, and local political leaders build their following by furnishing food for them.

Food and feeding are also a prominent feature of belief and imagination. When interpersonal suspicion mounts within the family or neighborhood, people fear that their enemies will poison their food. Ancestor spirits are often viewed as hungry or greedy, wanting to be fed through sacrifice. In many domains of behavior that do not involve actual feeding or oral activity—economics, sexuality, political succession—linguistic idioms, metaphors, and imagery derived from eating are widely used. It sometimes seems to an outside observer that the processes of eating and being fed are central to the symbolic interpretation of social reality in African populations.

Food is just one (although a basic) example of the concern for material transfer of interpersonal relations; among kinsmen land, cattle, and (increasingly) money are importantly involved, and in more transient relationships small gifts play a significant role. Something of the flavor of the material emphasis that can affect brother-sister relations is conveyed by the Acholi woman quoted below:

> If a boy sees his sister misbehaving in any way, he is authorized by his parents to give her a good beating. The sisters are very important to the brothers, whose future can largely depend on them. A brother whose sister has good manners and is married is sure to have a wife himself. The money paid to his father as his sister's bride price is the money he will use for his own marriage. Since he cannot marry until his sister is married, it is his real concern to see that she is well-behaved enough to be married early. (Apoko in Fox 1967, p. 67)

It is not possible to describe in any further detail the parts these goods play in African social life, but several points must be emphasized: (a) Some material giving is obligatory in a relationship, particularly a kin relationship, and is not dependent on how the individual feels about or even how well he knows the other person. (b) Persons are evaluated partly in terms of how much and how freely they give to others; those who give more than the obligatory minimum may be liked more as generous persons or may become special friends or leaders of others. (c) Failure to meet the material obligations of role relationships cannot be compensated by a friendly attitude or emotional warmth and support; since the relationships are conceptualized in terms of material transactions, attitudes and feelings are concomitants but not substitutes. (d) Relationships that have goals of obtaining valued resources (such as that of co-heirs to family property) generate competition, particularly when the resources are limited, the scope of obligations wide, and the rules for allocating resources somewhat ambiguous. Potential recipients or heirs are naturally competitive with one another, and Africans grow up in an interpersonal climate in which such competition is ubiquitous, although held in check by a variety of social controls. In novel institutional settings, Africans are sensitive to the material rewards offered and are ready not only to demand their promised share but also to compete with one another for preferment. Thus the obligatory giving and taking of resources as a major theme in social interaction has as its concomitant the nonobligatory, but inevitable, competitive striving for resources.

In the husband-wife relationship, babies are thought of as material goals for both spouses: a husband "gives his wife children" and she bears children "for him." It would be hard to exaggerate the personal importance of fertility to individuals of both sexes or the fear they have of being sterile. Giving and bearing children are absolutely obligatory no matter what the emotional quality of the husband-wife relationship. If the wife is barren, the husband takes another, and the first woman may eventually run away to try her luck with someone else. If the husband proves sterile or neglects her sexually, the wife most frequently leaves him for another; a young woman is likely to stay only if the sterile husband allows her to be impregnated secretly by another man. Africans generally want to have as many children as possible, so long as there is enough time between them to allow each one to thrive; children are often thought of explicitly as a quantitatively valued resource, parallel to property in the sense that "more" is unquestionably "better." They regard continued child-bearing to menopause as a sine qua non of the marriage, and no amount of conjugal love and understanding can make up for its absence. Occasionally, a couple will stay together without living children, but their attachment, however strong, is constantly interfered with by personal frustration and anxiety about not having children, and they lose the esteem of others. After the wife reaches menopause however, the spouses may have little to do with one another, as she is preoccupied with her grown and growing children, he with his younger wives. Finally, if cowives differ in their fertility, competition turns quickly into jealousy and suspicion, for there is no resource more valued among women than children, and their distribution is as invidiously calculated as the division of land is among men.

Functional Diffuseness of Authority Relations

Sociologists have described "traditional societies" as having "functionally diffuse" role relationships, by which they mean that whereas in a specialized and bureaucratic society like ours, social behavior between persons becomes limited to the specific function that brings them together (buyer-seller, employer-employee), in the traditional societies relationships are less narrowly defined by a single functional context. We have legislators, judges, and administrators in our government, but Africans have chiefs whose roles often include all three functions and are not even limited to "government" in our narrow sense of the term. This functional diffuseness is common to a wide variety of societies, but I want here to call attention to its characteristically African forms and to the expectations that Africans bring to authority relationships. (I do not use the word "traditional" because it seems to me that diffuse authority is at least as common in indigenous institutional settings in Africa.)

In Africa when someone is in a position of authority over others, there are characteristic demands and expectations he makes and has made upon him. He expects that his followers will obey his commands not only concerning the function that may have originally brought them together but for other purposes he deems significant. They must, for example, help maintain and enhance his social status by providing him with the conspicuous leisure appropriate to someone of high rank. In other words, they must perform menial tasks for him and serve him so that he can appear unencumbered in public and offer a degree of hospitality that is beyond his private means. The school is a striking example here, although parallel illustrations could be drawn from other institutional spheres. In schools all over anglophonic Africa, primary and secondary school pupils are pressed into service by their teachers, as domestic servants in their houses and as seasonal laborers in their fields and gardens. This may strike a Westerner as exploitation, but African parents do not complain except when the practice extends to using the female students sexually; then there is a public outcry and the teacher is dismissed. African parents who have had little schooling themselves often send their children to an educated kinsman, usually a schoolteacher, knowing that the boy or girl will be used as a house servant or in any other way the teacher wants, in the hope that the teacher will help the child with his schooling.

The situation in the schools is an extreme one because children are in no position to press their own demands upon the teacher (except for those girls who get teachers to reveal examination questions in return for sexual favors), but when adults are the subordinates, their willingness to serve in menial capacities is based on great hopes and expectations for personal advancement, which they make known to the leaders. From the Western observer's point of view, the very willingness to become a lackey to a leader and do his bidding might seem demeaning to an adult man, but Africans do not see it that way, and one must try to take the follower's point of view to understand it.

When a young African man becomes the employee, assistant, supervisee, political or religious supporter, or even student (in higher education) of someone in a relatively high position, he often does so with great hopes and expectations. First, he tends to exaggerate the power, wealth, and skill of his leader, in extreme cases believing him to have boundless power including magical means of escaping death. Second, he tends to have conscious fantasies that this great leader will use his power to raise his devoted follower from obscurity and make him into a great man too. He may actually propose this to the leader, while asking for help to support his (the subordinate's) self-improvement efforts in education or business. Third, more realistically, he expects the leader to be generous with food and drink when his followers spontaneously visit and to give them financial aid to meet urgent family obligations and pay debts. Every African of relatively great wealth is besieged by potential devoted followers seeking financial assistance and hospitality; a man with political aspirations must satisfy as many as he possibly can, straining his resources to the utmost. Finally, the subordinate will go to his leader for advice, guidance, and the use of influence, getting the leader to settle family quarrels, provide contacts and letters of recommendation, and give counsel on a variety of personal matters. In the hope that his relationship with someone of eminence will eventually lead him to prosperity and even greatness, the young man is eager to prove himself the dedicated servant, obediently carrying out his master's commands even when they involve menial and burdensome tasks. In his personal contacts with the leader he will temporarily fall into an attitude of respect and admiration, naive hopefulness, and dependence on the leader for advice, support, and protection. Hence the leader's diffuse and apparently limitless control over the labor of his subordinates has as its counterpart their diffuse and grandiose expectations of him as their patron. Rarely can he gratify their most grandiose expectations, but he can keep their hope alive through generosity and hospitality; if he did not do so, his followers might disappear in search of a more rewarding patron.

The Tendency to Blame and Fear Others When under Stress

Despite the placid and cheerful surface of interpersonal relations in most African communities, there are stong disruptive forces that must be held in check and socially regulated to maintain an orderly existence. These disruptive forces have their visible starting points in the personal disasters and interpersonal friction of African life or, more correctly, in the typical reactions of Africans to such difficulties. When a disaster befalls an African family—the death of its patriarch, sterility, insanity, a series of infant deaths, a crop failure—the most common reaction of the persons involved is to see it as resulting from the malevolent design of an enemy, often someone who is a competitor in a struggle for inherited property, job advancement, or educational achievement. Having decided that the misfortune is caused by someone else, through poisoning or a variety of magical practices, the afflicted family then takes steps to protect itself from the enemy's continued malevolence and possibly to strike back through public or private means.

From a psychological point of view, there are two particularly notable characteristics of this reaction to personal difficulty or disaster: the suspension of empirical criteria for interpreting natural events in favor of the attribution to unseen forces acting at a distance, and the choice of other humans in the immediate interpersonal environment as the causal agents rather than the self (as in a guilt reaction), malevolent gods or spirits (which do exist in some African belief systems but are less frequently blamed), or impersonal natural or cosmological forces. However one interprets this pattern psychologically, these distinctive features must be accounted for. Rather than attempt such an analysis here, however, I want to point out the relation of this stress reaction to social relationships as we have discussed them so far.

The emphasis on material transaction in social relations has been described, and the competition generated by it has been mentioned. There are many primary group relationships in African societies that engender competition for scarce resources: cowives competing for the favor of their husband and property he can allocate to them and their sons, brothers and cousins struggling for the patrimonial inheritance (especially land), neighbors quarreling over boundaries and damage to crops caused by each other's children or animals, peers in a variety of bureaucratic settings striving to become the favorite of their superiors. Intense feelings of jealousy and hatred accompany these forms of competition. The task of those in authority is to settle competitive disputes in a legitimate way that is recognized as just, so that the jealousy and hatred do not give rise to violence and conspiracy. To this end Africans spend a vast amount of time in mediation, adjudication, and litigation, not only in the courts but in judicial proceedings organized within extended families, lineages, compounds, and villages. But personal grudges do not necessarily end when the case is publicly settled, and even when disputants accept the impartial judgment of the elders or court, the stress of a sudden misfortune induces a regression from that mature acceptance to the deep-seated motives aroused by the competitive situation in the first place. When this regression takes place, the individual feels personally threatened by the hostility he attributes to his competitor. One sees this at funerals and public trials where suspicions of witchcraft and sorcery are first publicly voiced in the emotional atmosphere of the occasion.

The beliefs concerning witchcraft and sorcery so prevalent in African societies offer the threatened individual a definitive interpretation of his stressful situation that is compatible with his own personal motives, and they offer as well the feeling that there is something he can do about it—through a public witch trial, retaliatory sorcery, or emigration and subsequent avoidance of the designated enemy. In the past, these recourses to action appear to have functioned to keep interpersonal hostility within well-defined bounds, but in contemporary Africa witchcraft and sorcery are increasingly associated with disruptions of community life. What I want to emphasize here is that the personal reaction to stress involved in utilization of the witchcraft-sorcery complex is one that is widely characteristic of African populations, is generated in the context of interpersonal competition for resources, is precipitated by serious or sudden misfortune, and takes both normal and pathological forms. Only the normal form has been described. In its pathological varieties, common to many parts of Africa, the reaction involves delusions of persecution, and violence directed at persons in the immediate environment, sometimes with homicidal result. Although this is clearly a psychotic reaction and not to be confused with the typical reaction to stress described above, it shares with the latter the tendency to attribute malevolence to other persons and to move from fear to retaliation.

The Relative Absence of Separation Anxiety and Related Affects

We now turn from patterns of interpersonal behavior to affects or emotional states, which are difficult to compare across cultures—especially with objectivity—but can hardly be omitted in any attempt to assess patterns of personality. There are many possible contrasts in affects and their customary expression between Africans and Westerners, but I shall discuss one that I believe to be central for an understanding of social relationships. The Western desire for intimacy in social relationships, and its relative absence among Africans, has already been mentioned. The other side of that coin concerns separation and the anxiety that Westerners have about leaving or losing loved persons in their environment. We are accustomed to making strenuous efforts to avoid separating from our most intimate loved ones, to engaging in tearful departures and reunions, and to making the assumption that separation in physical residence—as when a child leaves home—has a final quality about it like a death and must be similarly mourned until the original emotional investment is irrevocably withdrawn or attenuated. These tendencies are not only widespread in our populations but are exalted in a variety of cultural forms ranging from sentimental literature and films to humanitarian ideologies with their concern about those who are rejected and abandoned, to domestic practices like the keeping of pet animals. Some of these cultural forms and practices involve such an exaggerated image of unconditional and everlasting love that they draw our attention to an unconscious function they have for the individual—the complete denial of hostility within the self and the transformation of the hostility that is surely there into an excessive concern about the well-being of others. In the affect of pity the unconscious hostility shows through most clearly; in fact "pity" has become a derogatory word in our culture because of this; but pity as an affect remains. Pathological separation anxiety as Anna Freud describes it for children with school phobias, for example, is due to the child's need to be constantly reassured that his unconscious hostile wishes did not magically kill his mother; a similar mechanism operates for neurotic mothers who get up innumerable times during the night to see if their children are all right. Much of our normal and culturally valued affectionate concern for others, particularly the most intense sentimentality in our culture, is reinforced by this tendency to convert hostility into its opposite. A related phenomenon is seen in relationships of a sadomasochistic nature in which two persons are bound together, so to speak, by the suffering that one inflicts on the other; both seem to need the emotional transaction, cannot give it up, and have come to think of the hostility as a necessary component of their love. Separation anxiety, sentimentality, pity, and sadomasochistic attachments are all ways that our culture, with its idealized concept of love, has of managing the unacceptable hostility necessarily involved in intimate relationships.

Many of these patterns of behavior seem to be absent among Africans: They appear to find physical separation from loved ones less upsetting emotionally and do not regard it as final. Sentimental attachments and their residues in longing, weeping, and nostalgia are not conspicuous in African communities, and the more sentimental outpourings of the Western mass media, if understood, have little appeal there. The reactions of Africans to the pet-keeping practices of Britons and Americans living in Africa is usually one of astonishment and amusement at the personalized concern and affection for animals. In caring for infants, the aged, and seriously disabled persons, there is a noticeable absence of the anxious concern and pity characteristic of Westerners, and none of the thinly veiled disgust that sometimes accompanies pity. Africans are not immediately drawn into an attentive and solicitously caretaking attitude by the sight of a weak, enfeebled, or helpless person or creature. Their casualness, relative to our attitude, often causes puzzlement and irritation in Westerners, who see this as an incomprehensible lack of humanitarianism.

African mothers rarely lavish on their infants the kind of affectionate attention that we think of as "instinctively maternal" behavior, and they are capable not only of carrying on conversations or tasks like trading while nursing their infants but also of inflicting necessary pain on them (in force-feeding and bathing) without hesitation, and without concern over the child's crying. Ainsworth (1967) made an intensive observational study of mother-infant interaction among the Ganda of Uganda. She states:

> In our American households the parents, loving relatives, and interested visitors alike bend over the baby as he lies in his crib, presenting him a smiling face, and waggle their heads and talk to the baby in an effort to coax a smile. This kind of face-to-face confrontation was not observed to occur in this Ganda sample. Indeed, it was rare for an adult even to hold a baby so that there could be a face-to-face confrontation. (1967, p. 334)
>
> In our society affection is ordinarily expressed—both ritually and spontaneously—by a hug, a warm embrace and perhaps a kiss. Many mothers encourage their babies to give them a hug and a kiss—or to hug and kiss the father, or a brother, or sister. By the end of the first year of life, babies in our society are able to return an embrace or kiss when it is given to them, perhaps clumsily, but in distinct response to the adults' affectionate

advance. That this is largely a culture-bound pattern of response—whether learned through reinforcement or through imitation—is suggested by the fact that Ganda babies very rarely manifest any behavior pattern even closely resembling European affection, and, indeed their mothers did not try to elicit hugging or kissing in the baby. (1967, p. 344)

Finally, Africans do not bring to social relationships the need to torment or be tormented that we see in sadomasochistic attachments in our society, and their interpersonal lives seem unusually free of these profoundly ambivalent motives. In this connection it might be mentioned that deliberate mortification of the flesh, as in the specialized asceticism of the West and India, is virtually absent in subSaharan Africa; Africans usually cannot understand what moral virtue there can be in extreme forms of self-denial and self-punishment.

To explain these differences in affective reactions and relationships between Africans and Westerners would take a great deal of psychological investigation; indeed, even testing the validity of my assertions about manifest behavior would be a big project. But we can try to understand them in relation to earlier observations on patterns of interpersonal behavior. For example, the social distance and formality of primary group relationships helps us understand the relative absence of separation anxiety; since the relationships are not as intimate as their Western counterparts, it is not surprising that they are more easily given up temporarily, and the greater social distance of daily interaction makes the loss of contact in actual separations seem less discontinuous, less final, more tolerable. Furthermore, the material obligations that are emphasized in role relationships can be fulfilled at a distance, with only occasional reunions, in a way that is difficult (even in intensive correspondence) if intimate emotional transactions are the goals. In other words, Africans can more easily keep up their primary social relationships at a distance than can Westerners, a point to which I return in the concluding section. At this juncture I want to stress that less separation anxiety must be understood in terms of the goals and means of interaction among Africans, which differ from those of Westerners.

As for pity, sentimentality, and sadomasochism, we must consider the way Africans handle their hostility. Social anthropologists have found that Africans all over the continent have a keen awareness of the hostility generated in social life and especially in jealous competition. Unlike Westerners, they do not deny—at least to themselves—the potential for hatred in even the closest of relationships, given failure to meet material obligations or the development of an irresolvable competitive dispute. In fact, many African belief systems contain the idea that unexpressed grudges cause disease and social disruption and that it is healthier to release the hostility than keep it pent up (which does not mean that the advice is always followed, but it does indicate public recognition of the problem). Without the need to deny and repress hostility toward others, there is no need to transform it into the anxious and excessive concern for their welfare, as we do in pity and sentimentality, or into the pretense that hostility is love, as in sadomasochistic attachments. Altogether, it would seem that for Africans the control of hostility tends to be managed through the institutional structure of their society, whereas for Westerners it is more frequently (though of course not entirely) managed through the structure of their personalities and particularly through the regulation of consciousness about hostile impulses in the self.

This is a rather glib formulation, but to go beyond it would take us too far from the main course of this brief outline. A more adequate formulation would have to deal with the representation of self for African individuals, the perceptual boundaries between self and environment, and the mechanisms of social and personal control.

Concreteness of Thought

A variety of pieces of evidence, none particularly convincing in itself, suggests as a whole that Africans in their indigenous cultures (like many nonliterate peoples) were more inclined to think and conceptualize in concrete rather than abstract terms, at least to a greater extent than is currently true of Western populations. This does not imply that complex thought processes were not involved, but that metaphorical communication, using concrete objects and actions, was preferred to communication using general qualities disembodied from their most familiar or striking context. Anyone who has asked an African elder to explain a difficult proverb (which abound in African cultures) has encountered this rich metaphorical wisdom in its full concreteness. Generalities have been captured in the proverb but are not discussed in general terms; the foreign inquirer unfamiliar with the detailed local context of behavior is likely to have a difficult time understanding the sage's explanation. Likewise, unschooled Africans, particularly children and youths who have not acquired a reservoir of generalizable experience on which to draw, often have a hard time understanding novel abstractions or switching over to thinking in abstract terms or solving abstract problems of an unfamiliar nature. Their cultural experience in the early years does not give them training or practice in the kind of abstract thinking used in the West. African children and adolescents who do go to school show more difficulties with abstraction than their Western counterparts, according to the reports of foreign teachers in Africa, and this is not surprising in light of their background. (See Cole et al. 1971, for discussion of this problem.)

The tendency to think in concrete terms is at the root of two characteristics previously discussed. The tendency to define relationships in terms of material expectations and obligations involves primary attention to the objects given and taken and to the actions of giving and taking, rather than to abstract dispositional qualities and mental traits of the persons. There is little interest in the idiosyncratic patterns of thought and feeling characteristic of oneself and others, patterns for which one needs abstract verbal labels before one can even notice them. In other words, the emphasis on material transactions and the avoidance of introspection in social relationships constitute a reflection in the domain of interpersonal cognition of the more general inclination toward concreteness of thought.

The tendency to blame and fear others under stress is another reflection of this general mode of thinking, in the sense that it establishes the causes of misfortune as familiar humans in the immediate environment. Africans are rarely satisfied with believing that disease, death, and disaster strike randomly in a community or are the results of forces beyond human understanding; they do not accept that degree of ambiguity. Instead, they insist that the causes can be identified with certainty as particular neighbors or kinsmen. Frequently, the neighbor or kinsman turns out to be a competitor in a dispute over material resources or obligatory transactions, another concrete element.

Without elaborating the point further, we can conclude that the concreteness of African thought noticed in teaching and other cognitive situations is an important, indeed necessary, characteristic of at least some of the interpersonal behavior patterns noted above. A deeper understanding of the relation between mode of thinking and interpersonal behavior must entail research into the development of infants and young children.

Having allowed myself to generalize in these seven points about characteristics I see as common to most Africans, I hasten to emphasize that Africa's populations are not psychologically homogeneous and refer the reader to the substantial and growing body of evidence showing psychological variations among African groups associated with variations in ecology (Edgerton 1971; Munroe, Munroe, Nerlove, and Daniels 1969), kinship organization (Clignet 1970), social mobility (LeVine 1966a), economic change (LeVine 1966b), and Western schooling (Doob 1964; LeVine, Klein, and Owen 1967).

ADAPTATION TO CHANGE

One could relate the foregoing discussion of uniformities and variations in African personality patterns to many aspects of change in Africa but I shall limit myself to illustrating how a few of the uniformities might affect personal response and adjustment to institutional change.

Personal Adjustment to Mobility

As discussed above, the formality of primary group relationships and the relative absence of separation anxiety make physical separation of husband and wives, parents and children, less painful and disruptive to the individual than in our culture, and the emphasis on material obligation makes it possible to maintain relationships during prolonged absences. For example, so long as a husband provides his wife with a place to live at home, a social group (his family) to live with, a livelihood (a piece of land or some capital for trading) and a pregnancy every two and a half years, his prolonged absence for economic or educational reasons is regarded as quite tolerable. This is not to say that husbands and wives separated by occupational circumstance do not experience the loss, but only that they seem more willing to accept long separations than their Western counterparts. This kind of relationship has allowed individuals to respond to economic incentives by moving themselves—in labor migration, for overseas education and vocational training, and when transferred to a better job—with a minimum of personal disruption.

African families do not have to be residentially intact in order to remain socially and psychologically real for their members; nor do the obligations of marriage and kinship diminish with prolonged absence. This was demonstrated ethnographically by Evans-Pritchard (1953) in his description of forms of marriage among the Nuer of the southern Sudan, but it is true through much of contemporary Africa, and provides an elasticity in relationships which is highly adaptive under modern economic conditions. Since there is never any pretense that the obligations of kinship are based on emotional intimacy or residential proximity, kinship groups are able not only to remain intact even when their members are dispersed but also to play a central role in the redistribution of economic resources. No matter how far away an individual has moved from his natal home, he is obliged to provide regular aid to his wives, children, and aging parents; to contribute when asked to the school fees and other important expenses of an indefinite number of more distant relatives; and to provide hospitality for an indefinite period to kinsmen who come to visit him or have migrated to his place. A mature man will also be called upon to return home occasionally for meetings at which major group decisions regarding internal disputes and collective property are reached. In rural homes and in the cities, the unemployed, the disabled, and the elderly are taken in by their kinsmen, whether or not they are well acquainted. These unfortunates may not have a great deal of attention paid to them but they *are* cared for, in societies that have few public welfare facilities. Thus the social distance, formality, and material obligation in African relationships operate at present to help preserve indigenous kinship organization in the face of increased mobility, redistribute income from participants in the modern economy to their less fortunate kinsmen, and provide care for the needy. None of these goals could be achieved if Africans made their obligations as contingent on intimacy and proximity as we do or allowed them to atrophy in prolonged separation.

The short-run adaptiveness of these behavioral patterns at the group or societal level is unquestionable, but what of the individuals involved? The advantages to them are obvious: they can count on their kinsmen for care, protection, and emergency relief even in a strange city and even when they have had no prior contact or acquaintance with the available kinsman. As the kin disperse, so does the spatial range of one's potential relations. Africans do take advantage of this potentiality, and it eases their adjustment in urban areas and in new settlements at home and abroad. The dangers of maladjustment and breakdown in personality functioning increase greatly when African individuals move outside the network of kin and ethnic affiliations (as happened to some students in America, see Muensterberger and Kishner 1967), where care and protection cannot be guaranteed.

But there are disadvantages too, experienced primarily by the wealthier and more successful Africans who find themselves on the giving rather than the receiving end in the network of kinship obligations. They are constantly called upon to help close and distant relatives, including many they barely know. Those wealthy Africans who are relatively unschooled and have not lived abroad take their donatory position for granted and even exploit it for political ends, but those who have become Westernized in their conception of social roles tend to resent not only the immense drain on their resources but also the intrusions on their privacy and limitless demands on their hospitality. These latter individuals sometimes see themselves as victims of an outdated system that coerces their participation and makes it more difficult for them to provide as adequately for their own children and immediate families as can their individualistic Western counterparts.

Response to Economic Incentives

The indigenous emphasis on material transaction in role relations, and the competition stemming from it, provided a psychosocial basis for African response to novel economic incentives introduced from the West. Although early colonial officials found it necessary to establish a compulsory tax to pull Africans into the labor market, such artificial devices have not been necessary in most areas for many years. Once Africans perceived the material advantages resulting from employment and the education fitting one for employment, they actively sought jobs, clamored for schools, and made sacrifices to obtain education. The strength of this response, as compared with "traditional" peoples in other parts of the world, results partly in competition: men want to do better than one another and each wants his own children to do better than the others' children. This competition is sometimes fraught with jealousy, suspicion, and hostile intrigues, but it has promoted among Africans a receptivity to innovations that have a demonstrable economic advantage and a high degree of readiness to participate in new economic institutions. In my opinion the deep-seated competitiveness as an aspect of individual personality has some of its roots in the polygynous family, where the intense striving of the cowives for equivalent or preferential treatment of themselves and their children provides an early model of jealous competition and invidious distinction.

Personal Adjustment to Intergenerational Differences in Acculturation

Another adaptive outcome of the pattern of interpersonal relations described above is the remarkable absence of serious conflicts between conservative and modernizing segments of families and small communities. Americans accustomed to the clash of generations in immigrant families and anthropologists acquainted with the schisms of American Indian communities along conservative and progressive lines cannot help but note the ease with which Africans manage this potentially troublesome problem. To understand it properly we must refer first to the competitive materialism just discussed: since Westernization almost always gives an individual an economic advantage over his less Westernized brethren, it also gains him their respect and dependence, and with this position they are not likely to question his values. More specifically however, there is the material aspect of role obligations and the relative unimportance of sharing thoughts and feelings. So long as the Westernized individual responds to the customary demands of his kinsmen described above, and provides financial assistance, gifts, and contributions where they are expected, he will be favorably regarded, even if he has left the home community, its way of life, and its beliefs and practices behind him. Neither his parents nor the others in his home village or town will expect him to share their values, opinions, or life-styles, and they may not even discuss their differences unless they affect the material obligations. The greater social distance between the generations in Africa allows culturally different parents and children to make their peace on the ground of formal obligation without invading each other's cultural domain. Hence we find a cultural relativism among Africans that would be impossible if closely related persons expected to be "of the same mind."

Reactions to Increasing Scarcity of Resources

Institutional and demographic change in Africa has not been completely unstressful by any means. Though unevenly spread across the continent, there is overcrowding of land in some rural areas, unemployment and overcrowding in the growing cities, and fierce economic and political competition in urban life. Responses to these stresses have varied, as they would anywhere, but the tendency to blame and fear others has been strongly evident, particularly where there is competition for scarce resources—land, jobs, occupational and educational advancement, political office, revenue for community improvement. When the resources are so scarce that an equitable distribution is impossible or when there is no institutionalized mechanism for distribution, competition has given rise to conflict, which has taken the forms described above, as well as other forms in political behavior. One of the most striking recent developments has been the apparent increase in witchcraft and sorcery accusations in many parts of the continent, particularly in some of the most overcrowded rural areas of East Africa and in South African cities. These are areas in which Western education and Christian missions which are antagonistic to magical beliefs have been most active; but they are also areas of the most stressful competition, in which people have fallen back more frequently on the underlying tendency to blame problems on the malevolent designs in their neighbors.

This brief discussion of adaptation to change has attempted to convey the way in which some indigenous behavioral characteristics of Africans function in contemporary settings. I shall end by warning that adaptation is relative to the time span over which one observes it; thus those behavioral characteristics that look highly adaptive now might prove disastrous in the long run, and those that look maladaptive now might prove their worth in time.

REFERENCES

Ainsworth, Mary D. S. 1967. *Infancy in Uganda: Infant Care and Growth of Love.* Baltimore: Johns Hopkins University Press.

Barry, Herbert H., III. 1968. "Regional and Worldwide Variations in Culture," *Ethnology* 7:207–17.

Clignet, Remi. 1970. *Many Wives, Many Powers: Authority and Power in Polygynous Families.* Evanston, Ill.: Northwestern University Press.

Cole, Michael; Glick, John; Gay, Jay; et al. 1971. *The Cultural Context of Teaching and Learning.* New York: Basic Books.

Doob, Leonard. 1964. "Psychology," in *The African World: A Survey of Social Research,* edited by R. Lystad. New York: Praeger.

Edgerton, Robert B. 1971. *The Individual in Cultural Adaptation: A Study of Four*

East African Peoples. Berkeley and Los Angeles: University of California Press.

Evans-Pritchard, E. E. 1953. *Kinship and Marriage among the Nuer.* London: Oxford University Press.

Fox, Lorene K. 1967. *East African Childhood: Three Versions.* London: Oxford University Press.

LeVine, Robert A., with the assistance of Eugene Strangman and Leonard Unterberger. 1966a. *Dreams and Deeds: Achievement Motivation in Nigeria.* Chicago: University of Chicago Press.

―――. 1966b. "Sex Roles and Economic Change in Africa," *Ethnology* 5:186–93.

LeVine, Robert A.; Klein, Nancy; and Owen, Constance. 1967. "Father-Child Relationships and Changing Life-Styles in Ibadan, Nigeria," in *The City in Modern Africa,* edited by H. Miner. New York: Praeger.

Muensterberger, Warner, and Kishner, Ira. 1967. "Hazards of Culture Clash: A Report on the History and Dynamics of a Psychotic Episode in a West African Exchange Student," in *The Psychoanalytic Study of Society,* vol. 4, edited by W. Muensterberger and S. Axelrod. New York: International Universities Press.

Munroe, Robert L., and Munroe, Ruth H. In press. "Population Density and Affective Relationships in Three East African Societies," *Journal of Social Psychology.*

Munroe, Robert L.; Munroe, Ruth H.; Nerlove, Sara B.; and Daniels, Robert E. 1969. "Effects of Population Density on Food Concerns in Three East African Societies," *Journal of Health and Social Behavior* 10:161–71.

Murdock, George P. 1957. "World Ethnographic Sample," *American Anthropologist* 59: 664–87.

Richards, Audrey I. 1932. *Hunger and Work in a Savage Tribe.* London: G. Routledge and Sons.

Sawyer, Jack, and LeVine, Robert A. 1966. "Cultural Dimensions: A Factor Analysis of the World Ethnographic Sample," *American Anthropologist* 68: 708–31.

Chapter 5

The Ethos of Insecurity in Middle Eastern Culture*

John Gulick

In 1934 Ruth Benedict published her book, *Patterns of Culture,* which had a powerful impact not only on succeeding generations of anthropologists but on specialists in many other scholarly fields as well. Probably the most widely received message of this book was that behavioral patterns in cultures other than our own cannot and should not be judged or interpreted in the same terms as they might well be if they occurred in our own culture. So, for instance, though the behavior of the Dobuans of New Guinea, as depicted by Benedict, seems clearly paranoid by the standards of our culture, we cannot judge it by those standards, but rather we must try to understand it in its own cultural context.

Patterns of Culture was a major contribution to the idea of cultural relativism, the idea that students of behavior must try to understand the behavior of any and all peoples relative to the other patterns of those other cultures, rather than to judge them (morally or functionally) in terms of the patterns of their own. Cultural relativism was consciously conceived

---

*Part III of this paper is a revised version of "Arab Societies and the Middle East" which was my contribution to the 1968 Hakone symposium. In extensively rewritten form, it was presented at the Conference on Psychology and Near Eastern Studies, Princeton University, May 7–9, 1973. This conference was chaired by L. Carl Brown and Norman Itzkowitz to whom I wish to express my appreciation. I would also like to thank John J. Honigmann and E. Terry Prothro for their critical comments on the penultimate draft of the present paper. I most particularly wish to thank L. Carl Brown for the editorial work he did on that same draft and for his graciousness in regard to the final disposition of this paper.

as a counter-concept to the ethnocentrism that was rampant and endemic in Western culture. It also fit consistently with the structural-functional concept that any culture is a steady-state system of subsystems ("patterns") which enable the human beings in the culture to cope and survive as members of groups or society. Thus, no matter how bizarre or repellent the behavior of a particular culture may seem to people in another culture, the latter should try to comprehend its functions in emotionally and ethically neutral terms.

Cultural relativism and structural-functionalism may have had some influence on educated people, at any rate, in Western industrial culture, making them somewhat more reluctant than their forebears had been to deride or condemn, let alone try to "reform," the patterns of other cultures. And these two concepts became working assumptions, if not articles of faith, for social scientists. Up to a point they still are, and properly so.

However, some limitations of these concepts as analytic tools have gradually become evident. In particular, the concept of dysfunction, central to the work of specialists in psychopathology within the context of their own culture, could not very comfortably be applied cross-culturally. Anthropologists attempting to apply psychoanalytic concepts to different cultures' child-rearing patterns, for instance, or to elucidate different cultures' worldviews by means of Rorschach tests, often diagnosed these patterns in what seemed like psychopathological terms. These approaches ran the risk of violating the nonjudgmental core of cultural relativism. The concept of dysfunction simply could not be fitted into the structural-functional framework unless the dysfunction were attributed to externally generated change. Since the ethnographic record was replete with the disastrous consequences to many nonliterate peoples of contacts with Western culture, this rationalization often seemed to suffice.

But not quite. Consider Nazi Germany. Are not governmental policies parts of the culture? Are not the parts of any culture to be analyzed nonjudgmentally in their own cultural contexts? Of course. Yet no American social scientist that I know of ever applied this value free logic to the Nazi government's policy of exterminating the Jews. Anthropologists, including Benedict herself, were able to cope conceptually, however, with Japanese militarism and its consequences, and ideas like situational (rather than absolute) ethics gained ground as a result.

Since the end of World War II, anthropology has grown greatly and has emphasized the study of large national cultures, rather than its previous concentration on small, tribal cultures. In the latter, change imposed by outsiders was often patently destructive, and thus change in the abstract became equated by anthropologists with disruption of what they thought to be the steady-state systems of traditional culture. But the "third world" national cultures themselves frequently confronted sociologists and anthropologists with a different view. Whether they liked it or not, social scientists increasingly found themselves studying people both at home and abroad who said they wanted to change some of their own traditional culture patterns in order to "modernize." One implication of this refrain was the new realization that certain behavioral patterns may become liabilities *in terms of their own cultural contexts.*

During the 1960s, American anthropologists and sociologists, to a far greater degree than ever before, began to perceive dysfunctional patterns in their own culture—specifically, militarism and violence in general. Some tried to explain them all away by asserting a genetic determinism that had supposedly affected all human beings since the Pliocene period. But one did not need to accept this simplistic and hopeless view in order to perceive that certain cultural patterns can become problem generators, and therefore that change, rather than being seen only as dysfunctional, can also be seen as functional insofar as it modifies the problem generating patterns. This point of view is difficult to reconcile with the old structural-functional approach. The further idea that increasingly dysfunctional patterns can persist for a long time and that the society can survive in spite of them (though at what cost and up to what point it is difficult to judge) is equally difficult to reconcile. Difficult or not, these ideas are now gaining ground.

The foregoing is intended to give the reader some idea of the changes, and anomalies, in professional environment that I as an anthropologist have experienced during the same period that I have been studying the cultures of the Middle East. Having originally been trained to accept cultural relativism and structural-functionalism as working assumptions, and not yet having rejected them completely, I have gradually and hesitantly come to the view that there is a subsystem in Middle Eastern culture that is apparently of long standing, that is stressful *in* the Middle Eastern context, and that may be dysfunctional for the achievement of cultural goals that have been set by Middle Eastern people themselves.

For the present, I am calling this subsystem the "ethos of insecurity," and I have an idea of where in the culture it is continually being regenerated. In this essay I will set forth these ideas, primarily drawing upon observations of Arabic speakers, though occasionally mentioning some non-Arab materials that seem particularly pertinent.

First, I wish to recognize a study that well illustrates the "ethos of insecurity," and does so in far more forthright terms than I am inclined to do: Marvin Zonis's study of the political elite of Iran (Zonis 1971). He did his field research from 1963 to 1965 and was presumably writing the book at the same time that I was working toward the formulation of similar ideas using entirely different source materials.

Zonis studied the Iranian political elite using questionnaires and analyzing them by factor analysis. He says that the political elite of Iran live and operate in an environment of cynicism, mistrust, exploitation, and, above all, insecurity. In connection with mistrust, he notes that children are trained early in the skills of dissimulation, that the work environment is perceived as being hostile and requiring constant vigilance, that the number of trusted friends is very limited, and that the immediate family is not a haven from mistrust, but, rather, involves parents' mistrust of their own children as well as sibling rivalry.

Zonis suggests that insecurity is indicated by the typical, protectively walled house, generalized individualism, independent familism and "lack of social cooperation." Insecurity due to the threat of arbitrary arrest and dismissal, financial manipulation and confiscation by the government, extortion and other instabilities are mentioned. More subtle is the idea that feelings of rejection are buffered by elaborate formal courtesies. More deepseated is the idea of "family disdain" that is, the low levels of trust prevailing among members of the nuclear family. And Zonis discusses the *doreh*, the small clique of people seeking mutual advantage, to several of which a particular individual may belong. James Bill, in another study of Iranian political behavior, leads from discussions of factionalism and the *doreh* to the observation that *dorehs* "encourage plotting and omnipresent interlaced antagonisms," though they discourage open confrontations (Bill 1972, pp. 45–48).

The findings of Zonis and Bill may not be peculiar to the Iranian political elite. They may well be extendable to non-Iranian, non-politically-elite Middle Easterners. I will not argue the point here, but their work serves as a useful preface to my discussion of the Arab ethos of insecurity.

THE PHENOMENON OF ARAB DIVISIVENESS

The predominant current image of Arabs in the eyes of Americans, as reflected in the mass media, is generally negative. This is of long standing, but it has been aggravated during the past quarter century since the establishment of Israel. The overwhelmingly pro-Israel bias can be illustrated in that the same members of the United States Congress who were most opposed to United States warfare in Indochina actually have actively promoted escalation of military support of Israel against the Arabs (Stone 1970) and that occasional exceptions in the mass media that attempt to be moderate and balanced are subject to attack (Stone 1967).

A conspicuous aspect of the problem has been the image of the Arab governments' difficulties in coordinating their efforts against Israel, accompanied also by indications of divisiveness within particular Arab governments as well as between them. Knowledge of this divisiveness in the face of a common enemy has been an indelible part of the American people's image of the Arabs during the period 1948–1973. The image does not on the whole incline those who hold it to feelings of understanding, respect, or compassion, but rather the reverse. This knowledge of Arab divisiveness contributes to the popular image of Arabs as unable to get along even with each other.

The purpose of this paper is not to intensify the *image* of divisiveness but to (1) explore what may be at the roots of it and (2) to examine certain changing aspects of Middle Eastern culture that may eventually ameliorate it. To these ends, this paper is primarily concerned with the tentative results of some efforts made by behavioral scientists to understand Arab (and Middle Eastern) culture while living and working in the midst of it.

These studies have shown an atomistic component in a large number of individual Arab personalities and an accompanying atomistic element in Arab culture that lies deeper than the widely recognized fact that Arab political behavior—international and intranational—is divisive. Further, it seems that denial processes (akin to reaction formation) and extra psychic rationalizations (such as "history") help to perpetuate the deeper, intrapsychic atomistic element in Arab culture.

When questions have been raised like "Why can't the Arab countries ever seem to get together on anything?" or "Why can't they even manage to work effectively together against their declared enemy, Israel?", a ready answer is the historical one above. And there is some truth in it.

Far-flung, from Morocco in the west to the Persian Gulf in the east, the Arabs, though having some cherished traditions in common, have many local differences—just as the various English-speaking peoples do. This is a divisive element which is sometimes formalized by the identities of the various Arab nations. During the several most recent centuries, nearly all of the present-day Arab nations were provinces of the Ottoman Empire, or *de facto* possessions of various European nations, until well into the twentieth century. Building strong independent national states on these colony-status precedents is an enormously difficult task. At times, in each case, building national strength seems to entail including them, but here regional differences and political rivalries may intervene. Either way, there is divisiveness. Running throughout is a pervasive distrust among the common people of government structures and activities—an attitude partly based on a long tradition of subjection to one conquest state after another.

The phenomenon of Arab divisiveness must be pursued further, into intrapsychic levels. I shall discuss it first as a self-perpetuating and stress-producing mental set. I shall then discuss the prospects for modification of it, and amelioration of the stress, through certain processes of culture change which are now taking place in the Middle East, particularly in the relationships between men and women in family structure. Because this mental set is simultaneously a source of stress and an integral aspect of centrally important interpersonal relationships, it tends to be denied, and this very denial tends to perpetuate it.

The purpose of analysing this Arab mental set is to clarify, in the hope that clarification might contribute to easing the predicament. This analysis cannot reveal to the Arabs' enemies any "secrets" which could be turned into a weapon to be used against them. The Israelis are already quite aware of what appears to be a significant atomistic component in Arab personality and culture (Harkabi 1967). Harkabi's article bears succinctly on this issue and is documented from experiences and published sources which are independent of and different from those used in the preparation of this chapter. It is worth noting, to his credit, that Harkabi, an Israeli general, writes in an objective yet compassionate tone which contrasts sharply with that in which too many Westerners thoughtlessly dismiss the Arabs.

I have already said that the basic assumption of this paper is that every culture is not only a set of on-going, problem-coping customs but also a self-generator of problems which, in turn, must be borne, for long periods perhaps, until they become overwhelmingly dysfunctional. The atomistic component of Arab culture is an example of such dysfunctionalism. While many of the details of this particular case are specifically Arab, the existence of this problem is certainly not peculiar to the Arabs.

A recent publication succinctly summarizes in larger context most of the cultural phenomena with which we are concerned, in what its author calls "the Pakistani-Peruvian Axis" of culture:

> The personality traits of this larger area tend to cluster around two points: (1) the restriction of personal trust and loyalty within the kinship group (usually the extended or nuclear family) with a consequent inability to offer loyalty, trust, or personal identification to residential groups (villages, neighborhoods, parishes), voluntary associations, religious beliefs, or the secular state, resulting in large-scale lack of "public spirit," combined with "corruption," and paralysis of those other kinds of associations. (2) The combination of powerful patriarchal social tendencies with female inferiority (except as a mechanism for producing sons) leads to many psychological ambiguities: strong emphasis on female premarital virginity (both as a symbol of family honor and as an economic good), segregation of the sexes in social life, fear of women as a threat to men's virility (witches and belief in "the evil eye"), the need to demonstrate male virility by social "touchiness" and other behavior, including fantasies of demonstrations of male

dominance over bulls, other men, and unattached women. (Quigley 1973, p. 319)

In intrakin-group relationships, including relationships between men and women, the ethos of insecurity is continually regenerated, and then ramifies to the more public behavior (such as associations and relationships with the state) in which individuals are involved. Doubtless there is mutual reinforcement here between the public and private spheres, and by concentrating on the latter, I do not intend to deny the importance of the former. For a closely reasoned and well-documented analysis of this public-private relationship, the reader is referred to Jane Schneider's article on circum-Mediterranean (explicitly including Arab) concepts of honor. A theme of her argument is that insistence on female virginity (or figuratively chaste behavior) is an attempt to give some strength to what are generally very fragile bonds of general social organization, that fragility being reinforced by the belief that female sexuality is evil and a constant threat to males (Schneider 1971).

THE KINSHIP GROUP AND ARAB DIVISIVENESS

Being patrilineal, the kinship system allows for the indefinite extension of generational depth to the name of one eponymous, male ancestor. In fact, depth of five to six generations is rather widely reported for situations in which lineages are actually functioning units. Usually noncorporate, such lineages occur in both villages and cities and are by no means exclusively found among the pastoral nomads (who actually constitute only about 5 percent of the total population yet are, on dubious grounds, widely thought to be prototypical of Middle Eastern culture in general).

Many Arabs apparently live in a social situation in which their lineage is little more than a name group. It is likely, however, that a majority of them are more deeply involved, at various times in their lives, in the three-generation extended family and/or the fraternal joint family, which are, of course, lineage segments, but it has been clearly demonstrated that the great majority of households consist of nuclear families. In other words, the majority of functioning extended families are not residential units.

One of the chief contexts of stress in the social system is in the relationships of extended/joint families and their component nuclear families. In this context there has been a persistent inability on the part of both native and foreign observers to recognize certain objective realities. They reiterate that the extended family *household* is "typical"; this is the theme not only in general works, but also in more specifically focused studies like Ammar's (1954), and Fuller's (1961).

Various censuses, sample surveys, and community studies have made clear that an average (or in some cases a modal) household size of five to six persons can be expected in Arab populations. Contrary to a widespread assumption, there are no significant rural-urban differences in this matter, and even the nomadic tent household is likely to be the same. The majority of households have fewer than six persons, and a survey of Egyptian villages indicates that only 3 percent of households with fewer than six persons include more than one married couple. This is not surprising, but what is surprising is that only 36 percent of households with six or more persons have more than one married couple—two married couples being the minimum for a stem family or a fraternal joint family household (Petersen 1967). Specific studies indicate that the proportion of extended or joint families ranges between 2 percent and 25 percent in particular communities.

While it is true that the incidence of birth, marriage, and death makes it impossible for many people ever to live in households consisting of three successive generations, as Petersen (1968) has demonstrated with demographic statistics from Egypt, demographic infeasibility alone does not account for this type of household's being in a minority; its very desirability is a highly debatable issue. Rosenfeld (1958), in his study of an Arab village in Israel, reveals that extended family households occur in two very different motivational contexts: (1) desire of a well-to-do elder to be head of a patriarchal ménage and (2) the sheer necessity for some destitute people to share their resources. In neither of these situations can one assume that all parties are happy about the arrangement.

Against the idealizations of paternal dominance, fraternal solidarity, and male superiority, which indeed are conventionally verbalized, there are a large number of contrary realities which result in tension, stress, conflict, and ambivalence (DeVos and Miner 1959). Maintenance of the conventional proprieties means maintenance of *sharaf al-^{c}a'ila* ("family honor"), and even the smallest children are constantly admonished to act only in terms of it (Tannous 1944). Maintenance of honor includes the denial of quarrels between parents and children, among siblings, and among their spouses. In the ideals of the culture, such quarrels (among many other things) constitute ^{c}*ayb al-^{c}a'ila* ("family shame"), and therefore they are concealed from outsiders (Bourdieu 1966). The apparent frequency and bitterness of these quarrels, coupled with the denial system concerning them, suggests a significantly high level of stress and conflict in these aspects of the culture.

Indeed, the role structure of the family itself seems to be conducive to this condition. Males are considered to be by nature fundamentally and immutably superior to females. One effect of this, as observed by Herbert Williams (1958), is a strong sense of inadequacy and worthlessness among many women. Yet mothers play a dominant role in child rearing, and Millicent Ayoub (1957) has observed that children are likely to support the mother, despite the father's formal authority, in her quarrels with him. Childrearing has been reported to rely heavily on negative reinforcement, including shaming and the stimulation of jealousy among siblings.

Brothers are equal in terms of the Islamic law of inheritance, and they are expected to be loyal and devoted to each other throughout life. In fact, however, elder brothers may be called upon to make sacrifices for their juniors, and this, combined with induced sibling rivalry, leads to conflict between brothers which extends to their wives.

This divisiveness, conventionally denied or concealed, repeats itself in the relationships of cousins and other members of the lineage more remotely related. It is reflected in the segmentary structure of Arab lineages which has been well documented, as has the frequency of their splitting into hostile factions (Gulick 1968).

Among the people in whom the greatest degree of trust and affection is conventionally expected (the only people, in fact, on whom the individual can theoretically count without question) it seems there are strongly ambivalent feelings: hostility, jealousy, and distrust masked by protestations of the opposite (see Khatchadourian 1961; 1962). In extended family households, such feelings may be exacerbated by proximity, and this is one of the reasons many people prefer nuclear family residence if it can be managed without any outward appearance of ill-feeling.

Dodd (1973) says that one of the characteristics of ^{c}ird (the type of honor that, unlike *sharaf,* cannot be acquired by appropriate conduct but can be lost by misconduct, mostly by women) is that it depends as much on maintenance of public reputation as it does on actual behavior. Offenses against ^{c}ird become serious when publicly seen. Therefore, family members are guarded and wary. Dubetsky (1972) has contributed some information from Turkey that may be pertinent here. He says that the belief is that the qualities of *dürüstlük* (trustworthiness) and *namus* (honor) can be acquired only by genetic inheritance (hence one reason for contracting marriages with close relatives assumed to have these qualities). However, *dürüstlük* and *namus* can be lost through misconduct. The same seems to be true of ^{c}ird among Arabic speakers. It is a controlling value that legitimizes family structure and the modesty code of both sexes (Dodd 1973, p. 40), and relatives (particularly females) continually pose a threat to other relatives because their actions may destroy it.

Paradoxically, the code which legitimizes family identity itself seems to generate anxiety and distrust among members of the family. Lawrence Rosen, in his study of dyadic relationships in urban Morocco, goes so far as to say that "the fundamental social unit is not some aggregate of persons, but simply the single individual as the locus of a particular set of personal ties and personal characteristics (Rosen 1972, p. 437). He finds that individuals establish advantageous ties with others who are very frequently only distant relatives or not relatives at all. It is easy to see such behavior as an adaptation to intrafamilial emotional sets that are frequently detrimental to the establishment or maintenance of trustful relationships.

We are, of course, talking about tendencies and not about absolutes. There is also genuine love and solidarity among relatives, and in contrast to the cases of outright desertion (Williams 1958) and refusals of help (Williams 1968) which have been documented, kinsmen remain the primary source of assistance in times of difficulty even under those modern regimes some of which, like that of Egypt, may be making efforts to provide some welfare services (Petersen 1967, p. 264).

Nevertheless, a widespread result of these influences appears to be a personality structure which—despite verbal assertiveness to the contrary—is emotionally isolated and distrustful. Herbert Williams (1958), using observations and psychodiagnostic tests, discovered such personality traits in a Lebanese Christian village. Judith Williams (1968) refers to the "impoverished" friendship situation, to the individual's tendency of necessity to keep his troubles and worries to himself, and to the very narrow circle of love and trust which is the lot of most people in a Lebanese Muslim village. Gulick (1967) has summarized the personality in terms of a hypothesized "vulnerable ego." This personality has certainly survived and reproduced itself, but events in the twentieth century have revealed its dysfunctional aspects.

Highly ambivalent forces are at work in this situation. The internally strained Middle Eastern kinship group has, despite its problems, survived because it has been essential to its members. Among nomadic, agricultural, and urban people, extended families (and sometimes lineages) have always been important sources of support in times of trouble and for mutual aid at various other times.

Migration of rural folk to towns and cities has always been a feature of the culture, but it has been greatly accelerated in the twentieth century by unprecedented population pressure, expansion of job opportunities in the cities, and modern means of transportation. Contrary to the usual assumption that a monolithic sort of urbanization causes great stress, the evidence from the Middle East is that the people seem to cope relatively effectively with the many necessary adaptations to city life. Perhaps the most important single reason for this is the way in which extensive kinship ties provide institutional buffers for the migrants. This is true even, and perhaps especially, in the shantytowns which now surround many of the largest cities (Gulick 1969).

True, a study of rural and urban Algerians using the Rorschach test showed more intrapsychic tension among the city-dwellers, but this could not easily be attributed to any trauma of urbanization itself (Miner and DeVos 1960). True also, that the *zar* ritual of Nubia is intended to reduce the depression and anxiety of women whose husbands have migrated to the cities of Lower Egypt (Kennedy 1967), but the Nubian situation is unusual for the Middle East, where it is generally either unmarried males or family groups who migrate to the cities. Many important behavioral patterns in the cities are not greatly different from those in the villages, partly because the degree of heavy industrialization is not nearly so great as it is in the West or in Japan. Nevertheless, many adjustments must be made in moving to the city, and positive actions of kinship groups, despite their negative features, apparently enable the average migrant to adjust to living in cities with less trauma.

Traditional experience with rulers who were accustomed to make heavy demands on their subjects but to provide few services has resulted in an attitude toward government which is typically a mixture of fear, evasiveness, and cynical opportunism (Gulick 1967). Such a mental set cannot easily be altered, certainly not simply by appeals to patriotic fervor and cohesion made by fledgling national regimes which must deal with desperate problems of survival at the same time that they try to establish new patterns of government. This mental set includes reluctance to take the risks involved in making commitments to new ventures and unfamiliar persons, as in service clubs, cooperatives, and labor unions. Consequently, while shielding people from risks, it also prevents them from establishing new alliances of trust and mutual benefit. Speaking generally of the political elite of Morocco, Waterbury says, "In sum, there is scant pressure . . . to open new paths, and individual initiative, while not discouraged, is not rewarded" (Waterbury 1970, p. 79). This mental set is both the result of the ethos of insecurity and an integral part of it.

Miner and DeVos (1960) refer to the idiosyncratic perceptions of Algerians, their egocentric thinking, and their insensitivity to group pressures. Gulick (1968) has summarized several different studies on the Arab Levantines which document their general inability to sustain group efforts, partly because authority seems to be defined as coercion-to-be-evaded. In other words, once again there is an important atomistic component in Arab personality structure.

The dysfunctional aspects of this personality structure have become apparent during the past twenty years. This period has seen the Arabs' repeated failures to defeat the efficient military organization of Israel or to win substantial popular support for their cause in the West. A serious search for the reasons for this situation is beginning to develop among some Arabs, and the hypothesized atomistic element in the personality structure might be included among them.

EFFECTS ON PERSONALITY OF ARAB CULTURE CHANGE

I have suggested that the atomistic component of Arab personality structure is continually being generated in the structure and functions of the kinship group and thereby perpetuated through time. Nevertheless, changes which are definitely taking place in relevant aspects of Arab culture might have the effect of ameliorating the stresses and lessening the atomism. Many of these changes are occurring in the extended family and in the interrelated roles of males and females.

An assumption of this paper is that Middle Eastern idealizing of the residential extended family, which conflicts with attitudinal realities, affects behavior regardless of actual residential patterns and is an important source of stress. Maximum stress is presumably to be found among those people who actually do live in residential extended families. Definitely in a minority even in the past, there is some evidence that such people may be decreasing in number. Petersen (1968) has shown that during the past fifty years, the number of extended family households in Egypt has decreased somewhat at the same time that Egypt's population has grown enormously. The reasons for this trend are not clearly understood, but population pressure on the land—forcing the members of many families to disperse—could well be one of them. Fundamental changes in the ideals of family structure seem less likely to be an important factor, for indications of explicit rejection of the extended family ideal seem to be limited to some of the extremely Westernized, upper-class people who are not representative of the Arabs as a whole.

The importance of the interactional extended family among people most of whom actually reside in nuclear family households appears to be the continuing general pattern at present. In his study of families in Beirut, Farsoun (1970) has shown that the majority of them are in very frequent interaction with their respective extended families even though there are strong tendencies in favor of nuclear family residence. Farsoun refers to "amoral familism" as a predominant value among those people, meaning that there is deep-running distrust of everyone except within a certain circle of kinsmen. One complication is that the boundaries of this circle seem to fluctuate, at one time including the extended family but at other times including only the nuclear family, which is at odds with other nuclear families in the same extended one. One of the Arabs' generalizations about themselves is that the divisiveness within extended families is due to the quarrels and jealousies of the women, especially among the wives of brothers and between them and their mother-in-law. There appears to be some validity to this generalization, but the brothers themselves are likely to be in conflict over property rights and various responsibilities which are ideally equally shared.

Counteracting these divisive elements are factors which perpetuate the interactional extended family. Farsoun has shown the significant degree to which members of his sample of interactional extended families depend upon each other in business partnerships, for loans, for finding jobs for each other, and even for help in securing social welfare benefits. These are residents of a large, modern city, and though they are undergoing great changes, they are still locked into extended family dependency, of necessity if for no other reason.

The continuing importance of the "family firm," as shown by such scholars as Samir Khalaf (1966), is evidence of the positive aspects of this phenomenon; for example, the mutual confidence of father and son are necessary for the success of the business (Benedict 1968). Petersen (1967) has made the same point concerning Egyptian businesses.

Among rural Arabs at the present time, there is evidence of the continuing necessity of the interactional extended family even under changing conditions. Rosenfeld (1968) has dealt with it in detail among Arab villagers in Israel; Saunders (1968) has shown it among Nile Delta villagers; and Williams and Williams (1965) have done likewise for villagers in the interior valley of Lebanon.

However, this continuing necessity of the interactional extended family in the midst of change may be only temporary. Rosenfeld emphasizes that one reason why the older dependency continues is that economic change has not yet been radical enough. For example, wage laborers are still underskilled, poorly paid, and so still mutually dependent. Saunders (1968) makes very much the same point for the Egyptian villagers she studied. The implication is that greater occupational diversification coupled with increased skills and pay scales will in the future tend to reduce people's dependence on members of their extended families and the negative effect which goes with it. Among the purposes of the various development, industrial, and educational programs in the Arab countries are, of course, diversification and upgrading of jobs. To the extent that these goals are achieved, less tense and stressful relationships among kinsmen might, eventually, emerge.

Economic change alone, however, will probably not be sufficient to reduce stress and counterbalance the atomistic character component, for stress is not purely determined by economics. If the denigration of women and the use of negative reinforcements in child rearing have anything to do with this character structure, then lessening of the denigration and greater use of positive reinforcements might also be necessary to effect changes in it.

Traditional Middle Eastern assumptions are that men and women are in every respect different kinds of creatures. Bourdieu's analysis of the totally bipolar cosmology of the Kabyles of Algeria is a good illustration. On the left hand is femininity, possessor of harmful and impure powers; on the right hand is masculinity, possessor of fertilizing powers. And the "principal imperative" of these people is "to conceal the whole domain of intimacy" (Bourdieu 1966, pp. 222–23). Another illustration of this general feeling is provided by Abou-Zeid (1966) who points out that among the Bedouin of Egypt, there are two different kinds of honor for men and women, and that on this principle, loss of chastity by a female is punishable by death at the hands of her own relatives. The psychological conflicts that are suggested here are epitomized in Hilal's assertion (1970) that Arab men simultaneously harbor exploitative and protective feelings toward women.

Antoun (1968) has recently added valuable information on this subject based on his observations in Jordan. He says that the basic concept of woman's modesty represents the family and that the man's honor depends on the defense of her modesty. It might be argued that this places the woman in a centrally important role which is far from being denigrated. The objection to this argument is that in fact it is the *burden* of family honor that is placed on the woman, and for the slightest deviation she is punished. This is accompanied by the idea that a woman's honor is in constant peril because she herself is "by nature" less capable of rationality than men and has an uncontrollable sexual appetite. This rationalization has been claimed by some to lie behind the practice of clitoridectomy among some Arab groups (Antoun 1968). One suspects that all of this is indicative of the men's projection and displacement of their own motivations. Whether or to what extent Middle Eastern women find this complicated situation denigrating is a subject on which they should in the near future find increasing opportunities to speak for themselves. Present sources are contradictory. On the one hand are, for example, des Villettes (1964), Hansen (1960), and Miner and DeVos (1960). Des Villettes says that Maronite women in a Lebanese village in the 1950s were entirely content with their domestic lives; Hansen concludes the same (also in the 1950s) concerning village women among Kurds in Iraq, adding that, indeed, she did not envy men among these women; and Miner and DeVos state their "impression of lack of dissatisfaction among Arab women over their subordinate lot in life and their rather easy going adjustment." On the other hand, three women observers present a very different view: Tillion (1966) sees the degradation of women as a very ancient circum-Mediterranean trait antedating both Christianity and Islam; M'rabet (1969) sees it as a very modern trait that has survived the independence of Algeria from France; and Papanek (1973) sees beyond mere sexual jealousy in her interpretation of it, linking men's "psychopathic rage" at the real or imagined sexual transgressions of their women to the possibility that those transgressions are an unbearable threat to the men's major claim on control over an uncontrollable social environment—seclusion of their wives, daughters, and sisters from a hostile world. Once again, the ethos of insecurity. A possibly more balanced, but no less complex, view of the situation is that of Judith Williams (1968) who found that adolescent girls in a Lebanese village do feel denigrated vis-à-vis males, but, because they can look forward to more certain (and limited) adult roles than men, seem more "contented" than boys do.

Whatever any individuals may feel on the subject of the "nature" of women, and therefore the "nature" of men as well, the fact is that changes are taking place in the roles of an increasing number of Arab women—changes which have repercussions for men and for the majority of the women whose role is still restricted to wife-housekeeper-mother (see Gulick and Gulick 1974 and Chapter 12 in this book).

Earlier in this paper, I alluded to the findings of Nadia Youssef. Based primarily on census data, they are that Middle Eastern women participate in the labor force (work outside their homes) to a considerably smaller extent than do women in Latin America, an area that in many ways seems similar to the Middle East in its cultures. Youssef relates this to Middle Eastern women's status and role in the family vis-à-vis men, and these phenomena I have related, in turn, to the ethos of insecurity. Nevertheless, Middle Eastern women do participate in the labor force to some extent, and it is necessary to examine this new development in more detail.

Women Working in Morocco

Type of Occupation	Percentage of Women in the Occupation
Personal care and health services	64
Handicrafts and industry	27
Goods-handling and transportation	8
Commerce	2
Administration and intellectual professions	2

(Forget 1962, p. 95. By permission of UNESCO.)

Forget (1962) reports on an attitude survey which was done in the cities of Rabat, Fez, and Casablanca on whether or not women should have jobs outside the home. Her general conclusion is that 60 percent of the women and their husbands were positive toward the idea of women working outside of the home.

Forget's more specific conclusions are also of great importance. Over 54 percent of the urban men and women who were questioned disapproved of women working as peddlers, hammam attendants, entertainers (except movie stars!), water carriers, and waitresses. But between 65 percent and 75 percent of the men and women approved of women being civil servants, embroidery instructors, and saleswomen, though only 42 percent of the men (as opposed to 65 percent of the women) approved of women as factory workers. Over 90 percent of the men and women approved of women being teachers, nurses, secretaries, and midwives; but only 65 percent of the men (as opposed to 100 percent of the women) approved of women being embroiderers.

Forget says, to emphasize the conflicting feelings of many people on this subject, that many women would like to work at home if they could, but that those who have some education should work outside the home. This is an interesting conclusion in view of what has been found in the case of urban immigrants from two Lebanese villages: the city attracts both the illiterate and the most literate women for virtually opposite reasons. Peasant women who have labored in the fields welcome the move to the city because there they can stay at home. Educated village women, on the other hand, welcome the move to the city because there they will have the opportunity to work outside the homes where they felt confined in the villages (Khuri 1967).

Reminiscent of traditional attitudes is the fear on the part of both men and women about jobs which will put men and women in constant contact with each other (Forget 1962; Nouacer 1962). Fear of the possibility of promiscuity, reiterated in so much of the literature on the Middle East, seems to be almost obsessive. Because of this fear of what family and friends may suspect, even the most highly Westernized urban adolescents and young adults do not go out on mixed dates (Muhyi 1963). The sources of conflicts in values, aspirations, and in interpersonal relationships are many.

Merely having a job outside the home is not the answer to the problem of women who feel the need to do more than only be wives and mothers. Forget found that in her sample of urban Moroccan women, 80 percent of the civil servants wanted to continue in their jobs but that two-thirds of the factory workers would like to quit.

A wholly new element in the Arab value system—the positive goal of striving for national unity and progress—is reflected in Forget's findings. The following categories of people were in favor of women working outside of the home because they saw it as contributing to this goal: 95 percent of the women civil servants and professionals; 75 percent of the men; 60 percent of the housewives; and 0 percent of the women factory workers. If, as some observers have suggested, an awakened national spirit is the only feasible way of developing among the Arabs a constructive "sense of community" beyond kin group and sect, findings like the above convey some idea of the many confusions and conflicts which need to be resolved in order to achieve such an awakening. For example, there is the possibility that many Arab men are only paying lip service to the extension of women's horizons, that they fear it and may in various subtle ways try to sabotage it (Muhyi 1969, p. 139). And when we further take into account findings—such as that in one attitude survey 53 percent of Muslim girls (in contrast to 28 percent of American ones) sometimes felt that they would be happier if they were boys—we see the possibility of an "identity crisis" of major proportions (p. 136). On the other hand, Prothro (1961) notes that where positive reinforcements in child rearing occur, they tend to be associated with greater modern education of the mothers. And Dodd (1968) has noted that in Egypt, the more mothers are educated, the more their sons tend to accept their mothers' emancipation. This trend suggests a potential reduction in the extreme polarization of male and female roles which significantly reinforces the denigration of women.

On the other hand, Dodd (1973) has also emphasized that there are various indications that ^{c}ird continues to be a powerful psychological force, even where "modern" influences are supposedly maximal, such as cities. Furthermore, the concomitants of ^{c}ird, such as early marriage for women and restrictions on their public activities including higher education, all point in the direction of continued high fertility. At this point, I will not attempt a discussion of the population problem in the Middle East. Suffice it to say that it is recognized as a problem by many of the Arab and other Middle Eastern governments. The problem is rooted in, among other things, the continuance of the system of values that has been the subject of this paper. Among urban Iranians, for example, whose concept of *namus* is apparently close related to that of ^{c}ird, the complexity and extensiveness of the problem have been clearly set forth (Gulick and Gulick 1973).

The facts are fragmentary, and our powers of prediction are not great. How close we have come to identifying the sources and nature of the apparent difficulties is a subject for discussion. Certainly, behavioral and mental traits very similar to those discussed in this paper occur in other cultures. Logically, it is not at all clear why this fact should detract from the importance of the phenomena in any particular culture; emotionally, the argument that it does so detract would appear to be a defensive reaction. Actually, the fact of similarities in itself gives added confidence that the diagnosis of the existence of stress factors, for instance, is not just an ethnocentric projection, but rather is consonant with the general recognition of conflict and ambivalence in human affairs. A complex of very similar traits in Brazil has been delineated by Bernard Rosen (1964), for example. And, as we have seen, other scholars have perceived cultural complexes, relevant to this paper, that occur in other areas than the Muslim Middle East. Indeed, Youssef's (1972) perception of similarities combined with differences between the Middle East and Latin America, highlights, rather than minimizes, the domestic seclusion of women in the Middle East, a phenomenon that is, as we have seen, an integral part of the ethos of insecurity.

Whether anything can or should be done about such difficulties is for the Arabs, and other Middle Eastern peoples, to work out. This will presumably require the development of an effective ethnic self-criticism (Sharabi 1963) which only they, ultimately, can generate.

REFERENCES

Abou-Zeid, A.M. 1966. "Honour and Shame among the Bedouins of Egypt," in *Honor and Shame: the Values of Mediterranean Society*, edited by J.G. Peristiany. Chicago: University of Chicago Press.

Ammar, Hamed. 1954. *Growing Up in an Egyptian Village*. London: Routledge, Kegan Paul.

Antoun, Richard T. 1968. "On the Modesty of Women in Arab Muslim Villages: A Study in the Accommodation of Traditions," *American Anthropologist* 70:4:671-97.

Ayoub, Millicent R. 1957. "Endogamous Marriage in a Middle Eastern Village," Ph.D. dissertation, Radcliffe College.

Benedict, Burton. 1968. "Family Firms and Economic Development," *Southwestern Journal of Anthropology* 24:1:1-12.

Bill, James A. 1972. *The Politics of Iran: Groups, Classes and Modernization*. Columbus, Ohio: Charles E. Merrill Publishing Co.

Bourdieu, Pierre. 1966. "The Sentiment of Honour in Kabyle Society," in *Honor and Shame: The Values of Mediterranean Society*, edited by J.G. Peristiany. Chicago: University of Chicago Press.

des Villettes, Jacqueline. 1964. *La vie des femmes dans un village Maronite Libanais: Ain el Kharoube*. Tunis: N. Bascone and S. Muscat.

DeVos, George, and Miner, Horace. 1959. "Oasis and Casbah—a Study in Acculturative Stress," in *Culture and Mental Health*, edited by Marvin K. Opler. New York: Macmillan.

Dodd, Peter C. 1968. "Youth and Women's Emancipation in the United Arab Republic," *The Middle East Journal* 22:2:159-72.

―――. 1973. "Family Honor and the Forces of Change in Arab Society," *International Journal of Middle East Studies* 4:1:40-54.

Dubetsky, Allen. 1973. "Kinship, Primordial Ties, and Factory Organization in Turkey: An Anthropological View," paper read at the Annual Meeting of the Middle East Studies Association, Binghamton, New York, 2-4 November 1972.

Farsoun, Samih K. 1970. "Family Structure and Society in Modern Lebanon," in *Peoples and Cultures of the Middle East*, vol. 2, edited by Louise E. Sweet. Garden City, N.Y.: The Natural History Press, 257-307.

Forget, Nelly. 1962. "Attitudes Towards Work by Women in Morocco," *International Social Science Journal* 14:1:92-124.

Fuller, Anne H. 1961. *Buarij: Portrait of a Lebanese Muslim Village*. Cambridge: Harvard Middle Eastern Monographs, No. 6.

Gulick, John. 1967. *Tripoli: A Modern Arab City*. Cambridge: Harvard University Press.

———. 1968. "The Arab Levant: an Annotated Bibliography," in *The Central Middle East,* vol. 2, edited by Louise E. Sweet. New Haven: HRAFLEX Books. New edition published by Human Relations Area Files Press, 1971.

———. 1969. "Village and City Cultural Continuities in 20th Century Middle Eastern Cultures," in *Middle Eastern Cities,* edited by F.M. Lapidus. Berkeley and Los Angeles: University of California Press.

Gulick, John, and Gulick, Margaret E. 1973. "Kinship, Contraception and Family Planning in the Iranian City of Isfahan," prepared for 9th International Congress of Anthropological and Ethnological Sciences, Chicago, September 1973.

———. 1974. "An Annotated Bibliography of Sources Concerned with Women in the Modern Muslim Middle East," Princeton Near East Paper, No. 17.

Hansen, Henny Harald. 1960. *Daughters of Allah: among Moslem Women in Kurdistan.* London: George Allen and Unwin.

Harkabi, Y. 1967. "Basic Factors in the Arab Collapse during the Six-Day War," *Orbis* 9:3:677–91.

Hilal, Jamil M. 1970. "Father's Brother's Daughter Marriage in Arab Communities: A Problem for Sociological Explanation," *Middle East Forum* 46:4:73–84.

Kennedy, John G. 1967. "Nubian Zar Ceremonies as Psychotherapy," *Human Organization* 26:4:185–94.

Khalaf, Samir, and Shwayri, E. 1966. "Family Firms and Industrial Development: the Lebanese Case," *Economic Development and Cultural Change* 15:59–69.

Khatchadourian, Haig. 1961. "The Mask and the Face: A Study of 'Make Believe' in Middle Eastern Society," *Middle East Forum* 37:15–18.

———. 1962. "Moral 'Make Believe' in Arab Society," *Middle East Forum* 38:16–20.

Khuri, Fuad I. 1967. "A Comparative Study of Migration Patterns in Two Lebanese Villages," *Human Organization* 26:4:206–13.

Miner, Horace, and DeVos, George. 1960. *Oasis and Casbah: Algerian Culture and Personality in Change.* Anthropological Papers, No. 15. Ann Arbor: University of Michigan Press.

M'rabet, Fadela. 1969. *La femme algérienne* suivi de *Les algériennes.* Paris: François Maspero.

Muhyi, Ibrahim A. 1963. "Women in the Arab Middle East," in *The Modern Middle East,* edited by Richard Nolte. New York: Atherton Press.

Nouacer, Khadidja. 1962. "The Changing Status of Women and the Employment of Women in Morocco," *International Social Science Journal* 14:124–29.

Papanek, Hanna. 1973. "Purdah: Separate Worlds and Symbolic Shelter," *Comparative Studies in Society and History* 15:3:289–325.

Petersen, Karen K. 1967. "Family and Kin in Contemporary Egypt." Ph.D. dissertation, Columbia University.

———. 1968. "Demographic Conditions and Extended Family Households: Egyptian Data," *Social Forces* 46:4:531–37.

Prothro, E. Terry. 1961. *Child Rearing in Lebanon.* Cambridge: Harvard Middle Eastern Monographs, No. 8.

Quigley, Carroll. 1973. "Mexican National Character and Mediterranean Personality Structure," *American Anthropologist* 75:1:319–22.
Rosen, Bernard C. 1964. "The Achievement Syndrome and Economic Growth in Brazil," *Social Forces* 42:3:341–53.
Rosen, Lawrence. 1972. "Muslim-Jewish Relations in a Moroccan City," *International Journal of Middle East Studies* 3:4:435–49.
Rosenfeld, Henry. 1958. "Processes of Structural Change within the Arab Village Extended Family," *American Anthropologist* 60:6:1127–39.
———. 1968. "Change, Barriers to Change, and Contradictions in the Arab Village Family," *American Anthropologist* 70:4:732–52.
Saunders, Lucie Wood. 1968. "Aspects of Family Organization in an Egyptian Village," *Transactions of the New York Academy of Sciences*, Ser. 2, 30:5:714–21.
Schneider, Jane. 1971. "Of Vigilance and Virgins: Honor, Shame, and Access to Resources in Mediterranean Societies," *Ethnology* 10:1:1–24.
Sharabi, H. B. 1963. "The Crisis of the Intelligentsia in the Middle East," in *The Modern Middle East*, edited by Richard Nolte. New York: Atherton Press.
Stone, I. F. 1967. "Holy War," *New York Review of Books*, 3 August 1967, pp. 6–14.
———. 1970. "When Doves Turn Hawk," *I. F. Stone's Bi-Weekly* 17:12:1.
Tannous, Afif I. 1942. "Emigration, A Force of Social Change in an Arab Village," *Rural Sociology* 7:62–74.
———. 1944. "Extension Work among the Arab Fellahin," *Applied Anthropology* 3:3:1–12.
Tillion, Germaine. 1966. *Le Harem et les cousins*. Paris: Editions du Seuil.
Waterbury, John. 1970. *The Commander of the Faithful: The Moroccan Political Elite—a Study in Segmented Politics*. New York: Columbia University Press.
Williams, Herbert. 1958. "Personality in Hadchite: A Study of a Maronite Village in Lebanon." Ph.D. dissertation, University of Pennsylvania.
Williams, Judith R. 1968. *The Youth of Haouch el Harimi, a Lebanese Village*. Cambridge: Harvard Middle Eastern Monographs, No. 10.
Williams, Herbert H., and Judith R. Williams. 1965. "The Extended Family as a Vehicle of Culture Change," *Human Organization* 24:1:59–64.
Youssef, Nadia H. 1972. "Differential Labor Force Participation of Women in Latin American and Middle Eastern Countries: The Influence of Family Characteristics," *Social Forces* 51:2:135–53.
Zonis, Marvin. 1971. *The Political Elite of Iran*. Princeton: Princeton University Press.

Chapter 6

The Cargo Cult: A Melanesian Type-Response to Change

Theodore Schwartz

The cargo cult was the "type-response" to rapid culture change induced by European contact in Melanesia during the period of colonial rule, which is now coming to an end. Through an analysis of this characteristic response we hope to gain further understanding of the mode of psychocultural adjustment generated by the Melanesian reaction to Western cultures.

The term "Melanesia" has been most often used to refer specifically to a linguistic area in which one finds populations speaking "Austronesian" languages. I use it, as do other authors, to refer to the peoples of the entire mainland of New Guinea as well as the surrounding islands including New Caledonia, the New Hebrides, the Solomons, the Bismarck Archipelago, and the Admiralty Islands (Manus). It applies to a culture area based on culture-wide criteria and includes speakers of both Austronesian and non-Austronesian languages. In spite of the extent and diversity of the geographic area termed "Melanesia," there are sufficient similarities on a macrocultural level to justify generalization (Schwartz, 1963). The main variation to be observed at this time is the degree of acculturation and incorporation into an emerging syncretic contact culture. There is a wide range of acculturation, from urban center to the yet remote regions of the mountainous interior of New Guinea.

In this chapter[1] there will be little reference to individual variation in adjustment; rather, personality adjustment will be examined in the context of collective social movements in Melanesia. Moreover, I do not assume, as will be indicated later, that the individual's or group's choice of roles or modes of social adaptation by an individual or a group necessarily indicates different degrees of good or bad internal psychological adjustment (*cf.* Introduction). My focus is on the complex whole that includes both cargo cult and non-cult responses to change and their interrelationships with one another.

This chapter analyzes the way cargo cults occur; the bases for the participation and nonparticipation of given groups and individuals; the content of cult belief and behavior; and the factors affecting persistence or decline of cargo cult-related behavior in the context of continuing rapid social change. In this analysis I will emphasize four basic factors which I feel are essential to an understanding of the cargo cult phenomenon in Melanesia.

First, one must have a holistic approach to cargo cults. One cannot understand a cult or a movement by studying only a specific occurrence within a given locality or in a brief cross section of its history. Cargo cults must be seen in the context of a theory of areal integration or of area-characteristic modes of psychological adjustment for the Melanesian area (Schwartz, 1963). Cults and movements are processes or vehicles for change, requiring longitudinal study.

Second, in considering psychological mechanisms in cult behavior, one must distinguish between what I term "pathomimetic" and pathogenically determined behavior.

Third, whereas psychological consistency theories have cited cults as mechanisms for dissonance reduction, I maintain that the dissonance and ambivalences of the cult belief system must be maintained by specific social mechanisms rather than reduced, if what I term "metastable" states of heightened excitement are to be prolonged.

Fourth, I wish to refer briefly again to what I have discussed elsewhere, that the cargo cult as a "type-response" occurs in the context of an area-wide underlying paranoid ethos that was inherent in traditional Melanesian (and many other) cultures (Schwartz, 1974).

This chapter is a critique and emendation of selected theories about the processes involved in magico-religious responses to culture contact and culture change. Although I refer to psychocultural adjustment throughout, I find it logically impossible to isolate psychological adjustment from cultural adaptation. When culture change occurs, it must, to an important degree, involve personal change of some depth within individuals. Otherwise, the change is not cultural change, but an unregistered environmental event (Schwartz and Mead, 1958; Schwartz, 1975b).

THE CARGO CULT AS A "TYPE-RESPONSE"

The cargo cults of Melanesia have attracted the interest of many anthropologists and other observers. Cargo cults are a "type-response"—one of the basic modes of reaction or adjustment to situations of rapid culture change characteristic of an entire area in a specific historical phase. These strikingly similar responses are extremely prevalent within Melanesia, but not in the same form or frequency in neighboring culture areas such as Indonesia, Micronesia, or Polynesia. I believe, therefore, that I can justify considering the cargo cult as a specific related to particular features of psychocultural adjustment in Melanesian cultures.

Cult responses to culture contact are not unique to Melanesia. They are comparable to forms of religious reaction to culture change, crisis, and domination reported throughout the world (Lanternari, 1963; LaBarre, 1974). What seems most characteristically Melanesian is embodied in the concept of "cargo." What is meant by "cargo" will be elaborated below (see also Lawrence, 1964). In addition to the well-reported cargo cult response one finds other types of more secular and political psychocultural responses to culture change in Melanesia for which I use the term "movements." Some of these, like the Paliau Movement (Schwartz, 1962), have been closely associated with cargo cults or have included cult phases, but are not themselves exclusively cargo cults. Although the distinction between cult and movement is often useful, its terms may be more precisely taken as components of a whole rather than as polar opposites. The relations between cult and movement components of a given social vehicle may be complex and may vary over time. I have tried to trace this relation in my 1962 monograph and in subsequent work.

The Melanesian cargo cult is a "type-response" because it occurs over a long time span and in widely scattered geographic areas within the Melanesian cultural boundaries. It occurs despite great ecological variability and despite highly divergent degrees and varieties of acculturation within specific areas in Melanesia. It seems probable that cult occurrences extend back at least to the mid-nineteenth century. The characteristics that early observers reported are very similar to those witnessed in recent times.

In spite of continuing intensive acculturation, the cults have occurred and continue to occur at almost all degrees of the acculturative continuum, ranging from peoples newly contacted (or on the fringe of contact) to peoples that have had intensive, perduring contact with Europeans for the past 100 years. In the 1970s, however, the remaining cults, active and latent, have diminished in importance as Papua New Guinea approaches independence and national politics develop. They cannot, however, be counted out. The cult beliefs were present in the most remote mountain areas of New Guinea where, until recently, people still lived largely by the technologically primitive modes of adaptation of their ancestors. Cult beliefs also appeared among Melanesians who had worked for Europeans on plantations, in towns, or who had acquired a variety of new occupations. Cults have appeared among Christianized Melanesians as well as among those who had been exposed to only the most remote concepts of Christianity as introduced by missionary activity or even by rumors thereof.

Cargo cults have occurred in virtually every ecological zone, from the highlands to the lowland coasts and swamps of New Guinea as well as throughout the various Melanesian Island groups. They have occurred among most of the major known culture variants of the Melanesian area. They have occurred among matrilineal and patrilineal peoples, among fishermen and gardeners, among small, isolated communities, and in larger, more complex settlements. The distribution of the cults and the high order of similarity both in content and process can in itself be offered as a strong argument for the unity of Melanesia as a culture area.

GENERAL CHARACTERISTICS OF CARGO CULTS

Although no two cargo cults were exactly alike, a number of basic beliefs recurred in most. The ancestors would return. The dead would be reunited with the living on a given day, suddenly and totally. The ancestors, when they returned, would bring with them a "cargo" consisting of the goods and wealth of the Europeans as well as the bounty of land and sea. In almost every instance, one or more prophets appeared who had received revelations from God, Christ, or the dead themselves. Prophets were able to describe the magico-ritual means to be employed to ensure the coming of the cargo.

It was believed that Europeans possessed a secret that gave them access to supernatural sources of cargo. The native believed that the coming of cargo would allow him also to realize some idealized form of European life, including enjoyment of wealth without work.

Some early cults were revivalistic in that they expected the advent of a state of affairs conceived within traditional concepts of wealth and welfare. Some elements were more variable. Often the ancestors were expected to arrive in ships or planes with the cargo. Occasionally the dead were to come up from a hole or cave in the ground where cargo was made. In some places such as Manus, people were told to destroy all their present belongings or to cast them into the sea in preparation for their replacement by European wealth. Often wharves, storehouses, airfields, or helicopter pads were built to receive the ships or planes.

After World War II the cargo was often envisioned as coming from America. The cargo, which God and the ancestors were to send to natives, was thought to be maliciously intercepted by Europeans. The labels were changed and goods redirected to European stores. Natives were forced to buy the meager amounts they could afford, to the profit of others. The outlines of a post-cargo world were only vaguely specified. In some cults, black skins were to be turned white. In others, natives were to become masters and the masters their servants. The whites were to be killed or driven out by the ancestors or by God. In other versions, native and European would "sit down together" as equals. Mountains would be leveled, the islands joined together, the seas calmed, and the fish made to leap abundantly into nets. In many cults, the arrival of cargo was to coincide with the imminent Second Coming of Christ.

Certain culturally stylized, extreme behavior occurred frequently in cults. Convulsive seizures were prevalent, as were "speaking in tongues" and "death and resurrection." These "symptoms" were considered firm signs of the nearness of God and the dead, and of the imminent coming of the cargo. There were sightings of ships manned by the ancestors. Natives sometimes reported the sound of cargo-handling winches in the night. Dreams and revelations further attested to the coming of cargo. Ritual marching, prayers, revealed songs, public rites of confession, purification, and baptism were employed in various cults as means to bring nearer the day it would arrive.

But the cargo did not come in the predicted time. The cult usually collapsed. Nevertheless, the beliefs did not die; instead they went into latency while the people gave up cult behavior and resumed their normal activity.

As for the cargo itself, the following list will convey an idea of its contents and of the imagined but unsystematized future based on it. The items listed are extracted from an "order" written by members of the Sua Cult in Manus in 1960. It was presented to the District Commissioner of Manus, along with about $50 as an inducement to him to send the order to the source of the cargo. The order was written by a native primary school teacher and a cooperative store clerk, members of the cult. Ninety-three items were listed in three columns (item number, quantity, and item). What follows is a nonconsecutive extract, as written, of part of the list: 500 pistols with cartridges; 5 bicycles; 10 motorbikes; 10 tractors; 1,000 sheets of iron; 500 window glass; 500 window shades; 10 mattresses; 18 mosquito nets; 1,000,000 sheets of iron; 8,000 bags of cement; 2,000,000 timbers; 500 boxes of tools; 28,000 chairs; 17,000 cases of nails in sizes 1/2", 1", 2", 3", 4", 5", 6", 7"; 30,000 tablecloths; 16,000 radios; 14,000 refrigerators; 8 storage batteries; 3 workshop buildings; 40,000 drums of kerosene; 40,000 drums of fuel; 4,000 warships; 5,000 cargo boats; 10,000 plates of rice; the same of sugar; the same of flour; 10,000 pigs; 16,000 writing pens; 2,000 grass-cutting machines; 4,900 sewing machines; and 9,000 razor blades.

Some explanations of why cargo cults occur will be considered below.[2] It is generally maintained that the Melanesian both admired and resented the European, envying the European's wealth and way of life and devaluing his own. He particularly resented that the European would not initiate him into the mystery of the acquisition of cargo; that he would not enter into a symmetrical, reciprocal relation with the Melanesian. The European told him that cargo was man-made, resulting from work and saving. Many Melanesians, through most of their experience in the contact culture, had worked hard for Europeans and acquired pitifully little cargo. Europeans, on the other hand, showed little evidence of engaging in physical labor. Instead, they wrote out orders to distant places and awaited the arrival of ships bringing cargo that natives unloaded but could not possess. The cargo mythology explained the gap between the Melanesian's own wealth and that of the European and offered supernatural means of instantaneously acquiring this wealth. Melanesians hoped Christianity would bring them to parity with Europeans when they adopted its beliefs, but it failed to produce the cargo. It was said to be "misunderstood" and transformed into the cargo belief.

THE CHARACTER OF CONTACT

The response to contact and consequent culture change in Melanesia is evident (1) in the cargo cult as the type-response of Melanesian cultures to disruption of their self-evaluative and cosmological schemes; (2) in the manner of their response to Christianity; and (3) in the manner in which pacification was accomplished. Each of these responses and adaptations is related to basic features in Melanesian culture and psychology.

There is little trace of any kind, even in native folklore, of the effects of three and one-half centuries of sporadic contacts from ships along the coasts of the Melanesian Islands. It must be kept in mind that European culture itself underwent a technological and social revolution during the period between early contacts and those during and after the last quarter of the nineteenth century. The sheer increase in impressiveness of technological power and manifest material wealth—from the days of visits by the men in sailing ships, through the more frequent steamers, to the massive force of men and material on the fleets and aircraft carriers of World War II—had its obvious effect. It roughly divided the period of contact into an initial period of gradual and sometimes resisted contact and the later period of virtually prehensile acculturation. Early accounts indicate that the aliens were received with little fear, with much curiosity, and with an avid desire for trade. Melanesians developed great respect for the weapons and power of the strange white men. But they seemed to show neither dread nor awe. Many reports, from the islands to the highlands, indicate an immediate interest in the material wealth and marvels possessed by the Europeans.

The warlike peoples of Melanesia fought one another, preferring unexpected attack or ambush to open combat (although open confrontation is of importance in "formal or ritual warfare" in the Highlands of New Guinea: see Gardner and Heider, 1968; Berndt 1964; Schwartz, 1963). Natives killed surprisingly few Europeans during the process of exploration, colonization, and pacification. Given their small numbers, the Manus of the Admiralty Islands probably exceeded most Melanesians in having killed some twelve Europeans at various times at trading posts and on ships. They, upon two occasions, captured ships and killed their native crews. Captured weapons were not used against Europeans but were used competitively to enhance the relative ascendancy and prestige of the most warlike native groups in waves of marauding against other native villages.

There are fuller accounts of the first stages of contact from those areas where contact was longest delayed (particularly in the Highlands of New Guinea and West Irian). These post-World War II reports have indicated that indirect knowledge of the white man and his power often preceded his actual appearance. Stories about the white man were carried in by rumor, on chains of narrative from group to group. In some areas where Europeans had not yet entered, some natives had gone out to neighboring localities seeking contact. Sometimes they traveled considerable distances to seek out native or European labor recruiters. I noted such occurrences in the Upper Sepik River area.

Contact since the 1880s has been far more intensive than the more casual contacts of the preceding centuries. Labor recruitment preceded government control in some areas. Missionaries used airplanes and more efficient river transport to penetrate into almost all of the most remote areas. European prospectors, crocodile hunters, curio collectors, and native loggers found it to their advantage to seek out the most uncontacted, unrecruited, and unsophisticated natives in as yet unevangelized, unstripped, unlooted, and unclaimed areas.

We are left to speculate on the cognitive content of these native contact experiences. Cognitive impact on native cosmologies did not depend on the intensity of contact viewed from the standpoint of the European. A ship, a first patrol, a single plane flying overhead could shake a cosmology. Melanesians experienced a flood of new wonders which had to be admitted to their cosmologies: sailing ships; men with pale "red" skins; strange clothing and weapons; marvelous, beautiful, and superior materials; the equally strange and often unpredictable behavior of the aliens.

The previously empty seas (which had been unknown to interior peoples) were now extended and peopled; the Melanesian's total perception of his place in the universe was challenged. What he had believed was broken and restructured on a new level of openness and uncertainty, demanding a new synthesis.

Cargo cults, as one of their functions, were an attempt at such a resynthesis.[3] The focus of conscious concern, however, was on some formula for the acquisition of the wealth of the white man. The appearance of the white man and his wealth caused a great sense of status inferiority that was intolerable to the Melanesian, whose sense of self depended so heavily upon the prestige derived from the manipulation of wealth. That which had previously been defined as wealth—native currencies such as dog's teeth, shell money, and pigs—now seemed sharply devalued compared to European goods.[4]

Although the early contacts were not intensive in the sense of frequency, numbers, and scale, they had profound effects. Some of the first changes occurred in the integrative core of Melanesian cultures. The cosmological changes already mentioned were part of the almost immediate conversion of traditional native cultures into what I call "contact cultures." In other words, from the time of contact onward, the groups became outwardly oriented. They sought to maximize opportunities for contact. Their interests turned toward new activities and new forms of wealth and, correspondingly, diminished for the traditional equivalents. Change was limited, of course, by the continuity of past learning. But the limitation was also importantly based on lack of opportunity—on the difficulty of acquiring the costly European goods, or simply on the remoteness of some parts of the area.

Conversion and Pacification

The greater the wealth manifested by the contacting Europeans, the easier was their task of conversion, pacification, exploitation, or administration. In the case of missionaries, relative success was often due to the natives' perception of the wealth that the missionary possessed or that he was thought to represent, rather than the cogency of the doctrine presented. The white missionary was conceived of as an inseparable component of the entire white society. Initially, between native and missionary there was very little mutual comprehension of what each sought from the other.

The Manus, with deliberation, decided to discard their own religion, which was based on ancestors and the household cult of the guardian ghosts. In its place they adopted Catholicism before any European missionary had come directly among them. The Manus discarded en masse the skulls of their ancestors, which had been kept in places of honor in their houses. They did this out of disappointment at the failure of their ancestors to provide as well for them as these new Gods and ancestors had provided for the Europeans. Yet their own ghosts hovered nearby, not so readily discarded, as the Manus tested the yield of the European religion. In light of later events, it seems likely that initial conversion may have been itself a "cargo cult" based on high expectations of imminent fulfillment of hope. Disappointment was inevitable.

Pacification also brought about a profound change touching the core of native culture. Yet it was accomplished in most areas with remarkable rapidity. The termination of warfare among a people trained to ferocity was another of the very first effects of contact and of the establishment of colonial administration. In places where there was resistance, Europeans carried out punitive expeditions, imprisonments, and demonstrations to establish the efficacy of European arms, and occasionally killed natives. In some places, such as Manus, a few Europeans were killed. But more often it was remarkably easy for the colonial administration to establish a monopoly of the use of force and to maintain peace by meager European personnel with small native constabularies. In many areas, virtual pacification was accomplished with the appearance of the very first European patrol, or even preceding it, based on rumors of the *Pax Imperii*. The ferocious warriors of New Guinea, still possessing their arms, ceased to use them against one another. In going through my collection of war stories, ballads, and accounts of pacification, I have sensed that a feeling of relief must have accompanied pacification, even though narration of war stories still lights all eyes. Melanesians welcomed the existence of state power, in this case an imposed colonial administration, that could settle disputes and retaliate for violence. They welcomed the cessation of many of the concomitants of warfare: the sneak attack, ambush, raiding, kidnapping of women and children, cannibalism, torture, extreme indignities inflicted on captives, and the continual need to be concerned with defense. In other words, a large element of rational appraisal on the part of Melanesians contributed to pacification.

Melanesians varied in the extent of post-pacification violence, but Manus was not unusual. Here a people trained to the adult role of warrior-raider were pacified by the German administration as early as 1911. Subsequently there were extremely few crimes of interpersonal violence. Manus natives often expressed to me that fear of the return of native warfare was one of their chief concerns in contemplating independence.[5]

Pacification was synchronous with the almost immediate conversion from traditional culture to a contact culture. All through the islands, people moved from defensive locations on the heights of the interior, from the lagoons, and from small islands to more exposed positions on what were once no-man's land: areas of trade and warfare on the beaches and the riverbanks. Everywhere, it seems to me, there was a wish to get into the exciting zone of contact—to be on a river or coast for the sake of seeing an occasional motor canoe or boat, trader, or patrol. Contact with other native groups, from whom attack was no longer feared, was now possible. There were great rewards to be realized immediately following pacification. Melanesians were deeply attuned to trade, ceremonial exchange, and the building of social networks. Pacification provided enhanced opportunities for such activities. Past hostilities and insecurity, however, left residues of tension and distrust.

In spite of new elaborations of old institutions into the space left by warfare, a culture geared to omnidirectional war cannot avoid profound modification in the advent of peace. All social expectations are altered. Socialization experiences that influence personality development are considerably modified by the diminished training toward an adult role involving prowess in combat, violence, and a continual need to defend oneself from the potential violence of others. The change that has occurred in Melanesia is apparent in photographs of three generations of Melanesians. The images in the first photographs extant are masks of ferocity, with knotted brows, with baleful and seemingly protruding eyes. The present generation regards the world from more relaxed countenances, reflecting perhaps puzzlement or suspicion, at times, but certainly not the defensive and vigilant ferocity of their grandparents.

There is no absolute discontinuity, however. Melanesians still carry within them the emotional training related to the competitive ethos which characterized previous generations. It is transmuted into new forms and new objectives. The past is not entirely lost. The now-suppressed excitement of warfare is experienced vicariously in the enjoyment with which tales of past horror and cannibalism are told by the elders to the young. Litigation, politics, competitive feasts and exchanges, gambling, and soccer carry some of the affective tone of past prowess in warfare. The present-day social and political divisions, the increasingly prevalent use of sorcery or belief in its use against one, provide channels for defensive-aggressive combativeness now expressed in forms of nonphysical violence (Romanucci, 1969).

Even with the adoption of Christianity, the discontinuity with the past has not been absolute in its implications for internal adjustment and social adaptation. The forms may be Christian, but the usages continue the ethos of the Melanesian past. In content as well, selective emphasis and elaboration lead to a distinctive Melanesian Christianity, reflecting the inevitable transformation whenever a religion is translated from one culture to another. Melanesians use Christianity pragmatically as they have used religion generally. It is judged continuously not by its abstract truth but by its seeming yield in terms of relative wealth, power, and longevity. The task, from the standpoint of the missionary, has been complicated by Melanesian expectations which make the missionary's outboard motor a more impressive argument than his attempt at emotional consolation. Defection from missions often occurred in the context of the cargo cults because the Melanesian was not willing to accept a religion of consolation or a promised afterlife as a substitute for a religion of fulfillment during one's lifetime (immediately, if possible). Today many missions that suffered from such defections in the past (particularly after World War II) are, in an attempt at modernization, turning to economic development and local autonomy as a major thrust of their efforts.

One of the profound side effects of conversion on Melanesian social organization was a restructuring of groups around mission membership. The many mission sects established new cleavages along new lines of religious intolerance. Marriage tended to follow common mission membership, often breaking lines of traditional bride procurement (Schwartz, 1975a).

With initial contact came profound economic and occupational changes. In some areas there was nearby urban development. In others, village life continued, but many men went away to work on plantations, in towns, in domestic service, on ships, or in the police force. In a pattern typical of much of the underdeveloped world, young men were often absent from their villages for years at a time. Cash crops, though often on a small scale for local markets, became increasingly important as a supplement to subsistence activities. Natives who had never left their own valleys or islands were often taken by ship or plane to work on distant plantations or as part of labor gangs in towns. They handled the cargo of ships, trucks, and planes, buying what they could in Australian or Chinese stores with their small wages. The currency of the early contact culture included tobacco, axes, knives, and cloth. More recently one finds increasingly such valued objects as watches, sunglasses, and transistor radios among the prestigious possessions acquired through wage labor. Previous patterns of distribution of wealth may interfere with the accumulation of property or capital. Kin still expect to share in what is brought back from the outside. The returned laborer manages to keep very little for himself. This remains a problem for even the most educated, salaried urban workers and civil servants.[6] Women tended to lag far behind men in acculturative experience (until the advent of government schools in the 1950s), particularly in areas away from towns where they could participate in market life.

Other aspects of the effects of initial and later contact will be taken up in the discussion of explanations of cargo cults, particularly racial, political, and economic relations to Europeans and the inflation of native standards of self-value.

THEORETICAL EXPLANATIONS OF CARGO CULTS

Explanations of cargo cults have ranged from sociohistorical attempts at specifying the conditions precipitating cargo cults to psychological theories of the behavior of cultists and of a cult's psychological functions for the individuals and groups.

Attempted explanations of cults in Melanesia, and of religious cults generally, make assertions about conditions that generate and sustain cults and movements. Many of these assertions suffer more from being incomplete than from being imperceptive. Taken separately, exclusive and sufficient explanatory force cannot be claimed for any of these approaches.

Sociohistorical Explanations

Sociohistorical explanations attempt to account for the pattern of occurrence and the content of given cults in terms of prior states (of the societies in which they occur) and specific local conditions. Starting from the specificities of each instance, such theories may attempt to derive "typical" cult forms and histories and the general situational determinants of cult recruitment of groups and individuals.

Stanner (1953, 1958) and Inglis (1957, 1959) discuss the possibility of a sociohistorical explanation for cult occurrences. Inglis apparently abandons the possibility of a general explanation of cargo cults and thinks that each occurrence must be explained through its historical particulars. The conditions under which cult phenomena occur seem entirely too varied. Any general set of conditions that one posits is too easily found also in villages and localities where such cults have not occurred. Inglis points out that satisfactory explanation must account not only for those situations where cults occur, but for their lack of occurrence elsewhere.

Stanner shares this view but feels that a general explanation of a determinate sort is still possible. Because the conditions under which cults seem to occur are far more widespread than the cults themselves,[7] Stanner would then say that cults occur where there is a person, usually in the role of prophet, who leads a group in the expression of these conditions. Cult formation will not occur where such a catalyst is lacking. For Stanner, the occurrence of a prophet is probably historically determined. Nevertheless, the hope that perhaps the prophet is the missing ingredient in a package of conditions capable of discriminating between occurrence and nonoccurrence of cults is in vain. The complex set of cults occurring as phases of the Paliau Movement offer a number of instances where some would-be prophets failed to generate a cult under conditions seemingly like those in which others succeed. Must we then posit another missing ingredient—insufficient charisma, perhaps? The prospect is dubious.

I do not wish to imply that the search for a set of general conditions of cult occurrence is in vain or that the differential local occurrence and nonoccurrence of cults can be accounted for without intensive study of specific local, historical circumstances. What I do maintain is that both approaches can lead only to frustration because they are based on selection of too small and particularistic a unit of observation in the local, apparently unitary cult occurrence. Such a particularistic approach makes every attempt at isolating a general set of conditions seem riddled with exceptions. I believe that a set of general determinants, relevant to cargo cults as a widespread phenomenon throughout Melanesia, can be defined if one studies larger interactive social areas over time instead of attempting to trace the historical process of each particular cult. How historical determinants operate with particular groups and individuals and how they interact with the more general determinants that affect whole areas must be demonstrated in intensive studies such as my investigation of the Paliau Movement (Schwartz, 1962).

In the larger units of observation that I am suggesting, general determinants emerge more clearly. Historical determinants are less apt to appear decisive. By historical determinants I mean the interstructuring of events; the effect of the specificities of previous states of a system on the specificities of subsequent states. On the local (village) level, the historical determinants seem so influential that it is difficult to discern, as one must, the operations of general determinants. Nevertheless, if they have been correctly ascertained, the general determinants are also to be seen at the local level. The challenge is to understand their effect on the contingent materials upon which they operate. This is only possible when one has a larger frame of reference within which to view particular events.

The failing of the approach that seeks out specific distributions—why this village, why not that one?—is that the unit of observation and of explanation is atomistically conceived. It is fallacious to assume that each cult outbreak was an independent occurrence. Cults were not even independent, parallel responses to a general set of circumstances. They were directly stimulated by the diffusion of the cargo cult idea over large areas. In each locality, and often in widely separated localities, there were a number of competitively contrasting versions of the cargo cult idea held by groups that frequently were well aware of one another's version of it. Elements from the repertoire of cult ideas recurred again and again in different combinations. Each version acquired a somewhat unique form as local innovators experimented with new variations. Most cult occurrences must be considered in the context of previous cult episodes in the same locale or elsewhere.

The social area I take as my unit of study has a historical as well as a spatial dimension. By the turn of this century, the idea of cargo cult was well established in the Melanesian contact culture. It would not be far amiss, in fact, to speak of it as a *cargo culture,* combining postulates of native Christianity and the revised native cosmology that developed in the process of contact.

For more than a year I lived among noncultists. I found that they interacted frequently with cultists, and that together they constituted a system of mutual reference. It was a typical Melanesian cultural reaction to respond antagonistically or competitively to what was happening among neighboring groups. The very fact that one group developed a cult immunized some others against cult behavior rather than stimulating emulation. I came to realize that, given some minor shifts in circumstances, those who joined and those who opposed might easily have been reversed. The determinants of cult occurrence must be considered as acting on both cult and noncult, not obscured by the contingency of differential recruitment.

Because of certain aspects of the Melanesian political system, when any given group joined a cult we could expect that some other groups would stay out (Schwartz, 1963). Cult membership took on the status of "property" to be matched by a contrasting property held by rival groups or leaders. The effect of this pattern of interaction was the spotty distribution of cults and the production of blocks of pro- and anti-cult villages, as well as pro- and anti-cult factions within some villages. It is not necessary to assume that cultists and noncultists were psychologically and situationally differentiated and that such differences accounted for the pattern of distribution of cult occurrences. In the larger areas of social interaction in which many distinct, often culturally differentiated groups were interlaced by lines of self-differentiation and identification, cult and anticult must be perceived as being locked into a single system of functional and emblematic contrast.

Melanesian cultures tended to differentiate from one another, even when contiguous and intensely interactive, by focusing attention on cultural and linguistic differences as "emblems" identifying groups. Even where these emblems of identity would seem to be minor or incipient differences, for group members they were emblems of constrastive solidarity and political autonomy. A fusion occurred of the two main senses of "property"—a fusion of what a group *owned* in a legal sense with what was "proper to" or distinguishing about an individual or group.

In Melanesian social organization, differentiation was always an act of insubordination—an assertion that a group was an autonomous, prestige-attaching unit—whereas emulation implied subordination. This basic feature governed patterns of recruitment to cults. The first recipients of a cult revelation in an area considered themselves the leaders or tutors of those who may come to emulate them. This forced potential cultists to choose between emulation (which would acknowledge their subordination) and the development of some counterpattern of differentiation (which would maintain their relative status and prestige vis-à-vis the cultists). Whether a particular group moved toward emulation or toward differentiation was determined partially by past group relations and other factors such as the prestige-status and rivalry of leaders or the level of excitation[8] reached in a particular phase of cult.

The intragroup dynamics of cult behavior in Melanesia required intergroup opposition. There was both exclusion of some potential members by the initiators, as well as self-exclusion by some potential members. For example, it was quite apparent that in the second cult on the South Coast of Manus (which I studied in some detail in 1953-1954), not all potential recruits were welcome. The studied exclusion of certain persons who were ideally qualified as opposition was socially generated in the very first steps taken in cult formation. In effect, recruiting was not indefinitely extended but was controlled. This view of the process of recruitment is relevant to our later discussion of inadequacies in Festinger's (1956) explanation of cult dynamics in terms of cognitive dissonance.

In summary, in studying the distribution of cult occurrences it is necessary to take not the cult village but the cult area as the unit of observation. One cannot concentrate simply on the social or psychological characteristics of cultists, assuming by their membership that they somehow differ from noncultists. One must seek out general psychocultural conditions governing recruitment in an area that develops cults.

It is only in considering the structure of a complex areal culture, such as that which united all of the Admiralty Island Archipelago, that one sees beyond a seeming political primitiveness to a much larger nonpolitical system of areal integration. It was such a system that brought relatively large numbers of people into a single, interactive unit (Schwartz, 1963). Similarly, this system should be observed over a longer period of time.

Many have studied cargo cults on the basis of accounts in the literature, most of which sample only a particular phase of a given cult. Longitudinal observation makes clear the hazards of inference from synchronic observation. For example, an apparently noncult situation could be a cult in a latent phase. Two groups studied repeatedly at intervals might be found to have interchanged positions, entering and leaving cult episodes.

In the dynamic circumstances of rapid culture change, a culture cannot be known from short-term observation. There are many aspects about which I would have been mistaken had I taken my 1953 observations in Manus to be unidirectional characteristics of change over a short run of even ten or fifteen years. Much that I thought was defunct later reappeared; some of what I thought was stabilized could no longer be seen on the next visit (Schwartz, 1975b). On each successive visit over a twenty-two-year period, not only the present but the past had changed. No culture is manifested all at once; its features are both recurrently episodic and productive. It must be viewed through time to be understood in any depth at all, although it is not thereby exhaustible.

Basic characteristics took on a quite different appearance as one moved from phase to phase of a continuing spiral of cult and movement interactions. Lack of fulfillment of the promise of a belief led to disappointment and a dropping off of cult activity. Yet, even as activity dwindled, a gradual restorative rationalization of the disappointment could already be in process, eventually spiraling back after some years into another manifest cult phase. The same oscillation over a longer period of time can be perceived in the more secularly oriented, sociopolitical movements. These movements passed through phases in which goal attainments were recognizably disappointing, and phases of high morale and vigorous activity. Even though such secular, goal-oriented activities had a longer, future time orientation, in terms of what they aimed to accomplish they, too, were unrealistically foreshortened and could not maintain heightened expectations, within their time perspective, without oscillations of hope and disappointment.

Oppression or Deprivation Theories of Precipitant Conditions

There seems to be very widespread agreement (perhaps more than there should be) on the social conditions precipitating cult activity. Cargo cults are often viewed simply as a response to a colonial situation. They are, as Lanternari puts it, "religions of the oppressed." They are a defense of a group against submergence in a lower caste position, a response of the disparaged. They are nascent or protonationalist movements when viewed in terms of power relations and political development.[9] This explanation is not specific to cargo cults but applies to religious cults and to many kinds of social movements generally. Such cults have also been called "redemptive," "revindictive," or "revitalization" movements, terms that imply a supernatural rectification of a situation of gross inequality of wealth, power, prestige, esteem, privilege, even health and longevity.[10]

Lanternari emphasizes oppression as the condition of occurrence for religious cults the world over in widely varying types of societies and situations. The argument is plausible. The struggles of the powerless are deflected into fantasy realizations of goals. Magical or supernatural means are used—the only means available to cast down the mighty and raise up the oppressed. History is replete with movements great and small that originated in local cults under such circumstances.

The oppression hypothesis is sometimes considered in the context of race relations (Valentine, 1963). Race relations assumed complex forms in Melanesian thought. The Melanesian felt excluded rather than inferior or incompetent. Hostility toward the white man probably developed quickly, mixed as it was with ambivalent identification. As mentioned before, the Melanesian explained the gap between himself and the white man by the unwillingness of the white man to share—to initiate the native into the mysteries of the sources of cargo. At a later stage, more secularly viewed, the resentment attached itself to the assumed unwillingness or tardiness of the white man to educate Melanesians to the kind of occupations that would yield a European standard of living. To Melanesians who have finally attained such occupations in recent years, the European is often seen as still holding back, refusing to pay natives on a wage scale comparable to that paid to European (Australian) expatriots.

Many of the whites with whom natives had most frequent contact prior to World War II were often the old type of racist colonial who considered "coon bashing" a good way to keep native labor in line and who professed to like his unspoiled "bushies" (unacculturated natives) but distrusted natives in proportion to their sophistication in the contact culture. Such were the plantation managers. Contact with liberal Europeans who related more personally to natives has become much more common since the 1950s, while floggings ceased and the more overtly brutal forms of racism were suppressed by a generally liberal and protective administration. In the 1960s, with Papua New Guinea moving toward independence, the administration attempted to eliminate discrimination generally as in rescinding the prohibition on native drinking of alcohol. Judged comparatively, in the context of modern colonialism, the Australian administration of Papua New Guinea after World War II was relatively benign and progressive. It moved toward self-government fairly rapidly, liquidating its own rule by intensive educational programs to place more and more natives into jobs once held exclusively by Europeans.

The armies encountered during World War II under situations that threw Melanesian and white together in interdependence, while achieving little depth of interpersonal contact, represented a new kind of relationship with peoples of the outside world. This was particularly so in contacts with white and black Americans, who are said to have treated Melanesians in a more egalitarian manner. Thus hope was raised that the Americans might break with the conspiracy of outsiders to withhold the cargo from the native. The sight of the black American soldier, working in various units but particularly in construction battalions, helped to dissipate whatever self-doubt there may have been about the potential of Melanesians for technical competence in the use and ownership of the white man's tools and wealth. Here were black people who were on the "inside," as natives perceived it. Natives in some parts of Melanesia saw American blacks build bridges, use bulldozers, create roads, and blast mountains as well as engage in combat and share in the use of force.

In areas of the most intensive contact, these effects of World War II diffused as traveling myths, reducing, fragmenting, and transforming the experience. But I would not want to overemphasize the effects of the war. Cargo cults long preceded it, continued to occur during the war, and have continued to the present. The war influenced the scale and content of the later cults. It contributed to the politicization of the movements with which some of the cults were associated, although the cult beliefs themselves remained essentially the same. America now became the land of the cargo, evoking even more grandiose dreams of sudden wealth.

Reaction to injurious race relations in the context of colonial domination was undoubtedly one of the elements expressed in cargo cults. Such conditions have been world-wide at various times, and religious cults have been a common form of response. Judeo-Christianity, embodying the salvation and revindication hopes of earlier dominated peoples, provided some of the messianic-apocalyptic imagery of the cargo cults. The cargo cult, however, in its full configuration, also had deep Melanesian roots. It is a subclass of the much larger class of religious cults and social movements. If we wish to account for the cargo cult specifically, we must consider its culture-areal aspects that require psychocultural as well as economic and political explanations.

Important among these, I believe, was the contact-induced inflation of preexisting Melanesian scales of value upon which the self-esteem of groups and individuals was based. Contact meant the rapid substitution not of new values but of new scales for the old values of prestige through competitive ceremonial enterprise in undreamed of new forms and magnitudes of wealth. The value system was not replaced or undermined so much as it was overwhelmed on its own terms. By their own previous standards Melanesians were suddenly impoverished, dominated, overpowered. I call this kind of situation "value dominance"—being overcome by others in terms of one's own values. Under value dominance there is no chance of telling oneself that the wealth of the other is of no importance compared to one's own spirituality or other values. The two cultures, broadly speaking, met on the common ground of materialistic, competitive striving for prestige through entrepreneurial achievement of wealth. Parity had to be not so much achieved as acquired. The supernatural was not so much a source of spirituality as it was a partner in enterprise. The missionary, whatever he himself believed, was taken as offering access to a supernatural partnership more appropriate to the new forms and scale of wealth and power. Thus culture contact with Europeans produced a situation of *value dominance* rather than of *value com-*

plementarity or *contrast*. This change in the scale of value and assessment of personal, group, and ethnic self-esteem was a fundamental part of the radical reordering of native cosmologies. Increased experience with Europeans brought home the enormity and the stubborn coherence of the extremely diverse content of European wealth, power, and knowledge.

Melanesians had been strongly oriented toward competitive striving for prestige and status. Their system was flexible. Birth to prestigious parents was advantageous, but prestige had to be personally and continually validated by feats of individual entrepreneurship in war and ceremonial exchange, or it was dissipated. The previous gap between the wealthy or important men and the poor and unimportant was minute compared to that separating natives from Europeans. As pragmatists, Melanesians judged their own traditional institutions and forms of wealth, their art and material accomplishments, their religion and magical means against this new scale and found them wanting. Over the past ten years there has been a strong drive by the waning Australian administration and by the nationalist *avant-garde* of politically advanced Melanesians to reawaken appreciation of selected, generalized construals of Melanesian traditions. More than superficial success, I believe, will depend on the degree of satisfaction of the longing for parity through acquisition and mastery of the prestigious manifestations of the European reference culture. These very recent developments will not be given extensive treatment in this paper.

If we apply the concept of oppression to the range of cult occurrences in Melanesia, we find inconsistencies at either extreme of acculturative situations. The formulation seems appropriate enough for explaining the middle period of contact history in Melanesia, when colonists and administrators thought they were there to stay and natives thought that this was the aim of those who dominated and exploited them. But when it is applied to the least acculturated groups and to the early days of contact, when cargo cults had already appeared, the oppression theory does not seem to work at all. In some areas where cults were reported, contact had scarcely been established and pacification had not yet been accomplished. The fact of a permanent, institutionalized, forcible dominance and economic exploitation by the outside group was probably not yet anticipated.

In such cases the notion of value dominance seems more applicable than the oppression theory. One can readily conceive of cults arising both in the known cases and all over the Melanesian area even if colonial domination had not been attempted. The mere presence of Europeans and their possessions and the early contact disturbances to Melanesian beliefs and scales of values were sufficient. Oppression was not needed as a determinant. I also believe that cults would have occurred even without the exploitation of native labor and the appropriation of native land (which in many parts of New Guinea was negligible, although important in others). In some localities, people in cults lost no land. There were even cults in Manus among those who had gained land and other advantages through their manipulation of Europeans.

Recently the more acculturated natives have believed that they are being exploited. Hostility has been directed against whites and Chinese. Every outsider has been viewed, by the mere fact of his presence, as making his fortune at the expense of the native. It may even be said that sensitivity to and perception of exploitation have increased as exploitation has decreased. Yet, until recently, there was a lack of interest, even fear, among New Guinea villagers at the prospect of independence as they understood it, even when they believed it to mean that most white people (Australians in particular) would probably leave. Again, the crucial question was access to cargo. Those who did not share it were resented, but there was fear that in the absence of the white man, even the cargo now penetrating the barriers to native ownership would be cut off. Fear of reversion to intertribal warfare in the removal of the *Pax Imperii* is also general. Some recent cults and movements hoped to replace Australians by Americans; sometimes black Americans were specified. At least there was a hope that they, more than anyone, might share the secrets of the cargo.

Also evidence of the basic orientation toward cargo was the indifference in cult areas to some administrative attempts to meet grievances. Agricultural extension programs were perceived not as cargo but as a long diversion—a tactic to distract attention and deceive the native. The apparent "oppression" to which the native of the contact culture reacted was that of deception and exclusion from cargo. The idea was quite widespread that the white man holds back cargo in order that the native, having no direct access to wealth, would be forced to purchase it from the white man. Because the native was kept in poverty, he would be forced to work for the white man to pay his tax and to buy the goods which he so fervently desired. Hence the cargo and the truth of its supernatural origins was withheld for purposes of exploitation.

A similar set of arguments could be used against the adequacy of the notion that the cults were revolutionary beginnings of a protonationalism. Such generalizations are easily derived from fragmentary accounts and have their measure of validity. When more is known of what actually happens in particular cults, one can see that in the cult phase, more than at other times, there was often a reversion to particularism of native traditional political organization. In fact only in the most recent postwar Melanesian cults and movements did one observe attempts at broader political groupings extending beyond the immediate locality. These recent movements also tapped the hope for cargo, but they saw in themselves much more than cargo cults. Paliau, the leader of one such movement, tried to unite as broad a segment of population of Manus and beyond as possible. He worked at building and maintaining extra-local networks. Network building is the natural (that is, cultural) activity of any Melanesian leader, but Paliau and some of the recent leaders set about it on a "protonational" level. Their movements were able to use cult residues to advantage, but they also had the cult to contend with as a perennial competitor, short-circuiting their political and secular programs with the promise of magical fulfillment.

As they persist in competition with more politically oriented movements, cults may impede political development. The unforeseen consequences of the cult experience lead to extension of solidarity for some, but in the social area they may lead to persistent factional blocs. Political development and the formation of wider groupings may be catalyzed by a cult episode (though such an episode is not indispensable), but to continue it must transcend its cult phase.

In the cargo culture, cult and political movement were by no means strict opposites. They differed in their means—the one magical, the other programmatic and secular—but again the differences were not absolute. The movements also showed unrealistically foreshortened time perspectives. On the other hand, to further diminish the opposition of cult and movement, Melanesian cults (like Melanesian religions generally) were not other-worldly. Immediate rewards were desired in this world. The dead were to join or remain with the living here—not in another world, far removed, idealized, and depersonalized. The cargo desired was not of a traditional content. The goal of both cult and movement was a standard of living and a way of life indistinguishable from that of Europeans. Many cultists shared with movement leaders the idea that there was nothing worth preserving in native tradition. Generally the past was regarded as a matter of hard work, sickness, and death (the real or historical past, that is, not the mythological past which was just the opposite). They saw their ancestors as playing at wealth with the valueless tokens of dogs' teeth and shells, which now could not buy a bag of rice in a store. The aesthetic value of native art was devalued when compared with such wonders as a tin can or a realistic photograph, drawing, or statue.

To summarize my objection to the oppression theory, when some natives as well as some scholars have said, "It's not the cargo—it's the principle," I repeat, it's the cargo. For Melanesia, the primary issue was not, "Are you a man or a woman, a white man or a black man?" The issue was "Are you a man with a name, a man who commands wealth, or are you rubbish?" I do not deny the fact of oppression—of colonialism, racism, and exploitation—to a degree that one would wish had been otherwise. I contend, however, that had Europeans come to Melanesia and applied neither force nor control, if they had not administered Melanesians and if they had taken nothing from the land and its people, there would still have been cargo cults. It was only necessary that there be contact between Melanesians and Europeans; that Melanesians be exposed to European wealth, technology, and material culture; that natives obtain their meager sampling of the least costly and least efficacious of European goods and be exposed to all that was beyond their ability to acquire; that Melanesians be psychoculturally endowed as they were, and finally—perhaps almost as necessary to the form and content of much cult behavior and belief—that Melanesians receive from its almost unwitting European carriers the messianic, apocalyptic, and revindicative messages of Judeo-Christianity.

Relative Deprivation

We are led from theories of oppression to theories of deprivation. These may be seen as transitional between theories emphasizing external conditions for the occurrence of cargo cults and those emphasizing internal psychological states. The oppression hypothesis of either political domination, economic exploitation, or racial degradation would indicate that the cults are a response to various forms of absolute deprivation. I believe that hypotheses of such absolute deprivation must be replaced by ones emphasizing forms of *relative deprivation.* For Melanesia, any relative deprivation involving differentials of power or wealth would take the specific form of status deprivation. Stouffer (1949), Merton (1957), and others developing reference group theory found it most relevant to consider the sense of relative deprivation as crucial to situations of intergroup discontent. Aberle (1962, 1966), who in his work on peyote religion presents the most systematic development of this concept, found relative deprivation to be the salient precipitating cause of cult recruitment (see also Hofstadter, 1952; Hagen, 1962).

Ideas of relative deprivation or its subtype, status deprivation, do appear quite commonly in interpretations of cargo cults. The hypothesis that the cults are a response to the acute sense of relative deprivation presents less difficulty than the more simplistic oppression hypothesis. Various writers, Stanner and myself among them, have spoken of a perceived differential and the Melanesian need to explain and to eliminate it. As long as it persists it is intolerable, directly and profoundly damaging to the self-evaluation of the Melanesian. For him, the person without wealth had neither name nor face, neither presence nor magnitude. Such a situation of contrastive wealth could affect any people. It may be particularly acute for the Melanesian, given the general psychocultural characteristics to which we allude. For more acculturated members of the recent cults and movements, political independence without cargo would also be meaningless for these same reasons. "Oppression" is experienced in the mere existence of the great disparity of obtainable wealth.

The theory of deprivation relative to reference groups seems, then, to be one of the well-established foundations for explaining the occurrence of religious cults generally in situations of change everywhere. Value dominance, as set forth earlier in this chapter, may be seen as a condition conducive to a sense of acute relative deprivation.

Theories of Psychological Stress: Rational or Irrational Responses

Only a short step separates theories of relative social or material deprivation from those considering psychological determinants or inner psychological states. To understand a situation of deprivation, one must comprehend the inner experience of the individual, including both the immediate and long-range emotional consequences of deprivation and the adjustive or adaptive responses they elicit. Further, one must consider how experiences of deprivation are related to other aspects of psychological functioning.

A sense of deprivation is generally thought to lead to inner states of frustration and stress. There is the possibility that some of the observed behavior characteristics of cult situations is stress induced, resulting in particular forms of psychopathological breakdown or the activation of stress-abating mechanisms (Wallace, 1956). Some commentators have also pointed to the stress that might result from cognitive confusion or inconsistency. F. E. Williams (1923, 1934) speaks of the possibly irreconcilable differences in ideas coming from native and European traditions. Stanner (1958), in his ideas of crisis and resynthesis, anticipates the thinking of Anthony Wallace, whose theory I will discuss shortly.

The early European response to cargo cults was to consider them as pathological manifestations of deranged or confused minds, a kind of temporary madness. Natives themselves readily used equivalent terms to characterize the extreme behaviors of the cult in its most intense periods. The term "hysteria" has been applied frequently to cult behavior within Melanesia and throughout the world. Sargeant (1957) likened cult behavior to abreactive therapies more directly related to hysteria in the psychoanalytic sense. In contrast to the theories that view cult behavior as pathological, a number of recent theories attempt to explain cult behavior in terms of rational cognitive patterns. In the simplest of these theories, cult behavior is considered to be rational misconceptions due to incomplete knowledge of causality. Such theories are to be distinguished from cognitive theories of consistency maintenance such as those of Wallace and Festinger, which I will discuss below.

Both the simple rationalist view and the consistency theories assume that the logic of cult belief can be judged by conformity with scientific logic. The view of epistemological relativism asserts the rationality of cult belief on the grounds of its own inner logic—that it is ordered and consistent in its own terms and realistic given its own construction of reality. The questions of rationality, realism, and effectiveness are relevant to evaluating the role of cargo cults in response to culture change, contact under dominance, restoration of value parity, and the development of Melanesia toward competence in its new world involvement. From a nonrelativist point of view, I question those explanations which see the cults largely as rational responses. It is true, as James Watson aptly put it to me, that the "cargo" belief is a "theory of underdevelopment." But internal consistency or congruence with cultural premises are not sufficient tests of rationality or realism. There is also the confrontation, over time, of theory with a changing external reality.

The argument is often put in these terms: The native has a limited experience of the European productive process. He often sees nothing produced, only the finished products. He sees white men write orders, send them off, and in a few months' time the fulfillment of that order when the ship comes. The white man uncrates it and claims it, perhaps signing a receipt for it. It is rational, therefore, in an island colony that so anxiously awaits each cargo ship, for natives to be immediately attuned to cargo and to seek some similar magical access to it so that they, too, may place their orders. Such cargo beliefs are said to be consistent with native experiences of discrimination and with native cosmological postulates. The view of the cults as rational explanation is obviously a partial truth.

To see the irrational component we must examine Melanesian postulates and experience, understanding that they are constructed from an external reality and are not simply a reflection of that reality. Experience of the world is, of course, culturally mediated. It may be "consistent" in terms of native canons of consistency, allowing for expressive functions of reality constructs in which ambiguity and inconsistency play a role. One cannot ignore the autistic shaping of explanations so as to leave some hope for instantaneous gratification in the form of wealth. We must further point out the persistence of belief in the face of accumulating counter-evidence. The cargo belief persists despite the acculturation process over years of increasing understanding of European technology. The persistence of belief varies in duration among individuals and groups, as indicated in my earlier discussion of recruitment. It is not interminable. When such features are examined, it is no longer useful to speak only of the rational component of cult belief.

In Manus, natives experienced more than eighty years of intensive contact. They worked in all manner of European enterprise; they at least observed many acts of on-site construction from imported materials and many of direct fabrication (as they did, for example, during World War II at the American installations), and many worked as helpers and mechanics or became clerks with some understanding of the ordering process. Over that time span, education, sophistication, overseas travel, and urban experience increased steadily. Recently many families could count among their near relatives some who gained previously inaccessible positions in the country's management. Here the persistence of cult beliefs *cannot* be seen simply as a rational construction of all the information available. The premises and postulates themselves were wish-constructed to make seemingly possible that which was so ardently desired. Native views of the past, present, and future of their culture and of Europeans were a series of constructs into each of which entered elements of experience, or perceived reality shaped by need and wish, rather than by a purely problem solving, instrumental attitude.

The question is often asked, Why do people persist in the face of the repeated failures of their cults? One answer is that they do not all persist. The recurrent series of cults in Manus among the same peoples showed a progressive shrinkage of active membership, some corrective tendencies, and avoidance of some of the pitfalls of the earlier cults. Nevertheless, they remained recognizably the same basic strategy even though fewer and fewer were recruited with each successive round. One might say that the threshold of recruitment rose steadily for the cults. In the first cult, virtually everyone was swept along within the affected villages, at least for a brief period. In the second, third, and fourth episodes, fewer and fewer joined. Probably as the threshold of recruitment rose, personality variables became more and more significant as the selective factor for cult recruitment. The person who was "in" and the one who was "out," however, were not necessarily different. Each was, in a sense, acting for the other. Each was ambivalently convinced of his position but also dogged by the possibility that the other might be right, and he was ready to switch if things started to go the other way. There were also important social-historical factors in the differential persistence of a shrinking cult. In Manus, the locale of the most stubborn cult persistence was also the point of its origin. These groups had, perhaps, the greatest stake in the cult and a sense of being its custodians.

Cognitive Inconsistency and Stress

Several current explanations of various aspects of cargo cults are based on theories about the effects of cognitive inconsistency. It is usually assumed that traditional cultures change relatively slowly and are characterized by the relatively consistent and mutually supportive ideas, values, and expectations of the members of a society. Under the impact of rapid, externally induced culture change, this consistency is thought to be increasingly replaced by inconsistent, incoherent, and conflicting sets of ideas, values, and expectations.

Wallace and Festinger are the most influential proponents of theories of cognitive inconsistency. Wallace assumes that increasing cognitive inconsistency leads to conditions of internal stress. Stress triggers a creative resynthesis in an individual who then becomes a cult prophet. This resynthesis produces a new, consistent set of cognitions for the individual and a reordered, consistent set of cultural constructs for the group. Festinger's theory employs the concept of cognitive dissonance and its resolution. He argues that given the necessary failure of cult prophesy, there are cognitive mechanisms that reduce the dissonance between continued hope of success and the fact of failure. Belief may then persist even though confronted by contradictory experience.

Wallace's use of consistency theory, with its assumed operation of physiological stress mechanisms as an explanation of a wide range of cult phenomena (Wallace, 1956), is well argued. But it seems dubious to me on the basis of my experience with the Manus cults. As Wallace sees it, the generally stressful situation in some members of a group is resolved by a crisis that provides an abrupt resynthesis; the process is aided by underlying physiological mechanisms that may be accompanied by such extreme symptoms as convulsions or coma. There is an unscrambling of what he terms the "cognitive mazeway." The individual achieves a consistent new view of the world by means of the dream or prophetic vision; he or she thereby becomes a cult leader. The individual may envision a new cosmology, a new plan of life, or new interpretation of group meaning that is satisfying and consistent, and includes a program for concerted action. According to Wallace, in this process there are marked alterations of personality in the prophet, for whom the crisis is an internal event. These events are part of a restorative sequel to crisis.

In my own studies of cults, I came to doubt this theory as a general reconstruction of the psychocultural processes in religious responses to change. The social and ideological reformulation by Paliau, and by other, more strictly cult-type leaders was a long, continuous process; it was not achieved via some single visionary episode, in spite of the fact that the cult myths commemorated such an episode. The seeming appearance of cognitive discontinuity—of a new ideology sprung suddenly from a moment of prophetic inspiration or revelation—comes from the dramatic forms used to communicate new schemes in a cult context. Such communication had to take the expected outer form of prophetic utterance as dream or vision, and it had to be properly validated by having the appearance of supernatural origin.

In the revelations of a cult, the prophet—the medium, the dreamer, or the visionary—invariably claimed that he spoke not for himself, but that supernatural powers spoke through him. The cult leader claimed to be a passive instrument favored only as a fit receptacle or transmitter of revelation. He used culturally prescribed forms of communication that previously had emerged from the contact culture to validate his claim to possession or revelation. This evolving contact culture, not the reconstructed traditional culture, was the relevant cultural system.

The dreams were not necessarily reported as they were dreamt, nor were they necessarily dreamt at all. In Manus, much was made of dreams in the cults. Incoherent dreams were rejected as uninteresting; true dreams were reported as long, discursive, coherent revelations. On hearing such dream narrations, one realizes that the dream or vision was long in preparation and finds its moment in the telling, not in the dreaming. Other cult formulations or syntheses were communicated through dramatized "deaths and resurrections," "speaking in tongues," and still others through seance.

I question, in the cult context, Wallace's contention that such extreme behaviors as convulsion, coma, and personality alteration are directly stress-induced and the result of chemico-physiological mechanisms. The situation of rapid culture change, of assimilation of a flood of new experience, of relative status deprivation, and especially the overwhelming of native standards of self-esteem should indeed be stressful, but this is an assumption. Current stress levels in the potential cult populations may be no greater or even less than in traditional precontact cultures. Melanesians with whom I have worked consider their lives easier and more secure than those of their grandparents. The end of native warfare and raiding, the establishment of a variety of new means of conflict resolution, and the availability of medical services have reduced stress. In general, assumptions about stress levels remain inferences without reliable grounds. They are possibly cross-cultural projections of presumptive rather than measured stress, and they ignore known cultural factors for hypothetical biological ones.

It would be of little use for us to infer stress from the cargo cults and then to explain them by it. I see little behavioral evidence of stress levels sufficient to precipitate an endocrinologically mediated crisis that would effect a cognitive resynthesis in some key individual. Nor do I think that the individual makes the cult. Too much attention is centered on the figure of the prophet or cult leader. The cult leader is shaped not only by his personal qualities, but by the response that he receives and the accuracy with which he times and shapes performance to the needs of his audience. He is a social fantasy producer and as such he is demand-oriented.

Pathomimetic Behavior

It is too easy to mistake the culturally required forms of cult behavior for the pathological equivalents on which they may have been patterned. Wallace has taken at face value the pathogenic nature of such behavior. The behavior I have observed in Melanesian cargo cults might more appropriately be termed "pathomimetic" (imitating pathological symptoms) in contrast to "pathogenic" (resulting from actual neurophysiological pathology). Some of the extreme behaviors observed in cults are *modeled* on pathogenic behaviors that occur under other circumstances. However, the coma and convulsive seizures appearing in the cults do not require that the enacting participant be either epileptic or under extreme stress. On the other hand, he may be self-selected—as well as group-selected—for that role as an expression and perhaps resolution of other neurotic or psychotic tendencies.

Cult "symptomatology" often exhibited features that contradicted the physiological, stress-mediated explanation and that pointed instead to culturally regulated behavior, which was expected and appropriately enacted. Convulsive seizures, shaking, trembling, and other aberrant body movements were invariably associated with the idea of possession. In the possessed state, the person was believed to be controlled by an ego-alien being, spirit, force, or powerful psychoactive substance. The person therefore was not responsible; it was not he, in fact, who was acting. Other culturally stereotyped behaviors of possession emerged, such as "speaking in tongues," mute speech, or charadelike behaviors. Seemingly marked alteration of personality validated possession, inspiration, or at least supernatural sponsorship. The person possessed was expected to show marked behavioral alterations—it was said that his eyes looked different, that he was a new man. He carried himself differently and dressed differently; he presumed to speak when he might not otherwise have spoken. He was accorded unusual respect and authority for as long as it lasted. In short, he behaved as a person assuming another role, with marked discontinuity from his habitual roles. If he was possessed, it was what I would call "role possession."

Hysteria, in its classic sense and symptoms of ego dissociation, can probably be included in this class of pathomimetic behavior. The observer cannot, in most instances, determine the degree of ego dissociation involving repressed awareness of ego control over the behavior, and perhaps repression of ego control itself. In cults, individuals manifesting the same behavior can vary widely in the degree to which the mechanism of repression is involved. This range extends from instances of (1) conscious "sham" involving collusion of the whole group, and in which the signs of validation of the cult belief are rigged; through (2) conscious or unconscious acting-out of culturally defined cult behavior, as in acting-out under "possession"; to (3) trance or autohypnosis. Assumptions about altered ego states generally have a methodological indeterminancy, in that present methods of field observation cannot help us resolve the actual state of the person observed; further, the nature of trance or hypnosis remains itself uncertain. In my judgment, what I observed is most readily accounted for by the second degree of dissociation operating in behavior at the levels of awareness that are most usual in culturally patterned behavior. The behaviors in question are defined as extraordinary. But the extraordinary is itself a cultural category of behavior, culturally marked and patterned. Pathomimetic behaviors, often dramatic and extreme, are not necessarily signs of social disorganization or breakdown, and they need not be external manifestations of acute stress or other abnormal physiological states. Although such behaviors may be modeled on actual pathogenic behavior resulting from disease, intoxication, or other abnormal physiological states, they become institutionalized behaviors detached from the pathogenic behaviors that might have suggested them.

For Melanesians, and possibly for all traditional cultures, the pathogenic and the pathomimetic are connected as reciprocals. A pathogenic behavior such as convulsion occurs occasionally, perhaps as the result of epilepsy or cerebral malaria. The symptoms are inherently frightening and dramatic. The pathogenic convulsions are interpreted in terms of possession. For example, in one Manus case they were seen as the spirit of a ghost trying to shake the "soul-stuff" out of a person. Under other circumstances, a person (or group) needing to believe he was possessed or the victim of a ghost would manifest pathomimetic convulsions of a sort which were acceptable to his group as validating his claim to possession. Displaying such symptoms might mark a claim to status in the cult, in the community, or as an object of therapy, depending on the situation.

It should be clear that by pathomimesis I am not suggesting simple sham or malingering. Sham may occur, but usually it is a kind of collusion between actor and audience, with a submerged or studied unawareness of this collusion on both sides. When possession is desired or required as validation of a claimed link to supernatural forces, pathomimetic symptoms are produced and culturally expected as signs with magical instrumentality. Cultists believe that pathomimetic behavior validates the reality or realizability of their goals and view it as a sign of (and therefore as helping to bring about) the nearness or interest of the supernatural agencies.

Cult symptomatic behavior does not occur without its cultural precedents. Melanesians generally became well aware of what behavior was expected when one finally had one's own cargo cult. Those who assumed the special roles in cults were the producers of social fantasy.

They were audience-oriented in their performances. The appearance and the acting out of pathomimetic behaviors depended upon the appropriate audience response. Even sham, as mentioned above, was collusive. No one was upset when it was revealed that it was not the spirits but the leader of a Manus cult who was ringing the bell in the spirit church (he used a concealed cord). There was no anger or feeling of betrayal. His position did not seem to be at all impaired by the exposure, which simply spoiled one good device for bringing men into contact with the spirits.

Some of the behaviors of cult symptomatology were supported in and perhaps derived from Christian beliefs. Cargo cults were often referred to throughout Papua New Guinea as "guria," a term applied to earthquakes, convulsions, or shaking of any kind. The "guria" of the apostles at Pentecost was well known to Melanesian Christians, and "death and resurrection" had its obvious precedent. It became a recurrent means of bringing the word from the land of the dead. Cultists also knew the Christian precedents for "speaking in tongues," for visions and possession by spirits, and for return of the dead en masse. Cultists showed me a woodcut in the Pidgin English catechism of the Roman Catholic Mission. It portrayed a cemetery with four angels blowing trumpets over the graves, and skeletons of the dead arising from their graves and assembling themselves (one with its skull in its hands, about to place it on its shoulders). Missionaries often became disconcerted when native converts believed and emulated quite literally, though selectively, what the missionary taught in his ritualized recitations. Clearly there was a direct infusion of Judeo-Christian messianic and apocalyptic ideas. Wilson Wallis (1943) traced the effects of this diffusion on religious cults around the world. There are obviously shifts of meaning in the transfer of ideas. The "delivery" that the Melanesians sought was not the one offered by the missionary. But aside from direct diffusion, there was also a parallelism, a resonance, between Melanesian beliefs and the premises that survive in modern religions from the early Christian cult (and its Judaic and earlier antecedents). Cultists seized upon those Christian elements that they recognized, both as suggestive models and as rationalizations supporting their own beliefs and wishes.

The Metastable State

A cult in its most heightened phase of expectation of imminent fulfillment, is in what I term a "metastable state" for both the group and for individuals. A metastable state of a system is one which it enters under special conditions of heightened levels of excitation. It is not "abnormal" but rather "allonormal" in the sense of being a potential, alternative state of that system rather than a breakdown or decompositional state.

Similarly, I view a culture as having a number of potential metastable, alternative states. The more extreme cult behaviors serve to evoke or to sustain the metastable cult state.

A metastable state tends to be transient. The required levels of excitation are difficult to maintain. The metastable cult state is reduced or incomplete in comparison to the normal state of the culture, in that some of the activities that normally sustain life over the long run may be suspended, awaiting the expected moment in which they will be obviated once and for all. In the normal state, magic is used to supplement otherwise effective activities such as gardening; in the metastable state, all activities become ritualized as magical means to the cult goals. The magic takes the rare substitutive rather than the normal supplementary form. Obviously the cult could not be maintained for long in this extreme metastable state. The very extremity of this reduced metastable state of the culture is itself a means to the cult's fulfillment through the magic of overcommitment, rendering nonfulfillment almost—but not quite—unthinkable. This state is a kind of "high" which, when it collapses, swings into a "low" state. In both Manus and in New Hanover I observed a depressed state in which sustenance activities were minimally resumed while village maintenance and other normal activities were neglected. The normal state, of which the cult state may be a latent component, is gradually restored.

Various allonormal, metastable states may be entered, depending on the level of certain variables such as expectation, morale, intoxication, commitment, and autistic intensity of the need to believe. Regardless of its failure to produce the cargo, the cult-state itself was so rewarding that the residual cultist became addicted to attempts to revive and relive its excitement. Although over time the level of excitement gradually diminished, the cult still continued as potential, offering intense feelings of hope and hostility, a self-righteous sense of election, unity, and solidarity within the group. It offered new opportunities for leadership and many distinctive roles. Finally, it offered the possibility of sudden fulfillment of inflated expectations and goals as an alternative to the long, difficult, economic development on the work-save-invest-educate formula offered by Europeans which seemed to have an uncertain outcome. The cult state itself acquired an expressive function that substituted for the actual instrumental fulfillment of its desired goal—the obtaining of cargo.

Cognitive Dissonance: The Functions of Ambivalence in the Metastable State

A number of other consistency theories appeared in the literature on Melanesia prior to Wallace; in the main they emphasized cognitive confusion. F. E. Williams, for example, attributed the so-called Vailala Madness in part to what he called "confusion of ideas" stemming from difficulty in assimilating a mixture of new and old ideas into a consistent scheme (1923, 1934). Williams also blamed missionary teachings for introducing ideas that confused the natives. What was most often embarrassing about the missionary ideas was not that the natives did not understand them, but that the missionaries themselves had not understood them.

Cross-labeling of the literal and the figurative was operative on both sides. Missionaries often presented in sermons what they thought they believed literally, only to find that when their ideas were taken literally by their new converts, it was evident that they themselves had been taking them figuratively all along. When natives repeated them and particularly when they acted upon them, the missionaries found that their teachings had not been taken as they intended. Natives just did not realize that such things as equality under God, the day of judgment, the redemptive promises of Revelations, and exhortations about the imminence of the Second Coming were not to be acted upon in the immediate present. Similarly, much that the missionary presented literally (or so he believed) was taken figuratively by native converts and was subject to reinterpretation in order to find the meaning beneath the apparent meaning, the truth beneath the surface of concealment. Finally, one might say that for the native, particularly the relatively unacculturated native, the entire world that he glimpsed around and through the white man was taken not as literal but as a new mythical cosmology, imbued throughout with magico-ritual potential. Thus, European mythology was literalized and European reality was made figurative, as an unreal or supernatural realm. The problem of native orientation to the unreal-real world around him was often one of overconsistency and premature consistency—of a reality shaped by his needs to compensate for and to overcome a hopeless envy of the European.

Generally, for Melanesians all discourse had both literal meanings and covert meaning and intention. This resulted in a "multilevel consciousness" (usually dual) which allowed for the coexistence of two or more levels of potential meaning or intention. The parties to communication might choose which level the speaker intended and the hearer understood. As a simple example, a man who argued for the removal of trees in the village cemetery might have been implicitly urging that his village participate in the most recent cult. Others might have opposed the tree removal, intending opposition to the cult. Still others who, given past commitments, could not admit their cult leanings, could argue for tree removal, submerging their support of cult participation while maintaining it in the exchange. A leader could speak on one level and be heard on the other in spite of his wish to control the level on which he was heard. This type of dual-level consciousness provides a perceived and often manipulated ambiguity that can be serviceable in adaptation.

Are consistency theorists correct in their assumption that thought and belief invariably strive toward consistency? To the contrary, there is much to indicate a useful, on-going social and psychological function for ambivalence, ambiguity, and dissonance. Festinger's theory of dissonance reduction attempts to explain the persistence of cults in the face of failure of their prophecies. He contends that when a cult is challenged by some obviously contradictory evidence, a dissonance occurs between the assertions of cult prophecy and the disconfirmatory evidence. Several things could happen: the cult belief could be dropped, the disconfirmatory evidence could be denied, or the dissonance could be tolerated. The disconfirmation can be rationalized or denied and the belief reaffirmed through various activities such as a renewed, more vigorous proselytizing.

Yet, one might argue that what occurs is not necessarily dissonance reduction. Cult persistence and the activities of which cults largely consist may not depend on dissonance reduction but instead may require its maintenance. The situation is more complex than suggested by Festinger's theory. Increased recruiting and the affirmatory and belief-validating activity that constitute much of the life of a cult can be cited as evidence of persisting dissonance, not its reduction. Most cults die, perhaps all when disconfirmation is overwhelming or repeated. But they would be dead in another sense if dissonance were effectively eliminated by dismissing the disconfirmations provided by failure of predicted events, or by repressing doubt in the consciousness of the believer. Affirmations of all sorts, the building of the case for belief, apologetics against real or implied adversaries, rituals of validation, the hedging of bets that shows up subtly in cults when belief seems firmest, the very fervor of commitment and overcommitment—all are evidences of the Janus figure of doubt and belief, of suspicion and credulity. Where there is an alternative to belief and to a wholly cult-committed life, as there was in the relations between religious cult and political movement in parts of Melanesia, there may be a slow oscillation in which the focal and subfocal levels of consciousness invert through a number of cycles. For some, often the generators of cults—possessed, so to speak, by the cult and by their role in it as the only possible way of being—there is no alternative and no inversion. Their struggle to maintain belief goes on indefinitely.

When cults persist, there may be some dissonance reduction in the process of routinization. The cult may have been modified to avoid disconfirmation (for example, by avoiding the naming of a particular date on which the cargo was to arrive). Such modification has several effects for the cultist. It avoids a confrontation that might risk termination of the cult. Cultists may institute controls limiting revelation or create ritual preparations that will never be complete or sufficient. Such measures anticipate and avoid the inevitable disconfirmation.

Such avoidance, at the same time, diminishes commitment. It lessens the effectiveness of the expressive magic of overcommitment that operates by making failure unthinkable. Correcting for errors also means being reconciled to cult behavior at a lower level of excitement, falling short of the heights of the metastable cult-state. There is ambivalence between the brief heightened excitement of the metastable cult-state and the prolonged hope and moderated excitement of a routinized cult-state en route to a perpetuable religion. The function of much of cult behavior is not necessarily to lessen dissonance or to overcome ambivalence. Rather it is to assure a certain level of persisting ambivalence that sustains cult excitement and activity, which becomes an end in itself.

In the Melanesian cults, there were patterns of behavior indicating the coexistence of belief and doubt in the consciousness of cultists. Contrary to Festinger's formulation, this dualism existed from the inception of the cult, not just at and beyond the point of failure of prophecy. In fact, *some features of cult behavior helped generate and maintain a level of dissonance essential to the higher levels of activity and excitement.* I have described some typically occurring features of cargo cults as "conspicuous secrecy," "ritual skepticism," and the generation and maintenance of opposition (Schwartz, 1962). Secrecy was used to recruit as well as to exclude, and skepticism was implicitly required of some entering cultists as part of the ritual of conversion to renew and attest to the dissonance on which the drama of conversion depended. Cultists not only recruited to add confirmation through additional numbers of believers; they also excluded and elicited opposition in order to add dissonance and oppositional segmentation which was necessary to their own morale and the maintenance of a high level of affirmative activity. While excluding some, they recruited others to form the larger interdependent system of which cult and opposition were both essential parts. For the majority in the Paliau Movement area, perhaps more than for others who declared the cults wrong from their inception, it finally became evident that the cult belief was not an efficacious means to cargo. Yet, for the former believers the idea is still attractive. They still feel the pull to levels of hope and feeling which the cult offered.

When cults persist, we are dealing in part with an addiction to expressive feeling states that contrast with the pallid lack of feeling or depressed feeling of plateau and drift states. For some Melanesians, the cult fixation was a counterdepressant. Hostility, even more than hope, may have been the dominant feeling of the cult phases. The hostility was directed in two ways: abstractly and ambivalently at the white man, who monopolized the cargo; and intensely and concretely at the noncult or anticult native, who was thought to spy, report, ridicule, and generally endanger the fulfillment of the cult. Government attempts to meet the public grievances and demands of cultists were met with resistance or apathy, not only because immediate access to cargo was not offered, but because such measures weakened the grievances and threatened the hostility that had greater value as feeling and as, perhaps, the main basis for the maintenance of cult solidarity.

Another basis for the fixation of some individuals in the cult is the personal gratification derived from the temporary exaltation of status. There was often a status inversion, such as women or adolescents becoming leaders, which was possible as long as the cult persisted. Those individuals who remained cult-oriented longer were frequently lower status or potentially higher status persons lacking either traditional or modern legitimacy. Just as the cult-fixated person may be described as "role possessed," the cultist without a cult is in a state of "role mourning."

PSYCHOCULTURAL FACTORS RELATED TO CHANGE: THE PARANOID ETHOS

I shall now consider the fourth category of theoretical explanations—how Melanesian psychocultural factors contributed to the occurrence and content of cargo cults. Melanesians were not simply responding to the circumstances of a contact situation and to the other conditions that contributed to the determination of cult occurrence. They were responding in terms of a distillation of past experiences arising out of determinative situations called culture. Cultural determinants are the learned continuities of past experience as well as the derivatives of culturally and situationally patterned experiences formed by each individual from the events making up his life history. Because the cargo cult was a Melanesia-wide phenomenon, strictly local cultural differences cannot bear weight in explanations of the general form and occurrence of the cults. The sociocultural factors involved must have been generally characteristic of Melanesia or at least widely recurrent. These cultural features are presented in the context of the justification of my argument that a paranoid ethos pervaded Melanesian cultures. I do not assert that the paranoid ethos or institutionalized paranoia was the cause of cargo cult occurrences. The ethos is part of the cultural context in which such cult occurrences were precipitated and within which they made sense to emotionally and cognitively attuned participants. The paranoid ethos, then, was a part of the nexus of causation of cults along with such causes as value dominance.

The paranoid ethos was not peculiar to Melanesia. It depended on universal psychological mechanisms. The intensity of expression of the paranoid ethos varies cross-culturally and from one historical phase of a culture to the next. One hopes its influence in Melanesian cultures is now diminishing in the course of recent acculturation, education, and modernization.

The paranoid ethos in Melanesia was related to many factors: the uncertainty of life, the high mortality rates, low longevity, high birthrate, and low survival rate for children. It was related to the uncertainty of the yield of productive activities in spite of technologies ingeniously diversified, within evolutionary and environmental limits. Perhaps most fundamental was its relationship to certain characteristic features of Melanesian culture: to the extreme atomism of social and political life, to the constancy and omnidirectionality of warfare and the fragility of all alliances, to the uncertainty even of village and clan solidarity. These ecological and cultural factors were all interrelated. They had to be conceptualized by Melanesians within a unified world view—a cosmology of animate and personal causation.

I venture this statement of a paranoid ethos, highly aware of the difficulties so often noted in using terms with psychopathological implications to characterize whole societies, let alone entire culture areas. Belief systems cannot be explained entirely on the basis of a rational calculus of experience. The social scientist who attempts such an explanation is rationalizing on behalf of the people he is studying because he takes the irrational as pejorative. But such an explanation does not have an invidious implication when the irrational is considered a potential component of all human behavior. The paranoid ethos, although culturally variable, has probably been characteristic of human experience through much of its history.[11]

The paranoid ethos that colored the world view of the Melanesian was intricately built on a structure of realism and autism, suspicion and credulity, fear and hostility, sensitivity to the intention and submerged meanings of others, fluency in layered discourse. In the resulting behavioral environment, realism or fantasy made little difference as far as the inner life of the person in the group was concerned. Persons alleged to have employed sorcery may or may not actually have taken magical steps against the injured person. Every sick man was believed to be an injured person—a victim of attack. Potential malice was felt to be almost omnipresent, beyond the narrow circles of relative trust within one's own lineage and affinal network. The effect was the same: each man's suspicion and hostile defense was justified. Projections might find some confirmation in actual interpersonal hostility, but nevertheless they remained projections. But even where there was ever present hostility, attack by sorcery, and, before pacification, the very real dangers of physical attack, the projected presence of enemies was subject to overgeneralization. It was a variable made constant—a principle that scarcely could be relaxed.

It is characteristic of a paranoid ethos that suspicion and cognitive rejection are coupled with extreme credulity. One is the obverse of the other, and under sufficient autistic pressure there is almost a reversal of the laws of evidence as we conceive them. The improbable is taken as probable, or certain, and the probable is rejected as a lie. These patterns became particularly visible in heightened states of Melanesian cults. They were a feature of normal life as well. In the cargo cult, the most improbable rumors or prophetic utterances running counter to native experience were accepted from persons who in a normal state would not be respected or given credence. Increasing disconfirmatory evidence could be readily rejected.

Just as credulity and suspicion are conjoined aspects of a single process, the perception by an individual or group of being the object of benevolent forces or beings is the positive counterpart of the negative perception of malevolence. The positive and negative aspects of paranoid perception have in common the delusion of self-reference. The behavioral universe is perceived as being focused on oneself, one's group, one's time. The perceptions "They are all out to harm us" but "God is on our side" may equally be delusions of reference—negative and positive paranoia usually fused into a single belief system.

The self is projected outward and reflected back in the form of persons, beings, and forces that embody one's hopes and fears. Such projected perceptions may reflect or distort, shape or be constrained by external reality. The relation between internal and external reality is, therefore, complex; it is variable across individuals and situations, and profoundly conditioned by culture.

There are many features of Melanesian culture that may have related to this paranoid ethos. I do not mean that the relationship is in one direction. Social structure is effected by the transmission, the inculcation, the ideological institutionalization of such an ethos. At the same time the social structure defines certain conditions which justify, gratify, condition, and prepare the individual to respond within this ethos.

Melanesian Cultural Features and Adaptive Practices

There are probably many other aspects of a Melanesian ethos to which I should give equal weight; exactly how they are integrated I could not specify. Traits such as "materialism" are often cited. Materialism, a concern with trade and exchange, a deep concern with wealth and invidious consumption or use of wealth are well known and are attributed by most commentators to Melanesian cultures generally. The term "entrepreneur" is commonly applied to Melanesians, who have been called the "capitalists" of the Pacific. References are made to the Puritan Ethic among Melanesians. McClelland (1961) has noted the high need-achievement and individualism of Melanesians, while others from a Marxist background have thought they saw a kind of proto-class society, an intra-societal oppression (Worsley, 1968). The openness and vigor of the Melanesian response to contact I have discussed elsewhere. One might go further to say that they are not merely open, but prehensile in orientation. Their wish to appropriate, to make their own, is intense.

One feature that I think is crucial to Melanesia is local multiethnicity. In relatively small areas, a large number of different languages associated with various degrees of cultural differentiation appear. But above all, such groups defined by linguistic differences and certain emblematic cultural features are, in effect, ethnic groups having a sense of commonality and usually a presumed, though untraceable, common origin and descent. The ethnic group tends to be predominantly endogamous, but there is a significant proportion of strategic scattering of marriages among other ethnic groups particularly across ecological lines that have an operational economic significance. As indicated, the differences of which people make much may seem minor to the outsider, but they seem greater, perhaps, to the native viewed against the scale of internal differentiation to which the peoples of a single areal culture, such as the Admiralties, are accustomed.

Local ethnic groups are not politically organized. They are not tribes in a political sense. Their one function, other than the probability of endogamous marriages and common language that I found in the Admiralties, was that of exophagy, "eating out" in the days of cannibalism. There was no barrier to warfare within the ethnic group. The rivalry of entrepreneurs made it likely that no cultural innovation entering the group would, in the short run at least, be diffused to the entire group. Differentiation was in itself a value. Would-be leaders have had to make a place for themselves by splitting some subgroup off from the village and beginning to establish a distinctive identity for that group. Relatively small degrees of dialect differentiation have been seized upon to create named dialect groups. Geographical distance was often insignificant compared to the self-created social separations. Such was the atomism and particularism of Melanesia that instead of the development of widespread interlanguages, multilingualism prevails. People know the surrounding languages and are sensitive to differences. They are able to furnish remarkably self-conscious statements of phonological and lexical correspondences.

The importance of Melanesian multiethnicity may be seen in contrast with Polynesia, where each subarea or island group represents an essentially monoethnic development with the retention of ties among groups as they grew and spread. I believe the common Melanesian experience of multiethnicity, of living within a mosaic of related as well as differentiated cultures profoundly conditioned Melanesian attitudes toward culture, that is, toward the perceived and abstracted behavior patterns which Melanesians associate with their own and other groups. They recognize the separability of culture, as a form of property, from race and/or genealogy. They recognize its transferability and at the same time its exclusiveness under informal patenting, licensing, and transfer arrangements. Whole ceremonial complexes and most of another group's art may be adopted to replace what previously existed. They recognize modifiability and associate innovation with entrepreneurship, leadership, and prestige. Such self-conscious awareness contributes to the general Melanesian openess to cultural importation and thus to the prehensile attitude toward change in the contact situation.

Ceremonies and magical or curative procedures can be transferred with some exchange of tokens that are a part of a larger cultural transfer deal involving return payments. In the case of cargo, a total transfer is desired. Melanesians seem to realize that the cargo—the property, the knowledge, the styles, the way of life of Europeans—requires a massive material transfer beyond the level that natives have as yet attained.

The Melanesian area manifests a preadaptation to change. Melanesians must often conceal from themselves a nostalgia for the past, particularly strong at certain stages of cults. The longing for reunion with the ancestors that is almost universal in the cults is stated as a longing on the part of the ancestors for a reunion with the living and for participation in modern life. The dead who will return are not like those who died: they are updated and upgraded; they have been Europeanized; they may even be white; they will come as the crews of ships and planes and as the masters of European technology. The past can be preserved only when it comes clothed in modernity and bearing cargo.

Networks and the Traveling Wave of Wealth Assemblage

It is particularly characteristic and important in the political structure of Melanesian societies and in the nature of leadership that a leader is a network builder. His relations are established through trade, marriage, and ceremonial exchange over a wide area. He builds his own potential for entrepreneurial feats by the building of others' obligation to him. Through the distribution of unstoreable goods, he accumulates storeable obligations. At the same time, he must handle relations with his public, a coherent group of supporters surrounding his own lineage and his network. He is used to the handling of complexly managed and timed affairs, so that many stored obligations will be redeemable simultaneously for the really big validating feasts and exchanges on which his leadership is based. Melanesian society motivates many to strive for the higher reaches of the prestige hierarchy. It trains and values aggression, verbal and oratorical skills, skills in war and exchange, and skill in technology. Such leaders are generally all-around men rather than narrow specialists. The legendary leaders of the early contact or precontact times, upon whose model the current leader is based, were men of ferocity, bigger than life, polygamists with many wives, many offspring, and extraordinarily ramified affinal exchange ties.

Throughout this area, in spite of the prevalence of warfare, the instability of alliances, the common history of villages split by acts of violence to make war among themselves, one finds this extraordinary network of trade, of specialization, even of warfare and aggressive relations which integrate large areal cultures. Various modes of relationship were cultivated to provide means for safe conduct for trading. These included kinship, cross-ethnic marriage, trade parternerships, and even the possession of common totemic names. All such channels were *unreliable.* Markets often became massacres, as did feasts to which important men over large areas were invited. War and trade and marriage existed in unstable oscillation. All junctures of normal intercourse were tempting opportunities for the entrepreneur to add to his list of feats and to even the past scores of others.

Concepts of wealth and consumption also relate to the ethos I am sketching. While the wealth is hard and material, nonmaterial traits are also treated as hardware; that is, they are negotiable. Wealth measured in terms of the largest accumulations that native society attained was not something that ever stood still. It moved in complex patterns along the overlapping networks of an integrative system, like a traveling wave now on this node of the thread of networks, now on another—not the same accumulation on any two nodes. Each time, a new assemblage is brought into being by one particular dealing of an entrepreneur and his dependents. This was the characteristic pattern of condensation and dispersion of large quantities of amassed wealth for public distributions. It was not the possession of wealth—a hoard in one's house—that marked the wealthy man, but the wealth that passed through his hands. Characteristically, in fact, he did not dare to store very much of this in his own possession. With property, there was a great concern about theft, and the malicious destruction of property both directly and in magical theft and damage was frequent. Property-attracting charms, and counter-magic against theft are still extremely common in Melanesia. Certain crops have recently been abandoned in Manus due to pests or other blights. This abandonment is attributed to the damage done by the evil eye of envious village mates and passers-by from other villages.

In attitudes toward work, most characteristically, there is a steady pace of individual chores. Few people may be found to spend an idle day, but work requiring considerable effort tends to be done sporadically rather than on a steady basis, and very often on a cooperatively communal basis. These peaks of work, and the exchange of work which accumulates these peaks, resemble again the condensation-dispersion cycle of the traveling wave of wealth in the exchange network. There are mythological fantasies in the Admiralties about a work-free existence that preceded native versions of the Fall of Man, the time before the violation of a totemic taboo or some other act of spoiling a good thing. I am not sure how widely represented they might be in Melanesia. A surprisingly large range of human activities are termed "work," so that one is led to think of an effort syndrome. This is probably widespread, to judge from the reflexes of this pattern in Pidgin English. Ceremonial exchange in all of its phases is "work"; even sexual intercourse and the production of babies, which requires multiple inseminations to fill the womb, is considered to be very hard work. It gradually consumes the male, contributing to his aging and decline. In the light of these conceptions of "work," the attractiveness of the no-work cargo state is evident.

SOCIALIZATION, KINSHIP, AND OTHER FEATURES

The question "Whom can one trust?" may be instructively directed at any culture. For Melanesia the reply generally was only the family or lineage of traceable consanguines. Rivalry among actual siblings of the same sex was muted. The tie to siblings of opposite sex—one might say the principle of solidarity of siblings of opposite sex—was dominant in many Melanesian societies, as it was perhaps in most unilineal societies. Through these ties of opposite sex a man had, in his sisters, the most important economic allies who would strive to elicit the rewards his affines owed him. The dispersed progeny of the outmarrying sex were allies, crucial nodes in exchange networks and potential recruits back to the group. The characteristic social form for Melanesia was the augmented unilineage; it constituted the reliable support group for the individual. This had a unilineal core in principle, with whatever additions that could be recruited through adoption, competitive recruiting, or even capture.

In the socialization process, males characteristically took important nurturant roles toward their children, particularly with their sons. Disciplinary, initiatory, and ceremonial roles were often displaced upon other relatives, or discipline was shifted from the living to the dead. Misfortune, illness, or death was interpreted as censure for some specific moral infraction—as disciplinary sanctions meted out by the ghosts of the lineage.

The child generally spent much of its preadolescent and early adolescent life in the play group, in an environment of minimal discipline. There was little rigidity in feeding and bowel training patterns. Weaning practices varied considerably among ethnic groups without seeming to effect the paranoid ethos. The frequency of adoption led to multiple and diffuse attachments. Genealogical reckoning was a matter of great flexibility. Certain formalisms of the kinship system were preserved even though relationships were restructured (aside from core incest prohibitions) whenever it was convenient to do so. Multiple attachments permitted the possibility of taking any number of ego positions in an overall genealogy.

Spiro (1967), in explaining Burmese patterns of suspiciousness, hostility, and projection that might well have been termed a paranoid ethos, stressed the importance of the child's sense of parental rejection in the transition from infancy to childhood. (See also Hitson, 1959.) While a variable degree of discontinuity in socialization occurring at this point is probably universal, it was not acute for Manus. There, when the next child was born the father, the community, and the play group took in the displaced child. I do not know how much weight to assign to the degree of discontinuity that remained. I believe the common core of pre-modern ideology, the atomistic sociopolitical system, and the evolutionary level of life security were the primary bases of the paranoid ethos to which a variety of socialized insecurities could attune the personalities of individuals.

The structure of trust and distrust, so important to the paranoid ethos, may have had one basis in the experience of the divided family. The dichotomy of owner and stranger found throughout Melanesia was exacerbated in a matrilineal context, such as that described by Fortune in Dobu (1935). In Dobu, the intensification of the paranoid ethos was well described. Distrust was intensified by a pattern of alternating residence and alternating roles of owner and stranger between the husband's and wife's villages.

Whether matrilineal or patrilineal (or possibly also cognatic but unilocal) the divided family was conditioned by unilineal organization and unilocal residence, and it left either the husband or the wife as a stranger and outsider, a possible spy, an agent of his or her family. Either husband or wife remained outside the circle of trust. Marriages were initiated in shame between husband and wife. The children were defined as having a different group membership from either the father or the mother, depending on descent. There was competition for the loyalty of the children. Marriage payments were often phrased as buying out the wife's relatives' claim to the children. The claim, however, remained.

In patrilineal societies, a sister's son could be a potential spy loyal to his own clan. In Manus the theme was recurrent (both in mythology and in historical accounts of war) of wives who had betrayed their husband's group, and of sisters' sons who spied for their own group in their mother's villages, or who were killed in distrust. The notion of spying was a prevalent one. Sorcery had a similar effect; a wife may have been suspected of using or transmitting substances (even the husband's semen) for purposes of sorcery.

This cleavage between husband and wife—between the person of exogamic sex and the community into which he or she married—and the competitive pull of loyalty between a father and his sisters, a mother and her brothers, must in some ways be registered and experienced by the growing child. But while the effects of the socialization process and family structure attune the child to the ethos and condition an appropriate personality structure, much of the work of transmitting the ethos was done in the absorption of the cultural ideology.

Other cultural features could be cited as implicated in a paranoid ethos—the commonality of specific shame, avoidance and joking relationships; name and word avoidances and their ramification in linguistic usages such as concealed, oblique speech; an attitude toward language that radically rejected homonymy. These linguistic features more broadly relate to the general cognitive rejection or nonrecognition of accident; all contingency had to be assigned meaning and intention.

Religion, Ideology, and the Paranoid Ethos

All parts of Melanesia probably had a similar core religion, despite the considerable diversities of local mythological elaborations. It is an error to read "religion" from the mythology.[12] When those aspects of the supernatural which were actually invoked in relation to sickness, death, and good or bad fortune are considered, I believe Melanesia manifests a high degree of commonality. Many of these common features relate to the general evolutionary level of "tribal" societies (Sahlins, 1958). In this religion it was primarily the dead who were actually operative in the affairs of the living, along with the lesser influence of spirits who inhabited most prominent features of the landscape.

The living and the dead, human and nonhuman beings, inhabited the behavioral environment of Melanesians. The dead of one's own group performed as moral supervisors, who employed sanctions of illness and threats of death. Attacks by the malicious ghosts of other groups and by murderous, deceptive, and cannibalistic ogre spirits that inhabited the bush provided common explanations of illness. Sorcery, a pervasive danger, was paired with countersorcery magic. Certain categories of one's own kin could curse one, inflicting barrenness, even death on members of one's family. Magic, both major and minor, was in everyday use by both laymen and specialists. In Melanesian religions, and in primitive religions generally, according to Firth (1955), there was a lack of interest in a differential reward for virtue or sin in an afterlife. The survival of the soul was transient, dependent upon the remembrance of the living.

The displacement provided by personalistic explanations of all misfortune eased the individual's moral burden and relieved local interpersonal relations of some strain. One way in which the patterning of the paranoid ethos varied among Melanesian societies was in the "displacement distance." Did one displace one's hostilities and anxieties upon neighboring groups, upon people who lived in the mountains behind the coast, upon members of other households or their ghosts? Perhaps Dobu, as described by Fortune (1932), represented displacement distance as zero, in which the limits of trust were at the boundaries of the ego. For Manus, one could even speak of negative displacement distance. The Manus characteristically professed distrust of and disclaimed responsibility for their own sensory reports, and spoke as if their emotions were autonomous. For most, the lineage defined the circle of trust and provided the social base for the particularistic cult of the ancestors.

The circle of trust was an enclosure outside of which fear reigned. Fear of ethnically "foreign" natives was general. The white man, an object of formal hostility, drew off little of this displacement to himself, for he was considered to be almost totally outside of the magico-religious system; more proximal enemies were needed. There may now be increasing recourse to explanation of major illness by sorcery due, in part, to the greatly increased travel by Melanesians among "foreign" natives as migrant laborers and as students.

I have mentioned that reward, safety, longevity, and wealth were the expected results of Melanesian religious practice. Many have commented on the pragmatism of Melanesian religions. The dead were not so much worshiped as they were conditionally respected and sometimes feared. The relation between living and dead accorded with the terms of a contractual relation, wherein the dead provided for the protection and welfare of the living in return for the maintenance of their memories and remains. The ghost who failed was replaced. Religion and magic were virtually coterminous, based on the use of supernatural instrumentalities for the attainment of the welfare of the living. Melanesians interpreted Christianity in their own way, absorbing many new concepts but rejecting with indifference the Christian heaven and hell. Both seemed remote and impersonal. The dead—whatever they did, so vaguely specified by Christianity—did not interact in a satisfactory manner with the living. Hell was exclusion from cargo. This was the significance of the doctrine of the Fall: not the sin of disobedience, nor of sexual knowledge, nor of presumption to Godly status, but exclusion from the Redemption that restored the cargo to the white man, who guarded his own monopoly of Grace. The conversions of group after group of Melanesians to Christianity must themselves be considered a series of cargo cults in terms of the beliefs and expectations of the converts.

The paranoid ethos was not confined to relations with supernaturals but was manifested supra-institutionally throughout the social, political, and economic life of Melanesian peoples. The individual was attuned to it in the socialization process and had absorbed it as an ideology, directly and indirectly, by the time he reached adulthood. There was individual variation in the embodiment of this ethos in the personalities of individuals, as there were variations in its patterning among Melanesian societies. Individuals most adjusted to the paranoid ethos, who were "hypernormal" in this respect, often found their way into cult-specific roles. Such individuals were the most univalent about cult beliefs. Only in the cult did such a person find a role fully expressive of his paranoid perspective. He developed the hardcore cultist role fixation, a veritable addiction to the cult experience. He was the nucleus for revivals and for cult nostalgia.

In the evolutionary transition to involvement in the emerging world culture, alternative modes of personal and group adjustment are becoming available. For the Melanesian, the paranoid ethos is no longer an unbroken enclosure. For him, like ourselves, it will remain a bedrock pathology of mankind to which we so easily return.

SUMMARY

The contact culture established in Melanesia took form rapidly in a cultural "evolutionary fold" that brought together traditional Melanesian cultures with technologically advanced Western cultures. Melanesian cultures were strongly oriented toward prestige economics and a status system based on entrepreneurial manipulation of wealth, assembled from the production of dispersed social networks. Feats of warfare also were counted but were soon precluded or yielded to the Europeans by the imposed and accepted *Pax Imperii.*

It is true that Melanesians have experienced the effects of oppression, exploitation, land alienation, and racism, all of which were present to varying degrees (depending on place and period) under the colonial system. But I have argued that value dominance, in itself, was one of the most important conditions giving rise to cargo cults. These cults, so widely distributed in time and space throughout post-contact Melanesia, demand equally general areal characteristics for their explanation. I have cited such general culture traits as the prestige-oriented value system and the cosmological-ideological system, with its affective counterparts that I have termed a paranoid ethos.

I have argued also that the cargo cults were precipitates of the contact culture, not of the traditional Melanesian cultures alone. It was equally essential that Europeans brought and seemingly withheld wealth of overwhelming magnitude; it is equally essential that they brought religious, messianic ideas and beliefs that they seemed eager to impart. It was "natural" (cultural) for Melanesians to assume that the religion was the key to the wealth. The European side of the evolutionary fold contained not only its technological wonders but also messages of imminent supernatural fulfillment, which it carried from its own remote past—messages scarcely legible to their donors but meaningful to their recipients. The cargo cults were a fusion of a Melanesian ethos and a Christian millenium.

The cults kindled great but unsustainable excitement and hope of achieving parity in wealth and estimable status. But they could not fulfill this hope. Outside of the cult episodes themselves, the contact culture more generally shared the cult's inflated expectations and foreshortened time perspectives, even when it looked to more programmatic, secular means rather than to supernatural intervention.

I have argued against considering cult beliefs as simply rational constructions based on Melanesian experience and premises. The cult's construct of the world was a highly motivated one on which autism and the perceptual, evidentiary effects of the paranoid ethos operated. Where cults persisted, I have argued against the adequacy of the theory of dissonance reduction and for the necessity of dissonance to the constant affirmations that constitute the life of a cult or religion. Some cult activities can be seen as dissonance maintaining. Effective reduction would mean a dead religion.

But cults do not necessarily persist. While hard-core residues are still to be found and a latency or potential for revival exists, the cargo cults of the 1970s are no longer as prevalent. The cults *are* subject to disconfirmation, transformation, and absorption in larger social-political movements, now on a national scale. The cults helped catalyze and anticipate these movements, even though they compete with and retard the latter where they persist. If the cults were well-grounded in the prenational contact culture, they have been left behind in more recent culture change in which, for many, a recalibration of expectations and a shift in choice of means is taking place. Further intense acculturation involves education and modernization in technological, economic, and political terms.

Like other nations, Papua New Guinea is achieving independence at an early stage in the process of development. The situation of value dominance remains and motivates the thrust toward rapid development. Papua New Guineans in government and in higher education are now debating the issue of rapid capitalization of development through the participation of foreign companies, which, it is feared, will compromise the independence of the country. The alternative is a much slower rate of internal development. The hope for "cargo" has shifted from the cults to national development for fulfillment or disappointment.

REFERENCES

Aberle, D. 1962. "A Note on Relative Deprivation Theory as Applied to Millenarian and Other Cult Movements," in *Millenial Dreams in Action*, edited by S. Thrupp. The Hague: Mouton.
_____. 1966. *The Peyote Religion Among the Navajo*. Chicago: Aldine.
Barkun, Michael. 1974. *Disaster and the Millenium*. New Haven: Yale University Press.
Belshaw, C. 1950. "The Significance of Modern Cults in Melanesian Development," *Australian Outlook* 4:2.
Benedict, Ruth. 1959. *Patterns of Culture*. Boston: Houghton Mifflin. (Originally published 1934)
Berndt, Ronald M. 1964. "Warfare in the New Guinea Highlands," *American Anthropologist* 66:4, pt. 2.
Burridge, Kenelm. 1969. *New Heaven New Earth: A Study of Millenarian Activities*. Oxford: Basil Blackwell.
Christiansen, Palle. 1969. *The Melanesian Cargo Cult: Millenarism as a Factor in Cultural Change*. Copenhagen: Akademisk Forlag.
Festinger, L. et al. 1956. *When Prophecy Fails*. Minneapolis: University of Minnesota Press.
Firth, R. 1955. *The Fate of the Soul: An Interpretation of Some Primitive Concepts*. Cambridge: Cambridge University Press.
Fortune, R. 1932. *Sorcerers of Dobu: The Social Anthropology of the Dobu Islanders of the Western Pacific*. New York: E.P. Dutton and Co.
_____. 1935. *Manus Religion*. Philadelphia: American Philosophical Society.
Gardner, R., and Heider, H. 1968. *Gardens of War: Life and Death in the New Guinea Stone Age*. New York: Random House.
Goodenough, W.H. 1963. *Cooperation in Change*. New York: Russel Sage Foundation.
Guiart, J. 1951. "Forerunners of Melanesian Nationalism," *Journal of Oceania* 22.
Hitson, H., and Funkenstein, D. 1959. "Family Patterns and Paranoidal Personality Structure in Boston and Burma," *The International Journal of Social Psychiatry* 5:3.
Inglis, J. 1957. "Cargo Cults: The Problem of Explanation," *Journal of Oceania* 27.
_____. 1959. "Interpretation of Cargo Cults—Comments," *Journal of Oceania* 30.
Jarvie, I.C. (1964, 1967). *The Revolution in Anthropology*. London: Routledge and Kegan Paul.
La Barre, Weston. 1971. "Materials for a History of Studies of Crisis Cults: A Bibliographic Essay," *Current Anthropology* 12:1:3–44.

_____. 1972. *The Ghost Dance: Origins of Religion.* New York: Doubleday and Co.
Lanternari, V. 1963. *The Religions of the Oppressed: A Study of Modern Messianic Cults.* New York: Knopf.
Lawrence, P. 1964. *Road Belong Cargo: A Study of the Cargo Movement in the Southern Madang District, New Guinea.* Manchester: University of Manchester Press.
_____, and Meggitt, M. (eds.). 1965. *Gods, Ghosts, and Men in Melanesia.* Melbourne: Oxford University Press.
McClelland, D. 1961. *The Achieving Society.* New York: D. Van Nostrand.
Mead, M. 1930. *Growing Up in New Guinea.* New York: William Morrow.
_____. 1934. *Kinship in the Admiralties.* Anthropological Papers of the American Museum of Natural History, vol. 34, pt. 2. New York.
_____. 1956. *New Lives for Old: Cultural Transformation, Manus, 1928-1953.* New York: William Morrow.
_____. 1967. "Homogeneity and Hypertrophy: A Polynesian-Based Hypothesis," in *Polynesian Culture History: Essays in Honor of Kenneth P. Emory,* edited by G. Highland et al. Honolulu: Bishop Museum Press.
_____, and Schwartz, Theodore. 1958. "The Cult as Condensed Social Process," Transactions of the Fifth Conference on Group Processes. New York: Josiah Macy, Jr. Foundation.
Merton, R. 1949. *Social Theory and Social Structure.* Glencoe, Illinois: Free Press.
Romanucci, Lola. 1969. "The Hierarchy of Resort in Curative Practices: The Admiralty Islands, Melanesia," *Journal of Health and Social Behavior* 10:3.
Sahlins, M. 1968. *Tribesmen.* Englewood Cliffs, New Jersey: Prentice-Hall.
Salisbury, R.L. 1970. *Vunamami: Economic Transformation in a Traditional Society.* Melbourne: University of Melbourne Press.
Sargant, W. 1957. *Battle for the Mind.* London: Pan Books.
Schwartz, Theodore. 1962. *The Paliau Movement in the Admiralty Islands, 1946-1954.* Anthropological Papers of the American Museum of Natural History, vol. 49, pt. 2. New York.
_____. 1963. "Systems of Areal Integration: Some Considerations Based on the Admiralty Islands of Northern Melanesia," *Anthropological Forum* 1:1:56-97.
_____. 1966. "The Co-operatives: 'Ol i-bagarapim mani . . .'," *New Guinea,* 1:8:36-47.
_____. 1968. "Beyond Cybernetics: Constructs, Expectations, and Goals in Human Adaptation," paper presented at Burg Wartenstein Symposium, No. 40, Wenner-Gren Foundation for Anthropological Research.
_____. 1973. "Cult and Context: The Paranoid Ethos in Melanesia," *Ethos* 1:2:153-74.
_____. 1975a. "Cultural Totemism: Ethnic Identity Primitive and Modern," in *Ethnic Identity: Cultural Continuities and Change,* edited by George DeVos and Lola Romanucci-Ross. Palo Alto, Calif.: Mayfield Publishing Co.
_____. 1975b. "Relations Among Generations in Time-stratified Cultures," *Ethos:* Special Issue Dedicated to Margaret Mead.

_____. In press. "Where is the Culture," in *The Making of Psychological Anthropology*, edited by George Spindler. New York: Holt, Rinehart and Winston.
_____, and Mead, Margaret. 1961. "Micro- and Macro-cultural Models for Cultural Evolution," *Anthropological Linguistics* 3:1:1-7; reprinted in Margaret Mead, *Continuities in Cultural Evolution*. New Haven: Yale University Press.
_____, and Romanucci-Ross, Lola. 1974. "Drinking and Inebriate Behavior in the Admiralty Islands, Melanesia," *Ethos* 2:3:213-31.
Spiro, Melford. 1967. *Burmese Supernaturalism*. Englewood Cliffs, New Jersey: Prentice-Hall.
Stanner, W. 1953. *The South Seas in Transition*. London: Australasian Publishing Company.
_____. 1958. "On the Interpretation of Cargo Cults," *Journal of Oceania* 29.
Stouffer, S. 1949. *The American Soldier: Adjustment During Army Life*. Princeton, New Jersey: Princeton University Press.
Valentine, C. 1963. "Social Status, Political Power, and Native Responses to European Influences in Oceania," *Anthropological Forum* 1:1.
Wallace, Anthony. 1956. "Revitalization Movements," *American Anthropologist* 58:264-81.
_____. 1966. *Religion: An Anthropological View*. New York: Random House.
_____. 1970. *Culture and Personality*. 2nd edition. New York: Random House. (1st edition, 1961)
Wallis, Wilson D. 1943. *Messiahs: Their Role in Civilization*. Washington, D.C.: American Council on Public Affairs.
Williams, F. 1923. "The Vailala Madness and the Destruction of Native Ceremonies in the Gulf Division of New Guinea," *Papuan Anthropological Reports*, No. 4, Port Moresby.
_____. 1934. "The Vailala Madness in Retrospect," in *Essays Presented to C.G. Seligman*, edited by E. E. Evans-Pritchard. London: Routledge and Kegan Paul.

1. This chapter is a revision of a much longer manuscript prepared for the Hakone Conference (Japan) in 1968. Much of the descriptive, ethnographic, and historical material has been deleted. It has been updated only in putting statements into the past tense which may no longer hold as firmly in the present context of rapid modernization and decolonization. As in any other study of emergent sociocultural phenomena, the assertions hold whatever degree of truth they may have achieved with respect to a given place and period. That period, for this chapter, runs roughly from the 1880s to the mid-1960s. A few more recent references have been selected for the reader who wishes to pursue the subject. Although I generalize to all of Melanesia, based on my experience and my readings, my view is strongly affected by my research in the Admiralty Islands (Manus), including more than five years of field work since 1953 with briefer periods in New Hanover and the Upper Sepik.
   The 1953-54 research was led by Dr. Margaret Mead with the sponsorship and support of the American Museum of Natural History in New York and the Rockefeller Foundation. I did further work on Admiralty Island areal characteristics (Schwartz, 1963) under a National Institute of Mental Health Special Research

Worsley, Peter. 1968. *The Trumpet Shall Sound: A Study of "Cargo Cults" in Melanesia*. 2nd edition. New York: Schocken Books.

Fellowship MSP 13,549. From 1963 to 1967 I conducted further field research with Dr. Lola Romanucci-Ross and extensive field consultation by Dr. Mead. This latter work was supported by a grant from the National Institute of Mental Health, MH07675. Additional field work in 1973 and 1975 has not substantially affected the statements in this paper.

2. For general works on cargo cults or on religious cults with extensive reference to cargo cults, see Burridge, Christiansen, Jarvie, Lanternari, La Barre, Lawrence, and Worsley.

3. Wallace (1956, and in subsequent works) stresses this function.

4. Among some peoples such as the Tolai of New Britain, native shell currencies continued to be valued and used in affinal exchange providing an important continuity between traditional and modern economies and value systems (Salisbury, 1970).

5. I have recently studied (1975) a near outbreak of warfare on Manus. Excitement over the prospective fight was intense among men raised long after the cessation of native warfare. The expectation is widespread that after independence native authorities will not be respected and violence will be frequent.

6. See Schwartz, 1975b, for discussion of more current developments, generational differences, and continuities.

7. Although cults have occurred very widely throughout Melanesia, their occurrence in any given region within Melanesia was spotty, even allowing for incomplete reporting in the literature.

8. "Level of excitation" refers to levels of excitement, commitment, expectation, recruitment, and extremity of behavior.

9. See Guiart 1951; Lanternari 1963; Valentine 1963; and Worsley 1968.

10. There are other important theoretical discussions that are not covered in this chapter. See especially La Barre 1971 and 1972, for his psychoanalytic approach and more generally a comprehensive eclectic analysis of "crisis cults." See also an insightful discussion by Goodenough 1963, and the analysis by Barkun of "disasters."

11. The "paranoid ethos" is not fully elaborated in this chapter. See Schwartz 1973.

12. I believe that this mixing of mythology and operative religious belief and practice accounts for some of the seeming diversity of Melanesian religions as described in Lawrence and Meggitt, eds. (1965).

PART 3

Urbanization: Adaptation and Adjustment

In many discussions of social change or culture change today, one finds somewhat loose usage of the terms *urbanization, modernization,* and *Westernization.* It might be well for us to make some distinctions among these terms. First, *civilization* relates to the appearance of cities as central foci of given cultures. Urbanization as a flow of population into large centers, therefore, is as old as the cities of ancient Egypt, India, the Middle East, or China and is not inherently related either to the modern age or to industrialization. Cities in ancient civilizations served as financial and administrative or political centers as well as central markets for internal and external trade. Then, as now, moving to a city may or may not have involved adapting to a change in cultural milieu. In this section, which looks at processes of personality adjustment and adaptation to urbanization, we shall discuss whether urbanization involves the necessity for considerable acculturative change by the individuals experiencing it.

Today, if not in the past, urbanization generally implies some extent of industrialization—the concentration of workers laboring with power machines. One must, therefore, distinguish between the effects of industrialization on preindustrial cultures, with established urban centers and patterns of urban life, and the effects of industrialization upon cultures that have developed cities only in the modern period.

There is a significant difference between modern industrial societies and premodern urban civilizations in the proportion of individuals working in agriculture. India and China, for example, were politically dominated from their populated political, social, commercial, and administrative centers. Nevertheless, their cultural patterns were continually influenced by the village life led by the majority of their population. Industrial cultures, in contrast, tend to have a relatively small agricultural population in the hinterland, which is peripheral to the cultural life of the city.

One may question whether the term modernization as it is used in modern social science can be sufficiently distinguished from that of industrialization to make necessary a separate term. Social scientists, such as Daniel Lerner (1964) refer to basic psychological and attitudinal aspects of living in an advanced technological, industrial, society. From this standpoint, one may argue that the term modernization refers to the world view which results from industrialization. The term industrialization, therefore, is more apt to refer to the technological, and the word modernization to the social-psychological. This is the way these terms are used in the following articles.

This brings us to the question of the appropriateness in many instances of the term Westernization in examining the movement into cities. One could argue that the processes observed as the consequence of industrialization do not necessarily involve heavy acculturative borrowing directly from Western patterns of life. The Japanese, for example, may have changed from premodern to modern Japanese without becoming Western. What is supposedly Western may be simply a modern life style reflecting the impact of industrialization upon a changing Japanese culture, rather than borrowings from an external Western culture. Another way of saying this is to recapitulate Caudill's argument that perhaps functional changes in social organization are the invariable concomitants of industrialization. These changes do not necessarily have a causal relationship to changes in culture or personality.

In industrialization, a change occurs in systems of production because of the development of a more scientific technology; it results in an increased division of labor, specialization in the use of mechanical and chemical transformations of energy, and the use of machine power to increase production. The change of living styles made possible by industrialization depends upon some portion of the population developing its organizational and intellectual capacities to maintain the more complex levels of technology. The application of new scientific knowledge to a matching technology vastly increases the possibility of primary production, allowing for radical increases in population in a smaller area. This leads, in turn, to the further development of the complexities of urban centers and a proliferation of service occupations within these centers. In this respect, industrialization has led to new forms of urbanization which appeared first in the West. It is too readily assumed that when, with the onset of industrialization, similar types of social attitudes appear in a non-Western culture that they are the direct consequence of diffusion of Western patterns, rather than an internal development within indigenous cultural traditions that have been modified by technology and demographic shifts.

Modernity, therefore, can appear in cultures other than the Western. Functional similarity does occur between some segments of different populations, such as similarities in certain class segments of modern industrial societies. That is, factory workers in every country may have many things in common because they work in very similar factories. This can result in increased capacities for cross-cultural communication and understanding, and the subsequent acculturative emulation of foreign patterns as a form of status enhancement. But this apparent acculturative emulation may be merely superficial, rather than a basic alteration of internal adjustive patterns or adaptive social mechanisms. For example, Japanese businessmen learn to play golf with Americans, but their golf game does not change the internal organization of Japanese business life.

Modernity, then, as it is used in social science literature, refers to a world view and a life style which includes the values of a modernized society. It refers, therefore, not only to instrumental processes in the political, economic, and structural components of the society but to processes of change in the value system, what Durkheim calls the "sacred" of the society. In the values of a modern society one notes continual secularization. Social and geographic mobility accelerate, albeit within a class-stratified social hierarchy. The forms taken by social mobility, however, may still be heavily influenced by previous cultural traditions, as we note in the case of Japan discussed by Sofue. In the economic realm, there is increased commercialization. Throughout the society increased segmentation runs both horizontally and vertically. People become directly concerned with improvement of living standards and the development of new formal institutions, such as school systems, to diffuse technical competence. The mass media expand, and production of recreational consumables increases. Finally, with technological evolution, electronic means are developed for participation by very large populations in events outside the face-to-face social system itself, such as political elections and news in distant places, so that the world view becomes global.

The processes of industrialization do affect basic institutions, such as the family, and traditional forms of socialization. The urban experiences that affect early psychosexual development are different from those in peasant or agriculture communities. As jobs change, the skills and traits which are valued by society change. The preconditions to successful modernization include bureaucratic talents, managerial talents, and the capacity for sustained work according to the fixed schedules which organize workers in efficient groups. These new types of skills and precision which are needed are not necessarily socialized in the experience of previous agricultural populations. Therefore, somewhere in the process of modernization some shifts in socialization are necessary for the assumption of the newly constituted adult work roles.

Both the preconditions for industrialization or economic modernization and the attendant results in the social structure have profound interrelationships with personality which call forth new types of competence: ways of problem solving, and perceiving; new types of interpersonal communication; new types of training, especially through formal educational institutions that take the place of the informal socialization practices within preindustrial family and community units.

Economists are becoming increasingly aware of the expressive, and the instrumental, motivations and functions in psychological systems that differ across cultures. For successful economic modernization a sufficient proportion of the population must be able to assume the emotional and instrumental capacities demanded first by entrepreneurship and subsequently by bureaucratic management. These techniques relate not only to the marshalling of capital investment on an individual or governmental basis but also to the management of emotional life so that it is not disruptive to efficient functioning.

Political leadership can never function independently of the motives and emotional patterns characteristic of a large proportion of the population. Not only do a sufficient number of leaders need entrepreneurial capacities, but they must also develop an emotional commitment to a more systematized form of labor based on a money economy—which is usually different from the exchange system prevailing in agricultural and hunting and gathering societies. There has to be sufficient congruence between the motives of individuals and the values of political leaders in order to promote successful economic development in an industrialized national state.

The increases in geographic and social mobility which accompany industrialization have serious effects on the nature of community and kinship organizations which held together the premodern society. These changes, in turn, have serious social-structural effects on patterns of marriage, of trust, and of interpersonal commitment. Disequilibria in any of these areas can lead to serious social maladaptations, as well as to internal maladjustments, such as alienation and intrapersonal stress. This internal maladjustment manifests itself in conflicts between particular social segments or individuals as well as in intrapsychic difficulties. Individual alienation and other forms of social instability can be seen in indices such as rising rates of delinquency and crime, increased violence, and other forms of societal conflict. We do not yet know how much deviancy or conflict is to be expected within very large urban complexes, or, more importantly, how much disequilibrium can be tolerated without collapse of the society.

URBANIZATION AS AN INFLUENCE ON ADJUSTMENT AND ADAPTATION

Such highly abstract conceptualizations need to be tested concretely in specific settings and cultures, which in previous ages were relatively cut off from external contact. We are interested in the human response, the patterns of adjustment and adaptation that occur and the various forms that change takes. In the following three chapters we are not concerned with the macro-issues involved in industrialization and urbanization, but with attacking the problems concretely. Does urbanization *per se* cause stress on in-migrants to a city? What happens to those who remain in the country?

In American sociological and psychological literature there is already considerable reference to the assumed psychological stress on rural populations that migrate into the city. In the United States, large scale epidemiological studies have been done in recent years which produce conflicting results. What does research reveal to be the case in different societies where urbanization within given cultures can be separated from acculturation compounded by urban migration? The following papers address themselves to this issue.

Chapter 7, by Alex Inkeles and David Smith, is an empirical examination of personal adjustment in six different cultures. Their evidence suggests that urbanization seems to be correlated with better mental health, not greater stress, and that increased education has a significant positive effect on adjustment.

Inkeles and Smith summarize their cross-cultural report by saying that psychosomatic symptoms in younger men in developing countries are caused by something other than the act of migration and subsequent exposure to modernizing institutions such as school, factory, city life, and mass media. The principal difficulty with the theory that urban transition is the cause of psychic stress lies not so much in an incorrect view of city life, as in a mistaken and romanticized image of village life. Inkeles and Smith challenge the view that the daily life of traditional villages in most cultures was inherently healthier than whatever village residents might encounter in urban industrial settings. It is quite easy to idealize the economic security enjoyed, the cooperative and affiliative nature of village interaction, and the availability of emotional support in times of personal need. An objective evaluation of the internal structures of village life in any number of cultures would attest to the relative infrequency of such idealized situations.

Edward Bruner in his report on the Batak, "Tradition and Modernization in Batak Society," raises several basic questions about the relationship of change to internal problems of adjustment.

In Bruner's interpretation of the anthropological data, he finds situations where rapid change produces internal conflict and others where no such symptoms of stress are reported. A central issue, therefore, is to determine what variables differentiate situations of change which induce stress from those which do not. One way to consider the difference is to generalize that rates of mental disorder may be a function of how successfully the host culture provides ways of handling the stress aroused. The research problem, then, would be one of intensively investigating the culturally provided solutions to stress. Mental illness simply becomes one alternative response made to resolve the aroused stress. Secondly, the concept of stress itself must be examined in its cultural context.

Bruner offers his case study of the Batak of Sumatra as an illustration of successful resolution of the possible stresses inherent in modernization. Bruner's explanation of why the Batak have adapted with facility points to a flexibility in role making rather than simply role taking. For example, the Batak headmen do not perceive the outsider's categories of traditional and modern. Seen through the subjective experience of the Batak themselves, one finds that a Batak headman flexibly adapts his behavior to changing situations and that the actors in his culture are, in this sense, creative agents interpreting the changing world in which they live and testing their interpretations by the feedback they gain from their behavior. If a people's adjustive mechanisms allow them flexibility and adaptability, then adaptation to modernization may proceed with considerable facility and minimal stress.

Bruner found the experience of the Batak to be quite different from that of American Indians. For them, renunciation of Indian identity seems to be necessary in order to take on change and become "white." It is not possible to identify as Indian and white at the same time, since, in the structuring of American society, these two categories are mutually exclusive. The Batak, in contrast, does not have to renounce his own social group or personal identity in order to urbanize, because no opposition between being a Batak and being a modern Indonesian is felt.

The final chapter in Part Three by professor Takao Sofue examines some of the new stresses faced by those left behind in villages and those who have moved to cities in Japan. Those left in agricultural life face serious readjustments, necessitated both internally and socially by a progressively devitalized rural life style. In the city, problems such as congestion and pollution are more serious than any yet faced in the United States. Within the urban environment are new forms of stress and resultant deviancy. In both city and country, a new series of tensions arises from redefinitions of the family and of the marital relationship. Sofue ends by indicating how generational stress in rapidly changing Japan is increasing as a new generation of Japanese attempts to adapt to an industrial culture.

Two conclusions can be drawn from these chapters. First, urbanization does not necessarily imply disruptive modernization. Second, there is a difference in the psychocultural effects of urbanization in situations where people move into cities that are part of their own culture as opposed to situations of immigration into a different culture.

The chapters presented by Inkeles and Smith and by Bruner point up the fact that, contrary to some notions, the processes involved in moving into urban industrial cities doe not seem directly to lead to internal adjustment and socialization difficulties. The evidence forwarded by these authors and by Sofue points in the opposite direction. The patterns of social adaptation and personal adjustment in the cities may be as good as or even better than the ones manifested by those who remain in the rural or traditional setting.

Inkeles' and Smith's cross-cultural survey of six highly diverse cultures would indicate that, in medical-psychiatric survey measurements of mental health, the urban dwellers in each instance compare favorably with control samples of the rural population. In Bruner's study in Sumatra, the natives' idea that there is cultural continuity in the law, or *adat,* makes for a smooth transition from rural to urban. Sofue notes the new social problems faced by those remaining in villages that have lost their vitality due to outmigration. It must be pointed out that in each of these studies the individuals considered are migrating to a city within the context of their own culture. That is to say, although the life styles of city and countryside may be quite different from one another, the illusion of continuity is maintained. The individual does not come into a situation where he must redefine himself as part of an ethnic minority or must change his language in order to make a new social adaptation. These latter problems are inherent in the problems of adaptation and adjustment discussed in Part Four.

REFERENCES

Lerner, Daniel. 1964. *The Passing of Traditional Society: Modernization in the Middle East.* Glencoe, Ill.: Free Press.

———. 1964. "The Transformation of Institutions," in *The Transfer of Institutions,* edited by William Hamilton. Durham, North Carolina: Duke University Press.

Chapter 7

Personal Adjustment and Modernization*

Alex Inkeles
and
David H. Smith

Few ideas have had wider currency among prominent commentators on social life than the belief that the city and its attendant industrial civilization are alien to "natural" man and inevitably breed social disorganization and personal confusion (see White and White 1962). Thomas Jefferson could see some good even in yellow fever since, as he said, "It will discourage the growth of great cities in our nation, and I view great cities as pestilential to the morals, the health, and the liberties of man" (White

---

*This paper was originally prepared for delivery at the 1968 Tokyo-Kyoto symposium as a report of the Harvard Project on Social and Cultural Aspects of Development, Center for International Affairs, Harvard University. The project has been supported by a number of different private foundations and government agencies, but this particular document could not have been prepared without the assistance of a Research Grant from the National Institute of Mental Health (#1 ROI MH 15646-01 SSR). The authors also express their appreciation to the Computer Sciences Laboratory and the Biomedical Sciences Support Program of the University of Southern California. We are indebted to Lucille Kurian for her research assistance.

Much of the material presented below was published earlier as "The Fate of Personal Adjustment in the Process of Modernization," in *The International Journal of Comparative Sociology*, Volume II, Number 2, June 1970. We have had to omit some of the tables and documentation appearing in the original. We are grateful to the editors of the journal and to E. J. Brill Publishers, Leiden, The Netherlands, for their kind permission to reproduce the material in this book.

and White 1962, p. 19). A century later Henry Adams saw New York City as a cylinder which had exploded to throw great masses of stone and steam against the sky, creating an air of "movement and hysteria" in which "prosperity never before imagined, power never yet wielded by men, speed never reached by anything but a meteor, had made the world *irritable, nervous, querulous, unreasonable,* and *afraid"* (p.72, italics added).

Such images of urban life and industrial civilization were also held by leaders of the burgeoning social sciences in the twentieth century. Pitirim Sorokin was profoundly convinced that the modern sensate culture was everywhere generating a great upsurge in mental illness (Sorokin 1957). Robert Park, leader of the dominant Chicago school of sociology, felt that the city, in the very process of its growth, "creates diseases and vices which tend to destroy the community." The peasant who comes to work in the city, Park held, is the prototypical case for observing the threat to individual integrity inherent in urban life. "Man, translated to the city," he remarked, "has become a problem to himself and society in a way and to an extent he never was before" (White and White 1962, pp. 162–66).

If Park's observation were true within the framework of already industrialized Western society, how much greater would be the impact on men in more traditional and isolated cultures whom life and circumstance had lifted from the quiet and security of their villages and cast into the maelstrom of urban industrial life? J. S. Slotkin spoke for many anthropologists when he asserted that no matter how compatible industrialism may *seem* to be, "its ramifications tend to produce cultural disorganization (Slotkin 1960, p. 31).

Not all anthropologists and sociologists accept the inevitability of the deleterious effects of migration, urban residence, and industrial labor which Slotkin seemed to assume. Some, like Oscar Lewis, have emphasized the relative transferability of socio-cultural patterns from the village to the city, patterns which protect the individual from exposure to excessive disorganization and consequent personal disorder. In his study of the migration of Tepoztecan peasants to Mexico City, he found "little evidence of disorganization and breakdown, or culture conflict, or of irreconcilable differences between generations." So far as the individual is concerned, Lewis reported, the Tepoztecan peasants "adapt to city life with far greater ease than do American farm families" (Lewis 1952, pp. 39–40).

Other analysts have stressed the need to differentiate adjustment according to the stages in a migrant's career and the quality and forms of his integration with his new urban environment. Deshmukh (1956), in his study of a floating population in Delhi, distinguished three stages in the life path of the migrant. In the earliest stage, according to Deshmukh, the migrant still enjoys a certain insulation from the impact of his new status. At the second stage, however, "he painfully learns about the difference in his own ways and the ways of the town; he is perplexed about everything in the town." According to Deshmukh this period is "the stage of crisis for each immigrant." In the third stage, however, some men acquire new skills and new ways, settle down comfortably in the town, and overcome their marginality. These are then presumably out of the crisis condition, and have achieved a new adjustment.

To resolve the controversy whether migration and subsequent modernizing experiences in developing countries are or are not deleterious to mental health, and to determine under what conditions such harmful influences as may result can or cannot be counteracted, required data in a form and on a scale not previously available. The materials collected by the Harvard Project on the Social and Cultural Aspects of Development permit a substantial advance in the assessment of the effects of migration, industrialization, and urbanization on psychic adjustment.

The Harvard Project, which is conceived as a sociopsychological contribution to the study of economic, political, and social development, investigates individual modernization in six countries: Argentina and Chile, East Pakistan and India, Nigeria and Israel. (Since we did not collect representative national samples, the habitual reference to countries in our tests and tables should be understood as a convention. For full details see Inkeles and Smith 1974.) This report will not, however, emphasize national differences, but will treat each country as another replication of the basic design. We assume that if something holds true for six such different countries, it must be a powerful connection indeed.

As part of our standard questionnaire, we included in every interview a Psychosomatic Symptoms Test (PT). In addition we asked more than fifty questions, in interviews of up to four hours each, which in various ways permit us to assess the validity of the test and to make independent evaluations of the psychic adjustment of migrant industrial workers in the six developing countries included in our study. The tests were administered to a highly purposive sample of cultivators (men who still work the land), newly arrived migrants to the city, urban workers earning their living outside large-scale productive enterprises, and workers in industry. Industrial workers are the largest group in each country, some 600 to 700; the other subsamples were to be 100 each. Our targets were not always reached; 720 men were interviewed in Nigeria and 1300 in India. Each respondent possessed certain common characteristics as to sex (all male), age (18-32), education (usually 0-8 years), religion, ethnicity, rural or urban origin, residence, and, of course, the occupational characteristics already mentioned.

Respondents were chosen within "sites," the most important being the factory. Up to one hundred factories were included in each country. In the smaller factories, virtually everyone meeting the sample criteria was interviewed. In the largest factories random selection procedures were used. Factories were selected on the basis of differentiation by size (five categories), product (seven categories), and relative "modernity" (two categories). Cultivators were chosen from villages which were the same or very comparable—in terms of culture, crop, ethnicity, religion, and the like—to the villages from which the industrial workers in our sample had originally come. The chosen urban, nonindustrial participants worked outside large-scale production organizations in the same cities as the industrial workers, and otherwise met the general sampling criteria. Like the industrial workers, this group included both skilled and unskilled workers, sometimes performing the same jobs as industrial workers, but in different working conditions.

PROBLEMS OF CONCEPTUALIZATION AND MEASUREMENT

The conceptualization and the measurement of "adjustment" pose difficult problems. The concept is defined in so great a variety of ways as to render it almost meaningless unless some particular measure or test is specified. So far as measurement is concerned, the situation is not much improved, because so many different and often unrelated measures have been used. In this study, we use the term "mental health" to refer to the relative success or adequacy of an individual's psychological and social functioning, within the limits of his constitutional capabilities and his environment. We emphasize that the criterion of successful functioning must be *relative to* one's physical body and to one's environment. We also stress that adjustment involves successful functioning in the *social* realm. For us, the concept is not limited to internal psychological processes. Broadly speaking, "adjustment" may be taken as synonymous with "mental health."*

The major criteria or indices of "adjustment" or "mental health" have been thoroughly reviewed by William Scott (1958). He found six basic research criteria in common use: (1) exposure to psychiatric treatment; (2) psychiatric diagnosis; (3) social maladaptation; (4) failure of positive adaptation; (5) subjective unhappiness; (6) objective psychological symptoms.

We could not afford to subject our interviewees to psychiatric diagnosis, even if they were willing, and we feared that records of psychiatric

---

*Editor's note: Inkeles' concept of "mental health" includes both adaptation and adjustment as defined in the Introduction to this volume (see pages 4–8).

treatment in developing countries might have little relevance even if they existed. Failure of positive adaptation, the fourth criterion, was also not suitable, at least given the design of our study. The usual test of successful "adaptation" is a man's ability to sustain a major social role, such as holding a job. Our research design required us to sample men who, at the time of the interview, were by definition successfully "adapted" in that they all were effectively employed. For the other three criteria of adjustment, however, we were able to include items in our test battery. In the report presented here we limit ourselves to analyzing our measure for the sixth criterion, namely objective psychological symptoms. To assess the presence of such symptoms we relied on a set of questions which had been widely used for this purpose in the United States and elsewhere. Sets of such questions are called psychosomatic symptoms tests (or scales). The items we used, in what we designate our PT test, are listed in Table 7.1.

Such a test recommended itself on the simple ground of precedent. Items such as those in our PT scale had been used in nearly every major study of the mental health or adjustment of groups (as against individuals) conducted since World War II, including the famous study of the American soldier, the midtown Manhattan study, a national sample reported in *Americans View Their Mental Health*, and others. (See Stouffer et al. 1949; Srole et al. 1962; Gurin, Veroff, and Feld 1960; Kornhauser 1965.) Even more important for our purpose was the fact that the test had been used with apparent success in cultures at least as different from the Western European as those included in our research—for example, with the Abeokuta Yoruba in Nigeria and the Zulu in South Africa (Leighton et al. 1963; Scotch and Geiger 1963–64).

A quick glance at Table 7.1 will make it clear why these questions are considered measures of psychosomatic symptoms and why they are judged to be indicators of psychic adjustment. Of course, everyone has a headache or experiences some nervousness sometimes. But we do not expect an individual who is well adjusted to report that he displays a large array of such symptoms, nor that he has them frequently or regularly. If a man tells us that he has trouble getting to sleep, *and* feels bothered by nervousness, *and* is afflicted by bad dreams, *and* has trembling hands, it seems likely that something is wrong. That "something" may, of course, be physical rather than psychic, but the questions included in the test seem inherently concerned with psychic adjustment as expressed in psychosomatic symptoms. They have "face validity."

The face validity of a test may, of course, be a false face. We note, therefore, that in a number of the cited studies which relied on some form of psychosomatic symptoms test similar to ours, the investigators validated the test against independent criteria of personal adjustment (see Kasl

TABLE 7.1 Percent of national sample reporting psychosomatic symptoms: by symptom and country

Percent of Respondents Reporting Symptom in:

PT	Test Question	Argentina (%)	Chile (%)	East Pakistan (%)	India (%)	Israel (%)	Nigeria (%)	Average Across Countries (%)
1†	Have trouble sleeping? Yes/No	12	23	20	54	37	21	28
2	Limbs tremble enough to bother you? Yes/No	—*	—	23	10	15	4	13
3†	Bothered by nervousness? Yes/No	33	36	36	27	48	9	32
4	Bothered by heart beating hard when not exerting self? Yes/No	—	24	16	13	13	45	22
5	Bite fingernails? Yes/No	—	—	15	6	14	—	12
6†	Bothered by shortness of breath when not exercising? Yes/No	8	15	9	6	8	22	13
7	Bothered by palms sweating when not exercising? Yes/No	—	—	—	—	22	22	22
8†	Often troubled by headaches? Yes/No	21	24	26	21	34	44	28
9†	Bothered by dreams that frighten or upset you? Yes/No	11	22	31	35	21	48	28
50	Health problems affect work in last 6 months? Freq./ . . . /Never	28	35	—	—	—	—	32
51	Couldn't get going to take care of things in last 6 months? Often/ . . . /Almost never	17	33	—	—	—	—	25
52	Bothered by body pains in last 6 months? Frequently/ . . . /Never	40	53	—	—	—	—	47
53	Difficult to get up in morning to face things you have to do? Almost always/ . . . /Never	15	26	—	—	—	—	21
N51	Ever thought you were being affected by witchcraft? Yes/No	—	—	—	—	—	26	26
	Average Percent of Symptoms Per Country	21	29	22	22	24	28	25
	Total Cases Per Country	(815)	(931)	(1001)	(1300)	(736)	(720)	

†Represents a "core" item, present in the scale for all countries. All others are "supplementary."
—* not included in country indicated.

and French 1962). The work of Kornhauser (1965), Bradburn (1965), and Leighton (1963) is particularly relevant. We ran our own independent tests to validate the scale, but before we present those results we should explain our particular method for scoring the adjustment scale.

Construction of the PT Scale

In our basic questionnaire we included a standard set of nine Psychosomatic Symptoms Test items which earlier studies had proved useful. However, each country's field director was left free to omit any question which he felt was clearly inappropriate in the culture setting in which he was working, and to substitute others where necessary. Sweaty palms may signal psychological stress in New England, but have little significance as a diagnostic tool in a very hot and humid country such as East Pakistan. Thus the final test was slightly different in each of the countries. We constructed two scales: one which was exactly the same for each country, but was limited to a few items and hence less reliable, and one which sacrificed strict comparability to take advantage of the distinctive items we had found to be especially useful in some particular country. Since the two scales yielded highly similar results, we decided for this analysis to blend them in a composite scale. This composite stresses both strict comparability—represented by a core set of five items which held together most consistently across all the countries—and national diversity, as represented by the addition for each country of supplemental questions which seemed to cohere with this basic set. Table 7.1 identifies the items as core or supplementary, and indicates which were used in the composite scale for each country.

It will be noted that cultural differences were manifested in the variable "popularity" of particular symptoms in the diverse national groups. Trouble with sleeping, for example, was one of the most popular symptoms in India, reported by over half the respondents, whereas it was cited by only about 10 percent in Pakistan and Argentina. For this report, however, we did not consider the significance of specific questions in particular countries. We were, rather, seeking for an array of symptoms which would distinguish one man from another *within the same culture*. As we added to the set of symptoms, moreover, these cultural differences tended to average out, as in the fact that in all six countries the average proportion citing the symptoms in any national scale was about 25 percent, although the distribution of prevalent symptoms varied.

On the basis of his answers to the PT test, each person in our sample received an adjustment score which could be as low as zero or as high as one hundred. One hundred was the perfect score—it represented a man who claimed not to have any of the symptoms. Any man who reported having *all* the symptoms presented in the PT test for his country received a score of zero. The scores obtained in each country covered the entire possible range from 0 to 100, except for India, where the lowest was 13.

The resulting scales seemed to be of good quality. The item-to-item correlations were in a range which compares reasonably well with results obtained in similar studies in the United States. In addition, a principal components factor analysis found that a strong first factor of "general adjustment" emerged in all six country samples. This predominant first factor consisted of the set of items we had already designated as constituting the composite PT scale for each country.

Validity of the PT Scale

The results of the verbal material we recorded and of our several statistical procedures, reported in full elsewhere, confirmed the impression that the PT test is indeed a valid measure of adjustment (see Inkeles and Smith 1970). We saw quite clearly that frustration, disgruntlement, disappointment, and anguish—as revealed in attitude questions—are reflected in the manifestation of more psychosomatic symptoms by the individuals who express those feelings.

Men who were relatively satisfied with their condition, who felt that they were getting a decent break in life, and who judged that others were treating or had treated them well, less often reported multiple symptoms. Multiple symptoms were manifested by those who felt the chances for a poor man to get ahead were decreasing, who felt their social standing was low, and who were unhappy in their work. In some cases the increase in the proportion with extreme symptomatology doubled, or more than doubled, as we moved from the men most satisfied with conditions to those least satisfied with themselves or people around them. In fifty-two out of sixty comparisons we were able to make, those experiencing less satisfaction showed more symptoms.

It should be recognized, furthermore, that validating the PT scales by the use of single items makes a very stiff test. The more common method is to use a scale. When we used a summary satisfaction scale, we found that in five of the countries the observed association between dissatisfaction and multiple symptoms was significant at the .001 level, and in the sixth was significant at the .01 level. These findings based on attitudinal measures argue in favor of accepting the PT test as a valid measure of the psychic adjustment of our subjects. Admittedly, the negative sentiments expressed by those with more symptoms are not the equivalent of hospitalization, nor do they carry the same weight as a clinical diagnosis based on a psychiatric interview. Nevertheless, it seems reasonable to assume that men who more often and more vigorously expressed feelings of powerlessness, anger, hostility, neglect, and deprivation, as described above, would be rated by psychiatrists as more "poorly adjusted."

TESTING THE HYPOTHESIS: THE IMPACT OF MODERNIZING EXPERIENCES

The main modernizing influences measured in our research are education, urbanism, mass communications contact, and experience in factory employment. In addition, we are in a position to test how far geographical and occupational mobility, particularly as expressed in the move from the countryside to the town and from agricultural to industrial pursuits, act to produce psychosomatic symptoms. We sought to determine if migration, education, contact with radio and television, exposure to urban life, and work in modern factories conduce to psychic disturbance in anything like the degree they have been alleged to. To effect this test we relied mainly on the results of our "matched" groups of respondents. The matches have the virtue of permitting us to examine the influence of any single variable while the other main variables are simultaneously controlled.

Where relevant, we have also presented correlations between the several modernizing forces and the PT test, so that any marked differences between those results and ones obtained with the matches will be readily apparent. In addition, we have supplemented the rather stringent match procedure by the use of partial correlations and regression analysis.

Education and Psychosomatic Symptoms

Emile Durkheim identified popular education as a factor contributing to "the weakening of traditional beliefs and the state of moral individualism resulting from this" (Durkheim 1951, p. 168). He linked the widespread diffusion of literacy to higher rates of suicide. Others have linked it, for similar reasons, to the greater incidence of psychic strain. However in our data there is a consistent, and at times substantial, trend for higher education to be associated with better adjustment as measured by the PT scale. In all six countries the zero-order correlation between education and adjustment was positive, and in three significantly so at the .01 level. When this relationship was examined separately for cultivators and factory workers matched as high versus low on education, thus controlling a number of other possible confounding influences, the difference persisted. A median correlation of approximately .11 was observed between education and adjustment. This pattern was substantially reversed only in Nigeria, where more education went with less adjustment in the factory worker group. Neither in this case, nor in any of the others, however, did the more stringent match test reach acceptable levels of statistical significance. Detailed figures on the results of the match test as used with large sets of independent variables may be found in Inkeles and Smith 1970. We may tentatively conclude that insofar as educational upgrading is a common component of the experience of modernization, then the effect on the individual's psychic adjustment is positive and favorable, even if quite modest in intensity.

We suggest that education plays two roles: it equips men better to understand and thus deal with their own inner problems, stresses, hopes and fears, enabling them to turn their energy into more constructive rather than self-destructive channels; and it similarly enables men to deal more effectively with their social and physical environment. This is not to say that there are not many stresses and strains to which the more educated man is subjected, especially since he may be expected to assume more responsibility. Yet, on balance, the better-educated seem to be the more favored by good psychic adjustment.

Urban Experience and Psychosomatic Symptoms

The impact of urbanization on adjustment has been examined in the past few years by several scholars. Perhaps the two most relevant studies are those of Scotch and Geiger (1963-64), and Leighton et al. (1963), both of which are often cited as proving that the experience of urbanization, in Africa at least, is associated with stress and consequent psychological maladjustment. However, we read the evidence somewhat differently.

In our opinion, neither of these two studies, the best known and most careful of their kind, can be cited as providing striking evidence that cities and towns in developing countries have greater concentrations of young men with many psychosomatic symptoms and other signs of psychic distress (see Inkeles and Smith 1970). In both studies the authors pointed out that it was not urban life *per se* that seemed responsible for maladjustment, but rather the rapid cultural change and especially the "social disintegration" that is presumed to accompany urbanization in developing societies. Urban areas in transition may often be characterized by the disintegration of extended kinship ties, loss of religious values, erosion of traditional economic interrelationships, and the like. Yet this disintegration is not an inevitable accompaniment of urbanization and need not be a permanent quality of urban life.

If we compared cultivators and city workers and found them differing in adjustment, we could not tell how far the difference was due to the factor of residence, and how far due to their contrasting conditions of employment. If, however, we restrict ourselves to men of rural origin now employed as factory and nonindustrial workers, we can compare those who have been long in the city with those whose stay has been short. The zero-order correlations (in line 2 of Table 7.2) suggest a negative impact of city life, with three of four countries indicating more symptoms with more years in town, the relationship being statistically significant in two of the four countries. Using the match of all those who originated in the countryside but differed in having "few" as against "many" years of city residence, we can make the comparable match test in five countries.* In four of the five there is an appreciable tendency for those longer in the city to have more symptoms. In no case, however, did the correlation coefficient reach acceptable levels of statistical significance (see Table 7.2). On this basis, therefore, one cannot claim absolutely that more years in the city are likely to produce more psychic symptoms, although some suspicion is certainly pointed in that direction.

The "years urban since age 15" match allowed us to judge the effect of a given *quantity* of urban experience. We could also test the effect of differences in the *quality* of the urban environment. If urban life produces psychic stress, the more intensely urban a place was, the greater should have been its negative impact on adjustment. We could test this assumption with the match which pitted the larger, more modern, cosmopolitan urban complexes in each country against smaller and less cosmopolitan cities.

The results of these comparisons of urban *quality* rather strengthened the conclusion we reached on the basis of the measures of *quantity*. Despite the presumably greater social disorganization, impersonality, confusion, and discord in the larger, more cosmopolitan, and more rapidly changing urban conglomerates, they evidently did not produce significantly more personal disorientation, individual stress, or psychic disorganization.

Factory Experience and Psychosomatic Symptoms

Ever since Dickens wrote his devastating accounts of life in the industrial milieu of nineteenth century England, the smoke, dust, noise, danger and intense time pressure in factories have all been identified as likely to generate nervous disorder as well as physical disease. The physical conditions of the nineteenth century factory are no longer so common, even in developing countries, but the image of the factory as an unnatural place, demanding a pace and a style of work alien to human nature, still lingers on.

*In Israel nearly all of the respondents were considered of urban origin; hence, the origin test could not apply.

TABLE 7.2. Correlations of PT Adjustment scores with selected variables measuring "modernizing" experience:† by country

Modernizing Experience	Argentina	Chile	East Pakistan	India	Israel	Nigeria
Formal Education	.05	.02	.13***	.16***	.09*	.11**
Years of Urban Residence	-.13*	-.07	-.11**	.02	n.a.	-.04
Months of Factory Experience	-.13**	-.08*	-.06	.10**	-.14**	.13**
Factory Size	.04	.05	-.06	.04	.07	.08
Factory Modernity	.09*	.07	-.02	n.a.	.14**	.04
Mass Media Contact	.02	-.00	.05	.10**	.03	.04
Minimum Numbers††	(663)	(716)	(654)	(700)	(544)	(520)

†The modernizing experience variables are scored from low to high. Adjustment (PT) is scored so that those with *fewer* symptoms earn *higher* scores. Positive correlations, therefore, indicate that having more of the modernizing experience is associated with better adjustment (or fewer symptoms). Negative correlations indicate more of the modernizing experience goes with poorer adjustment.
*Indicates correlations significant at the .05 level; those designated by ** are significant at the .01 level; those designated by *** are significant at the .001 level or better. All others are not significant.
n.a. = not available in the country indicated.
††N given applies to the subsample of factory workers only, reported on lines 3, 4, 5. The N for lines 1 and 6, based on the total sample, is given in Table 7.1. In Argentina, Chile, and Nigeria, the N for line 2 differs from that for lines 3, 4, 5, being, respectively, 239, 305, and 184. The difference is due to the fact that in line 2 the cases are limited to men of rural origin only.

If work in a factory makes a man nervous or otherwise distressed, the longer he continues at this trade the worse his condition should become. Other studies of the relations of industrial labor to mental health have, surprisingly, not given much attention to the length of time a man has worked in industry. In our samples from developing countries, factory experience does not have a powerful effect on adjustment as measured by the PT scales and, perhaps more important, the effect is not consistently in the same direction. It is indeed the case that in four of the countries those longer in the factory manifest more symptoms. In two others, however, the reverse is true, with an equally strong association linking few symptoms with more years in industrial employment.

Since such correlations often cover up more complex relationships, we regrouped the industrial workers into three sets consisting of "new workers" who had been in industry less than seven months, those who had worked in industry between one year and five, and highly experienced workers with six or more years in the factory. In addition, we introduced controls for education and migratory status. Furthermore, following clinical opinion on the diagnostic significance of different PT scores, we considered only those having multiple symptoms.

The results gave almost no support to the assertion that factory employment in developing countries is regularly associated with increased psychic stress. If this claim had been correct the predominant rank order pattern for the percentages should have been 1, 2, 3, with the largest proportion of long-time employees having multiple symptoms. In fact, that pattern appeared in only four of the eighteen instances in which we had complete information. Moreover, these cases were offset by two instances of the opposite pattern, indicating that longer factory employment was associated with fewer symptoms. In the great majority of cases, there was no definite progression as men moved up the factory experience ladder. New workers most often had the smallest proportion claiming multiple symptoms, but beyond that no consistent progression over time was evident. In the relevant comparisons, the long-term workers showed a larger proportion with multiple symptoms about half the time; in the other half the workers of middling experience had the less healthy profile.

We are led to conclude that for the new workers, especially those who are migrants, finding a job may have been such a source of relief and gratification that they scored unusually low on the Psychosomatic Symptoms Test. The rosy glow may wear off in a year or two, but that does not presage a *steady* decline. As our comparison of the middle-experienced and high-experienced workers indicates, the psychic health of the industrial worker in developing countries does not consistently deteriorate year by year.

When we considered the factories in the study in terms of their size and modernity, we found no basis for concluding that the larger, and presumably more formal and bureaucratic, factories induced men to develop more psychosomatic symptoms. If anything, the larger the factory and more modern, the less probability of finding a high proportion of men with many psychosomatic symptoms.

Mass Media Contact

The mass media are often accused of contributing to social disorganization and personal stress: they are said to undermine traditional leisure time activities, encourage wild fantasies and unrealizable hopes in their audience, remind people constantly of the luxury goods they cannot have and the places they can never go. Our data, however, did not confirm this view of the effects of the media.

In five of six zero-order correlations, more exposure to the radio and newspaper went with *fewer* symptoms, significantly so in India. In the stringent match test these trends held up. All six countries showed those with more exposure to the mass media to have fewer symptoms, although in no case were the results statistically significant.

The Effect of Geographical and Occupational Mobility

One theory sees the source of personal stress in the modern institutions such as school, factory, city, and cinema. Another considers the source of psychic disturbance to be the dislocation of the individual's primary ties which comes with the shift from the countryside to the city and from rural to urban occupations.

To test this second theory we compared the test scores of those still living in their traditional villages with those who had moved to the city for factory work. The most relevant comparison was obviously that between new workers, that is, those who had been working in the city seven months or less and the men who had continued to live in the villages. Israel was not included in this part of the study because of very different migration patterns.

The new city worker had a better PT score in four out of five comparisons, although none of the differences were statistically significant. The edge held by the new factory workers seemed to decline as time passed and the euphoria of having found a job diminished, but the old time workers did not have significantly more symptoms that those who continued in farming. Indeed, in India we found the only instance of a relationship in this set which was somewhat significant at the .05 level and it showed those who had moved to the town to have fewer symptoms than those who had not.

The picture was not much altered by matching factory workers of rural origin with those of urban origin. The matches showed that the factory workers who had been born and raised in the countryside were not significantly more prone to psychosomatic symptoms than their fellow workers who had been born in town. Much the same impression must be drawn from a systematic comparison of the groups of workers alike in education and length of factory experience but different in their status as migrants or nonmigrants. Out of twenty-six applicable comparisons, the migrants had more symptoms fourteen times and the nonmigrants had more ten times, the remaining two being ties. This hardly makes a compelling case for the proposition that migration has a consistently negative effect on adjustment.

Taking all the measures into account, moving from village to city itself seems to have no striking effect on psychic health. Perhaps the critical factor is whether the postmigratory status permits one to become integrated into a stable, meaningful, and rewarding role in a new environment. It seems that it is not the fact of moving, but more the kind of reward the migrant wins *after his move,* which determines the presence or absence of psychosomatic symptoms (see French 1963, pp. 39–56).

CONCLUSIONS

Of the modernizing experiences frequently identified as likely to induce disruption of personality, none consistently and significantly brought about increased maladjustment as measured by the Psychosomatic Symptoms Test. In our analysis we did find some instances, in some countries, in which a particular modernizing experience seemed to produce more symptoms, and to do so at statistically significant levels. These instances were almost always offset, however, by other findings going as strongly in the opposite direction. The patterns observed in relation to adjustment were not only weak but were also decidedly lacking in consistency across the six countries. We are not dismissing the occasional evidence in favor of the theory that modernization is inimical to good mental health, but we feel the *general* thrust of our results is quite unmistakable. Keeping in mind our reservations, we may summarize our findings as follows.

Increased education, long ago identified by Durkheim as counterproductive of social integration and as more likely to lead to suicide, had a fairly consistent, and sometimes significant, positive effect on adjustment, both among workers and cultivators. Exposure to the impersonality of urban life, to its plethora of stimuli, to its frenzied pace, and to its crowded conditions did not consistently and unmistakably induce psychosomatic symptoms. The jangling flood of music, desire-arousing advertisements, and distressing world news presented by the mass media also did not seem to injure psychic health. Men born in the urban centers were not significantly less well adapted than those born in the countryside; men who have lived long in town did not have significantly more symptoms than men with fewer years of exposure; those living in the larger and more cosmopolitan cities such as Lagos, Santiago, Buenos Aires, and Ranchi were not psychically worse off than those living in the smaller and often more traditional cities of Ibadan, Valdivia, Cordoba, and Khalari.

Neither can we say that employment as a factory worker is conducive to psychosomatic complaints. Men who have worked longer in industry do not have consistently more psychosomatic symptoms. Indeed, for the more successful men who have technical skills, and especially for those who have been able to buy more goods, there is a fairly consistent and often significant tendency toward better adjustment. Working in large factories—often supposed to be more impersonal, bureaucratized, and dehumanizing—was not more conducive to psychosomatic symptoms than working in small factories; if anything, the contrary was the case. But in any event, the relations were not statistically significant. Much the same lack of differentiation was evident when the factories were classified as more and less modern in technology and personnel policy.

Whatever may cause psychosomatic symptoms in younger men in developing countries, *it is apparently something other than exposure to modernizing institutions such as the school, the factory, the city, and the mass media.* Finally, we found no evidence that migration itself brings about psychic distress, as measured by the development of a large number of psychosomatic symptoms. Men who had moved and taken industrial jobs in town did not consistently have more symptoms than those who remained in their home villages, nor did they seem significantly less adjusted than their fellow workers who were raised in the town and hence came to work in industry without the necessity to migrate.

Challenges to Our Conclusion

We made a great effort to salvage the hypothesis that factory work and urban life are detrimental. In the numerous match tests very few of the results reached significance, but a certain number did indicate that modernizing institutions might be sources of personal tension. By studying these influences one at a time it is possible we have obscured the fact that their impact was in important degree *cumulative,* producing a significant effect only when one negative experience was piled on another. To test that idea we grouped the respondents in each country according to how much they had been exposed to any or all of the modernizing experiences shown in Table 7.2. If the effects of modernizing experiences were indeed cumulative there should have been a steady increase in the proportion showing multiple symptoms as we moved up the scale from minimum to maximum exposure.

Nothing of the kind occurred. In five of the six countries there was no visible pattern of any kind. India was the only country which showed a statistically significant pattern: each step up the scale of increased exposure to modernizing influences brought with it a *decrease* in the number of psychosomatic symptoms. The one clear-cut result, therefore, argued that if exposure to modernizing influences had had any effect, it was to *improve* personal adjustment.

In order to decrease the likelihood that we were overlooking significant relationships because of the small size of our matched groups, a multiple regression analysis was undertaken, using all of our subjects. If the theory about modernization experiences cumulatively leading to maladjustment was correct, all, or at least most, of the signs in the regression analysis of the PT test should have been *negative,* that is, they should have shown a decline in adjustment associated with more exposure to modernizing experiences. In fact, only one third were negative, and, quite contrary to theoretical expectation, two thirds were positive.

Finally, as a last resort, one might argue that even if contact with modern *institutions* does not conduce to more psychosomatic symptoms, *personal* individual modernization does. In other words, it might be argued that what is important about the individual's modernization is not what *made* him modern, but rather just *how* modern he has become. Several of the more popular theories certainly assert quite firmly that the more modern a man is, that is, the further he has come from his traditional cultural roots, the more under stress he should be.

This proposition could easily be tested by correlating each individual's score on the OM Scale (the Project's general measure of individual modernity) with his score as to psychosomatic adjustment. Except for the statistic for Israel, all the correlations were positive, indicating that greater attitudinal modernity went with better adjustment, that is, with fewer symptoms. Although the correlations were very modest in size, four of the six were statistically significant (at the .05 level or better). If, therefore, we were stating our conclusions independent of the theory we have been testing, we would be forced to say: "The more modern the individual, the better his psychic adjustment as measured by the Psychosomatic Symptoms Test." We set out to test the null hypothesis: that there are no significant differences between groups which have been much or little exposed to the city. Since that was our original aim we restrict ourselves to saying: "We found no basis for asserting that individuals more exposed to modernizing experiences, or who were more modern in attitudes, values, and behavior, were less well adjusted than those whose modernization was less advanced."

Interpretations

The meaning and significance of the findings we have presented depends greatly on the assumptions with which one initially approached the interaction of social change and modernizing influences with psychic health and personal adjustment. Those who assert that the experience of extensive social change is inherently profoundly disturbing to the individual and who believe that the forces of modernization—such as urbanization, industrialization, and mass communication—are invariably deleterious to individual psychic adjustment, will find little evidence here.

But in our view the results we obtained should be considered as particularly weighty because the design of our research was rather precisely attuned to the requirements of testing relevant theory, the number of cases involved was quite substantial, and the research was repeated in six developing countries involving a wide range of cultural and structural variability.

There is the possibility that our results were mainly an artifact of our method, and in particular of the instrument on which we based our diagnosis. While acknowledging that the PT test is not a maximally refined or precise instrument, we affirmed its value on the basis of clinical evidence from numerous other researches and the extensive evidence presented in this study that the test had substantial validity.

The second line of defense against our findings would be to accept the facts but question our particular formulation of the theory we claimed to have placed in scientific jeopardy. Everyone in our sample was gainfully employed. This meant that even those who were migrants had had the good fortune to find jobs, despite the fact that they lived in countries and in times in which very large numbers of their compatriots were without employment. Everyone in our sample might, therefore, have considered himself fortunate, and this, in turn, could have been reflected in a generally low number of symptoms in all the subgroups of our research. In addition, whether migrant or not, all the men in our samples were, by the mere fact that they held jobs, defined as successfully coping with the requirements of daily life. And it is precisely this fact of successful coping which the PT test was expected to reflect.

From Jefferson through Dickens to Sorokin and Slotkin the assumption has been that the source of trouble lay in the very institutions of modern life, in industry, in urban life, and in rapid communication.

We did not mean to challenge the conclusion reached by many anthropologists that the small, isolated, technologically backward tribal groups they studied had frequently been physically overwhelmed and culturally disoriented and disorganized, with the result that their members had been driven to a condition of despair reflected in serious psychopathological symptoms. But these conclusions should not be mistakenly generalized to apply to the situation of citizens in developing *nations*, where industry, cities, and mass communications are introduced by their own governments as symbols of national development.

In the light of our findings the only form of the proposition now acceptable is: "The experience of social disorganization *may* breed individual psychic stress," or, alternatively: "Failure to become integrated in an urban industrial setting *may* generate psychic strain." These revised formulations carry very different policy implications from those arising from the assumption that individual stress is an inherent and more or less universal accompaniment of industrialization and urbanization. If industrialization and urbanization can occur without increased psychic stress, as our results suggest, the jeremiads against industrialization and urbanization as dangerous to mental health must be seen as mere projections, not resting on any firm foundation of fact.

Finally, we wish to point out that the difficulty with the theory that urban transition causes psychic stress may lie not so much in an incorrect view of city life as in the mistaken image of what village life is typically like. The theorists believed—one is almost inclined to say they imagined—that the individual in the traditional village more or less invariably enjoyed great economic security (even if at a low standard), willing and helpful cooperation from others, certainty as to his status and rights, dignified treatment in accord with his position, and ample emotional support in times of personal crisis. But in many peasant villages, the average peasant suffered and continues to suffer not only ignorance and poverty but also deep insecurity both in his relation to nature, to which he looks for his sustenance, and in relation to the powerful figures in his village, be they more powerful peasants, rich landowners, or government officials. Under these conditions the villager, more often than not, cannot rely on the support of all others when he is in need. Family and group quarrels, indeed feuds, are often the norm. Mistrust is frequently rampant, and fear expressed in witchcraft and sorcery belief may be endemic. Insult and abuse are as common in the village as elsewhere. In short, traditional village life is not necessarily so different from the life of the simple and the poor anywhere else, including towns, cities, and industrial centers.

However dismal urban life and industrial employment may be, therefore, they will not necessarily lead to greater psychic distress if the village left behind by the migrant is quite a stressful place to live. Our investigation suggests that in developing countries security, calculability, support, trust, respectful treatment, and the like are as much enjoyed by those who have moved to the city and have taken up industrial employment as by those who continue to pursue the bucolic life of cultivators in the bosom of their traditional villages. *The upshot of the matter is that the theory which sees the transition from village to city and from farm to factory as inherently deleterious to mental health must be, if not wholly discarded, at least drastically reformulated.* We recognize this assertion to be one which many will find not only implausible, but perhaps outrageous or even slightly heretical. The facts at hand, however, leave us no alternative but to make the statement, and to invite our critics to undertake those further studies which may prove us in error.

REFERENCES

Bradburn, Norman, and Caplovitz, David. 1965. *Reports on Happiness.* Chicago: Aldine Publishing Co.

Deshmukh, M. B. 1956. "Delhi: A Study of Floating Migration," in *Social Implications of Industrialization and Urbanization: Five Studies of Urban Populations of Recent Rural Origin in Cities of Southern Asia.* Calcutta: UNESCO Research Center on Social Implications of Industrialization.

Durkheim, Emile. 1951. *Suicide.* Translated by J.A. Spaulding and George Simpson. Glencoe, Ill.: Free Press.

French, J.R.P., Jr. 1963. "The Social Environment and Mental Health," *Journal of Social Issues* 19:39–56.

Gurin, Gerald; Veroff, J.; and Feld, Sheila. 1960. *Americans View Their Mental Health: A Nationwide Interview Survey.* New York: Basic Books.

Inkeles, Alex, and Smith, David H. 1970. "The Fate of Personal Adjustment in the Process of Modernization," *The International Journal of Comparative Sociology* 11:81–114.

———. 1974. *Becoming Modern.* Cambridge: Harvard University Press.

Kasl, Stanislav V., and French, J.P.R., Jr. 1962. "The Effects of Occupational Status on Physical and Mental Health," *Journal of Social Issues* 19:67–89.

Kornhauser, Arthur. 1965. *Mental Health of the Industrial Worker.* New York: John Wiley and Sons.

Leighton, Alexander T. et al. 1963. *Psychiatric Disorder Among the Yoruba: A Report from the Cornell-Aro Mental Health Project in the Western Region, Nigeria.* Ithaca, N.Y.: Cornell University Press.

Lewis, Oscar. 1952. "Urbanism Without Breakdown: A Case Study," *Scientific Monthly* 75:39–40.

Scotch, Norman A., and Geiger, H. Jack. 1963–64. "An Index of Symptom and Disease in Zulu Culture," *Human Organization* 22:304–11.

Scott, William A. 1958. "Research Definitions of Mental Health and Mental Illness," *Psychological Bulletin* 55:29–45.

Slotkin, James S. 1960. *From Field to Factory: New Industrial Employees.* Glencoe, Ill.: Free Press.

Sorokin, Pitirim A. 1957. *The Crisis of Our Age: The Social and Cultural Outlook.* New York: E. P. Dutton & Co.

Srole, Leo et al. 1962. *Mental Health in the Metropolis.* New York: McGraw-Hill.

Stouffer, Samuel A. et al. 1949. *The American Soldier: Adjustment During Army Life: Studies in Social Psychology in World War II,* vol. 1. Princeton: Princeton University Press.

White, Morton, and White, Lucia. 1962. *The Intellectual Versus the City: From Thomas Jefferson to Frank Lloyd Wright.* Cambridge: Harvard University Press.

Chapter 8

Tradition and Modernization in Batak Society*

Edward M. Bruner

> [A]ny line of social change, since it involves change in human action, is necessarily mediated by interpretation on the part of the people caught up in the change—the change appears in the form of new situations in which people have to construct new forms of action. Also . . . interpretations of new situations are not predetermined by conditions antecedent to the situations but depend on what is taken into account and assessed in the actual situations in which behavior is formed.
>
> (HERBERT BLUMER 1962, p. 191)

This paper examines theoretical problems involved in the study of culture change from a symbolic interactionist perspective. It deals with social psychological concomitants of rapid change, and uses as illustrative material field data gathered among the Toba Batak ethnic group of Sumatra and among American Indians.

Current theories of modernization and acculturation tend to view persons as passive recipients who "adjust" to historical changes imposed from without. Symbolic interactionism, however, sees persons as actively engaged in constructing interpretations and in attributing meaning to the changing situation in which they find themselves. People reflect upon their predicament, make selections, and choose among new lines of ac-

---

*An earlier version of this paper appeared as "The Missing Tins of Chicken: A Symbolic Interactionist Approach to Culture Change," *Ethos* 1:2:119–238. I am indebted to Niels Braroe and to Herbert Blumer for helpful suggestions.

tion at the same time that they preserve the familiar. Most crucial is the act of interpretation, but it is precisely the analysis of this act that is omitted from most culture change studies, even psychologically oriented ones.

Tradition, in this perspective, is not a given, nor can it be inferred from study of the old culture. Rather, tradition is created and constructed anew in contemporary situations; as the situations change, the socially constructed conception of group tradition may also change. The positions taken by defenders of native tradition should not be viewed in terms of their historical accuracy, for that is really of secondary importance. More to the point is that statements of group tradition create an identity that is *currently* meaningful to the participants and to those with whom they interact. The content of tradition, that is, of culture, varies according to time, context, and audience. Further, we cannot assume that modernity is an objectively defined, universally applicable concept, nor that it has exactly the same meaning everywhere. Modernity, like tradition, is socially constructed and is a product of interaction.

The Batak construction of their tradition and of their identity is limited by the social structural circumstances of Indonesian society. The interpretative act occurs in a societal context. A Toba Batak in Sumatra or an American Indian in Arizona is not completely free to choose his cultural symbols or his slot in the structure; there are limitations inherent in the situation. In this sense there is no opposition between structuralism which defines what is possible within the social arena and symbolic interactionism, which focuses on the interactions and images that emerge within it. In this chapter we shall be concerned with the differences between Indonesian and American society and with how these differences influence the emergence of group identity and culture. We begin with a brief introduction to Batak history and society.

BATAK HISTORY AND CULTURE

The Toba Batak are an Indonesian ethnic group with a total population of about one million, whose homeland is in the interior mountain region of North Sumatra. They are wet rice agriculturalists with patrilineal descent, patrilocal residence, a segmentary lineage system and affinal alliances. Before Western contact, which began in the 1860s, the Batak were at a tribal level of organization: each village was relatively autonomous, intervillage warfare was frequent, and there was no centralized political authority.

The Dutch military forces achieved complete control of the area in 1907, and from that date until the Japanese occupation early in 1942, the

Dutch government in conjunction with German missionaries had an uninterrupted period in which to bring political stability, Christianity, and Western education to the Toba Batak. Very few foreigners or even members of other Indonesian ethnic groups came to live in the Batak highlands. Most European settlement was along the coast, which developed into a vast plantation area. Many Toba Batak received an elementary level education in local government or missionary schools and some went on for further training in Java or even in Holland. Educated Batak found employment with the European plantations on the coast, with the colonial government, or in town-based business enterprises. On the lower level of stratification there were Batak clerks and elementary teachers. Some Batak were trained as medical doctors and lawyers, and a few held high positions in government and commerce.

By any standards that one might apply, cultural change among the Batak has been rapid and extensive (Bruner 1959a, 1959b, 1961). In less than a century the Batak have emerged from a relatively primitive tribal existence to occupy an important position in contemporary Indonesian society. But change has not been uniform, nor has it affected all persons to the same extent. There is a striking contrast between a Batak who has received a Ph.D. in economics from an American university and a rice farmer who lives in the highlands, is pagan, and does not speak Indonesian. Some Batak enjoy the material advantages of Western civilization in that they have access to all of the goods that might be found in a Southeast Asian equivalent of the Sears Roebuck mail-order catalog. Others live in traditional rectangular huts raised on stilts with palm-thatched sloping roofs, without electricity, running water, or modern conveniences.

Regardless of individual differences in level of economic achievement, the Batak have retained their family and kinship systems relatively intact, and indigenous ceremonials continue to be performed in the village and in the city. Even the most educated urban-based Batak participate in the ceremonies sponsored by their kin group. I have seen a chauffeer-driven er-driven limousine bearing a very cosmopolitan and wealthy Batak official from his office in a coastal city to the highlands to participate in a traditional ritual to rebury the bones of a lineage ancestor. Despite changes in many areas of life, there is still considerable respect for traditional Batak ways, particularly in the social-ceremonial sphere.

The situation of very rapid change combined with the juxtaposition of new and old ways would appear to be one that might generate conflict on both the cultural and intrapsychic levels. Rather than deal with the issue in the abstract, I choose to begin with an example—or rather an anecdotal presentation—of an incident that occurred shortly after my wife and

I had established ourselves in our own household in a Batak village in the highlands. The incident started me thinking about alternate ways of conceptualizing processes of change in Indonesia.

We discovered early one morning that two kerosene stoves and four large tins of chicken had been stolen. We mentioned the incident to a neighbor and within minutes our house was full of people milling around, asking questions, and examining the room in which the theft occurred. We were advised to report the matter to the police who were located in an administrative town about five kilometers away. I did so and was informed by the officer that someone would come later to investigate the crime. I stopped off to buy another stove and returned to the village. It was then suggested that the incident should also be reported to the village headman. Two other men of the village and I went to his house and, after drinking a glass of palm wine, we told him about the theft.

By eleven o'clock all work had stopped and almost everyone in the village was gathered outside our house, sitting on the ground on woven mats. The theft was the only topic of conversation. Visitors arrived from nearby areas, and even those traveling along the adjacent road would stop for awhile to inquire about the theft and offer their opinion. It was generally agreed that the crime had been committed by some "bad young boys" from another district. The implication was clear that no one in our village could possibly have been guilty. The members of our village were indeed embarrassed by the incident. As they had accepted us into their community and had adopted my wife as a daughter of the lineage, the theft was taken as an insult to them and to the entire clan. We were told by the villagers as well as by a number of government officials that had the thief been caught he would have been severely beaten. I learned later that a noted diviner had been employed to determine the identity of the guilty party, but without success.

Before noon the assembled spectators had reached sizable proportion but it was clear that the investigation of the crime was to be conducted by a smaller group. Three uniformed policemen, all Batak, arrived from town, the village headman appeared in ceremonial dress, and they were joined by the three eldest men of the senior lineage of the village. Together they constituted the investigating group and stood apart from the others. I had to repeat to them, again, the events leading to the discovery of the theft and they conducted a careful examination of the house and surrounding area.

At the end of the investigation we invited the policemen, the headman, and the village elders for a cup of tea. We assembled in our house and spent over an hour discussing a variety of topics including local politics and Batak traditions. After tea they went home, the crowd dispersed, and everyone returned to their normal activities. The next day the headman visited again and eventually became one of our best informants. The thief was never caught.

TWO APPROACHES TO CULTURE CHANGE

I propose to examine this many-faceted incident from two different points of view. I begin with the conventional way such phenomena are routinely treated in the literature on modernization and culture change (see Fallers 1955 for one outstanding example). I will then analyze the same incident from a symbolic interactionist perspective and compare the two approaches.

We start with the conventional approach by examining the structure of the investigating group. The three elders represent the traditional element in Batak society, while the policemen represent the modern component. Further, the sphere of operations of the elders is purely local, while the policemen are the representatives of a national institution. The Dutch colonial government introduced a uniform criminal code throughout the archipelago and the police, as part of a larger bureaucratic organization with headquarters in Djakarta, today enforce that code.

Structurally then, the elders stand for the traditional and local in opposition to the police, who represent the modern and national. There is also an ideological difference. The elders resolve conflicts by traditional means in that they strive to restore harmony and reestablish good relationships among disputing kinship groups. If the thief had been caught and beaten the elders would have called a meeting of all parties to settle the matter. The appeal would have been to traditional custom *(adat)*, the aim would have been to compensate the lineage and clan for the offense to a member, and if successful, the meeting would end with the sharing of a common meal. The police, however, operate with a very different set of rules and have the official duty of enforcing an impersonal code. If the thief had been caught by the police he would have been formally arrested and taken to jail to await trial in court.

The role of the village headman is most interesting in that it is a point of articulation between the two systems. The headman is a direct descendant of the most powerful lineage segment of the clan that founded the village; his ancestors were chiefs, and he has a traditional right to rule. He is also the lowest level civil representative of the national Indonesian government, and he receives remuneration for his services as a public official. The post he occupies is an elected office, but the people of the village have chosen a man with the traditional prerequisites. He is considered to have magical power *(sahala)* and is an expert in Batak tradition and customary law, but at the same time he speaks Indonesian well and both interprets and enforces directives from the national and provincial government for his fellow villagers, who are his kinsmen.

I could continue the analysis along these lines, but the perspective utilized thus far should strike a familiar note to students of culture change. The central notions recur in many studies in many parts of the world. There is a striking resemblance to Faller's (1955) work on the predicament of an African chief who has one set of values, beliefs, and motivations in the traditional system of patrilineal kinship and another set in the modern system of civil service. In the African case and in my Sumatran example, it is not that there are completely separate persons or groups, some traditional and others modern, nor is it possible to compartmentalize behavior in such a way that traditional roles can be played in a traditional context and modern roles in a modern context. According to Fallers, the predicament is one of handling simultaneous but conflicting demands in the same situation. Consequently the African chief, who believes in both ideologies, experiences conflict and suffers from his own sense of remorse as well as from the application of social sanctions.

A recurrent theme in the literature of social and cultural change is the psychic conflict experienced by persons in traditional societies which are in the process of becoming modern. The conflict is usually seen as the result of a simultaneous commitment to incompatible roles in the old and the new cultures. A classic example is that of the native entrepreneur attempting to maximize profits and accumulate capital for his business at the same time that he attempts to fulfill his kinship obligations and assist his many relatives. The incipient businessman may attempt to keep the two contexts separate but compartmentalization frequently is difficult—at some point a village relative may come to the office to request employment. Aspects of the two systems, traditional and modern, have a way of coalescing in a single context. The businessman may of course choose between his business or his extended family—he can give one up—but if he is committed to both and cannot compartmentalize, he experiences inner conflict. Or at least this is what the literature tells us is supposed to happen. These notions have become so ingrained as modes of analysis that the absence of conflict is taken as an "exception," one that requires an explanation. One of the most frequently offered explanations for the absence of conflict is that the two preexisting systems were in some sense compatible, which is a neat trick in that it means the two systems may combine without changing.

What I have done thus far is to examine a body of data in terms of a distinction between traditional and modern aspects, selecting for emphasis the historical origin of the elements in the situation. I depict the incident as a mixture of two different systems, one indigenous, local, and traditional, and the other imposed, national, and modern. Both structural and ideological components are segmented and allocated to their system of origin. The points of juncture are depicted as leading to conflict on both the social and intrapsychic levels. The anthropological field worker interested in culture change is, of course, oriented in this direction. His objective is to make statements about the old and the new, about how social and cultural institutions which formerly took form "A" are now moving in the direction of form "B." He is sensitive to trends and reads history into contemporary ongoing events.

Having made the case in terms of conventional modernization theory, I submit that a more illuminating interpretation of these events is based upon symbolic interaction theory. The participants do not view the world in terms of two separate systems, one traditional and the other modern, nor do they see "brokers" as points of articulation between local and national institutions. For the Batak the elders, the headman, and the police are part of the here and now; they operate in a contemporary context. To regard the elder as traditional is misleading for it implies that his role is aboriginal or historically prior; such is not the case, as the elder functioned in a very different context in the historical past. Nor are the policemen more modern or recent from the perspective of the present day Batak, who have lived long in a society in which there were policemen. An informant will, of course, provide an answer to the anthropologist's questions regarding historical origin but he does not ask such questions of himself. The Batak have their own categorizations and they make a major distinction between the adat and the nonadat sphere of life, but their distinction does not correspond to traditional-modern nor even to indigenous-Western.

The traditional-modern dichotomy and the role conflict usually assumed to be generated by it implies that past centuries of historical events are embodied in the minds of each person, as if a particular individual carried in his head the burden of history. The encapsulation of the past in a single mind does, of course, have meaning, but not as a factual record. We carry within us not the reality but the myth, based upon the distortions, selections, compressions, and recombinations of the past, so as to serve contemporary needs. The Batak have their myths, but the traditional-modern dichotomy is the anthropologists' fiction.

There is no such thing as a modern role or a traditional role. The position of elder or policeman is not a fixed institutional slot, with prescribed behavior that must be enacted. The occupant of a role devises a performance in reference to all the significant others in the particular context. As Turner (1962) has suggested, this is role making rather than role taking. The headman is continually testing his role and revising his behavior in terms of the reactions of others.

The important thing about the headman role is not that it is part of two supposedly separate systems, as the headman has for a very long time had to relate internally to his villagers and externally to supralocal authorities. The important point is rather that the headman devises behavior as a creative solution to the changing position in which he finds himself. He engages in an act of interpretation and constructs his contemporary role. The shifts from a period of relative autonomy to colonial and Japanese domination, and to the contemporary era of Indonesian independence have represented massive political change, but this does not mean that the specifications of the headman role have been revised and spelled out in detail with each historic shift. There has been no step-like official redefinition of the headman role by successive political authorities. Rather, the headman and his constituents have adjusted their behavior to the new conditions. The headman role, as most roles, is not well defined, even in the best of circumstances, and the headman must devise a performance intelligible to others and appropriate to the changing situation. He does not respond passively to external stimuli; he acts in ways that shape the direction of change and thereby reinterprets "tradition." This simple but creative act is the basic stuff of culture change and the process by which it occurs.

If the social scientist approaches his study with the notion of a traditional system and a modern system including the roles that supposedly accompany each, then the articulation of the two become points of turmoil and conflict. The result is that moral dilemmas tend to be seen as a direct consequence of changing cultures rather than as a part of the human condition. This perspective has a dampening effect on our perceptions of innovation and adaptability even on a small scale, as the actors are depicted as being moved by impersonal historic forces rather than as creative agents interpreting the changing world in which they live and testing their interpretations by their behavior.

I should like to present another example of creative behavior recorded in my field notes on the theft incident. Shortly after his arrival in the village, the head police officer stated that he was a member of the same clan that had adopted my wife as a daughter. Therefore, she was to address him as *amang* (father) and I was to call him *tulang* (mother's brother). There were further conversations between the other policemen and the village elders in which everyone in the group used Batak kinship terms in both address and reference even though all conversations were in the Indonesian language. Although the use of kin terms is a familiar alternative in Batak society it was innovative behavior in this situation because it created a means of encompassing everyone—an American anthropologist and his wife, three policemen, three village elders, and the headman—within one familiar frame of reference. During the entire interaction over a period of hours there was no necessity to label anyone by status terms such as sir or professor or officer. In Batak society when you say, for example, "Would you please pass the rice," the word "you" is the appropriate kin or status term, so kinship is quite prominent in all interaction. Every time I spoke to the head policeman I called him father and he responded to me as son, which had an impact on the relationship. In a situation of potential conflict among relative strangers the use of a kinship framework had a soothing and leveling effect and was certainly not a part of the formal definition of any "role," nor does it add very much to call such usage "traditional." In this problematic situation the participants creatively took a novel line of action in utilizing kinship categories to encompass newcomers. They worked out a definition of the situation which connected the old and the new without disagreement.

Subsequent discussions with the village headman, the police, and others involved in the theft incident did not yield any evidence of psychic conflict because of culture change. Many of the headmen complained about the lack of firm articulation with the Indonesian administrative structure; there is and always was considerable competitive maneuvering among lineage brothers for status and power; and there were other dissatisfactions—but no indication of inner conflict directly attributable to processes of change and modernization.

Beyond this one incident, our observations among the Toba Batak in rural and urban areas over a one-year period indicate that they are a vigorous and active people who are making a successful adjustment to the modern world. In our ethnographic work we found few indications of internal stress resulting from the predicament of being in a rapidly changing culture. The question arises of how one gathers firm empirical evidence to prove the point, evidence that is not only convincing but which has cross-cultural validity. I do not have a satisfactory answer to this question, but beyond my own observations we did have one independent view. We systematically gathered psychological data consisting of life histories, TAT's, and Rorschach protocols from a total of thirty-two persons, divided between our villagers and a matched sample of the Batak urban elite. Our thought was that if modernization processes did increase stress it should appear in our city sample, an upwardly mobile group subjected to all the pressures one finds in an urban environment. The data were analyzed by a clinical psychologist, Alan O. Ross, whose independent finding is that there was some slight evidence of psychic conflict owing to culture contact in a few persons, one of whom lived in the village, but that it was not at all prominent in the records. Overall, there was no evidence that the city sample was any more or less maladjusted than the village group.

An additional factor that contributes to my confidence in our observations in Sumatra is my comparative research experience with American

Indians (Bruner 1955, 1956), among whom I feel there is appreciably more intrapsychic conflict caused by culture change. In the next section I accept this impressionist observation as a working hypothesis and contrast the Indonesian and American Indian cases with the objective of isolating some of the processes that generate internal stress.

AFFECTS OF MODERNIZATION ON THE AMERICAN INDIAN AND THE BATAK

The most striking difference between the two areas is that American Indians, until quite recently (Witt 1968), have had to renounce their Indian identity in order to change their culture, but the Batak do not have to change themselves in the process of becoming more modern. The distinction is of the most general relevance. Spindler (1968, p. 343), for example, assumes that identity is challenged by the confrontation of different cultural systems, Berreman (1964) and Chance (1965) emphasize shifts in self-identification, and Hughes (1958, p. 27) is quite explicit in stating that when people begin to think of themselves as "part of the outside group" a "watershed has been crossed in the process of psychocultural change." My point is that this may be a valid statement for American Indians, but it is not a universal process. At least it is invalid for the Batak, primarily because there is no "outside" group with whom they can identify and aspire to emulate. Their model of a modern person is a modern Batak, whereas the American Indian model is a white man.

The mechanisms involved in perceptions of group affiliation are well known for American Indians, American Negroes (Kardiner and Ovesey 1951), and other lower status minority peoples (DeVos 1965), who come to identify with the superordinate group but who are unable to join or fully emulate it because of some barrier such as caste, color, or culture. They do incorporate the superordinate group's negative evaluation of themselves, which leads to feelings of shame, personal inadequacy, dependency, and hostility. To the extent that Indians or Negroes try to become "white" they may be accused by their own people of being traitors or Uncle Toms, and they become dissociated from their own group. The critical dimension for our purposes is that there is an opposition between being Indian and being white, and that a person has to make a choice; he cannot be both at the same time.

Precisely along this line the Sumatran case differs: one can be Batak and modern at the same time. A Batak does not have to renounce his own social group or personal identity to change his culture, because there is very little opposition between being Batak and being a modern Indonesian. The Batak moves through an ethnic category to become more modern, not from one ethnic category to another. Every citizen of the Indonesian state is simultaneously a member of one or another of the three hundred or so different ethnic groups that, taken together, constitute the population of the archipelago. A Batak who becomes more educated and wealthy and moves to the city does not strive to change his identity; he cannot become a member of another ethnic group such as a Javanese, for membership in such groups is determined by birth, and he does not "become" an Indonesian because he has always been one (see Bruner 1974). Yet modernization is not accomplished without difficulty. It involves new learning, as indicated in the following example.

There is a distinction in Indonesia between *halus*, refined, and *kasar*, crude. Among the Javanese the upper class and nobility are known as halus and the village peasants and urban working class as kasar. Among the Batak the distinction is applied to entire ethnic groups and the Javanese, as a whole, are considered more refined than the Batak. The latter, however, acknowledge that they are kasar with some pride. The Batak say about themselves that they are a hard people, who speak too loud, fight among themselves, and get angry easily. But they say, you always know what is in our hearts whereas the more halus Javanese may be polite and refined, and they speak softly, but one can never tell what they are thinking. The Batak may be kasar but they consider themselves smart, crafty, and tough.

Despite this ethnic pride in kasar features the Batak do change their behavior in the city and in other modern contexts in the halus direction. The distinction is important in Indonesia, because persons are evaluated from this perspective, and, in some respects being halus is a criteria of modernization (Peacock 1968). To be halus means not only to have refined manners, but also to control and channel aggression, a problem area for the Batak. In the city, aggression is expressed in more indirect and subtle ways and there is considerably less arguing and fewer direct verbal attacks than in the village. My wife, who learned to speak Batak in the village, acquired the manner of shouting and the gestures characteristic of village women. Her mode of speaking invariably brought embarrassed laughter to urban Batak audiences, because of the incongruity between an otherwise halus person whose speech patterns resembled those of a village bumpkin.

A villager who has recently migrated to the city may be ridiculed for his country ways, and he may feel uncomfortable in the more cosmopolitan urban milieu. New learning must occur before he is fully accepted in urban society, but there is no barrier to such new learning and it occurs with the support and cooperation of his family and kinship groups. That he has to modify ways of handling aggression in the city does represent a change in "self" in the process of becoming modern, but both selves, the old and the new, are equally Batak.

To summarize thus far, for the American Indian there is an opposition between traditional and modern ways, in that traditional is equated with Indian, and modern with white. Items of culture or styles of life become symbolic of structural opposition between groups. For the Batak there is no such structural opposition between traditional and modern. Chewing betel nut and wearing a sarong are different from smoking a cigarette and wearing pants, but a Batak man may do both, depending on personal preference and context, and these cultural items are not so symbolic of group and hence self-identity, as they are with Indians and whites in America.

The distinction has many implications for students of cultural change and psychological adjustment. If the model of a modern person is someone like yourself rather than a member of another ethnic group it is easier to identify with him and hence to become more modern. Among the Batak, extensive changes can occur very rapidly, even in one generation. There are few barriers to change, and the process generates a minimum of inner conflict because one's identity is not called into question. Items of culture or behavior are not rejected simply because they have been labeled modern or associated with an outgroup. Models of change are readily available and may be derived from multiple sources from immediate family to extended kin to the mass media (Bruner 1956). The villagers today tend to emulate those Batak who became successful one generation ago by accepting lower level positions with the government and on the plantations, whereas the more sophisticated urbanites now realize that the more direct routes to upward mobility have shifted, and they tend to prepare themselves for careers in business and commercial fields. This process, which Friedl (1964) calls "lagging emulation," represents a stratification difference in perceptions of the best strategies for mobility, but all occur within a Batak context.

The American Indian situation in which traditional Indian and modern white ways become symbolic and meaningful to the people tends to facilitate compartmentalization. Items are labeled Indian or white, or native terms are applied such as hopi and kahopi, and the role structures tend to be kept separate. There are clearly marked Indian contexts and white contexts with behavior appropriate to each (Dozier 1951). Terms such as Indian or traditional, of course, are purely symbolic and may or may not have historical validity. What is labeled Indian does not refer to the aboriginal past but is rather a term applied by the Indian people to various aspects of culture and behavior in the contemporary context. Batak compartmentalization may also occur, but it takes place along the lines of a structural opposition inherent in Indonesian society between the members of different ethnic groups *(suku bangsa)* such as Batak, Javanese, Malays, and Minangkabau.

THE BATAK THEORY OF CHANGE

Although there is no structural opposition among the Batak between traditional and modern, they do live in a rapidly changing world and it is not unexpected that they are aware of change, they talk about it, they contrast various life styles and even rates of change, and they have what I choose to call a theory of change. By theory I do not mean a systematic and logically connected set of propositions but rather a set of assumptions and beliefs, widely shared among all segments of society, which serves to make sense out of the changing circumstances in which they find themselves and which serves as a guide to action and as a basis for decision. During periods of directed change in which force might be utilized by a superordinate authority, such as during the Japanese occupation, the Batak theory is less effective as a selective mechanism: decisions about what to accept or reject are not apt to be made in terms of the theory. But for those aspects of culture not subjected to force, and during periods of nondirected change, the Batak theory does operate and is effective.

The Batak view of change was formulated by me and not by the people, but those with whom I discussed the matter tended to agree that my formulation was an accurate characterization of the Batak position.

The theory is simple. The basic distinction is between the nonadat domain, which has changed and will continue to change rapidly, based upon considerations of utility and convenience, and the adat domain, which, according to Batak testimony, has not changed in the past and will not and indeed cannot change in the future. The nonadat domain includes anything technological, such as all economic concerns and ways of earning a living—rice farming, agricultural pursuits, commercial, business, and governmental activities—material objects and goods, regional and national politics, education and the school system, and universalist religions, both Christianity and Islam; all are nonadat. The nonadat sphere is defined negatively in that it includes everything not encompassed by the adat, which has a narrow and restricted domain. The adat is sometimes equated with customary law but it is more than that—the adat defines ways of relating to kinsmen and to the social-structural arrangements among consanguineal and affinal relatives. It includes the family, lineage, and kinship systems, the affinal alliances and relations between wife-giving and wife-receiving groups, as well as all the ritual, life-crises, and ceremonial activities that embody and express these relations among kinsmen. In essence, the adat tells a man how to relate to people, who in the highlands are almost equivalent to kinsmen. The adat applies only to Toba Batak and not to foreigners or members of other Indonesian ethnic groups unless they have been adopted into the Batak system.

All Batak are quite explicit about the adat/nonadat distinction and there is little hesitation in deciding which sphere is which in any given case. It should not be thought that adat relations are based entirely upon mutual cooperation, personal warmth, or love. Frequently brothers are very competitive, and in the marketplace a man will try to bargain with any relative for the most advantageous price. It is rather that relations among kin are encompassed by the adat, and these adat activities are among the most meaningful and expressive aspects of the life of the Batak. I have heard of one Toba Batak who disregarded the adat, moved to Java, married a Sundanese and changed his name, but my informants could not identify any Toba Batak in North Sumatra, in either the country or the city, who did not participate in the adat life to some extent, and this included such varied people as a law professor, a lieutenant governor, and the local Volkswagen importer.

The Batak insist that the adat does not change. I indicated to my informants that a funeral ceremony that takes five days in the country is completed in one day in the city, that new social groups such as the clan association have emerged in urban centers, that kinship usage has shifted, and that there have been an equal number of significant changes in village society. In each case the Batak informant would acknowledge the particular change, and one man quoted a proverb to the effect that the adat is different in each different locality while another, a well-educated gentleman, casually informed me that as an anthropologist I should realize that customs that arose in rural society would necessarily change in the urban environment. Apparently I had missed the point—the Batak explained that particulars may change but it is the principles of the adat which are fixed. A principle, for example, is that a man shows respect to his father-in-law and to the male members of the lineage from whom he received a wife; there are a multiplicity of ways in which that respect can be demonstrated. When my Batak informants made the distinction between particulars and principles, I was reminded of the Constitution of the United States, which is reinterpreted as circumstances change, but which in our mythology is thought to be the fixed and permanent basis of our form of government. The Batak adat is like the American Constitution in that both are thought to be based on fixed principles, and both are sacred to the members of the respective societies.

One consequence of these beliefs is that although the Batak are actually changing rapidly, they do not think that they are changing in any essential (adat) respect. Their belief system *enables* them to change extensively and rapidly. They modernize at the same time that they preserve continuity with the past, which facilitates change and reduces psychic stress. Their principles allow for flexibility and adaptability, and make it possible for them to renegotiate their culture without jeopardizing their sense of integrity. As long as the Batak continue to retain what they call their adat principles along with faith in their particular theory of change, then their culture and identity are not threatened.

The Batak actually have a double basis of support and security for, on the one hand, there is the security provided by maintaining meaningful ties within a familiar circle of extended family and kinship groups, and on the other hand, there is an ideological component providing security within a known historical tradition. The security function provided by social groups is well documented in the literature but the security-providing function of an ideology has not been extensively considered. In any case, the net effect is that the Batak are secure enough to modernize rapidly.

The kinship network and group life of the Batak have further implications for our understanding of psychic stress. Batak society is achievement oriented and many individuals strive for success. It is to be expected that some fail completely and for many others there is a wide discrepancy between their goals and level of achievement, a situation that in the United States has been described as leading to internal conflict. But in the context of the group life of the Batak it patterns differently. Let us take as an example the man who fails in his efforts to be successful in the city and who has no alternative but to return to his village to work the rice fields. He may say of himself that rice farming is dirty, that he has to work as hard as the water buffalo, and even that he is stupid, but he is still a valued member of his lineage and part of a meaningful social order. If his daughter is married, his urban relatives will come to the village to attend the wedding, and he in turn will be invited to participate in the urban adat rituals. Indeed, when he journeys to the city he may be given a most prominent role in the ceremony and his advice will be sought, for as a village elder he will have more knowledge of genealogies and Batak traditions than his urban counterparts. If his son proves himself to be particularly gifted in school, the son will move to a relative's house in the city while he is given an opportunity to attend an urban university, and the cost of his education will be shared by the members of the lineage. The kin group helps not only in education but in extending credit, establishing new business enterprises, finding employment, arranging suitable marriages, and in many relationships with governmental agencies. The lineage wants the son to be a success as they all benefit, and they expect that when the son achieves a position of prominence he in turn will do favors for his kin and will contribute toward the cost of educating some other son of the lineage.

The man who lives permanently in the village has a special role with reference to his lineage relatives who reside elsewhere in that he is considered as a "caretaker" of the lineage property. The land and houses belong to the kin group and one's inherited rights are not lost or diminished by migration to the city. In times of crises there may be a return migration to the village, and every Batak is aware of the possibility that he may come back some day to his highland home: The Batak were subjected to Dutch rule until 1942, to three years of Japanese occupation, to the fight for independence between 1945 and 1949, to the 1957–1958 uprising in Sumatra, and to the Communist massacres in 1965 and 1966. These have been troubled times and the alternative of returning to the village is a meaningful one.

The relationship between rural and urban members of the lineage is thus reciprocal, irrespective of degree of wealth, education, or social position. The consequence is that there is a multiplicity of potential social niches for each individual, who has the possibility of finding the particular niche most congenial to his ability, training, and temperament. He may reside in the village or the city, and he may engage in a wide range of possible occupations, but he still retains his place and his prerogatives in the lineage.

Batak society is also one that finds a place for everyone and takes care of its own, and in this respect might be characterized as a society that is forgiving or considerate of individual differences. Becker (1963) tells us that it is social groups that create deviance, but the Batak tend not to label behavior or conditions as deviant, except for gross physical abnormalities. The only reason for expulsion from Batak society is for committing incest by marrying within the clan or for flagrantly violating the adat in some other respect. Otherwise, most persons who clearly have very low intelligence or who are in a seemingly unstable condition are not labeled as deviants, but are accepted in society.

THE FUTURE OF THE BATAK SYSTEM

The objectives of this paper have been to apply symbolic interaction theory to the analysis of culture change and to compare the social structures of Indonesia and America as contexts within which ethnic groups construct an identity. The Batak were seen as active agents attributing meaning to their world and devising a theory of change which enabled them to adapt at the same time that they preserved the integrity of their tradition. Examples were selected to show that change is managed in terms of a series of small interpretative acts, made every day, which do not in themselves require any cataclysmic renovation of underlying world view or psychic structure.

The Batak adaptation would probably not be possible in the United States, where minority ethnic categories are attacked and denigrated, or at least challenged, precipitating defensive reactions as well as capitulations. I am not sure, however, how far one may generalize the Batak data to other Indonesian societies or even how long the conditions I have described based upon my field experiences will continue.

A number of factors have the potential of generating tremendous stress in Batak society. Indonesia has experienced political instability, high inflation, and unfulfilled promises of the revolution. Although there have been great advances in some fields, particularly in education, there has been considerably less economic progress than many had anticipated and hoped for. These conditions create frustration and dissatisfaction in daily life, on all social levels.

The Toba Batak appear to have made a relatively successful adaptation thus far. As a group they fought well in the struggle for Indonesian independence, they are loyal nationalists, and they have contributed in many ways to contemporary Indonesian society. That severe psychological stress is not prominent among the Batak may be attributed in large part to the combination of their social system and their ideology, which has served them well in the past. One may, however, question how long this can continue.

The negative position could be developed as follows. It is obvious that the Batak theory that combines rapid technological change with the retention of the basic premises of the older social-ceremonial order is not in accord with Western theories of modernization. Max Weber might have pointed to the contradiction inherent in a condition that combines the principles of "rationality" in the nonadat technological domain with a traditional principle in the adat expressive domain, in which decisions are made in accordance with how it was done in the past. Marx might have regarded the adat sphere as a frosting on the cake of economic reality and political power, and he might have considered the Batak theoretically naive, as they do not view the social-ceremonial-expressive culture as a reflection of the means of production. And many sophisticated social scientists today would claim that with increasing modernization and rapid change it is inevitable that the Batak kinship system and ritual organization will break down. The arguments and the evidence are well known, and it would appear that my formulation of the Batak theory of change is in opposition to some powerful European and American theorists.

I am inclined, however, to agree with DeVos et al. (1965), who claim that classical Western economic theory is itself culture bound, and with Gutkind (1968, p. 136) who says that the basic data of change on which Western theories were based are quite different from the kind of changes now occurring in many African societies and, by extension, in Asian societies. Cultural change in Indonesia has not been due primarily to industrialization, but rather to education, to revolutionary nationalism, and to aspirations for a better life. Batak modernization has not been the result of changes in the mode of production, and there is relatively little industry. Nor have Western theories that see the traditional and the modern as polar opposites or as ideal types on a continuum (Lewis 1952) taken full account of the extent to which traditional principles may be utilized in the service of the modern.

To continue speculation about the future, I am more concerned about the Batak view that they can change one part of their adat after another, yet retain the basic "principles." If they change enough particulars, the accumulation of separate modifications may reach the point where the structure itself is transformed and the principles themselves are no longer recognizable. Of course this is partly subjective, and if the Batak continue to perceive the structure to be "their" adat, whatever it actually may be, then it will continue to serve a similar function.

It is difficult to know who will prove to be correct in the long run, the Batak or Western theorists of modernization. We may, however, gain some insight into the problem by comparative study in which we examine the same processes in other contemporary societies in other areas. I suggest that for the investigation of these questions the symbolic interaction viewpoint has much to offer.

REFERENCES

Becker, Howard S. 1963. *Outsiders: Studies in the Sociology of Deviance.* Glencoe, Ill.: Free Press.

Berreman, Gerald D. 1964. "Aleut Reference Group Alienation, Mobility, and Acculturation," *American Anthropologist* 66:231–50.

Blumer, Herbert. 1962. "Society as Symbolic Interaction," in *Human Behavior and Social Processes*, edited by Arnold M. Rose. Boston: Houghton Mifflin.

Bruner, Edward M. 1955. "Two Processes of Change in Mandan-Hidatsa Kinship Terminology," *American Anthropologist* 57:840–50.

———. 1956. "Primary Group Experience and the Processes of Acculturation," *American Anthropologist* 58:605–23.

———. 1959a. "The Toba Batak Village," in *Local, Ethnic, and National Loyalties in Village Indonesia: a Symposium*, edited by G. W. Skinner. Southeast Asia Studies, Cultural Report Series. New Haven: Yale University.

———. 1959b. "Kinship Organization Among the Urban Batak of Sumatra," *Transactions*, New York Academy of Sciences, 22:118–25.

———. 1961. "Urbanization and Ethnic Identity in North Sumatra," *American Anthropologist* 63:508–21.

———. 1974. "The Expression of Ethnicity in Indonesia," in *Urban Ethnicity*, edited by Abner Cohen. ASA Monograph 12. London: Tavistock.

Chance, Norman A. 1965. "Acculturation, Self-Identification, and Personality Adjustment," *American Anthropologist* 67:372–93.

DeVos, George A. 1965. "Assimilation and Social Identity in the Japanese Former Outcaste Group," in *Mobility and Mental Health*, edited by Mildred B. Kantor. Springfield, Ill.: Charles C. Thomas.

DeVos, G.; Murakami, E; and Murase, T. 1965. "Achievement Orientation, Social Self-Identity and Japanese Economic Growth," *Asian Survey* 5:575–89.

Dozier, E. P. 1951. "Resistance to Acculturation and Assimilation at an Indian Pueblo," *American Anthropologist* 53:56–65.

Fallers, Lloyd. 1955. "The Predicament of the Modern African Chief: an Instance from Uganda," *American Anthropologist* 57:290–305.

Friedl, Ernestine. 1964. "Lagging Emulation in Post-Peasant Society," *American Anthropologist* 66:569–86.
Gutkind, P. C. W. 1968. "African Responses to Urban Wage Employment," *International Labour Review* 97:135–66.
Hughes, Charles C. 1958. "The Patterning of Recent Cultural Change in a Siberian Eskimo Village," *The Journal of Social Issues* 14:25–35.
Kardiner, Abram, and Ovesey, Lionel. 1951. *The Mark of Oppression*. New York: W.W. Norton.
Lewis, Oscar. 1952. "The Effects of Technical Progress on Mental Health in Rural Populations," *América Indígena* 12:299–307.
Peacock, James L. 1968. *Rites of Modernization: Symbolic and Social Aspects of Indonesian Proletarian Drama*. Chicago: University of Chicago Press.
Spindler, George D. 1968. "Psychocultural Adaptation," in *The Study of Personality*, edited by E. Norbeck, D. Price-Williams, and W. M. McCord. New York: Holt, Rinehart and Winston.
Turner, Ralph H. 1962. "Role-Taking: Process versus Conformity," in *Human Behavior and Social Processes*, edited by Arnold M. Rose. Boston: Houghton Mifflin.
Witt, Shirley Hill. 1968. "Nationalistic Trends Among American Indians," in *The American Indian Today*, edited by S. Levine and Nancy O. Lurie. Deland, Fla.: Everett Edwards.

Chapter 9

Psychological Problems of Japanese Urbanization

Takao Sofue

CHANGES IN RURAL LIFE

Immediately after World War II a remarkable change took place in rural Japan, particularly in formerly impoverished agricultural villages. Beginning in 1946, a general land reform program was carried out. By a single law the former tenant farmers were changed into landowners. This program met with enthusiastic success. Farming techniques generally improved and mechanization of agriculture by small machines greatly boosted agricultural yields. But the problem of very limited amounts of land for each cultivator remained a barrier to further development of Japanese agriculture, especially to any large-scale mechanization.

Agricultural income has not been able to catch up with the increasing income of urban dwellers who are benefiting from the major development of Japanese industry. While the average income for each farmer in 1955 was 83 percent of that of the industrial worker, this decreased to 67 percent by 1960 and has continued to decline. On the other hand, consumption of modern products by villagers is rapidly increasing. The use of television sets, refrigerators, washing machines, and so forth now is almost as widespread in villages as in the urban areas (Tsukiji 1965, pp. 8–10). To afford these new necessities many farmers are moving out into industrial work. In 1941, 41.5 percent of the agricultural households had no members holding outside jobs. This decreased to only 15.6 percent by 1970 (see Table 9.1).

In villages near cities, the customary response of the male farmer is to seek additional part-time employment, or to take full-time employment

TABLE 9.1 Percentage of households specializing in agriculture without side-jobs

1941	1950	1955	1960	1965	1970
41.5	50.0	34.8	34.3	21.5	15.6

Source: Fukutake 1972, p. 66.

in industrial plants. Holding onto his land, however, is a sacred duty, for it is inherited from his patrilineal ancestors. He therefore believes that it should continue to be farmed by some members of his family. Then, too, the income he gains in the city is often insufficient, and his wife or elderly parents must continue farming. Small tractors and other machines have aided this change.

In villages distant from cities, on the other hand, the contemporary tendency is still for the eldest son to remain in the village and farm while his brothers and sisters may go to the cities. Some eldest sons would prefer to work in the more attractive cities, but are obliged to farm the lands inherited from their fathers. A serious problem for these eldest sons is finding a bride, since most rural girls today are attracted to white-collar men and do not wish to become country wives. Under these frustrating pressures a disproportionate number of eldest sons commit suicide (Okuda 1966, p. 96).

A decrease in villages' youth population is a common phenomenon almost everywhere. On the other hand, in the past few years some youngsters, though still a minority, who have become disappointed with city life (after several months to a few years) return to their home communities, a move commonly called "U-turn," which has become Japanese slang for return home. Those who do return may soon find their homes very dull after the city's excitement and again try to find jobs in cities; many end up moving periodically between their home towns and the big cities, unable to find a comfortable place to stay.

In some isolated mountain villages facing unfavorable conditions, more and more people are so pessimistic about the future of country life that many entire households have moved to the city to find new lives as city workers. The number of half-deserted villages is gradually increasing, especially in the area facing the Japan Sea. Some villagers have been compelled to move. Gamō's TAT-card study of the psychological reactions of villagers compelled to evacuate their town when the government decided to build a dam there is one of the very few available on the psychological effects of change in rural Japan (Gamō 1960, pp. 77–112).

Similar problems are found in fishing communities. In many villages, junior sons and daughters have left their homes to work in cities. As a result, traditional forms of social organization are disappearing. For example, in most of the fishing communities of the Izu Peninsula (in central Honshu), the male youth groups, which used to play an important role in the social life of these communities, were dissolved during the early half of the 1960s because of the decreasing number of young people. Traditional folk dances and other festivals are less and less attended. This situation is a cause of psychological distress for those remaining in the villages. Irritation, frustrated wishes, anxiety, and loneliness are more or less commonly expressed psychological problems, especially among the aging.

In villages where deep-sea fishing is still economically rewarding, the young men remain, but even in such communities there is considerable change. The youth group was, in the past, very useful for the training of the young fishermen, since those entering it learned various techniques from the senior members. Today, they acquire the newest knowledge formally, in the schools. In one fishing village which I visited, in Yamaguchi Prefecture in the southwestern end of Honshu, the young men's group does still exist, but without many of its traditional social functions.

The attraction of urban culture has been increased by the mass media's recent emphasis on the attractiveness of city life. Today, nearly all village households own television sets. Even in the most remote rural areas, most youth wish to live in cities.

For those who remain in the villages, the "other-directedness" and a high sensitivity to social pressure and social conformity—which are often pointed out as psychological characteristics of the Japanese—are exploited by commercial advertising. Each family competes with its neighbors to buy a better television set or to change its bathroom or even the whole house. This competition may involve borrowing large amounts of money. As a result, keeping up with modernization often brings about serious economic and interpersonal problems for a family. For instance, the number of car owners has recently increased in poorer areas, as well as among the economically better off. This new "necessary" item puts an additional strain on the household budget (Sakamoto 1968, pp. 72–73). The following anecdote typifies the interpersonal problems resulting from modernization.

In a village of Iwate Prefecture, in the northeastern part of Japan, the sons of an old woman decided to rebuild their shabby house. Their old, traditional, thatched farmhouse was replaced by a new, concrete and steel square house of Western style. But this old lady now visits her neighbors and friends every day weeping and complaining that she is very unhappy to have bad sons; she now feels as if she were living in a prison. She says she can never relax in this modernized house. Although the former house was shabby, it had an *irori* (hearth made in the floor) in the center of a large room around which all members of the extended family could gather. In the new house there is neither a large common room nor an irori, and family members are separately housed in their own rooms, each heated by a propane gas stove. Her old friends used to sit almost daily around the irori and chat. Without it, they feel quite ill at ease, none of them drop in as before, and this elderly lady feels very lonely (Ōmura 1969, p. 123).

Another factor affecting the traditional villages is the gradual extension of suburban residential areas, and particularly the increasing number of large, government financed apartment houses which have brought villagers into very close contact with city people. This contact often seems to cause villagers to feel inferior and results in covert hostility toward city people. In rural communities situated in this kind of "rurban" area, a husband very often works in a company in the city, while the wife farms alone and these commuting husbands can cause anxiety for wives and tension between spouses. One wife confessed to me, "Everyday when my husband comes back from his work in a neat suit and tie as an ordinary white collar worker, I am covered with mud and dust and feel very sad about it. Probably he is working every day surrounded by beautiful office girls. Whenever I think about it I have a very strong anxiety that he might gradually be disappointed with me and leave me."

On the other hand, some farmers living in the suburbs of Tokyo and similar huge cities, which are becoming total white-collar workers' residential areas, are now enjoying much prosperity from selling their land, a situation recently called the "New Gold Rush." Since the price of land is fabulously high in Tokyo, each peasant can now get tens of millions of yen (300 yen equals $1) for his land. Many use the money to build westernized, air-conditioned houses with fine gardens, and have luxurious lives as landlords of many homes or apartment houses. Some of them, however, attempt to become merchants and fail; others lose most of the money by gambling or spending it on women. Very often their children acquire a habit of wasting money on luxury which may contribute to juvenile delinquency and family disorganization (Asahi Shimbunsha Newspaper 1969). In short, one finds numerous examples of anomie and social dislocation as by-products of rapid urbanization.

According to statistics compiled by the Ministry of Agriculture and Forestry, the total number of farmers in 1972 who temporarily left their homes to work elsewhere was about 341,300. Among them 263,800 stayed away for one to six months, but 77,500 were gone longer. According to statistics compiled by the Ministry of Labor, however, the total number is estimated to be about 600,000 (Asahi Shimbunsha *Yearbook* 1974, p. 336). Extreme cases of family disorganization result when some of them are attracted by city life and city women and refuse to go back to their homes even after the work is finished. They simply disappear or hide themselves in the midst of the city, never telling anyone their new addresses. This phenomenon is called *jōhatsu*, which means "evaporation." Although the total number of farmers who have suddenly "evaporated" is uncertain, it seems to be increasing yearly. In the case of Aomori Prefecture at the northeastern end of Honshu, about 90,000 farmers become temporary laborers every year and about 50,000 of them work annually in the Tokyo-Yokohama area. Among them, 103 were reported missing by 1967 (Mitsukawa 1967, pp. 186–87). The deserted families suffer economically and socially and lack funds for the children's education. Possibly, their "evaporation" is related to a previously existing covert tension which becomes visible only when the man is given the opportunity for defection.

INTERPERSONAL RELATIONSHIPS IN THE FAMILY

In rural Japan the most serious traditional source of family disharmony has been disharmony between the eldest son's bride and his mother, since the young couple is supposed to live with the husband's parents and the young bride has to be strictly obedient to them. This tradition was particularly strong in the northeastern part of Japan where the patrilineal family has been most emphasized. Very often the son's mother forced him to divorce his bride if she did not bear a child or displeased the mother. Immediately after World War II the suicide rate among rural young women increased; mother-in-law tension was reported as a major cause. This situation has been changing; young brides are now in a much freer position. Since a democratic ideology has become more prevalent, the veto power of young women over choice of a partner has become greater, and thus they can, for example, refuse to marry farmers.

It should be remembered that change of actual interpersonal relationships is much slower than change in the ideal images youth have about family structure. Before the War, "feudalistic" relationships were taken as the natural order by brides and they were resigned to them. Today even actually improved relationships are frequently considered unsatisfactory, since they fall short of expectations (Matsubara 1961, p. 79; Ōhara 1965, p. 45). This discrepancy between ideal forms of change and the actual change occurring seems to be a very important factor in post-war family tensions, not only in rural areas but also in cities.

In upper-class families there are problems of psychological adjustment because of lost status and power resulting from land reform and other concomitant changes.

CHANGES IN THE URBAN AREA

The most serious problems of those living in large cities are caused by urban overpopulation and congestion. The rate of population increase for the five years between 1960 and 1965 averaged 9.2 percent in cities with more than one million population, and in Yokohama the rate reached 30 percent. The average was 23.7 percent among cities with a population between five hundred thousand and one million. In some suburban areas, a 100 percent rate or higher has prevailed.

In the great cities, and especially in Tokyo, land for dwellings commands fabulous prices. For this reason much of the urban population is housed in quarters much smaller than the country homes left behind. Many apartment houses, built by private entrepreneurs, offer tiny, shabby apartments that would be regarded in western countries as slum dwellings. Since 1956, an increasingly large portion of the urban population has been relying upon government-financed housing. Complexes of the government-built apartments, sometimes quartering thousands of people, have sprung up adjacent to all the major cities. Most people are eager to rent their small apartments, for the rentals are moderate but in general, discontent over housing is high. In a public opinion poll conducted back in July 1964 25 percent of the subjects living in Tokyo were complaining about the increasingly difficult housing situation (Asahi Shimbunsha 1968, p. 532). Indications are that this dissatisfaction has not decreased.

Another related problem is the necessity of commuting on congested trains from a distant suburban area into the city. This difficulty increases yearly. According to a study in 1960, about 73 percent of those working in Tokyo spent from 90 minutes to four hours commuting, substantially longer than the time spent by most American commuters. Long hours on extremely crowded trains during the daily rush-hour is a continuing cause of irritation, restlessness, and exhaustion (Okuda 1966, pp. 188–89).

The problems created by traffic jams, noise, and smog are widely recognized and often discussed in newspapers and journals. Many university students who came from the countryside or from small towns suffer maladjustment problems because of these conditions and because of the high cost of food and the coolness or unkindness of city people (Sofue 1964). Quite a few freshmen from the country develop strong symptoms of homesickness and neurosis in May, often called "May sickness," one month after the beginning of the Japanese academic year.

These conditions have led to changes in political taste among the city people. As a consequence of the recent elections (1971–73), mayors of the six largest cities (Tokyo, Yokohama, Nagoya, Kyoto, Osaka, Kobe) are now renovationists (supported both by the Japan Socialist Party and the Japan Communist Party), who replaced the former conservatives (supported by the Liberal Democratic Party). A similar shift is taking place in many smaller cities. It is often said that the larger the urban population becomes, the more critical people become of the established policy of the government. In the election of the House of Councillors in the summer of 1974, conservatives were defeated by renovationists even in many rural districts. Thus a critical attitude appears to be gradually extending beyond the cities.

SOCIAL CHANGES

Changes are indeed occurring in the Japanese family, but as noted by Caudill in Chapter 1, the manner of these changes reflects Japanese culture, as well as the exigencies of modern city life. While statistics reveal new trends, they also reveal the continuity of Japanese patterns.

Changes in Living Patterns

Smaller families are replacing extended family residences. There is a notable tendency for married couples to establish a new residence in contrast to the tradition of residing in the husband's father's house. According to 1960 statistics, population increase during the five years between 1955 and 1960 was 4.6 percent, yet the number of separate households increased by 13.2 percent. The increasing number of apartments and particularly of government-financed apartments, has promoted the separation of nuclear family from the extended family as has the Western idea of individualism. Hence, while in 1954 92.0 percent of the aged lived with their sons, in 1964 the percentage decreased to 78.7 percent; this trend is continuing (Mitsukawa 1967, p. 195). Still, more than half of the young couples continue to live with the husbands' parents. While many might prefer to live separately, they cannot do so either because they cannot find an inexpensive, suitable place to live, or because they have had to comply with parents who complain that they are too lonely. A resulting repressed, covert tension between the two generations is not unusual. In spite of this tension, patterns of family responsibility are still largely observed.

In the relationship between husband and wife, considerable changes are taking place. There is evidence that there is increased intimacy as the position of wife, especially in middle class families, becomes more equal. In Japanese society in general, and especially within families of a more traditional nature, male superiority is often a covert if not overt source of hostility. Kuwata (1966) pointed out that both the husband's and the wife's role-expectations are changing but at different rates; thus there is a resulting disparity in expectations which becomes the grounds for family tension.

Attitudes toward divorce still reflect a general hesitancy to dissolve family ties, since laws today make dissolution a relatively simple legal matter. Nevertheless, divorce remains emotionally difficult for most Japanese. The divorce rate in modern Japan was highest in 1890 (2.70 per one thousand persons) and showed a subsequent decrease to its lowest (0.63) in 1938. After World War II, it increased to 1.02 in 1947 remaining constant around 1.01 until 1951. More recently, another gradual increase has been noted. This pattern of changes in the divorce rate is considerably different from that in Western countries, where the divorce rate seems to rise consistently with modernization (see table 9.2).

Table 9.2 Divorce rate in Japan and Western countries (per one thousand persons)

Country	1930	1966	1970	1971
Japan	1.60	0.80	0.93	1.00
U.S.A.	1.59	2.52	3.51	3.72
Britain	0.09	0.82	1.17	1.50
Sweden	0.36	1.32	1.61	1.69
Denmark	0.65	1.40	1.93	—

Source: Compiled from Shikata 1966, pp. 257–58; Kuwabatake 1973, p. 113; and United Nations 1973, pp. 634–35.

In prewar Japan it was not uncommon for an autocratic husband or his mother (sometimes his father) to seek divorce when either were not satisfied with a bride. After the war, however, divorce has been caused more often by the wife's condemnation of the husband's extra-marital love affairs, his insufficient income, his lack of sexual prowess, or by temperamental differences. The divorce rate is now much higher in urban areas (Kuwata 1966; Mitsukawa 1967). Thus two kinds of divorce—Japanese sociologists call them the "traditional" or "feudalistic" type of divorce and the "modern" type—coexist in Japan, the latter gradually replacing the former. The process of change is not unlike that reported in other countries. In 1951, 20.0 percent of the divorces were caused by the wife's conflict with the husband's parents, compared with 3.1 percent in 1964; the most important cause cited in 1964 was temperamental difference (49.7 percent) (Shikata 1966, pp. 258–63).

Finally, the increasing problem of "*jōhatsu mama*" (mothers who have "evaporated") should be mentioned. This term has appeared in newspapers since 1968. Like husbands from rural areas who disappear while working in large cities, some urban housewives are reported suddenly to run away, leaving their husbands and children behind. The number of such cases remains small but seems to be showing a gradual increase. Most of these runaway wives are from the lower-middle class; the principle causes of such desertions seem to be disappointment with husbands and the unattractiveness of home life.

Closely related to changes in the direction of smaller household units is a change in child-rearing patterns. Traditionally, as was pointed out by Benedict (1946, pp. 253–55), child discipline in Japan was very permissive during early infancy and increasingly strict after about six years of age. This pattern has recently been replaced by a more lenient type of rearing, and hence children tend to be over-protected; this may exacerbate the traditional strong dependency ties Japanese maintain with their mothers (Doi 1962, 1963).

Changes in Crime and Delinquency

The incidence and type of juvenile delinquency found in post-War Japan, also reflect forms of cultural continuity as well as changing trends in city and rural life.

Table 9.3. Number of crimes by youngsters and adults

Year	Number Crimes by youngsters (under age 20)	Per 1000 persons	Number Crimes by adults	Per 1000 persons	Proportion (%) of crimes by youngsters
1951	126,505	12.1	380,142	8.2	25.0
1956	89,684	8.3	336,660	6.5	21.0
1961	131,044	11.7	278,810	4.9	32.0
1966	141,333	10.6	254,541	4.0	35.7
1971	102,335	10.0	227,096	3.2	31.1
1972	97,031	9.7	224,442	3.1	30.2

Source: Adapted from Hōmushō 1973, p. 258.

The number of juvenile crimes increased gradually until the middle 1960s and then started to decrease. It increased briefly in 1970 and 1971, but dropped in 1972. On the other hand, the number of crimes by adults has been decreasing every year since 1951, reaching the lowest post-War level in 1972. Such a tendency is more clearly indicated by the statistics in the city areas. If we set the rate of crimes per one hundred thousand persons in 1963 in each city as 100, then it rose to 298 in New York (1971), 206 in West Berlin (1972), 164 in London (1971), 157 in Los Angeles (1971) and Hamburg (1972), and 130 in Chicago (1971), while it was only 87 in Tokyo (1972) and 63 in Osaka (1972) (Hōmushō 1973, p. 104). Thus, while the number of crimes is increasing in most American and European cities, it is decreasing in Japanese cities.

The Criminal White Paper suggests several factors as probable causes for the trends noted. First, the Japanese police are very strict about regulating guns, other weapons, and narcotics. Second, Japanese society contains relatively few individuals in minority status; hence there are fewer total crimes by Korean and former outcaste minority groups, although these groups commit a high proportion of crimes. Third, the development of education and the extremely low illiteracy rate might be another factor. Fourth, because of economic prosperity unemployment has usually been low. Fifth, family ties are still much stronger in Japan than in some Western countries. Finally, the Japanese are traditionally quite obedient to the laws (Hōmushō 1973).

Although it is impossible to predict whether this low crime rate will continue, since it seems to reflect numerous social, cultural, and psychological variables, I would like to emphasize the last two factors as particularly important. Even though the traditional idea of family is becoming weaker, especially among youngsters, family ties are still strong and the sense of familial obligation remains the most important connection among members of Japanese society. Second, Japanese obedience to the law is the product of three hundred years of feudalism, which lasted until the Meiji Restoration in 1868. The feudalistic, traditional psychology of obedience is part of every Japanese person's cultural heritage.

The most noticeable post-War shift in crime was the increased reporting of injury, assault, incendiarism, threat, and especially rape. In 1946, the reported number of rape cases was 600, compared with 6,857 reported in 1964; the number of reported physical assaults was 410 in 1946, compared with 47,000 in 1964. Most of the rapes and assaults were committed by youth below 25 years of age.

This trend toward an increasing portion of criminal activity by youth is a general one. Most of the brutal crimes now tend to be perpetuated by those between 16 and 19 years of age; the rate of crimes committed by youth is almost twice that of adults. In addition, the number of youthful first offenders is increasing rapidly: since 1960, more than one hundred thousand youngsters have been arrested as first offenders. (Due to a low recidivism rate, the total incidence of crimes still remains relatively low. [Ed. note]) The proportion of these delinquents from intact homes with true parents rather than from broken homes is increasing every year. It was 84 percent in 1965, in contrast to 75 percent in 1956. This is due to the decrease in broken homes which were caused by war time dislocation. More and more of the delinquents are from what is termed the middle class rather than from the lower class. As indicated in Table 9.4, since 1964 so-called middle class youngsters are more likely than lower class youngsters to become delinquents.

This may be due to improved economic circumstances among Japanese generally. But the number of thefts committed by the very young is in-

Table 9.4. Classes of Japanese juvenile delinquents

	1956	1963	1964	1964
Middle class	33%	47%	51%	56%
Lower class	58%	48%	45%	45%

creasing as is the number of crimes committed by high school students. (Again this reflects the fact that more Japanese go to school longer because of social expectations and opportunity.)

Continuities and Change in Rates of Suicide

The trends in suicide are another important measure of the effects of change in Japan. Even before the War, the suicide rate was very high among the Japanese people. Although it decreased somewhat for a few years after the War, it increased again to the world's highest rate of suicide from 1954 through 1958. After that peak, the rate dropped to 15.35 per 100,000 in 1970.

Several characteristics of the suicide rate are distinctively Japanese. (see Naka 1973, pp. 18–19; DeVos 1973). Age and sex distribution of suicide have maintained a remarkably distinct pattern in spite of fluctuations in overall incidence. The suicide rate remains particularly high among the youth, especially among those between the ages of fifteen and twenty-five. Although in other countries men commit suicide much more often than women (the ratio ranges between 3:1 and 5:1), the overall ratio in Japan remains about 2 men to every woman. After the age of sixty, the female suicide curve continues to climb roughly parallel to the male curve. According to World Health Organization figures aged Japanese men have one of the higher suicide rates in the world, though seldom at the top, but the older Japanese females have been in first place for female suicides for a decade.

Another important fact is that in Western countries, suicide is more prevalent in urban areas and seems to be closely related to urbanization. In Japan, however, the urban suicide rate is not always higher than the rural one (Naka 1973, pp. 18–19).

CONTINUITY AND CHANGE BETWEEN TWO GENERATIONS

So far I have briefly reviewed various aspects of the changing Japanese society. The final problem is that of change in the fundamental structure of the Japanese psychology, or more specifically, change in the Japanese personality.

The most noticeable side of the Japanese people's daily life, manners and customs, has changed considerably, not only in the cities, but in the villages as well. Many young men now wear loud-colored sport shirts and ties, young lovers walk arm in arm in public, and youngsters have adopted the habits of gum chewing and eating while walking in the street. They simply wave hands and say "bye-bye" (in English) in lieu of bowing to each other. All these acculturative changes resulted from contact with American soldiers during the occupation. Hippie styles, with long hair and blue jeans, have been introduced more recently. There is a replacement of honorific terms with simpler ones and a tendency for girls to use masculine words previously allowed only for boys. All of these changes, as well as a loss of respect for the Emperor and a strong antipathy toward the rearmament often suggested by older conservatives, are the subject of long disputes between the old and the young. Many old people feel both irritated and lonely. As a result of the disputation, the word "danzetsu" (discontinuity), referring to the rift between younger and older generations, has become quite common since 1970. Discontinuity is a popular subject in newspapers, magazines, and books and is also a frequent topic in management seminars.

In the Japanese company, traditional paternalistic types of management are gradually being replaced by more democratic types. As a result, however, some managers and foremen lose self-confidence and have greater difficulty controlling younger employees. Social tensions between older and younger employees are increasing in work situations; conflicts are more frequent and there may even be some resultant neurosis (Yokoyama 1966).

Young women are frequently angered and frustrated by the traditional ideas of male-superiority and the continuing exclusion of women from many spheres of Japanese society. They are often seriously handicapped by discriminatory hiring practices and pay policies. The more intellectual and more educated they are, the more disillusioned and angered they frequently become.

Such changes can, however, be overemphasized. I doubt that the gap between the generations is generally as wide as is commonly believed. Many of the overt changes in behavior are only modifications in institutionalized patterns of behavior and should not be mistaken for real changes in the Japanese modal personality. Continuity and change coexist between generations.

One continuity is in the most basic characteristic of the Japanese personality which is "uncertainty about oneself." The result of this characteristic is the "other-directedness" and "group-orientedness" of the Japanese which have been frequently pointed out by scholars (De Vos 1973). The Japanese are very sensitive to others and like to behave in a group as the other members do. Another aspect of uncertainty is the sensitivity to "vertical relationships"—superior-inferior relationships, or ranking order (see Nakane 1972). This feature is connected to or overlaps with the very strong dependency need, or *amae*, discussed by Doi (1962, 1963, 1971).

Sensitivity to vertical relationships has been considerably weakened among the youth since the War. Negation of traditional manners and customs, especially politeness to superiors, and the indifferent, sometimes even scornful, attitude toward the Emperor are the result. Traditional emphasis upon the *sempai-kohai* (seniors-juniors) relationships discussed by Nakane (1972) is becoming much weaker among the youngsters, especially since the late 1960s. The extremely radical, world-famous student revolt after the War, especially around 1969, reflected this change. (At the same time, these student movements probably accelerated the change in relationships.)

A most noticeable change has occurred in heterosexual relationships among the young, at least in large cities, since around 1970—just after the year of the most radical student revolts. Confucianism, which was emphasized by the Feudal Government as the national ethic for three hundred years through the Meiji Restoration in 1868, influenced the traditional form of Japanese heterosexual relationships. Since the Feudal Period among the upper class and since the end of the 19th century among the middle and lower class, friendship between the sexes and love marriages have been strongly condemned. Traditionally, men and women were cast into superior-inferior relationships. Heterosexual relationships are now much freer, horizontally oriented, and love marriages are becoming much more prevalent. (From my personal observations, I would guess that love marriages may account for more than 80 percent of the marriages among college graduates in Tokyo today.) The number of young lovers in the same college or in different colleges who just "live together" *(dosei)* without getting married has been increasing sharply since 1970. This phenomenon seems to be the result of student movements, participated in by female students almost as actively as male students; when they took over the university buildings for a few months, males and females stayed together inside. Thus the student revolt seems to have been a factor in the change. In addition, the influence of the changes in postwar education based upon democratic principles has been considerable.

The effect of coeducation in primary and high schools is especially important. This system, although started shortly after the War, tended to be disliked or not well accepted in many regions. Only since around 1960 has coeducation started to work smoothly in most places, although it is still not fully accepted in some conservative areas. Those who attended coeducational institutions came to have more equalitarian attitudes toward the two sexes.

So far, I have dealt mostly with the changes in vertical relationships. On the other hand, the fact that juvenile delinquency has not increased as much as it has in Western countries and that the incidence of recividism remains low testifies to the persistence of traditional Japanese obedience to the law (or to anything required from above). This obedience indicates that respect for vertical relationships may still be a strong characteristic of the Japanese.

But changes have occurred because the *institutionalized or expected patterns of behaviors* have altered, due to the drastic change from pre-War militaristic and totalitarian "Imperial Japan" to post-War "democratic Japan." It should be remembered, however, that these changes were imposed from outside and were not the result of Japanese initiative. Thus, the most basic personality trait seems to have remained largely unchanged. But to make sweeping generalizations about "average" Japanese would be misleading, especially since the number of more individualistic and more independent youngsters seems to have been gradually increasing in the past few years. More and more students do not want jobs as ordinary salaried men after graduation: instead they demand something unique or meaningful to the society. Charles A. Reich (1970) pointed out that youth in the United States were concerned with "liberation" and "being true to oneself." This new consciousness became prevalent among some youngsters in post-1970 Japan as well. To take one example, which I heard from an executive at a leading bank in Tokyo, three graduates of the University of Tokyo who had worked there for a few years as elite junior executives recently quit their jobs, because they could not find real satisfaction or happiness by being bankers. Two of them joined volunteer social service organizations, and another became a volunteer in a Christian group. Although the number of such young people is still small, there were fewer youths like this before 1970, and these few should have an important impact. Their numbers may increase in the future or this phenomenon may be only momentary.

These undergraduate students were all born in the first half of the 1950s. They frequently complain that they cannot understand today's high school students born after 1955, and never get along well with them, because "they are too individualistic and independent." They claim that there is a very wide generation gap between them and the high school students. If this is true, it might be related to the fact that Japanese economic conditions improved after 1960, and television became popular around then. Those born in the early 1950s would not have come into contact with TV until elementary school age while those born after 1955 watched TV from childhood or even infancy, and hence its influence was probably much deeper. Most of the TV dramas and cartoons for children show very independent and quick-reacting heroes and heroines who are non-traditional and do not respect the traditional vertical relationships. They are not obedient to their parents or teachers. Sometimes "superman" child detectives, for instance, are much more efficient than the adults, and help the adults in investigating many difficult criminal cases. These influences might make today's high school students less vertically oriented and less other-oriented, or group-oriented than the university students.

It is interesting, however, that these undergraduate students are themselves deplored by graduate students, because, they claim, the former "are more individualistic, independent, etc., ..." So in this way, there may be some kind of difference in character between each generation which indicates that the number of Japanese individuals with more certainty about themselves may increase in future generations.

REFERENCES

Anonymous. 1969. "Kinkō nōson ni miru shin gōrudo rasshu" [New "Gold Rush" in the suburban area], *Asahi Shimbun News Paper*, January 6–10.

Asahi Shimbunsha [Asahi News Paper Agency]. 1968. *Asahi Nenkan* 1968 (Asahi Year-Book 1968). Tokyo: Asahi Shimbunsha.

Benedict, R. 1946. *The Chrysanthemum and the Sword: Patterns of Japanese Culture*. Boston: Houghton Mifflin.

DeVos, George A. 1973. *Socialization for Achievement*. Berkeley: University of California Press.

Doi, T. 1962. "*Amae:* a key concept for understanding Japanese personality structure," in *Japanese Culture: Its Development and Characteristics*, edited by R. Smith and R.K. Beardsley. Chicago: Aldine.

———. 1963. "Some Thoughts on Helplessness and the Desire to be Loved," *Psychiatry* 26:266–72.

———. 1971. *Amae no Kōzō* [Structure of *amae*]. Tokyo: Kōbundō.

Fukutake, T. 1972. *Genda: Nihon Shakarion* [Contemporary Japanese Society]. Tokyo: University of Tokyo Press.

Gamō, M. 1960. *Nihonjin no Seikatsu-Kōzō Josetsu* [Introduction to the structure of the Japanese life]. Tokyo: Seishin Shobō.

Hōmushō [Ministry of Justice]. 1973. *Hanzai Hakusho* [Criminal White Paper]. Tokyo: Ministry of Finance.

Kuwabatake, Y. 1973. "Rikon" [Divorce], in *Gendai Shakai Byōrigaku* [Social Pathology]. Tokyo: Seishin Shobō.

Kuwata, Y. 1966. "Kazoku kaitai" [Family disorganization], in *Shakai Byōrigaku* [Social pathology], edited by K. Ōhashi and J. Oyabu. Tokyo: Seishin Shobo.

Matsubara, J. 1961. "Sengo shakai to kazoku" [The post-War society and the family], in *Nippon no Shakai* [The Japanese society], edited by T. Fukutake. Tokyo: Yūhikaku.

Mitsukawa, T. 1967. "Toshi no kazoku kaitai" [Family disorganization in the city], in *Toshi Shakaigaku* [Urban sociology], edited by K. Ōhashi and T. Omi. Tokyo: Kawashima Shoten.

Naka, H. 1973. "Jisatsu" [Suicide], in *Gendai Shakai Byōriga Ku* [Contemporary Social Pathology], edited by K. Ōhashi, T. Shikata, and J. Ōyabu. Tokyo: Kawashima Shoten.

Nakane, C. 1972. *Japanese Society*. Berkeley and Los Angeles: University of California Press.
Ōhara, K. 1965. *Nippon no Jisatsu* [Suicide in Japan]. Tokyo: Seishin Shobō.
Okuda, M. 1966. "Ohiiki shakai to shakai byori" [Community and social pathology], in *Shakai Byōrigaku* [Social pathology], edited by K. Ōhashi and J. Ōyabu. Tokyo: Seishin Shobō.
Ōmura, R. 1969. "Korega nōson no kindaika ka?" [Is this the modernization of the village?], *Ushio* Autumn 1968:118–26. Reprinted in *Nihonjin: Sono Kozo Bunseki* [The Japanese: Readings in Culture and Personality], edited by T. Sofue. Tokyo: Shibundō, 1969.
Reich, Charles. 1970. *The Greening of America*. New York: Random House.
Sakamoto, J. 1968. "Seinen yo, den'en ni kaero!" [Youngsters, let's go back to the country!], *Ushio* Autumn 1968:70–79.
Shikata, T. 1966. "Rikon, iede" [Divorce and runaway], in *Kazoku Shakaigaku* [Sociology of the family], edited by K. Ōhashi and K. Masuda. Tokyo: Kawashima Shoten.
Sofue, T. 1964. "Tokyo no daigakusei ni okeru tekiō katei no ichibunseki" [An analysis of the process of adjustment in Tokyo college students], *Nempō Shakai Shinrigaku* [Japanese Annals of Social Psychology] 5:133–60.
Tsukiji, B. 1964. *Nōson Kakumei: Gijutsu Kakushin wa Nani o Motarasuka?* [Revolution in agricultural villages: What will the technical innovation bring to us?]. Tokyo: Chūō Kōronsha.
United Nations. 1973. *Demographic Yearbook*. New York: United Nations.
Yokoyama, S. 1960. "Shokuba Kinchō" [Social tensions within enterprises], in *Shakai Byōrigaku* [Social pathology], edited by K. Ōhashi and J. Ōyabu. Tokyo: Seishin Shobō.

PART 4

Minority or Subordinate Status and Change

In the previous sections a number of authors dealt with situations of change stemming from a variety of political and social stimuli. In this final section, we consider change occurring within and between social segments of complex societies. Part 4 in some sense is the converse of Part 2: in Part 2 we examined similarities in responses to change in areal cultures that had no political or social cohesion; in Part 4 the reverse is true. Political unification, voluntary or forced, has created complex pluralistic societies whose ethnic or social segments respond differently to change.

Unfortunately, we cannot present examples of each possible type of social subgroup or variety of response to change. Some other papers presented at the original conference or submitted later could not be included due to space limitations. I shall refer to these in this introduction and in the general conclusions, as it is essential to consider the issues they raised.

Represented directly or indirectly in this section are questions of ethnic groups in such pluralistic societies as the United States and India. First, particularly in the United States, are the individual and group responses to change of voluntary immigrants who became members of ethnic minorities in a new society. Second, there are groups in the United States that have become minority enclaves by conquest, either recently or long past, and maintained their ethnic integrity. Such groups manifest different responses from those groups who have entered a pluralistic situation voluntarily. A third type of response to change is shown by the members of different occupations, castes, or social classes as they experience modernization. There is notable contrast between what happens in a class-segmented society and the social changes visible in a caste society such as India.

Finally, change in society cannot but help bring about shifts in status and in the role characteristics that differentiate the sexes in family and other interpersonal relationships as illustrated in Egypt. These shifts are bound to have psychological consequences on both men and women.

ETHNICITY AND SOCIAL PLURALISM

In the first paper in this section, Nathan Glazer suggests how American society is segmented by ethnicity as well as by social class. It is an inherently pluralistic society where every group of a different origin, whether or not it is racially or physically distinct, tends eventually to be treated as an "ethnic" segment of the population. It is difficult to explain the reasons for differential adjustive or adaptive responses made by ethnic groups, as their origins are so diverse and the patterns of immigration so varied. As a result, the community and family responses to acculturation within American society manifest a wide variety of historical adaptations.

Every ethnic group member in the United States must adapt to a general, widely recognized pattern of relative social rankings. Pejorative or discriminatory social attitudes are particularly difficult for members of groups when the family and community patterns of socialization have failed to protect the individual from the harmful personal effects of chronic social discrimination.

Glazer's chapter warns us of the difficulties inherent in attempts at an easy comparison of the relative adjustment of American ethnic groups given the diversity of variables to be considered.

POLITICAL DEFEAT, SOCIAL STATUS, AND ACCULTURATION

Theodore Graves' contribution to the conference addressed itself specifically to problems of ethnic identity for the American Indian minorities in North America. Graves discussed the widespread appearance of individual and social pathology in the socially dispersed Indian and Eskimo minorities. Using a "decision theory" framework he centered on four problem areas of acculturation: first, limited access to the valued goals of the majority society; second, the anomic breakdown of normative goals and social controls within Indian cultures; third, the disorganizing effects of competing reference groups, especially in childhood and adolescence; fourth, the problems of a negative self image that is passed on from one generation to the next.

The basic question which Graves addressed is: under what conditions does acculturation create psychological adjustment problems and under what conditions does it not? He has examined in his own ongoing research the drinking problem of the Navajo immigrants to a large American city as it is related to difficulties in occupational adaptation. He claimed that the Navajo are caught in a situation of desire for access to the material goods of American society and an inability to obtain them, resulting in internal stresses which are resolved maladaptively by drinking. This theory emphasizes "means-goals" disjunction as an essential dynamic of social pathology, that is, insufficient means to obtain the desired goal. Graves presented results of direct psychological measures which demonstrate that those experiencing a "means-goals" disjunction do, in fact, display higher levels of psychic stresses and more symptoms of psychopathology. Therefore, he finds support for the argument that drinking rates and court convictions are a response to psychological difficulties, rather than to a lack of "stake" in the dominant society's norms.

Graves' second argument was that there are indeed some "basic incompatibilities" between the traditional values of Indian culture and such highly espoused capitalist values as individual accumulation of wealth. This conflict of values makes it impossible for some Indians to take on the necessary occupational roles. For example, it is difficult to act as a storekeeper, since generosity toward kin is directly opposed to the necessity of running a capitalist business.

The third feature which he spelled out is the related problem of competing reference groups, which make for highly differential responses to education. (A reference group sets the values and attitudes which an individual desires to emulate, whether or not he is actually a member of the group.)

Finally, he discussed problems of self-concept and social self-identity. As has been reported by a number of other psychological anthropologists observing problems of adaptation among American Indians, Graves reviewed the forms of negative self and social image that contribute heavily to social pathology: occupational failure, negative mothering of infants, a horrendous suicide rate as well as the problems specific to alcoholism.

The psychologist C. J. Lee contributed a paper to the Hakone conference entitled "Culture Change and Psychological Adjustment Among the S.E. Bantu." Lee examined the adjustive and adaptive responses of the defeated Zulu of South Africa, former proud warriors living in a present-day demeaned socially subordinate caste status under white domination. He contrasts patterns of adjustment and adaptation of the nineteenth and twentieth centuries in respect to two psychological variables: that of achievement and of aggression. It must be noted that these are essential interpersonal variables to be found expressed in every culture within the adult occupational role behavior of both men and women.

The Zulu male received adult status recognition in the past for his military prowess, courage, and dignity. Status was gained by military exploits. In contrast, the achievement orientation of women was expressed solely in terms of childbearing and rearing in a definitively subordinate role. Interestingly enough, as in many other societies there were rituals of licence where role reversal occurred and women and girls don male attire, sing obscene songs, and take on other attributes of the male role forbidden women. Lee indicates that in the prior culture there were alternative modes of adjustment and adaptation for those individuals who suffered both internal difficulties and external role conflict. Traditionally intrapsychic problems had several cultural outlets around such as the use of divination, sorcery, and other practices of a similar nature. For example, anxiety could be allied and converted from "free floating" forms to definite fear of a known sorcerer. Anxiety could be allayed by the use of countermagic and protective rituals. Conversely, recourse to a sorcerer would provide a very satisfactory outlet for aggression such as that engendered by jealousy.

Lee then turns to the twentieth century where the political structure and its security system no longer exists. The Zulu have been defeated by South African whites. They have become a minority exposed to western medicine and education. Gulfs of understanding have widened between the uneducated traditional leaders and the more literate young men. Patterns of achievement and aggression have changed. The status of warrior no longer exists and occupational achievement is being defined in terms of a modern industrial economy in which the black man plays a subordinate, demeaned role. He is denied opportunity, occupational and personal development and yet he has internalized the values of a modern culture. By means of the TAT Test Lee presents evidence of a covert aggression and hostility felt towards superordinate whites—a feeling of need to support one's own community and yet a sadness and despair about an incapacity for successful actualization.

Some specific forms of breakdown appear, especially among women related to culture change. This is evident in dream material systematically gathered by Lee. Magic is still available to help ease the stresses of modern life. Sorcery has not disappeared, but is still used as a recourse in interpersonal difficulties. There is evidence for considerable internalized conflict related to difficulties in realizing its role expectations for both men and women.

In another paper, Professor J.E. Cawte discussed the result of a more classical psychiatric approach to the present minority status of the Australian aborigines in assessing psychological responses to culture change. He contrasts the more passive responses of the Australian aborigines to the more active and successful responses of the natives of New Guinea. Those living in New Guinea are still a majority in control of their own lives, whereas the Australians live either in missionized enclaves or in what amounts to reservations.

As in the case of many of the other groups that might be considered, the rampant political injustices incurred make it seem somewhat academic to consider the problem solely in its psychocultural dimension. Perhaps more than any other group, the Australian aborigines, including the Tasmanians who are now extinct, were subjected not only to foreign diseases, but to total status degradation by white settlers. Their previous forms of social organization were totally disrupted. More recently, the Australians have relented and sought to protect the "Blackfellow." Nevertheless, the case for assimilation or incorporation of the Bushman into modern life has been considered hopeless.

Among the Australian aborigines sorcery and possession are culturally available for the external expression of internal adjustive problems. Recourse to their use, as Cawte indicated, is one measurable index of anxiety and disturbance. The compelling influence of sorcery among aborigines is indicated by the phenomenon of "thanatosis," the medically inexplicable death of individuals who have been socially condemned to death by sorcerers.

Clinical study of the present day cultural use of sorcery reveals that it becomes more prevalent in situations of culture contact, rather than less prevalent, as some might expect. In reservation-like living conditions in Australia, it appears more common in multitribal aggregations than in single tribe cohesive communities. This suggested to Cawte that social fragmentation and resulting personal insecurity is a direct determinant of the rising incidence of sorcery complaints.

Cawte singled out the high density of internment camps as the most disruptive problem of aboriginal life. He believes that many of the traits attributed to aborigines may actually be the result of this externally-induced camp life. Occasional brawls and violence, some forms of drunkenness, and disputes over women are all used by the whites on the outside to form negative stereotypes of the native personality.

Concentrated efforts are now being made by European Australians to help rehabilitate the aboriginal family and make them more Western through welfare, mental care, education, and social-economic support. He reports that these efforts have met with limited success.

Related to Levy's discussion of the time phases to be found in responses to change, Cawte briefly reported also on his previous study of a three-generational group in which the older generation characteristically manifested paranoid states and had a concentration of aggressive personalities while the middle generation had more organic disorders of a type that would have proved fatal if they had been living a more traditional life. In the younger generation, he found more evidence of schizophrenic disorders. These observations suggest some evolution in the type of mental disorder taking place with culture change. In the first generation, assertive opposition had been adaptively expressed; in the second, more apathy had been felt along with physical deterioration, subnutrition, and disruption of family life. In the more recent, third phase there is further fragmentation in the family relationships and characteristic features of withdrawal and failure to become involved in any way with European society.

In brief, this volume suggests forcefully how much clinical work awaits systematic attention. There are unavoidable psychological concomitants compounding the maladaptive responses of defeated groups that have been forcefully incorporated by more complex societies. Subsequent restitutive social policy should not ignore what has occurred and is occurring on the psychological level. Comparing various instances world wide, one notes functional similarities in reactions wherever situations have been studied, psychologically as well as politically, be it the American continent, Australia, South Africa, or Eastern and Northern Asia. Even well-meaning, humane policies very often neglect to consider such psychological determinants and therefore fail in their ameliorative efforts.

INTRAGROUP DIFFERENCES IN CULTURE CHANGE

The final concern of this section is how social change within a culture may affect a given occupational class or other social segment. In a previous publication with Bauer (1956) on adjustment to the Soviet socio-political system, Inkeles used a modal personality concept to sketch forms of conflict and incomplete communication between the political elite and the majority of the Russian population. The framework they use suggests a concept of differential socialization: the intrafamily experiences of children growing up in the various segments of society differ in such a way that differences in subgroups tend to be perpetuated. The authors found that differences in response to government policies were related to citizens' educational and occupational levels. There is a self-perpetuating tendency evident within the managerial class; many of its members grew up in families of similar status. Children in those families are reared differently from those in typical peasant or worker families. These differential early socialization experiences, according to the authors, produced enduring effects on personality formation prior to exposure to common educational experiences in the schools. Mobility out of the lower classes occurs mainly among individuals whose personality is somewhat different, for whatever reasons, from that of the majority of their class of origin. These differences express themselves in stronger drives for education and for a position of status. This is not a conscious "natural selection," but an automatic process based on affinity between certain personality types and opportunities for membership in the elite categories within the Soviet system.

In Chapter 11 Gerald Berreman takes on a very complex situation in

India today, a society segregated for much of its history by considerations of caste defined both occupationally and in terms of ritual purity. Berreman's interactional orientation focuses on the political and psychocultural problems of differential status. Whereas one could generalize briefly that social trends in the United States (as suggested by Glazer and others) have caused caste increasingly to be defined in ethnic terms, in India the converse is true. Ethnic differences become, somehow or other, defined within a caste ranking system. Studies in India by Srinivas (1966) and other social scientists have described a process termed "sanskritization," which occurs when those in an inferior position take on behavior patterns of those in a superior position in order to emulate the superior status. Berreman in his chapter raises the major issues related to change around this dynamic in Indian society. There is a strong social inducement for individuals to emulate what they see as socially rewarded as well as rewarding behavior. Such emulation is visible both in a situation of social mobility in subordinate social segments of a population, and in acculturative forms of change in which an individual enhances his social position by taking on behavioral patterns borrowed from another group.

Berreman points out how mobility in India tends to be on a group basis rather than on an individual basis (as it is in the United States), for caste structure necessitates the movement of a total group rather than an individual in order to enhance relative status. Patterns of status emulation based on an implicit cultural acceptance of status hierarchy impede government attempts at equalization of status for all Indian citizens. Again, as was demonstrated in the instances of China and Japan, the cultural ethos persists in spite of deliberate attempts at amelioration by legal means. Despite changes in social forms, the implicit patterns of hierarchy remain and indeed operate in such a way that there is keen frustration on the part of the socially disadvantaged. Berreman points out that only at the highest levels of economic influence is there satisfaction with the status quo in India today. For the elite, the economy, the political system, and the social organization have worked advantageously. Threats of radical political or economic change from the right or left cause them some anxiety, but they generally maintain a complaisant unrealistic wish that change will not occur.

Berreman's chapter illustrates a very general socioeconomic condition in large parts of the world. Modernization has brought abject poverty and status loss to some. There are enormous economic and social disparities in many societies. Such a status quo cannot long persist, and social mobility on the part of some (as in India) is not a viable answer. People cannot leave the resolution of such problems to impersonal forces without risking disaster. Fundamental changes in social and economic structures are called for, and in one way or another will eventuate. This sense of social urgency prompts many social scientists to consider the niceties of concern with the subjective, human experience or with the working of psychological determinants as irrelevant.

Without negating a need for political action, a major purpose of this volume is to point out that should we at any time neglect to consider the psychological as important, we may embark on retrograde policies borne of the best intentions. We may institute political policies that are doomed to failure because the considerable collective force of human psychological motivation is ignored or ill considered. If change is to be accomplished by deliberate policy, the intimate patterns of human socialization within primary group experiences must somehow become part of any genuinely scientific equation assessing all the variables contributing to social change.

THE RELATIVE STATUS OF THE SEXES AS A MAJOR DETERMINANT OF HISTORY

In the final chapter contributed to this volume, Cynthia Nelson describes how, according to many observers of modernizing societies in the Middle East, the women's aspirations, demands, and successes are causing a basic transformation. The entire pattern of social interaction between the sexes is changing with increasing rapidity. Literacy and independence among Moslem women is not a twentieth century phenomenon, but in the past it was limited to a very small segment of the upper class. Nelson is concerned with present forms of psychological adjustment and social adaptation in a society which has, in the past, reinforced beliefs in the inferiority of women. Her chapter complements Chapter 5 on the problems in the Arab world.

One of the recent influences for change has been the educational and occupational opportunities given women in Egypt. This has come with great difficulty due to obstacles such as chronic unemployment among the male population, which limits the employment of women even in jobs where they are manifestly more productive and efficient than men. Economic needs and traditional attitudes can conflict, causing a dilemma for men, some of whom, for example, are willing to accept a working partner for a wife and at the same time maintain ideas of subservience in other areas.

Male-female relationships have to be viewed in the context of the historical confrontation between cultures caused by patterns of dominance and submission and the ambivalent types of emulation between conqueror and conquered. The Middle East did not develop castes in its pattern of social stratification but, until recently, kept women in a subordinate role on explicit assumptions of biological inferiority. The adjustive psychological effects of these relationships upon both sexes have been profound.

Elsewhere, Miner and DeVos (1960) have written about the psychological effects of subordinate status on the dominant and the subordinate grouping, based on the findings of projective test material obtained in Algeria. Miner and DeVos argued that institutionalization of a concept of biological inferiority in women produces difficult psychological problems for men, perhaps even more than for the subordinated women. Defense systems emphasizing masculinity perpetuate difficulties in relating to women. Status subordination of women is an indirect cause in many men of latent, if not overt, homosexuality. Paranoid type defenses are frequently used to bolster threatened masculinity.

DeVos and Wagatsuma (1967) have contended that there are basic functional similarities between sexual and caste subordination patterns when they are based on the same premises which causes a dominant group to fear and repress another. Paranoid fears of the sexual and aggressive propensities of the exploited group occur. Such displacement of qualities that are personally disavowed by a majority or some majority onto a subordinate group, like the American blacks and Japanese outcastes, parallels some of the problems resulting from basic inequalities in the social relations of men and women.

As Berreman has pointed out in respect to those subordinated in India, there are certain mythologies in stratified societies that people are content in their subordinate role. This belies the facts of political history as well as psychodynamic psychology.

REFERENCES

Bauer, Raymond, and Inkeles, Alex. 1956. *How the Soviet System Works: Cultural, Psychological, and Social Themes.* Cambridge, Mass.: Harvard University.

DeVos, George, and Wagatsuma, Hiroshi. 1966. *Japan's Invisible Race.* Berkeley: University of California.

Miner, Horace, and DeVos, George. 1960. *Oasis and Casbah: Algerian Culture and Personality in Change.* Ann Arbor: University of Michigan.

Srinivas, M. N. 1956. "A Note on Sanskritization and Westernization," *Far Eastern Quarterly* 15:481–96.

Chapter 10

American Ethnic Groups: Identity, Cultural Change, and Competence

Nathan Glazer

THE DIVERSITY OF AMERICAN ETHNIC GROUPS

A fantastic kind of diversity is now implied in the United States by the term "ethnic group." To bring this diversity together with the general theme of culture change and psychological adjustment is to approach a topic so broad that even the most selective and idiosyncratic approach can be justified. The theoretical problems in considering the adjustment of these very varied ethnic groups are enormous.

In the United States the term "ethnic group" originally was applied to the major European immigrant groups, whose steady and massive immigration into the United States became a feature of American history for a hundred years after about 1820. The major immigrant groups included, in roughly chronological order, Irish, Germans, Norwegians, Swedes, Czechs, Jews, Italians, Poles, Russians, Hungarians, Slovaks, South Slavs, Greeks, and many others. Originally called "immigrant groups," they became "ethnic groups" as the numbers of immigrants declined, and the numbers in the second and third generations increased, while some sense of group identity and group character persisted.

A second kind of group now considered "ethnic" consists of those immigrants who are listed in the census as "races"—including Japanese, Chinese, Koreans, Indians (that is, from India), and other smaller groups that are not European and yet scarcely classifiable as "races" by any scientific criteria of race. In the mysterious processes of American group formation, they have also become "ethnic groups," and the fact that the Japanese are a "race" and that Greek-Americans are an "ethnic group" only moderately affects, whether in the consciousness of members of these groups or the consciousness of other Americans, their general status as two of the many groups of a generally ethnic type into which Americans are divided.

Between the core "ethnic groups" and the "races" there are a variety of groups from Western Asia that are not simply ethnic and certainly not racial—for example, Syrians, Lebanese, and Armenians. Typically, they immigrated later than European ethnic groups, and in American (that is to say, old American) consciousness, they have been seen as less European than European ethnic groups (since they came from Asia), and not quite so different as the Eastern Asian "racial" groups (since there are substantial numbers of Christians among them). Still, in the American hierarchy of group preferences they have generally stood near the bottom, above the races and non-Christian groups, but below the European ethnic groups. One must also point out that many of the Eastern and Southern European ethnic groups, during the first few decades of their mass migration, were also seen as very different, indeed racially different, from the Northern and Western European immigrants. Thus the southern Italians and the Jews were considered racially distinct and inferior during the first two decades of this century.

We have already referred to "old Americans." They, too, are now, for scholarly and increasingly for popular purposes, yet another "ethnic group." It is characteristic for studies of various kinds of phenomena which require the distribution of a population into ethnic categories simply to place those without a specific ethnic identification, the white Anglo-Saxon Protestants, into a category variously called "British," "Yankee," "old American," "white Protestant," or "WASP" (white Anglo-Saxon Protestant). By now, politicians, pollsters, magazine writers, and the public are not astonished to see the descendants of the founders of the American republic referred to as just another ethnic group.

We have already referred to one religious group, as well as a number of racial groups, as being in some degree also "ethnic," that is, Jews. A few years ago, one had to make an argument in order to treat religious groups as ethnic groups—that is, groups felt to be connected by descent, values, some common identity, so considered by others, and showing various distinctive traits. Today, it is fairly common in research to consider a religious group as a kind of ethnic group. Religious denominations have tended to be ethnically based, their membership drawn from a single ethnic group. Jews, one major religious group, are simultaneously a major ethnic group. Actually, American Jews are divided into a number of important ethnic variants—German Jews, East European Jews (who also vary by country and region of origin), and Sephardic Jews from Mediterranean countries. But one variant, the East European, is dominant, and the entire group is merged to form what is conceived of as a single ethnic group, "American Jews," even though each subgroup maintains a number of important cultural variants.

The various denominations of Protestantism were also ethnically based—(such as the Lutherans who were primarily Germans, Swedes, or Norwegians). Similarly, the Catholic Church in each area tends to reflect the ethnic group or groups which make it up—Irish, Italian, Polish, German, and so on. Even after these ethnic divisions were in part overcome—Protestant denominations have been merged, and the different ethnic groups within the Catholic Church are being brought more effectively within a common religious structure—the larger "supraethnic" church itself tended to act in some ways as an ethnic group. Will Herberg argued that religious identity replaces and serves the same function as ethnic identity. Ruby Jo Reeves Kennedy documented how intermarriage between persons of different groups was more common if they were within the same religion. Thus the larger religious group served as the boundary for marriage partners (Herberg 1955; Kennedy 1944, 1952.) The religious group becomes in some measure a descent group, with some common cultural attributes. Aside from the mechanism of social change which tends to make religious groups seem like ethnic groups, in any local area each religious group will be composed of only a few ethnic groups. Thus, Catholics in New Haven are either Irish or Italian, in Buffalo they are largely of Polish origin, and so on.

Mexican Americans form another distinct type of "ethnic group." If immigrants, they have migrated from over a land border, and maintain close contacts with the mother country. In this respect, as in others, they are like French Canadians, in that they show a low rate of social mobility and a relatively low rate of acculturation and assimilation. But the Mexican Americans are distinct in that part of the population was acquired by conquest. Some of those who came as immigrants identify with this older group, seeing themselves as a conquered and exploited people, rather than one which has come willingly for greater opportunities, for they live and work in states that were once part of Mexico.

Somewhat different is the case of the Puerto Ricans. They have not been conquered in direct conflict with the United States, nor have they drifted across a land frontier. They have been acquired as a colony, but have come to the continent as free migrants. Whatever the ambiguities of their political status, most Puerto Ricans tend to see themselves as an ethnic group, though they may yet come to see themselves as a colonized group demanding political independence.

Even the American Indian, descendants of another conquered people, finds when he comes to the city that the general form "ethnic group" gives him his identity, for he is forced to act as members of ethnic groups in the city before him were forced to act. He associates with other Indians, formally and informally, fights for recognition of his problems, and becomes, in general consciousness, a member of another ethnic group.

Finally, we come to the American Negro. Here perhaps the category of "ethnic group" is most uncertainly applied and most strongly fought. At one time the American Negro wanted to be only another American, an old American, certainly, for he had come as long ago as the oldest Americans. Perhaps there were moments when, in northern and western cities, Negroes saw themselves as part of the pattern of American ethnic groups. Certainly American social scientists have often analyzed the Negro and his problems in northern cities in the context of the prevailing patterns of ethnicity. Whether they considered economic achievement, educational level, cultural development, or political participation, they might well have found it most convenient to compare the American Negro not with the faceless category of "whites," but with specific ethnic groups in the various cities in which Negroes settled (see Glazer and Moynihan 1970).

Perhaps this was only an optimistic illusion. American blacks, it appears, will not be satisfied by being enrolled, with latecomers, in the array of American ethnic groups. If they are not to be fully incorporated into American society, on the level of old Americans, then they demand a special recognition of their character as a people—a recognition distinct from the informal kinds of recognition of ethnicity that have prevailed up until now for European ethnic groups.

Still, if we speak of American ethnic groups, we must also speak of the American Negro. Even if Negroes are not to be considered an ethnic group, the key questions that concern social scientists and Americans in general in connection with black Americans can only be settled by understanding in what way blacks *differ* from other ethnic groups. If we are concerned with the question of their occupational advancement into skilled working class, white collar, business, and professional spheres, then we will want to see how their progress or lack of progress compares with that of various ethnic groups which have faced problems similar to, if drastically less severe than, those blacks faced. If we are interested in their psychological health, once again we will want to see how various ethnic groups and other races have adapted or failed to adapt to the stresses of discrimination and prejudice. To understand the cultural development of black Americans, the rise of strong feelings of specific cultural identity, and of a strong desire for the recognition of the separateness of Afro-American culture, we will want to compare it with the cultural development of other ethnic groups in this country: their acceptance or refusal to accept their separate identity, their relationship to the culture and language of their homelands, their adaptation to American culture on various levels.

The blacks' place in American society—owing to their special involvement in American history, the special obligation of American society to them because of hundreds of years of slavery and of exploitation, the size and consequent weight of the Negro group, its political significance, and its power to disrupt the society—will always be of special significance. But our understanding of the American Negro must take place within the context of American Ethnicity.

The chief confrontations of black Americans and white Americans are ethnic. The black does not confront an undifferentiated white society, which in any case hardly exists. He deals with Jewish teachers in New York, Polish homeowners in Chicago, Irish and Italian political power in Boston, old American suspicion and hostility in a host of suburbs, and so on. American Negroes are evaluated by ethnic groups in terms which ethnic groups draw from their own experience: "We made it in the face of prejudice, why doesn't he?" So whether or not American blacks consider themselves an ethnic group, their relationship to the other ethnic groups will be a key element in their future history. The beginning of this interplay is perhaps best indicated in the fact that the President's Commission on Civil Disorders devoted a chapter of its report to a specific comparison of Negro and immigrant experience (National Advisory Commission on Civil Disorders 1968, Chapter 9).

We have raised briefly, very briefly, some of the key theoretical questions involved in the concept of the American ethnic group: its relationship to *race*; its relationship to *religion*; its relationship to the descendants of the early settlers, who were called "colonists" before the Revolution and the establishment of the American republic, rather than "immigrants," as those who came later are called; its relationship to the descendants of the American slaves, to the conquered people of the Southwest, and to the original Indian inhabitants. All these categories begin to take on the character of ethnic group, which becomes a fundamental category for the understanding of American social structure and the American population.

Ethnic group is no longer a category determined by taking the European immigrants of various geographically defined countries and including them and their descendants within a single group. For it is not only a demographic category but also a social category, involving the same complexities in its understanding and measurement as does social class. Just as classes merge and diverge, with some borders between them becoming less distinct (for example, the line between the "old upper class" and new recruits through higher education), others becoming more distinct (the line between working class and welfare poor), and with varied consequences for consciousness and social change, so, too, with ethnic groups. Some ethnic groups have been formed out of the merger of groups that were and felt themselves to be distinct in Europe; some have been formed out of races; religious groups have taken on some of the characteristics of ethnic groups.

The ethnic group is a form in American society, one may say an institution, that is available to define the character of various groups as they enter and become a part of that society. Just as class at different times seems to have been more closely linked to family, or to education, or to profession, so ethnicity has on occasion had a sense of racial difference, on other occasions of cultural or linguistic difference, and in its most attenuated forms it seemed a certain symbolic attachment. And just as class consciousness waxes and wanes, so does ethnic consciousness; since 1965, and the rise of black power, we have been, it seems, in a phase of waxing consciousness (see Glazer 1954, 1965).

A full understanding of any American social phenomenon must involve attention to the ethnic factor, just as it must involve attention to the basic social category of class. Indeed, these two crosscutting characteristics increasingly become the two dominant elements for the categorization of the American population for purposes of social analysis, and for many problems ethnicity is more significant than class.

EFFECTS OF ETHNICITY ON ADAPTATION AND ADJUSTMENT TO AMERICAN LIFE

Obviously such an enormous diversity of groups forms a great natural laboratory for studying the problems of adaptation and psychological adjustment under cultural change. But it is a laboratory of enormous complexity. The number of individual studies which throw some light on this matter runs into the thousands. Relatively few studies have focused directly on ethnicity, but large numbers categorize their population by class and race, and many by religion. In some cases, such categories correspond to ethnic groups, but concentration on ethnic group, as such, as a research variable is relatively limited. There is an enormous body of literature on the American Negro and a considerably more restricted body of literature on American Jews. All other ethnic groups come far behind, as far as research literature on their psychological adjustment under conditions of cultural change is concerned, except perhaps for the large Italian American communities in New Haven and Boston which have received a good deal of attention from scholars at Yale and Harvard. For most groups, however, the literature is fragmentary.

Differing Patterns of Adaptation

It is clear that different ethnic groups have had radically different patterns of adaptation, which we may crudely measure by achievement within the society, and adjustment, which we may crudely measure by the degree of psychological disorder they have suffered. While it is hard to measure adjustment, the statistics of economic advance in the form of income and occupation, of educational achievement, and of political prominence and significance are unambiguous, though complicated. But we cannot compare ethnic groups simply from the census, for the census only records the foreign born of an ethnic group, and, for some statistics, the second generation, that is, those born in this country of foreign parents. Thus from the census we can only study the achievement of the first two generations—and often only the first—of immigrant ethnic groups. The census does, however, record all members of a racial group, regardless of generation, and so we have better statistics on Negroes, Japanese Americans, Chinese Americans, and other groups recorded as races. Nor does the census record religion. But from the fragmentary information of the census, and from detailed specific studies of ethnic groups in various communities, we do know, beyond any doubt, that certain groups have shown a remarkable ability to advance economically, educationally, and politically; others have been less successful, and still others have lagged disastrously (see, for example, Warner and Srole 1945; Glazer 1960; Glazer and Moynihan 1970; Strodtbeck 1958b; Petersen 1971; Light 1972).

Recently, the census has begun to collect some data for ethnic groups, although its definition is radically defective. Thus, the "Russian" and "Polish" groups in these initial census efforts to get at ethnicity include an indeterminate number of Jews, and it is undoubtedly for this reason that "Russians" lead in median years of school completed (16.0, as against 12.9 for English, Scots, Welsh, and lesser figures for all other groups) and in median family income (U.S. Bureau of the Census, 1971–72a).

The data on the position certain ethnic groups in American society hold in those spheres that we use as indices of adaptation are quite clear: certainly blacks, Mexican Americans, Puerto Ricans, and American Indians form the lower strata of American society (though a good number of poor whites of a variety of groups keep them company there). But how we may explain their position is far more complex than is generally realized. Racism, discrimination, prejudice, the stress of living in a society where one is not only disvalued but faces concrete barriers, are certainly one part of the story. However, when we disaggregate the category of blacks, let us say, we find some groups, such as West Indians, who show higher rates of achievement in the measures of adaptation than others. While all Spanish-surnamed Americans are considered disadvantaged by government agencies, and must be included in censuses of employees and students so that these agencies may determine whether a pattern of discrimination exists, the differences between groups of Spanish-surnamed Americans are substantial: Cuban families in 1971 had a median income of $9,371, Mexican American families $7,539, and Puerto Rican families $6,210. The educational pattern of each group was quite different (U.S. Bureau of the Census 1971-72b).

The Relationship Between Adaptation and Adjustment

We can take three approaches to conceptualizing this ethnic variation in adaptation. First, we can analyze the structure of opportunity each group has met, and we can match against that its resources in terms of certain social measures that qualify it to take advantage of this opportunity. The structure of opportunity includes such factors as the nature of the economy at the time the group entered the society; the measures of resources include the group's wealth, education, skills. It is quite clear that this is not enough to explain what has happened to the various groups. We can then add a second element—the degree of discrimination and prejudice the group has faced which has limited its using its capacities to achieve. While it is clear that discrimination and prejudice have played an enormous role in American society, groups that faced a considerable degree (and actual incarceration, as in the case of the Japanese) have sometimes done better than groups that have faced less prejudice and discrimination, and that have entered the society with apparently similar resources.

This drives us to a third level of explanation, the psychological and cultural factors, which we can demonstrate differ from group to group, though not as easily as we can demonstrate the differences in the opportunity structure, in initial resources, and in prejudice, discrimination, and oppression. Nevertheless, these are real and significant elements, elusive as they are, for nothing else will make sense of the facts. (The studies of the Japanese Americans are perhaps the most impressive demonstration of the significance of psychocultural factors. See, for example, Caudill and DeVos [1956].) This is perhaps an overly elaborate argument for something most social scientists accept, but I make it because this approach to the understanding of the competence and adaptation and achievement of different ethnic groups in American society is now strongly challenged.

Before examining the adjustment of different ethnic groups in the United States, we should note that there are various points of view about the relationship between adjustment and adaptation, that is, successful achievement. The earlier psychological researchers, under the influence of W. Lloyd Warner, wavered between a commitment to an open society, in which all have the opportunity to advance and achieve, and the feeling that striving to achieve will exact psychological costs and that it can thus be psychologically beneficial to maintain a stable class position in which, presumably, a good adjustment would coexist with modest achievement.

Some psychologists, too, are re-evaluating certain pathological symptoms as being in some sense adaptive, or if maladaptive, representing a "healthier" psychological adjustment, because the society itself is "sick."

The Difficulties of Studying Adjustment

American social scientists studying the characteristics of various ethnic groups have focused on one psychological aspect, the drive or motive to achieve. This is true not only of those who have studied the achievement motive itself, but in a large measure also true of those studying child rearing practices in different classes. These studies, too, have been oriented to a psychological predisposition to achieve: how does discipline affect the child's capacity for independence, for emotional distance from parents, for self-initiated and sustained activity, and the like?

Much of the research on psychological disorder bearing on ethnic groups tries to find relationships between geographical mobility, social mobility, achievement, aspiration, and mental illness. The clearest finding is that the downwardly mobile show a higher rate of treated mental disorder than the higher socioeconomic groups. The story on geographical mobility is more mixed. While some research has shown a relationship between migration and mental illness, the best studies are unclear (Hollingshead and Redlich 1958; Srole et al. 1962; Malzberg and Lee 1956).

The attempts to understand the problems of psychological adjustment through studies of the distribution of mental disorder are surrounded by pitfalls that make even the very best studies suspect. Studies of treated disorder, the most common, raise the difficult problems of the relationship between the treatment rate and the availability of treatment facilities for different areas and different socio-economic levels and, even more importantly, the effect on the treatment rate of groups' attitudes toward symptoms of mental disorder and toward the treatment of mental disorder.

Studies of prevalence raise other problems, such as the severity of the psychological disorder used as an instrument to determine prevalence. Contradictory findings can often be reconciled, but only by subtle analysis. Thus, the New Haven study, a study of treatment, showed much *higher* rates of treated disorder for Jews, though the difference was largely made up of treatment for psycho-neuroses. The Midtown study showed *no* difference in treatment rates. Earlier studies by Malzberg had shown a lesser degree of psychosis among Jews, measured by admission rates to hospitals. Many psychoanalysts—who do not use statistics—believe Jews are *more* neurotic. On prevalence, the Midtown study shows Jews less impaired, but also less "well"—they bulge in the "mild symptom formation" group (Srole et al. 1962; Rinder 1963).

But one wonders how much confidence one can place in these findings, except insofar as they seem to fit with experience. The Dohrenwends, reviewing some twenty-five studies of prevalence, determined that the only consistent finding is that social class and psychological disorder are inversely related in fourteen of eighteen studies (Dohrenwend and Dohrenwend 1965). It is not unreasonable that one possible response to the greater strains and pressures of economic insecurity and low status is a higher rate of psychological disorder. Yet even such a finding is not indisputable. There is sufficient evidence that ethnic groups vary widely in various health matters, and in aspects of family life which affect physical health and, presumably, mental health. There is no reason to think that all groups of the same socio-economic level will show the same features of psychological disorder, if the ethnic factor is an independent one. One of the most striking studies of these differences is Minako Kurokawa's of the reasons for grossly different patterns of childhood accident rates between Japanese American and other families (Kurokawa 1966a, 1966b; see, too, Glazer 1955, on Jewish illness and accident rates).

While I would argue that differences in adjustment between ethnic groups are significant in the American context, and these differences affect adaptation, it would be pointless to underestimate the enormous difficulties involved, methodologically and theoretically, in establishing this position. One could go through a good deal of literature and point to conflicting studies in which, in one, ethnic factors are reduced or disappear when class, rural-urban, and other social variables are held constant; in others, ethnic factors remain when other social variables are held constant. A fascinating article by Bruce Dohrenwend demonstrates the complexities of trying to establish unambiguously the role of ethnicity, as against class and other factors in determining psychological disorder. His exploration begins with one of the most striking findings of the Midtown study in the area of ethnicity, the far greater degree of impairment found among Puerto Ricans in New York than among other groups. Dohrenwend reports other studies show the same (Srole et al. 1962, p. 290; Dohrenwend 1966).

But if psychological disorder really reflects social position, as seems reasonable from the findings on social class, then why, Dohrenwend asks, in the Washington Heights prevalence study, using the same instrument that the Midtown study used, did Negroes show no greater degree of psychological disorder than the Jews and Irish of Washington Heights? If mental disorder is a reaction to stress, to social status, then why do the Puerto Ricans show it, and not the Negroes?

He shows where one of the problems lies by a careful analysis of the instrument used to detect psychological impairment in the Midtown study, and by the response to the items in this instrument by both Negroes and Puerto Ricans. Puerto Ricans do not consider certain conditions on which they are requested to give personal information so undesirable as Jews and Irish do; Negroes consider them somewhat more undesirable. Thus Puerto Ricans may admit to more symptoms than Negroes. His argument indicates that items in tests trying to assess psychological disorder cross-culturally or cross-ethnically can only with great difficulty be decontaminated of cultural factors that make responses in one group aberrant while the same responses in another group are commonly accepted.

But, Dohrenwend continues, how far have we gotten if we find that an aberrant response in one group is considered somewhat normal in another, so that people do not resist acknowledging it? Even if a response is considered normal, does it not retain its character as a sign of mental ill-health—does it not perhaps reflect an ill-health that is common to an entire population, and which it would thus be foolish, in an excess of value-free cultural relativism, to label as "normal," or even "good," as well as "common" for that population? That is, if members of one ethnic group are freely willing to admit the presence of some psychological symptoms while members of another group who have the same symptoms do not admit that they have them, is there any reason then to conclude that the former group is "healthier"?

The willingness or unwillingness of groups to admit symptoms is somewhat related to a general problem with cultural-level psychological analysis: it inevitably focuses on invidious distinctions that members of the groups involved cannot accept with the same equanimity as they can analyses of structures of opportunity, of measures of resources, and of prejudice and discrimination. If a group migrated into the cities at a time when unskilled labor was a declining possibility, if its background meant that it came without money and education and occupational skills, if it faced prejudice, discrimination, and oppression, then the members of the group will not find, in an analysis of opportunity structure anything that is damaging to its self-image and respect. If, however, analysis focuses on the values of its culture, if it focuses on the relations within the family, if it emphasizes differences in capacity based on damaging family experiences that are *characteristic* of the culture, then we are in a completely different area of social science. The group will frequently not admit these characteristics nor accept with objective dispassion such judgments upon it—unless, of course, the group comes out "well" in the comparisons, in terms of commonly accepted values in the society; or unless the group is illiterate and unaware of what the social scientists are doing to it. Thus, the people of Alor could not fight back when Cora Du Bois and her associates presented a devastating picture of their culture and their psychological adjustment and capacity—the people of the United States can fight back, and increasingly are.

American Ethnic Groups   289

Fifteen years ago, when Fred Strodtbeck analyzed differences in family structure and achievement motive between Jews and Italians, he was already aware of this problem—after all, Italians in New Haven were not preliterates or peasants. He wrote:

> It is hoped that no reader will impute an evaluative tone to our comparison of Italians and Jews—the two differentially achieving groups chosen for study. In the first place, status mobility, used as the criterion of "success" in this study, should not be perceived as the only criterion for recognizing activities of social value. . . . Our own choice rests primarily on the fact that status mobility is a societal means of evaluating people which applies to a broad range of social activities in the United States today.
>
> In the second place, we are not primarily interested in studying these subcultures *per se*, with the aim of predicting which groups would show the most status mobility from now on. Rather, our interest was in the extent to which each of these "old cultures" was *initially* adaptive to the social setting as we analyzed it. There is considerable evidence in our data, in fact, to support the notion that, whatever differences in values and family interaction originally existed, they are disappearing as both groups are assimilated into American life. For example . . . we found no qualitative differences in family interaction between Italians and Jews . . . with effects of socio-economic status removed. . . .
>
> Finally, we know that socio-economic status affects socialization and the power balance in the family, both of which are related to subsequent achievement. But both ethnic groups are changing in socio-economic status. . . . [A]s an illustration: more Jews are moving into high status where the fathers are more powerful and may therefore, according to our data, tend to produce sons who have values less conducive to upward mobility. On the other hand, more Italians may be moving into medium status, where family power may be more conducive to mobility than in the lower status where many of them are now (Strodtbeck 1958a, pp. 185–86).

This is a valiant effort to reduce the invidiousness in such comparisons, but not completely effective. First, it is true that if status mobility should decline as a means of evaluating people, then the invidiousness in this distinction would also decline. If we had means of distributing income other than economic achievement, means which in no way affected the respect in which people were held, then indeed there would be no invidiousness in such an analysis. Many intellectuals argue against the use of "social mobility as a societal means of evaluating people," but it will be a long time before they succeed. If they do, or if, going even further, refusal to participate in workaday economic activities becomes a means of achieving even higher status (as it is now perhaps in hippie communities), then invidiousness would again return to such an analysis—but this time it would be perhaps the Japanese or the Jews who would protest at the image the analysis projected of them, as possessing the values that made for work, achievement, and social mobility.

Second, despite Strodtbeck's data, it is not clear that ethnic differences in values and family interaction are indeed declining. Lenski's *The Religious Factor* suggests that a number of key values may diverge between religious groups (which as I have said, are linked to ethnicity) with increasing generations in the United States. We have generally thought that, as ethnic groups rise from the working class to the middle class, they lose their original cultural attributes and thereby become more alike. They do, in some respects; but in other respects they maintain differences or become more different, in part because they are free to develop certain characteristics, since they are no longer under the common pressures of poverty or working-class status. This is at any rate one plausible interpretation to explain Lenski's findings (Lenski 1961). There are other striking demonstrations of the maintenance of differences between ethnic groups in the face of social mobility (see Stodolsky and Lesser 1967; and Greeley 1971.)

But whatever the possible reactions of Italian Americans to Strodtbeck's analysis, they pale before the actual reactions of American Negroes (and other deprived groups) to social scientists today. The most striking example of the difficulty of making potentially invidious analyses is the explosion that followed the publication of the Moynihan Report on the American Negro family, which said nothing more—indeed, considerably less—about the American Negro family than E. Franklin Frazier, John Dollard, Allison David, and many others had said years before (Rainwater and Yancey 1967). But these earlier examinations occurred at a time when it was taken for granted that social science devoted itself to analysis without consequences. Thus, when E. Franklin Frazier wrote about the Negro family, he never dreamed that government could or would do anything about it (Glazer 1966).

To these earlier writers, the Negro family was a social phenomenon to be *explained*. The audience for the explanation was not large, and it was not expected that the analysis would lead to political consequences. Today, both of those conditions have changed, and we work under conditions that soon may not permit the kinds of analyses in which we have freely engaged in this volume on the character of Arabs, Burmans, Melanesians, Indians, and many other groups. What this means for social science is a serious and much debated question, to which I do not have the answer. But, returning to the United States and American ethnic groups, perhaps more important than what this development may do to social science is what it may do to social policy (see Moynihan 1968; Glazer 1969). It may become impossible to study honestly the differences between ethnic groups, not only on the gross level of their achievement but on the more subtle level of aspects of their psychological adjustment, their culture and values, their family structure, and what in history lies behind all this. If it does, one wonders what that will do to the relations between groups, the quality of our culture, and our chances to devise effective policies to overcome inequality.

REFERENCES

Caudill, William, and DeVos, George. 1956. "Achievement, Culture, and Personality: The Case of Japanese Americans," *American Anthropologist* 58:1102–26.

DeVos, George. 1968. "Achievement and Innovation in Culture and Personality," in *The Study of Personality: An Interdisciplinary Appraisal*, edited by Edward Norbeck, Douglas Price-Williams, and William M. McCord. New York: Holt, Rinehart and Winston.

Dohrenwend, Bruce P. 1966. "Social Status and Psychological Disorder: An Issue of Substance and an Issue of Method," *American Sociological Review*, 31:14–34.

Dohrenwend, Bruce P., and Dohrenwend, Barbara S. 1965. "The Problem of Validity in Field Studies of Psychological Disorder," *Journal of Abnormal Psychology* 70:52–69.

Glazer, Nathan. 1954. "Ethnic Groups in America: From National Culture to Ideology," in *Freedom and Control in Modern Society*, edited by Monroe Berger et al. New York: Van Nostrand.

―――. 1955. "Social Characteristics of the American Jews, 1654–1954," in *American Jewish Yearbook*, vol. 56. New York: The American Jewish Committee and the Jewish Publication Society of America.

―――. 1960. "Social Characteristics of American Jews," in *The Jews*, edited by Louis Finkelstein. 3rd edition. New York: Harper.

―――. 1965. "The Peoples of America," *The Nation* 201 (20 Sept 1965): 137–41.

―――. 1966. "Introduction," *The Negro Family in the United States*, by E. Franklin Frazier. Chicago: University of Chicago Press.

―――. 1969. "Ethnic Groups and Education: Toward the Tolerance of Difference," *Journal of Negro Education* 38 (Summer 1969): 187–95.

Glazer, Nathan, and Moynihan, Daniel P. 1970. *Beyond the Melting Pot*. 2nd edition. Cambridge, Massachusetts: M.I.T. Press.

Greeley, Andrew. 1971. *Why Can't They Be Like Us?* New York: E. P. Dutton.

Herberg, Will. 1955. *Protestant, Catholic, Jew*. New York: Doubleday.

Hollingshead, A. B., and Redlich, F. C. 1958. *Social Class and Mental Illness*. New York: Wiley.

Kardiner, Abram, and Ovesey, Lionel. 1962. *The Mark of Oppression: Explorations in the Personality of the American Negro*. Cleveland: World.

Katzman, Martin. 1968. "Discrimination, Subculture, and the Economic Performance of Negroes, Puerto Ricans, and Mexican-Americans," *American Journal of Economics and Sociology* 27: 371–76.

―――. 1969a. "Ethnic Geography and Regional Economies, 1880–1960," *Economic Geography* 45:45–52.

———. 1969b. "Opportunity, Subculture, and the Economic Performance of Urban Ethnic Groups," *American Journal of Economics and Sociology* 28: 351-66.
Kennedy, Ruby Jo Reeves. 1944. "Single or Triple Melting Pot? Intermarriage Trends in New Haven, 1870-1950," *American Journal of Sociology* 49:331-39.
———. 1952. A subsequent article with the same title in the *American Journal of Sociology* 58: 56-59.
Kurokawa, Minako. 1966a. "Childhood Accident as a Measure of Social Integration," *Canadian Review of Sociology and Anthropology*, 3:67-83.
———. 1966b. "Family Solidarity, Social Change, and Childhood Accidents," *Journal of Marriage and the Family* 28: 498-506.
Lenski, Gerhard. 1961. *The Religious Factor*. New York: Doubleday.
Light, Ivan. 1972. *Ethnic Enterprise in America: Business and Welfare Among Chinese, Japanese, and Blacks*. Berkeley, California: University of California Press.
Malzberg, B., and Lee, E. S. 1956. *Migration and Mental Disease*. New York: Social Science Research Council.
Moustafa, A. Taher, and Weiss, Gertrud. 1968. "Health Status and Practice of Mexican Americans," Mexican American Study Project, Division of Research, Graduate School of Business Administration, University of California, Los Angeles, Advance Report 11.
Moynihan, Daniel P. 1968. "Sources of Resistance to the Coleman Report," *Harvard Educational Review* 38: 23-36.
National Advisory Commission on Civil Disorders. 1968. *Report of the National Advisory Commission on Civil Disorders*. Washington, D.C.: Government Printing Office.
Petersen, William. 1971. *Japanese Americans: Oppression and Success*. New York: Random House.
Rainwater, Lee, and Yancey, William. 1967. *The Moynihan Report and the Politics of Controversy*. Cambridge, Massachusetts: M.I.T. Press.
Rinder, Irwin D. 1963. "Mental Health of American Jewish Urbanites, A Review of Literature and Predictions," *International Journal of Social Psychiatry* 9:104-09.
Rosen, Bernard C. 1961. "Family Structure and Achievement," *American Sociological Review* 26: 574-85.
See, Joel J., and Miller, Kent S. 1973. "Mental Health," in *Comparative Studies of Blacks and Whites in the United States*, edited by Kent S. Miller and Ralph Mason Dreger. New York: Seminar Press.
Srole, Leo, et al. 1962. *Mental Health in the Metropolis*. New York: McGraw-Hill.
Stodolsky, Susan Silverman, and Lesser, Gerald. 1967. "Learning Problems in the Disadvantaged," *Harvard Educational Review* 37:546-93.
Strodtbeck, Fred L. 1958a. "Family Interaction, Values, and Achievement," in *Talent and Society*, edited by David C. McClelland, et al. Princeton: Van Nostrand.
———. 1958b. "Jewish and Italian Immigration and Subsequent Status Mobil-

ity," in *Talent and Society*, edited by David C. McClelland, et al. Princeton: Van Nostrand.

U.S. Bureau of the Census. 1971–72a. *Current Population Reports*. P-20, No. 249. "Characteristics of the Population by Ethnic Origin: March 1972 and 1971."

U. S. Bureau of the Census. 1971–72b. *Current Population Reports*. P-20, No. 250. "Persons of Spanish Origin in the United States: March 1972 and 1971."

Warner, W. Lloyd, and Srole, Leo. 1945. *The Social Systems of American Ethnic Groups*. New Haven, Connecticut: Yale University Press.

Chapter 11

Social Mobility and Change in India's Caste Society

Gerald D. Berreman

"Upon my back the burden of screaming blood-stained pain . . ."
(Umakant Randheer 1973)

"The cure of their ills can only come from a sea of change affecting the whole of Hindu society."
(N.K. Bose, Commissioner of Scheduled Castes and Tribes, 1970)

Indian society is widely known as one made up of corporate groups which are ranked relative to one another and in which membership is ascribed by birth, in short, a caste society. It is also a society made up of many other kinds of groups organized on different principles—regions, languages, religions, classes—socially and culturally distinct from one another, in continuous but limited interaction. There is perhaps no other nation, region, or culture area in which group memberships have been such a dominant theme in scientific studies and social commentaries; no other way in which the variety of groups has been so great.

India is also generally described as a traditional society and a sacred society: one in which ways of life are prescribed by custom and endorsed by religion. Yet no one today would be likely to claim that it is static. In fact, the major contribution of empirical studies spanning the more than twenty-five years since India's independence is documentation of change—of movement and flexibility in this uncompromisingly hierarchical, culturally and socially plural society. This change has been analyzed as social mobility, as status emulation, and in its distinctive and traditional Hindu manifestation as Sanskritization (Srinivas 1956). Governmental programs have been described as various kinds of development, reform, and abolition. Massive social and cultural processes have been discussed under such terms as casteism, communalism, regionalism, and nationalism, all of which focus on group identity and solidarity. Equally pervasive changes of recent vintage are described as westernization, urbanization, modernization, and secularization. Organized, militant efforts toward fundamental social, political, and economic change are increasingly referred to in the media and analyzed in the literature as revolutionary movements and emancipation movements. In this chapter, some of these dimensions of change in contemporary Indian society will be identified and discussed. Attention will be paid to both traditional and emerging modes of mobility and change, the latter often growing directly out of the former as new opportunities and new perceptions occur.

CONTEMPORARY TRADITIONAL INDIA: PROCESSES OF SOCIAL CHANGE

The bases for change in India are implicit in the very description of the society as hierarchically stratified and plural. Hierarchical stratification implies differential advantages for the constituent groups. Differential advantage means differential access to the necessities and rewards which make life possible and enjoyable. When, as in the case of India, some people are denied these things or are severely limited in their access to them and other people have them freely or in quantity, those who are deprived will inevitably attempt to change their situation (Berreman 1967, 1973; Gough 1973a). A comparison of India's caste system with America's system of race relations suggests that "no group of people is content to be low in a caste hierarchy—to live a life of inherited deprivation and subjection—regardless of the rationalizations offered them by their superiors or constructed by themselves" (Berreman 1960).

Cultural pluralism implies different ways of life among people who are in contact with one another, very often with specific and complementary economic roles. In such circumstances, diffusion of ideas and behavior is inevitable. The nature of the relationship among groups affects the kind and rate of this diffusion but does not prevent it. Consequently, change is inherent in the very juxtaposition of differences as a result of the inevitable communication between those harboring differences. Cultural distinctiveness is likely to be highly valued and consciously perpetuated. When it is associated with advantage it is often stringently enforced, but even then some degree of emulation is inevitable.

As a consequence of hierarchy and pluralism, change is inherent and constantly apparent in Indian society. Peasants, urbanites, and tribal peoples, poor and rich, educated and illiterate, high caste and low, Muslim, Hindu, Christian, Sikh, Jain, Parsi and Buddhist, linguistic and regional groups, and many others, all are in constant juxtaposition and interaction. Peoples of differing status, culture, language, religion, region, and experience meet in cities, on transportation routes, on pilgrimage, in schools, in administrative, political, economic, and religious contexts. There are social and physical barriers to social interaction, some of them formidable, but none of them impenetrable. Frequent and intense communication diminishes intergroup distinctiveness.

In India, contact among diverse peoples, though ubiquitous, is usually narrowly defined and rigidly patterned. People often seem to be threading their way between one another rather than mingling. This characteristic feature is significant in social change there. In almost any Indian relationship, one person dominates and the other submits; one controls and the other is controlled; one takes advantage and one defers; one profits and one loses. Who does which is usually determined by the social groups to which the participants belong and this, in turn, is often determined by birth. Common membership implies shared status, shared interactional patterns, and shared attributes. All members of ascribed groups are considered to be alike in contexts where group membership is relevant; behavior is expected to correspond to group status; individual variations are ignored or suppressed. This does not mean that the individual is without alternatives, however, for he is a member of several types of groups at the same time: of a caste, a religion, a language group, a regional group, an occupational category, a class, and subgroups of all of these. In traditional, small-scale settings—especially rural ones—these are likely to be highly correlated with one another, leaving little room for choice, movement, and manipulation. But in less personal settings such as urban ones, they are not so tightly bound. Which membership or identity will be relevant depends upon the situation and the participants. To some extent one can choose which identity is to be presented and how, even though he is unable to change the repertoire of identities available to him.

The prevalence of birth-ascribed statuses, the high correlation among these statuses, and their crucial role in determining access to rewards and the nature and quality of interpersonal relations, have important consequences for the dynamics of the social system as well as for the self-definition, group image, and life experience of those who live it. The system allows for little individual mobility; if one is to move, he must move with his group or leave the system. But the system does not function easily or automatically. It works to the extent that it does, and is stable to the extent that it is, at great cost. The amount of physical and psychic energy devoted to keeping people in their respective places—to maintaining status and privilege by those who have it, and to seeking advantage and mitigating disadvantage by those to whom it is denied—is staggering. This is apparent even in the most traditional settings; it is all the more evident in settings where traditional controls are not readily applied.

Indian society, with its enormous population, its overwhelming poverty and limited natural and technological resources, together with its ethnic diversity, its rigid social hierarchy and interethnic friction, is—more conspicuously than most—one wherein people live in the diverse ways they do, and occupy the diverse statuses they do, because they can and must, more than because they want to. They experience change more often in the directions in which they cannot avoid it than in the directions in which they seek it. The disadvantaged persist in seeking change to escape the privations of the status quo more often than not in full awareness that the likelihood of achieving that change is slim. It is testimony to the depth of their disadvantage, as well as to their courage and the pervasiveness of resistance to oppression, that they persist in the attempt to throw it off.

Emulation and Mobility

Many social changes and their attendant conflicts in India have resulted from attempted changes in group identity, in group status, and in sources of values or standards of behavior. People want to be recognized as Kshatriyas rather than Sudras, as Buddhists rather than Harijans, as Santals rather than Hindus, as plainsmen rather than hillbillies, as Nagas rather than Indians, as Indians rather than Muslims, as sophisticates rather than villagers. In these aspirations, individuals' attitudes and behaviors are influenced by sets of norms which they assume are held and exhibited by others whose attributes and behaviors they emulate and whose approbation they seek, who therefore constitute reference groups for them (Damle 1968; Turner 1956). Mobile members of any group may attempt to change the self-images of their fellows and/or the public image of their group by changing their attributes, their behaviors, and especially by changing the nature of their interaction with members of other groups in such a way as to be consistent with the image they seek, and inconsistent with the image they wish to alter. This is the essence of reference group behavior and of status emulation.

The correlation between rank and privilege on the one hand, and its symbols on the other, is sufficiently strong that groups of people characteristically seek higher rank simply through adoption of the symbols of high status—through status emulation. This has been most commonly referred to as "Sanskritization," a term coined by M. N. Srinivas (1956), and now widely used in the sociological literature of India. It refers specifically to the adoption by people who are of relatively low status of behaviors and attributes identified in the Sanskrit literary tradition as indicative of high status and as meriting the rewards of high status—specifically, Brahmanical or priestly status. Such characteristics as vegetarianism, elaborate ritual, detailed attention to purity, non-violence, celibacy of widows, and avoidance of polluting activities, contacts, and occupations are included. In a broader sense, this process also occurs without the Sanskritic component, that is, without the literal derivation from classical injunctions recorded in Sanskrit literature. Thus, the status attributes of the highly ranked warrior-ruler category (the Kshatriya *varna*) serves as a model for at least as many upwardly mobile groups in India as does the priestly (Brahman) model. The Kshatriya model requires styles of life and demeanor in which vegetarianism and non-violence are irrelevant. Similarly, among non-Hindus the model may be one of pristine Islamic culture (Islamicization) or the emulation of any other esteemed tradition regardless of the specific model. Mountain people of all castes and religions in the lower Himalayas often adopt some behaviors and attributes of the socially superior plains people in an effort toward what might be called "plainsward mobility" (Berreman 1972). In addition, rural people often emulate urbanites; Indians have emulated Englishmen under British rule; those who had been apolitical have emulated the successful and esteemed political activists of the pre- and post-independence period. The pattern is for an entire social group to adopt ways identified as *exemplifying* high status in the belief that they also *confer* high status. Thus, a caste whose traditional occupation is defiling and whose members eat meat and allow their widows to remarry, may back up a claim to higher status with a move to abandon these defiling practices. At the same time they may adopt ritual forms and even dress characteristic of a higher caste status. Without altering their coherence as a group, they will claim for their group a higher rank than society has been willing to grant them—one with which their newly purified behavior is consistent. Whether or not the model is Sanskritic, the process is one of status emulation. This process is traditional in India. I know of no low caste which does not cherish a claim to higher status and which has not made some overt efforts to realize that claim—whose members are unable to cite behaviors and attributes meriting higher status than that accorded them.

Power and Mobility

In practice, emulation is insufficient to earn members of the group attempting it the status to which they aspire, for they display only the expressions of status. They lack the criteria by which the society awards it. High rank and its rewards are associated directly and instrumentally with control and exercise of economic and political power. They are only symbolized and legitimized by behavior and attributes. Virtually every behavior or attribute can be rationalized as consistent with high rank so long as it is accompanied by power, and almost no behavior or attribute warrants high status among the powerless (with the exception of some traditionally designated priestly roles). The history of claims to higher status is a sad one from the point of view of most of those making the claim. Usually they are simply denied the opportunity to express it. If they persist in the attempt, punishment is quick and decisive, for their claim is a threat to the status quo and those who profit by it. If punishment is ineffective—if the claim cannot be denied—it is because those expressing it are too powerful to be denied. If that is the case, they will be accorded the status they claim, for it would be too incongruous and threatening to the system to have a powerful and wealthy group being treated as low in status. Its members would be in a position to challenge such treatment, and a successful challenge by a denigrated group would undercut the rationale for the system and deny its legitimacy and inevitability.

Therefore, if a group cannot be prevented from pressing its status claim, that claim will be recognized and legitimized by appropriate authority—the group will be promoted. This is not admitted to be a move in status, for the system depends upon the theory that status is immutable. Instead, it is said that a deserved but hitherto unrecognized status will henceforth be recognized. The basis for the ability to make a successful claim and bring about a change in accorded status may be acquisition of land or other property, change in occupation, or in the degree to which an occupation is remunerative. Similarly, the elimination of traditional monopolies on particular goods or services may change the fortunes and hence the status of an entire group. Change may also result from the acquisition of the vote or other means to political representation and power, and from education or other means of access to the sources of power and decision making in the society. It is clear that in contemporary India, the likelihood of these kinds of changes has increased with rapid and nationwide economic, technological, political, and social change. The universal adult franchise, political representation for disadvantaged peoples, and other provisions of the democratic and socialist constitution under which India functions have enabled groups in several areas to assert themselves which were heretofore relatively powerless. As we shall see, this has often been done—could only be done—outside of the traditional status hierarchy, and in some instances in direct opposition to it.

That such change, and the motivation for it, is not new is indicated by the fact that almost every major religious movement within the recorded history of India has based its appeal to the oppressed and to intellectuals concerned with the oppressed upon a promise, a philosophy, and an organization emphasizing freedom from caste discrimination, beginning with Jainism and Buddhism about 500 B.C., followed by Christianity, Islam, Sikhism, various Hindu reform movements such as Brahmo Samaj and Arya Samaj, and the modern resurgence of Buddhism among tribal peoples and untouchables.

During the period of British rule a government census was taken every ten years, beginning about one hundred years ago, in which caste was recorded irrevocably. This gave an unparalleled opportunity for asserting and legitimizing status claims. Prior to that time, the only source for legitimation of a group's claim to status was public opinion (or in rare cases, royal decree) affirmed by priestly endorsement. The census required British officials to record the caste of every person and therefore, in effect, to decide whether a group's status claim was valid or not. They were besieged with appeals, complaints, and counter-complaints. William Rowe cites one indicator of the magnitude of the problem: "The volume of such petitions may be appreciated if we consider the statement of one harried census official who, writing in the Bengal census of 1911, states: 'Hundreds of petitions were received from different castes—their weight alone amounts to 1 ½ maunds (120 pounds)—requesting that they might be known by new names, placed higher in the order of precedence, be recognized as Kshattriyas, Vaisyas, etc' " (Rowe 1968). An understanding of the courts, access to legal counsel, and facility in writing and interpreting the rules, to say nothing of knowledge of English, were tremendous advantages to those involved in this kind of status claim. But the underpinnings of social and ritual status, access to wealth and power, antedated the British. They were fundamental to the caste system.

Tribal groups—those people outside of Hindu social organization—have been incorporated into Hindu society throughout India's history as a result of contact and assimilation. Most often, these unsophisticated peoples, without significant sources of wealth and without political power, were incorporated at the bottom of the traditional hierarchy. But a few exceptions make the true basis for status readily apparent. Those few groups who retained control of the land or other primary and productive sources of livelihood and those who maintained political control of significant regions were incorporated into the caste system with high rank. One of the most famous instances is that of the Gonds, a large and widely dispersed tribal group of Central India. In most areas, Gonds were adopted into the caste hierarchy, if at all, as untouchables. In some regions where they had held on to the land, they were dubbed "Raj Gonds" (ruling Gonds), and their status in the caste hierarchy was equivalent to that of the warrior-administrator (Kshatriya) groups of Hindu society—esteemed and privileged. In some tribal groups, particular lineages—ruling lineages—were called Kshatriya and their members formally inducted as such while their fellow tribesmen of less powerful affinities were called low caste.

Solidarity

No amount of emulation achieves mobility in a system where status is birth-ascribed. Only the threat or use of power brings about the redefinition of relationships upon which enhanced status can be based. Emulation is a convenient, frequent, and sometimes required concomitant, but it is never sufficient. Solidarity, on the other hand, can bring enhanced status without emulation if the balance of power permits (see Orans 1965). Blacks in America have learned this, as have untouchables in India. The parallels are readily apparent. Blacks and other denigrated ethnic minorities in America have long been told to act like members of the dominant society with the implicit or explicit promise that if they do so, they will be treated and rewarded as full members. They have found that this is not the case—they are treated in ways which they consider acceptable only when the alternative for the dominant society becomes too painful for it to countenance. Thus they have banded together in solidarity movements. That the parallel is evident to India's dispossessed as well as to outside observers is evidenced by the emergence of the Dalit Panthers, an untouchable emancipation movement of Western India (discussed below) which draws explicitly on the American Black Panthers as a precedent.

Indian society is so heavily dependent upon corporate groups (those named, bounded, self-aware, and easily recognized) in defining relationships among people that it is not surprising to find that new ones emerge as traditional ones diminish in relevance. Caste is often a basis for such new groups even when it does not define their membership. The Rudolphs (1960) have commented upon the form and function of "caste associations" in contemporary India, formal organizations which often encompass several endogamous castes or *jatis* of similar name, occupation, and rank. Sometimes the constituent groups come from a more extensive region than that within which strict status equivalence is demonstrable through frequent interaction. In other instances even more disparate groups may unite in such an association. Caste associations provide a mechanism for political or economic activity and status enhancement and comprise an interest group for people who, in their individual families and castes might be too few, too poor, or too powerless to achieve their ends. Generally such associations have a governing body operating under a constitution, they publish newspapers advocating the cause and reporting the activities of the association and its members, hold meetings, negotiate internecine disputes, represent the association in its relations with outside agencies, endorse political candidates, and the like.

Caste associations are by no means the only politically oriented groups that have existed for some time in Indian society. In the city in which I worked, almost every conceivable bond among people was translated into corporate group membership. There were innumerable religious associations and ethnic associations representing almost every major region, language, and culture of India. Almost every occupation and business in the city organized its practitioners into unions or associations ranging from barbers to liquor store owners, from coolies to truck drivers, from millers to doctors. Political parties appealed for votes on the basis of endorsements by, and the promise of patronage to, groups and associations of every type. At election time the political commitment of nearly every such group was a matter for speculation, comment in the press, and ultimately of public record. In short, these associations were important agencies for the mobilization and coordination of collective effort to achieve the goals of their members.

CITY AND VILLAGE: CONTINUITY AND CHANGE

More striking than new opportunities for group mobility within the traditional status hierarchy has been the appearance in recent decades of new status hierarchies—new arenas for status competition. They have emerged from the impact of urbanization and westernization, but are not independent of the traditional social organization in which they are based.

Urbanism is nothing new in India, but rapid urbanization is new. The emergency of industrial employment, of easy communication over long distances, of increasingly efficient distribution of goods and services, and of more effective centralized administration has made urban living a more accessible alternative to more people in India than ever before, and the expansion of urban employment has made it increasingly attractive. Urban life affords a measure of independence from the ties and constraints of membership in rural-based social groups by granting a degree of individual anonymity and mobility quite unattainable in rural communities. Caste, religion, ritual, tradition, and the social controls implicit therein are not as rigid or pervasive in the city. People are increasingly able to seek status and other rewards on an individual or small family basis, largely independent of caste or the other larger social entities of which they are also a part. They do this primarily by going to the city, although the values of the city also extend into the countryside and have loosened the hold of tradition even there. Nontraditional, secular criteria of status such as occupation, income, education, urban life-style, and sophistication, have become increasingly important, relevant, and available. To an increasing extent urban Indians can achieve status as a result of behaviors and attributes rather than simply as a result of birth. Such status supplements, and in many contexts replaces, caste or other ascribed statuses.

In his excellent discussion of industrialization and stratification, Harold Gould observes that "industrialization brought about the transfer of specialized occupations of all kinds from the context of kin groups [in India, castes] to factories organized on bureaucratic principles. This meant that henceforth, and increasingly, occupational role and role occupant would be *in principle* separated; that the preponderant criteria for determining occupations would be 'performance qualities'; and that economic rewards and social mobility would constitute the principal standards for evaluating the worth or status of any given role" (Gould 1971, p. 14). This is the basis upon which the undermining of traditional ascriptive (caste) criteria is founded.

Generally the old and new systems, the traditional and secular, operate simultaneously, in complementary spheres. Traditional status—caste status, for example—does not disappear in the city. It remains important in the most private contexts: the family and neighborhood. Some neighborhoods essentially reproduce the village setting in personnel as well as social structure; others do not (Rowe 1964; Vatuk 1969). A very large proportion of city-dwellers are in close touch with their natal villages. Tradition and ascription are especially important in the city in those relationships upon which the day-to-day functioning and future composition of the family (and its extensions in the lineage, sib, and caste) depends, of which the epitome, of course, is marriage. In rural India, these primary relationships are virtually all of the relationships a person experiences. In the city, these primary relationships occupy a diminishing proportion of most people's time, attention, and energies. The individual is much of the time outside of his home territory, interacting with people other than those with whom his relationships are lasting, total, and traditional. Much of his interaction is fleeting and takes place on the basis of particular or even fragmented roles, entails limited commitment, and is with people whose lives intersect with his own in only very limited ways. In these circumstances he is not accountable for his total behavior, and his identity is less easily discernible. He can often behave in a way consistent with the requirements of the situation without reference to his group membership. He is even able to "pass," if that is his desire, by learning the superficial symbols of the status to which he aspires or which he finds rewarding—a status such as that of white collar worker, student, middle class householder or professional man (Isaacs 1964). In these statuses, skill in handling the language, in pursuing the occupation, or success in acquiring money or an appropriate lifestyle may be socially recognized and rewarded irrespective of caste and family, although the latter will remain important in other contexts.

Contrasting Patterns of Social Relations

Changes which have occurred in the move from traditional culture and social structure to a more secular society can therefore be illustrated by examining contemporary urban social relations as contrasted to rural ones.

Rural villages, where 85 percent of India's population lives, are composed of people whose statuses are largely a consequence of their membership in corporate groups such as families, lineages, and castes. People spend most of their lives in familiar settings interacting with others they know well. Statuses are consistent: well-to-do people are politically powerful people with high ritual and social status; poor people are relatively powerless and of low status. As a result, there is rarely a novel social situation to be dealt with. Relations with people of groups other than one's own—with groups of higher or lower status—are highly stereotyped and at the same time highly personal, since individuals know exactly who their fellow villagers are in terms of family history, group memberships, and personal qualities. Thus they knew exactly the kind of behavior which is appropriate to each person in each situation.

In the city ethnic diversity is great. A large proportion of the city resident's social relations take place with strangers or casual acquaintances. Even people who are not strangers may know little about one another and may see one another only in limited situations for short periods of time. Acquired status results in a wider range of combinations. Urban people, therefore, continually have to figure out how to relate to others on the basis of minimal information and in highly specific, impersonal situations, rather than responding upon the basis of thorough knowledge and consistent statuses as occurs in the village.

This does not mean that the city is socially unstructured or even that it is less structured than the village, rather it means that the structure is less conspicuous, lying largely in the regularity of responses to subtle cues about social identity and about the situational relevance of that identity in face-to-face, yet impersonal and often fleeting, interaction. This difference is exemplified in the differences between the social knowledge and skills of the "country bumpkin" and the "city slicker," each of whom may be a laughing stock in the other's milieu, where his hard-won social knowledge and skills are as inappropriate and irrelevant as they are effective and appropriate on his home ground. Both survive socially by reacting to the social identities of others, but the definition, recognition, and expression of those identities, and the appropriate responses to them, are quite different.

Urban residential neighborhoods are often relatively homogeneous and stable over time, so that social relations there approximate—even reproduce—those in villages. Indian cities therefore have been sometimes described as agglomerations of villages, and the rural-urban contrast minimized. The social relations in the work-a-day world of the city—in the bazaar, places of work, commerce and administration—are conspicuously different from those in villages, neighborhoods, and other relatively personal settings.

In attending to urban social relations one must be careful not to confuse the casual but frequent relations such as those of customer and proprietor, civil official and applicant, student and fellow student, student and teacher, with the interactions of employer and employee, creditor and debtor, and so on. The latter instances entail long-term relationships, heavy commitment, and fateful consequences. In these kinds of relations, ethnic, religious, caste, and family ties may play crucial roles just as they do in the intimacy of the family. The reason seems to be that these relationships are fundamental to the welfare of those involved. Even in the middle and upper classes, and even in the impersonality of city life, such welfare is regarded as the responsibility of the group to which the individual belongs and as a reflection upon that group. K. N. Sharma (1969) has described how traditional ties may be called upon in non-traditional circumstances to provide support or advantage to members of the group or within a range of closely associated groups comprising a resource network or resource group. Whenever possible, therefore, a person in a position of influence must attend first to the well-being of those to whom he owes his primary responsibility. A sophisticated man may mingle freely with people of other groups and may deal easily with a wide variety of people, but he is obligated to see to the welfare of his family, his sib, his caste-fellows, and his coreligionists before committing himself to others. Such primordial attachments take precedence over school ties, class interests, or abstract notions of impartiality. To the foreigner or the bureaucrat, such support might be regarded as nepotism or corruption; to the participants it is simply an expression of traditional social ties which represent superordinate commitments and therefore comprise the paramount moral obligation.

Impersonal urban interaction requires the ability to recognize a wide range of social identities on the basis of minimal cues and the ability to select and react to various aspects of identity in appropriate circumstances. The audience to interaction and the total situation in which it occurs can determine the aspects of individuals' identities which are relevant to their interaction. There is considerable room for manipulation of one's own identity as well as for control of one's response to the identity of others. In the traditional setting, on the other hand, be it the rural village or the urban family and neighborhood, this latitude is not present. In the impersonal city setting a tremendous variety of social categories and social situations must be taken into account in formulating behavior, but impersonality, anonymity, and brevity of contact make the stakes small in any given encounter. In the intimacy of the village, the social variables are few but the stakes are high because every interaction is part of a continuing, virtually inescapable relationship which carries the weight of group commitment and group status. One can manipulate the former types of relations with far greater ease and less risk than the latter.

CONSEQUENCES OF GROUP MOBILITY STRIVING

The consequences of group mobility-striving are largely contingent on circumstances. Contemporary urban life has available more means to mobility, and perhaps suggests to those who seek it a greater likelihood of success, than the highly structured, closely controlled traditional village setting. Nevertheless, mobility occurs in all settings. Some low status groups have been victims of technological displacement with the result that their economic, political, and social statuses have declined. They drift either into the status of rural, landless laborers or into unskilled urban employment, both of which are overpopulated and underpaid. The result is underemployment, unemployment, poverty, and lack of opportunity for improvement. Water-carriers, for example, comprise a caste whose members have been displaced in many parts of Northern India with the advent of hand pumps; goldsmiths have been displaced by the influx of commercially produced jewelry; carpenters and potters, on the other hand, have found their services in continued demand in most of rural India and so have stayed with their traditional jobs in approximately their traditional status. The occupation of tailor arose in some regions in village India, for example, during the period of British rule, providing income and status to a variety of relatively disadvantaged people. In some instances new occupations have been created and with them opportunities for enhancement of economic and perhaps social status for those fortunate enough to fill them. Contemporary industrial employment has created new jobs and therefore has had something of the same effect in urban areas. The literate castes found new scope for their skills and new rewards in the British bureaucracy.

Room at the Bottom

In my urban research, the comparative condition of two of the most despised caste groups, leatherworkers and sweepers, proved an illuminating instance of the effect of occupational importance and status.

In a medium-sized North Indian city, leatherworkers have been to a large extent occupationally displaced because commercially produced shoes have replaced their handmade products in the urban market. Not all of the many people of leatherworker caste can make a living at their traditional occupation, since they face extreme competition. Others were landless laborers before coming to the city and have never done leather work. Most have sought to make a living in the city in a variety of unskilled occupations, but their denigrated status, their lack of education and other resources, and the lack of opportunity to learn new skills has kept most of them from acquiring a secure livelihood. They are disorganized, deprived, poverty-stricken, depressed, oppressed, and despondent.

Sweepers, on the other hand, are essential to the functioning of the growing city. They are its only sewage and garbage collection system. Their despised occupation assures them a vital role. The city has grown faster than their numbers, and people of other groups are unwilling to do their defiling work. Therefore, virtually all of them are employed. Most sweeper families have the guaranteed income of municipal employment supplemented by the less reliable income of employment in private households. Perhaps most importantly the municipal employees are effectively unionized, with a professional bargaining agent and the viable threat of strike against their common employer always available. As a consequence, these people are reasonably secure, though not prosperous. The difference in outlook between sweepers and leatherworkers looks very much like a difference in personality. Sweepers as a group are self-confident, optimistic, outgoing people. Sweepers would generally volunteer to talk, speaking volubly about their work, caste, caste discrimination, or whatever might come up. Leatherworkers, on the other hand, are characteristically despondent and evasive, exhibiting feelings of insecurity and inferiority in out-group interaction. Leatherworkers would often say, "I am not fit to answer your questions," or "I do not know anything about these matters." Leatherworkers were especially loath to talk about caste, untouchability, and related issues, and were ready to take offense or feel threatened.

Sweepers reported taking consistent advantage of the compensatory legislation for untouchables, and they could cite relatives and acquaintances from among their number who had achieved success in the army, the civil service, and in institutions of higher education. Among leatherworkers, to whom such legislation is equally applicable and for whom such opportunities are by law equally available, the opportunities were unknown or untried, and almost none could cite people of their group who had achieved significant social or economic movement by these routes. Yet, in the rural countryside, where sanitation is a less vital issue, where sweepers are entirely dependent upon high caste landowners for their livelihood and where their numbers are often greater than required by the demand for their work, they are a typically deprived and depressed group, no better off than leatherworkers. In rural areas where leatherworkers have not yet felt acute competition from commercial shoes, those who follow that occupation are, if anything, somewhat better off than sweepers, for their job is slightly less defiling, cleaner, and the market for their work somewhat more profitable. In city and countryside sweepers and leatherworkers are theoretically comparable in status—at the bottom of this rigidly stratified society. Fate has treated them differentially as times and technology have changed.

Status Abhors a Vacuum

Urban migration, urban influence, and secularization, with their attendant new statuses and new sources of rewards, not only afford new opportunities for mobility among those privileged with access to them, but also open the possibility of mobility within the traditional system to those formerly denied it. For example, if members of groups with traditionally high status come to value secular avenues to prestige and privilege, they are likely to be less protective of traditional expressions of status (Rowe 1968; Cohn 1955). In such circumstances, low castes in many areas have found an opportunity to display attributes and behaviors consistent with long cherished claims to higher status. They have found the opportunity to do so not because they are at last accorded their status claims, but because high caste individuals in a position to deny the legitimacy of their claims simply do not care any more. Such high caste members may be no longer interested in protecting their traditional status attributes because they are seeking status in a new, secular system where caste and its perquisites are largely irrelevant—where occupation and middle class lifestyle are the means to, and symbols of, success. Aggressive low status groups are therefore able to move into the vacuum left in the traditional hierarchy. They move up as those at the top move out. The rewards of doing so may prove to be quite illusory. While such status striving goes on among formerly depressed groups, their superiors are likely to have become disinterested in traditional caste status symbols. Where traditional symbols of status remain salient, however, the barriers to displaying them remain formidable, defying even constitutional guarantees and legislation.

Statutory Status

An interesting permutation of the process of upward mobility can be seen in the consequences of modern compensatory legislation on behalf of oppressed groups. Upon achieving independence, and in fulfillment of promises and expectations, the government of India sought to counteract the oppression which the caste system has visited upon its lowest groups by granting special privileges to them (Dushkin 1972; Galanter 1972). Those groups designated as oppressed are now guaranteed seats on governing and legislative bodies, both local and national. They are accorded reserved scholarships in educational institutions and reserved positions in public employment. Thus, in some circumstances it has become an advantage to be defined as disadvantaged. The complaints from people of high status are numerous as they see their offspring fail to achieve admission to colleges and universities, fail to acquire scholarship aid, fail to be appointed in coveted jobs, while those who do less well in examinations are admitted under the quota for disadvantaged groups. Interesting legal contests have ensued. Ironically, a member of a low caste who has long claimed high caste status may insist militantly that he is indeed low in order to benefit from government policy. In such instances, concrete rewards are at stake: political representation, education, and employment. Economics and politics outweighed ritual and tradition in the ensuing dispute. It is worth noting that the courts have quite consistently ruled that de facto or accorded status, rather than claimed status, is the factor which determines eligibility for such compensatory advantages (Galanter 1968).

Escape from Status

Escape to the city is sought by many rural poor and low caste members in the hope of finding jobs and avoiding caste oppression. Many find their hopes unrewarded and find it impossible to leave the village or to survive in the city. Some seek escape within their traditional environment. I noted contrasting modes of escape from the rigidities of the traditional caste and class systems, as distinguished from attempted upward mobility within them, in my study of a rural mountain village of North India. There, low caste people had little opportunity for upward or urban mobility. The status hierarchy is rigid and there are no avenues by which they can find suitable employment outside.

Yet individuals do occasionally escape the consequences of their birth to a significant extent. Three young men did so in the ten year interval between my initial two periods of research (1958–68). One had simply moved to a nearby village whose residents were mostly of his own caste, thereby avoiding most interaction with caste superiors and the denigration that entailed and the resentment it engendered. He was still near enough to continue to make his living as a tailor for people of all castes in the area. Another, a blacksmith, had been deemed crazy. He gave up the responsibilities and commitments of normal social and economic life and simply lived as a drifter, collecting and selling forest produce to derive his meager income, moving from place to place, responsible to no one, accountable to no one. (He was certainly deviant, but crazy only if acceptance of oppression is considered evidence of normality.) The third individual undertook the most elaborate, even spectacular escape, by becoming a practitioner of the supernatural—a miracle-worker and temple-keeper—wherein his status was primarily dependent upon his ability to deal with the supernatural convincingly and successfully (Berreman 1972). His caste status, while not forgotten, was secondary to his supernatural prowess and enigmatic behavior in daily life. He did none of the traditional work of his caste (blacksmithing), and suffered few of the privations of his inherited untouchability, while receiving public acclaim both locally and from afar, he lived well on the proceeds of his supernaturalism. He was well aware of the worldly advantages which derived from his other-worldly way of life. In fact, his rather conspicuous enjoyment of them seems to be jeopardizing his hold on the public esteem.

In the same village, some high caste young men have become dissatisfied with village life as such—with its rusticity and other limitations and deprivations. Education and contact with urban life styles and mass media have led them to aspire to an easier, more varied and sophisticated way of life. Several of them have made overt moves to escape the village. Unlike their untouchable village fellows, they regard migration to urban areas and urban occupations as realistic possibilities. Through schooling and with the economic and often the moral support of their parents, they have had the means to enter and cope with that environment. Two young men had joined the army, two had emigrated to jobs in factories, one had acquired a part-time job in the postal service in a regional market town, one had undertaken training as an auto mechanic in the city, and three had been, or were being, trained as school teachers. These were attempts to escape the traditional milieu of village, caste, and family by turning to non-traditional ways of life and secular sources of rewards and status.

CHALLENGES TO TRADITION: CONSENSUS AND CONFLICT

Anthony Wallace has contended that "the cultural relationship is based not on sharing but on a complementarity of cognitions and motives" (1961, p. 41). People get along with one another not so much because they agree, or act from the same motives or in the same ways, but because they are able to predict one another's behavior and, as a consequence, adapt to it and articulate their own behavior with it. This is demonstrated clearly in India where social organization is based not primarily on value consensus, but on insight and understanding as to the nature of the social world.

On the individual level this means knowing relevant social groupings, recognizing them in the people one meets, knowing what behaviors such people expect and what behaviors they are capable of, how they can be expected to act and react in particular circumstances, and what resources are at their disposal. This is especially characteristic of the heterogeneous urban setting, as we have seen, but it is also characteristic of any situation (including the rural one) where there is conspicuous diversity in values and interests. To the extent that social stability is manifest, it is largely a consequence of the balance of power and rewards, not agreement on the desirability of, or the rationale for, the system. No stigmatized, oppressed, or even relatively deprived ethnic group or social category that I have encountered accepts its status as deserved or legitimate, but many, probably most, people in such statuses accept their status as fact and accommodate to it, while cherishing a hope or nursing a plan to alter it. No such group accepts justifications for their own group's deprivation, no matter how convincingly the beneficiaries of the system portray the alleged justification in religious or philosophical terms. That this is the case is amply attested to by India's long history of social conflict, social reform movements, and the recurrence of religions and ideologies advertising themselves as caste-free. India's institutionalized inequality, rigid as it is, has generated a long, sad history of resistance against overwhelming odds. Fractionation into small, competing social cells, together with highly concentrated sources of power and wealth, have been the major factors enabling continuation of the system by minimizing the likelihood of concerted or successful remedial action on the part of the oppressed. As social, economic, and political circumstances change, these characteristics of the society may change as well.

Social change in India cannot be understood completely in terms of consensus; a model based on power, conflict, and pragmatic appraisals thereof is essential. Yet it cannot be understood without some reference to consensus. This statement is less enigmatic than it may appear to be, for the consensus is not of the kind that is usually described. It is not consensus on status assignment, on the legitimacy and desirability of social forms and social relations or even on the values underlying them; instead, it is a fundamental consensus on the nature of the system and of the power relations which maintain it. In the welter of conflicting traditions, values, and interests the necessary consensus—that which makes successful interaction possible—is on who has the power, and how and under what circumstances and for what purposes it will be used. On the interpersonal level this means agreement on the nature, membership, and identifying characteristics of the various social groups of which the society is comprised, and how they and their members behave, interact, and react. When this minimal but crucial consensus breaks down, conflict is likely to become overt and the ever-present potential for drastic change is likely to be realized.

The precipitating change may be the acquisition by low status groups of economic, political, or supernatural power, through land reform, wage labor, unionization, universal franchise, direct political representation, civil rights legislation and its enforcement, education, the appearance of a compelling ideology of change, the appearance of a powerful and convincing religious or political leader or movement, or some other influential advocate of the cause of the oppressed. It may also occur through the emergence of group self-esteem and self-confidence as a result of any of these or other changes, with a consequent willingness by the group to assert whatever power is available to it.

The traditional mechanism for handling such threats to the status quo, and to the interests of those who benefit from it, has been to prevent the opportunity for depressed groups to effectively assert their claims by denying them independent income, political influence, education, and other means. The breakdown in the effective employment of these repressive mechanisms accounts for many of the social changes in recent years and promises far more drastic changes in the future.

Reform and Good Intentions

There is a long history of reformist sentiment and activity in India directed at mitigating the worst inequities of caste and class. It has emanated largely from those in positions of privilege, often with a distinct paternalistic flavor. It was epitomized in the ideas and actions of Gandhi, who sought to outlaw untouchability and to dignify the occupations associated therewith without eliminating the caste system. In his aims he differed from the Untouchable Buddhist leader B. R. Ambedkar, whom he worked with and supported (see Zelliot 1972).

The constitution of independent India is replete with anti-untouchability and anti-discrimination provisions including Article 17, which states that "Untouchabilty is abolished and its practice in any form is forbidden. The enforcement of any disability arising out of 'Untouchability' shall be an offense punishable in accordance with law." In Article 15, discrimination in public places "on grounds only of religion, race, caste, sex, place of birth" is proscribed. Civil rights legislation is supplemented by compensatory legislation providing for "protective discrimination," whereby disadvantaged groups are provided reserved seats in local, state, and national governing bodies, reserved seats and scholarships in educational institutions, reserved employment, loans, grants, and the like.

Not surprisingly, implementation has lagged far behind legislation in these matters, as it has in the United States and elsewhere. Caste discrimination and the practice of untouchability flourish still, especially in rural areas and, in fact, among all but the most enlightened urban dwellers.

Revolt, Emancipation, and Reaction

The poor and the oppressed in India have recently mounted a number of militant movements whose aim is fundamental social, cultural, political, economic, and sometimes religious change. These essentially revolutionary movements focus on emancipation from the consequences of low caste and class status through revolt against the entire system which reserves wealth, power, and privilege for the few at the cost of poverty and oppression for the many. Their means are often regarded as drastic, but those who employ them are convinced that only drastic means hold the possibility of success.

A few recent and contemporary movements can be cited to indicate the nature, the impetus, and the portent of these movements.

Maharashtra has been a center for emancipation movements for many years, among the best-known being an anti-Brahman movement of the 1870s among primarily middle caste Marathis under the leadership of Jotirao Phule (Omvedt 1973). Untouchable caste emancipation activities in the region emanated largely from the populous and untouchable Mahar caste. Dr. B. R. Ambedkar was of this group. In the 1920s and '30s, he pressed for the rights of untouchables, an effort which he channeled through the Scheduled Castes Federation during the 1940s, and through the All-India Republican Party during the 1950s. Dr. Ambedkar's aim was to win for untouchables not only respect, but full equality. He had sought the same end as chairman of the committee which drafted the Indian Constitution and as Law Minister in the first cabinet of independent India. Zelliot (1972) points out that "Ambedkar's final resolution of the Untouchables' religious dilemma [namely, that Hinduism defines, justifies, and endorses their oppression] was adopted in 1956 when he converted to Buddhism in an attempt to link untouchables to the greatness of India's past while denying the contemporary concept of caste." Some three and a half million untouchables followed him in this conversion (Fiske 1972).

In the same region, arising also from the large and aroused Mahar untouchables, has come a new movement founded in 1972, calling itself the Dalit Panthers (Padgaonkar 1974; Malik 1974). The name combines the Hindi and Marathi word *dalit*, meaning oppression, with the name of the militant black organization of the United States. Its supporters see caste exploitation as economic rather than religious in origin. They aim at mobilizing far beyond the Mahar caste to unite ". . .all scheduled [Untouchable] castes and tribes, converted Buddhists, workers, landless labourers, small farmers and nomadic tribes." Thus, they are moving from a caste-based movement to a class-based one. And they are for "all-around revolution" because "compartmentalized change is impossible." Supporters of the Dalit Panthers have already produced an impressive literature of protest including poems, songs, short stories, essays, memoirs, and novels, some of which were published in English translation in the *Times Weekly* (of the *Times of India*) as an eight-page "Special Issue on Dalit Literature" (17 November 1973). This literature has publicized their grievances and their program, and has proselytized new members. As Malik (1974) pointed out, there are about eighty million untouchables and forty million tribals in India who, if they could unite politically, would comprise a formidable political force. He went on to say that "such an eventuality is remote indeed, but recent developments could mean that the young untouchables of India, the Harijans and the tribals, are going to make life tough for those who have counted on their meek acceptance of injustice as a permanent condition. They may provide the national cohesion to a radical revolt young Marxist-Leninists have so far lacked."

Revolutionary political activity directed toward social, cultural, and economic reform has a venerable history in India. The Communist Party of India (CPI) has existed for more than forty-five years. In the past ten years two splits have occurred, leaving three Communist parties: one, the CPI, is pro-Moscow; another, the CPI-Marxist, is independent; the third, the CPI-Marxist-Leninist, is pro-Chinese (Maoist) (Ram 1973).

Kathleen Gough (1973b) has observed a strong connection in India between poverty and Communism. Those states with the greatest proportion of starving citizens and landless laborers give the most electoral support to the Communist parties. Right-wing parties win strongest support in states with much smaller percentages of underfed people and landless laborers, possibly because people who have attained some degree of comfort are afraid of losing what they have. Gough does not posit a direct causal link between poverty and communism, but suggests that years of deprivation make acceptance of revolutionary ideas more likely.

The Congress Party, which has been in power since independence, has gradually been losing control, in favor of the more extreme parties, both far-right and far-left. In some areas, support for revolutionary movements has resulted in armed revolt, led mainly by Maoist Communists.

Support for right-wing parties such as the Jan Sangh and Swatantra has no doubt been enhanced by middle and high caste and middle and upper class fears of Communist, Dalit, and other revolutionary and emancipatory activity on the part of the poor and the oppressed and their sympathizers. It is a reaction in part to caste and class revolt, just as revolutionary activity is a reaction to caste and class oppression. In Maharashtra, for example, home of the Dalit Panthers and of anti-Brahman and Mahar emancipation movements, an extreme Marathi nationalist and Hindu chauvinist organization called the Shiv Sena has been prominent, virtually dominating the city of Bombay for some time with its near-fascist tactics and ideology. Directed more at non-Marathi speakers and non-

Hindus than at untouchables, it represents a right-wing effort toward solution of severe social, cultural, and economic problems revolving around employment opportunities.

Clearly, inequities in livelihood, power, and privilege in India are the genesis of profound social conflict—conflict which will be resolved only if the inequities are resolved. Even the advocates of drastic means to change, however, are not optimistic. The society is so divided by differences of caste, religion, region, and language, the economy is so firmly in the hands of the elite, the poor and landless are so very poor and powerless, that the requisite fundamental change seems all but unattainable in the near future. Having discussed the fact that the polarization of the Indian peasantry (into the rich, landed and the poor, landless) and the "green revolution" in agricultural productivity which occurred in the 1960s are mutually reinforcing and are detrimental to the poor, H. P. Sharma concludes: "Metaphorically speaking, one can say that the present situation in rural India is like a watermelon—green on the outside and red inside. Whether the watermelon rots and eventually bursts, with all the redness wasted, or whether it is cut at the appropriate time depends upon effective Left leadership, the prospects for which do not seem very promising at the moment" (1973, p. 16).

PROSPECTS: THE OMINOUSLY CLOUDED CRYSTAL BALL

Indian society is one of many in which secularization, urbanization, westernization, and industrialization are powerful forces. It is one in which the legacy of colonialism is strongly felt and in which power, whether conferred via colonialism or indigenously derived, largely determines who prospers and who suffers. There is no headlong rush among Indians, even in cities, to emulate Western society (except among some of the small middle and upper classes), except for the desire for certain material goods and the basic rewards of a secure life and livelihood, which are increasingly thought to require some Western technology and Western institutions. Self esteem and confidence, based on that which is closely identified with one's own group and hence oneself, is a major value that Western influence has not greatly altered. Communal values, as they are called in India, are championed at least as often as they are suppressed. Hindu nationalism is almost as prominent as secularism in contemporary political rhetoric, and is far more prominent in daily life despite the nation's official commitment to secularism. Demands for ethnically based states, usually defined in terms of the constitutionally sanctioned criterion of common language, but often reflecting deep-seated cultural cleavages, have proliferated and are as frequent as pleas for national unity. Ethnic solidarity is as often sought as national integration. These sentiments are manifest in interpersonal relations as they are in intergroup relations, in solidarity and conflict, in loyalty and prejudice, in chauvinism and discrimination. They are expressed in behavior ranging from votes to riots, and from social etiquette to social oppression.

The lines along which people mobilize for action are both traditional and modern, both religious and secular, both caste and class. As society changes, new identities and new groups emerge, leading to new bonds and new schisms, some replacing, some supplementing; the old Pluralism, cultural and social, persists. The result of this diversity—whether divisive or not—will depend upon the ability of the nation to encompass and respect its heterogeneous peoples, traditions, and values, to radically diminish the disparity in economic and political rewards among them, and to enhance social justice.

Economic development has not resulted in widespread economic democratization in India. The gap between the masses of poor and the few who are well off has, if anything, increased. In combination with increased political sophistication and enactment of the universal franchise, this leads to increased importance in the social structure of bonds among people who share common economic and political characteristics. In the Northeast and in the South, radical political movements of the left have gained massive strength. In Maharashtra and especially Bombay, and in some other areas, ultra right-wing, communalist parties have gained large followings, as have radical leftist parties advocating emancipation of the oppressed. In both instances, failure of the democratic and mildly socialist Congress Party—the party of Ghandi, Nehru and independence—to achieve a higher standard of living and social justice has led to these alternative paths. The oppressed poor are joined in their efforts to change the status quo by disillusioned people of all walks in life, including the many educated, unemployed young men of the cities. Almost any alternative seems better to them.

The "green revolution" in agricultural production simply emphasizes this problem. Although it does represent an increase in productivity, that increase is limited to certain sections of the country, notably the Gangetic plain. Even where increased productivity has occurred, it has benefited primarily those who were already well off, those who control the land. Laborers, tenants, non-agriculturalists, and urban poor are not significantly better off than before. Inflation counteracts what little rise in income they may have experienced. Land reform has eliminated some large landlords, but has not noticeably benefited the rural poor. The revolutionary "Naxalite" movement of Northeast India is a vehement response to economic and social inequities by the landless agriculturalists whom land reform legislation was supposed to help and did not.

Consequently, there is little hope and little enthusiasm for governmental programs among India's poor. Among rural land holders there is little motivation to share any increase in productivity of the land—they keep it to themselves. There continues to be a strong impetus among the advantaged to achieve a life-style which excludes manual labor. Their young men continue to seek urban employment, especially the prestige of white-collar jobs, by acquiring an education. As a consequence, they contribute to the surplus of B.A. and M.A. economists, engineers, lawyers, and others who comprise the embittered, educated unemployed. Recently, food shortages in many parts of India, exacerbated by raging inflation, have increased social and political unrest drastically across caste, class, and ethnic lines.

Among the urban middle class there is a strong current of pessimism. They see the limitations inherent in their status, given the realities and prospects of life in India. To them the right-wing solution has considerable appeal in that it promises to protect what they have, and identifies particular alien groups as the culprits responsible for their difficulties in a threatening world. The depth of anti-Muslim feeling, and the extent to which it is played upon in this context, is startling to the uninitiated. Many middle class people would like to see their children escape—leave India and seek education and employment elsewhere in the United Kingdom, Europe, or America. Many of them attempt a less ambitious move in the same direction by sending their children to Indian schools for advanced technical or professional training to give them a chance for suitable employment in the government or private enterprises in large cities.

Most urban people of lower status and lesser prospects see no possibility of escape and have little to protect. They try to maximize the meager opportunities available to them within the system—to seek jobs and some of the amenities of urban living, just as people of low status in rural areas attempt improvement of their life chances via traditional avenues, including Sanskritization. Those who are employed in industry often become strong supporters of their unions, and of political parties which work through organized labor—the parties of the left and radical left. Those of very low caste and of minority status tend to support the parties of middle and left, partly because parties of the right make scapegoats of them. They support movements and parties advocating emancipation because right-wing and communalist parties victimize them. The high caste poor, and almost poor, together with those who have property, frequently seek security and exaggeration of their traditional status in right-wing and communalist parties. Some small minority groups, peripheral to the larger society, find their very uniqueness rewarding. Instead of attempting political activity or social mobility, they maintain their distinctive identity in order to capitalize on their unique role in society. They comprise such colorful groups as itinerant puppeteers, musicians, tinkers, and others whose reputation and clientele depend as heavily on their distinctive dress and manner as on their skills.

The relationship between politics and social status is suggested, in the city of my research, by the fact that in the 1969 local election, the victorious right-wing party was supported financially by Hindu business interests including small shopkeepers, and was voted for by Hindus of all but the lowest castes. The Communist candidate was supported by organized labor, several unions having been the basis for party activity. The Congress party, with its liberal tradition, was supported by Muslims, untouchables, and many of the educated who believed it to be the best hope for a just and democratic society, and one with a realistic chance of being elected. The Socialist candidate was supported primarily by his own ethnic constituency, which included some organized labor in which they predominated.

Only at the very highest levels of economic affluence—among the incongruously rich—has there been any semblance of satisfaction with the prospects for the future in India, and even for them recent economic trends have been sobering. For them foreign education and employment is irrelevant. The economy, the political system, and the social organization have worked to their advantage, and many of them persist in seeing continued affluence for themselves and their offspring in the future, deriving from the institutions and mechanisms already at hand which have served them so well. The threat of radical political and economic change from the right or left—especially the latter—is cause for anxiety among them, but they are accustomed to having things go their way and many retain naive but perhaps diminishing confidence that somehow, disastrous change will not occur. Their complacency is unlikely to persist as the right-wing communalists of Bombay and Maharashtra, the Dalit Panthers of the same region, and the revolutionary Communists of West Bengal and the southern states become increasingly powerful and increasingly active.

If the abject poverty and enormous economic and social disparities among India's people are not quickly, effectively, and thoroughly diminished on a massive scale within the present institutional framework, as seems highly unlikely, alternatives such as those described above will surely be sought. The status quo cannot long persist. Mobility—of castes or individuals—is not a viable answer. That it has traditionally been the focus of social change, to the point of preoccupation, is not surprising in a society where status determines virtually everything in life. But it has proved a hopeless kind of change, and this is increasingly recognized. More fundamental changes in the social, economic, and political structure are called for, are sought, and in some form or other will inevitably come.

The question now is whether it is not already too late to make the necessary changes in a democratic context. If it is, or if remedial actions are not rapid and decisive enough, the response will be either the application of increased force from above in an attempt to maintain some semblance of order within the framework of the social and economic status quo—perhaps through an outright military takeover—or rejection of the status quo and drastic changes initiated from below. Either would be painful and humanly costly, but the status quo is already both for many people, and they would not regret its disappearance. The former course would be temporary at best, and ultimately hopeless, for it would not resolve the problems but only cover them up. No amount of force is likely to keep the lid on the boiling cauldron of poverty and unrest which is contemporary India. The other alternative, drastic change from below, seems to offer a more viable prospect for the resolution of India's problems if the human cost of its achievement were not to prove prohibitive, and if a new elitism did not emerge.

That drastic change has not happened yet in India is most likely a result of the inhibiting effect of the poverty, powerlessness, and hopelessness of most of India's people—of those who would benefit most from change—in relation to the concentration of power, land, wealth, and education among the privileged few. The fractionation of the poor into many competing and dependent groups has prevented effective mobilization for large-scale change. Slight improvements in their standard of living, together with new access to means of mobility, to economic resources, to sources of power, and to agents of decision-making, and access to education, mass media and other sources of information, may well lead to redefinitions of their chances in society—to the emergence of hope, determination, and consequent demands for change and the formation of alliances enabling effective action for change. The likelihood of this is enhanced by increased political awareness and participation on the part of the poor and oppressed. They have not been unaffected by the equalitarian, democratic, and socialist rhetoric of Indian politics, nor by the failure of that rhetoric to result in effective action. These experiences generate awareness of common interests and alternatives, and provide an understanding of the means to change and the possibility of achieving it.

Urban India is the wellspring of change and the arena in which it is happening most rapidly. There the social structure is loose enough to allow experimentation with various alliances, social structures, political mechanisms, and economic arrangements which have been elsewhere inhibited by the rigidity of traditional social organization and the unitary relationship between that social organization and the distribution of power. Effective mechanisms for change in the society, and in the life chances of its members could presumably emerge from newly mobilized interest groups growing out of urban experience or organized by those with such experience. Some such groups have been described above.

These events cannot be understood without reference to world-wide political and economic trends. In particular, they cannot be divorced from events elsewhere in South Asia. The emergence of Bangladesh with the political and economic instability which has followed both in Bangladesh and in Pakistan; the turmoil in Sri Lanka (formerly Ceylon); instability along the Himalayan frontier; changing relations with Afghanistan, Iran, Middle Eastern nations, the Soviet Union, the United States, and China—all of these impinge crucially on events in India and have their consequences in the lives of even the most humble Indian citizens.

If India's problems cannot be solved at the national level—if a viable social revolution cannot be effected—then people may well revert to reliance upon communal groupings for security and status. Rivalry and conflict among them could become the characteristic mode of social relations and social change. The experience of enhanced but frustrated aspirations in the post-independence period would make return to the *status quo ante* out of the question. Extreme divisiveness would result, violence would no doubt play an increasing role in intergroup relations, and India's nationhood would be in jeopardy. Totalitarianism or fission would almost surely follow.

REFERENCES

Berreman, Gerald D. 1966. "Caste in Cross-Cultural Perspective," in *Japan's Invisible Race: Caste in Culture and Personality*, edited by G. DeVos and H. Wagatsuma. Berkeley: University of California Press.

_____. 1967. "Caste as Social Process," *Southwestern Journal of Anthropology* 23:351-70.

_____. 1972. *Hindus of the Himalayas: Ethnography and Change*. Berkeley: University of California Press.

_____. 1973. *Caste in the Modern World*. Morristown, N.J.: General Learning Press.

Bose, N. K. 1970. *Report of the Commissioner for Scheduled Castes and Scheduled Tribes, 1969-70*. Delhi: Government of India Press.

Cohn, Bernard S. 1955. "The Changing Status of a Depressed Caste," in *Village India*, edited by McKim Marriott. Chicago: University of Chicago Press.

Damle, Y. B. 1968. "Reference Group Theory with Regard to Mobility in Caste," in *Social Mobility in the Caste System in India*, Comparative Studies in Society and History, supplement 3, edited by James Silverberg. The Hague: Mouton.

Dandekar, V. M., and Rath, Nilakantha. 1971. "Poverty in India: Dimensions and Trends," *Economic and Political Weekly*, 2 Jan. 1971, pp. 25-48.

Dushkin, Lelah. 1972. "Scheduled Caste Politics," in *The Untouchables in Contemporary India*, edited by J. Michael Mahar. Tucson: University of Arizona Press.

Fiske, Adele. 1972. "Scheduled Caste Buddhist Organizations," in *The Untouchables in Contemporary India*, edited by J. Michael Mahar. Tucson: University of Arizona Press.

Frankel, Francine. 1971. *India's Green Revolution: Political Costs of Economic Growth.* Princeton: Princeton University Press.
Galanter, Marc. 1968. "Changing Legal Conceptions of Caste," in *Structure and Change in Indian Society*, edited by Milton Singer and Bernard S. Cohn. Chicago: Aldine.
_____. 1972. "The Abolition of Disabilities—Untouchability and the Law," in *The Untouchables in Contemporary India*, edited by M. Michael Mahar. Tucson: University of Arizona Press.
Gough, Kathleen. 1973a. "Harijans in Thanjavar," in *Imperialism and Revolution in South Asia*, edited by Kathleen Gough and Hari P. Sharma. New York: Monthly Review Press.
_____. 1973b. "Imperialism and Revolutionary Potential in South Asia," in *Imperialism and Revolution in South Asia*, edited by Kathleen Gough and Hari P. Sharma. New York: Monthly Review Press.
Isaacs, Harold. 1964. *India's Ex-Untouchables.* New York: John Day.
Malik, Harji. 1974. "India's 'Untouchables' Step Up Protests," *The Christian Science Monitor*, 24 April 1974, p. 3.
Mamdani, Mahmood. 1972. *The Myth of Population Control.* New York: Monthly Review Press.
Omvedt, Gail. 1973. "Cultural Revolt in a Colonial Society: The Non-Brahman Movement in Western India." Ph.D. dissertation, University of California, Berkeley.
Orans, Martin. 1965. *The Santal: A Tribe in Search of a Great Tradition.* Detroit: Wayne University Press.
Padgaonkar, Dileep. 1974. "The Dalit Panthers, Passion Without Programme," *The Times of India*, 23 Jan. 1974.
Ram, Mohan. 1973. "The Communist Movement in India," in *Imperialism and Revolution in South Asia*, edited by Kathleen Gough and Hari P. Sharma. New York: Monthly Review Press.
Randheer, Umakant. 1973. "Heirs." Translated by Gauri Deshpande. *Times Weekly (Times of India)*, 17 Nov. 1973, p. 8.
Rowe, William L. 1964. "Caste, Kinship and Association in Urban India." Burg Wartenstein Symposium No. 26. New York: Wenner-Gren Foundation for Anthropological Research.
_____. 1968. "The New Chauháns: A Caste Mobility Movement in North India," in *Social Mobility in the Caste System in India*, Comparative Studies in Society and History, supplement 3. The Hague: Mouton.
Rudolph, Lloyd I., and Rudolph, Susan H. 1960. "The Political Role of India's Caste Associations," *Pacific Affairs* 33:5–22.
Sharma, Hari P. 1973. "The Green Revolution in India: Prelude to a Red One?" in *Imperialism and Revolution in South Asia*, edited by Kathleen Gough and Hari P. Sharma. New York: Monthly Review Press.
Sharma, K.N. 1969. "Resource Networks and Resource Groups in the Social Structure," *The Eastern Anthropologist* 22: 13–27.
Srinivas, M. N. 1956. "A Note on Sanskritization and Westernization," *Far Eastern Quarterly* 15: 481–96.
Times Weekly (Times of India). 1973. "Special 8-Page Issue on Dalit Literature," 17 Nov. 1973.

Turner, Ralph. 1956. "Role-taking, Role Standpoint and Reference Group Behavior," *American Journal of Sociology* 61: 316–28.

Vatuk, Sylvia. 1969. "Reference, Address, and Fictive Kinship in Urban North India," *Ethnology* 8: 255–72.

Wallace, Anthony F. C. 1961. *Culture and Personality*. New York: Random House.

Zelliot, Eleanor. 1972. "Gandhi and Ambedkar—A Study in Leadership," in *The Untouchables in Contemporary India*, edited by J. Michael Mahar. Tucson: University of Arizona Press.

Chapter 12

Social Change and Sexual Identity in Contemporary Egypt*

Cynthia Nelson

Most discussions of the changing status of women in Arab societies of the Middle East begin with the assumption that the processes of modernization are the most powerful forces for change in the family and the larger society (Lerner 1958; Goode 1963; Berger 1964; Berque 1964; Polk 1965; Patai 1969, 1973). Writers vary on the use and meaning of this term, but some agree that it involves the imitation and adaptation of Western values and institutions.

This chapter will address those questions that have been left virtually unexamined in discussions about modernization and the rising status of women in the Arab world. To wit: (1) What are the traditional assumptions that Arab men and women hold about the nature of masculinity and femininity and how do they influence their conceptions of the relations between the sexes? (2) What are the broader social and historical crises occurring within the society that are linked to the status change of women? (3) What are the conflicts, dilemmas, and paradoxes confronting men and women as the latter seek to equalize their status? Implicit in the fol-

---

*I should like to express my deepest appreciation to my students—both men and women—who over the past ten years have so patiently and generously instructed and guided me into the subtleties and complexities of Egyptian culture. Also I wish to acknowledge the excellent technical assistance of Jane Tabata Usami who typed the many drafts of this manuscript.

lowing discussion is the assumption that Arab women's aspirations, demands, and successes have transformed and will continue to transform Arab society profoundly and permanently.

The central perspective for my interpretations of the subjective experiences of men and women in contemporary Egypt is what DeVos calls "emic understanding," or what I call a "phenomenological understanding." By this I mean an attempt to discover the essential structure of phenomena through recourse to the sources of subjective experience. This assumes that everyday life presents itself as a reality (or multiple realities) interpreted by human actors in a subjectively meaningful way. Our task as social scientists is to understand from the actor's standpoint what it means to him or her to "be a man" or to "be a woman" in the context of lived experience. We must approach our subject matter as actors meeting other actors living in real life situations and attempt to understand how they construct their social worlds. We must suspend Western assumptions and try to grasp how others construct their worlds and in so doing try to link this common sense world to the broader social and cultural configurations within which lived experience occurs (Schutz 1953, pp. 1–37). It might be helpful to draw attention to certain historical processes of culture contact as they have occurred in the Middle East and their relevance to the understanding of the status of women in Egypt.

The Arab conquest of Egypt in the seventh and eighth centuries resulted in the subsequent development and dominance of Islamic civilization throughout the Middle East and North Africa. A second phase began in the late eighteenth century with the Western colonialization of this same region and its subsequent impact on traditional Islamic conceptions of masculinity and femininity. During the Arab conquest, a type of sexual caste system developed in which the women, in effect, remained the biologically, legally, socially, and morally submerged inferior group (DeVos 1966, 1967; Berreman 1972, pp. 402–04). As Berreman has cogently argued:

> . . . the nature and quality of segregation of the sexes has not been defined by sociologists as comparable to that of other ascriptive social categories discussed here. Nevertheless, most of the characteristics of birth-ascribed separation and stratification (racial, caste, ethnic, colonial and pluralistic characteristics), and virtually all of the psychological and social consequences of inborn, lifelong superiority-inferiority relations are to be found in the relationship of males and females in most societies (1972, p. 404).

I would also argue that the basic psychological attitudes that developed over the centuries as a result of this rigidification of sex role relations conforms to what DeVos has defined as "expressive" exploitation.

As I define it expressive exploitation is related directly to the irrational and unconscious psychological processes and motives characteristic of man's complex mental advantage. . . . Expressive exploitation is most visibly institutionalized in societies stressing the basic social inferiority of women (1966, pp. 11–12).

THE HERITAGE FROM THE PAST

Some of the traditional cultural premises underlying the sexes' conceptions of each other are expressed not only in the Quran (Koran) and the traditional Islamic literature, but also in Arabic poetry and the documents of travelers, historians, and observers of the region. (The Islamic and traditional cultures are not identical. Islam supports the segregation and seclusion of women, but it is not the sole cause of women's low status. See Saleh 1972a, 1972b.) The most striking pattern that emerges from this material concerning the sex role relationship is the view that a man's honor and self-esteem are intimately connected to a woman's sexual purity. Woman is viewed as frail and easily seduced, therefore needing man's protection; at the same time she is seen as sexually insatiable and lacking willpower, therefore needing seclusion. This notion of protecting and secluding women is expressed in the symbolic act of veiling.

The phenomenon of veiling and the seclusion of women existed in the circa-Mediterranean societies long before early Christianity and Islam, but was almost unknown among the pre-Islamic Arabs of the Arabian peninsula. The rise of Islam and the conquest of the circa-Mediterranean region by the Arabs in the seventh and eighth centuries rigidified this pattern of veiling and seclusion of women. Contrary to popular Western belief, for Arab conquerors the act of veiling expressed values of status and prestige, not subjugation and enslavement.

The Prophet Mohamed had one purpose in mind when he asked his women to speak to other men only through a paravan or some sort of separating object—to distinguish them from other women of the community and preserve special status as his wives. Implicit in this injunction to veil and seclude the prophets' women is the idea that the religious purity of the Prophet and his descendants is endangered by the free social intercourse of his women with the "dishonest among men." Women were secluded to protect them from contamination as well as to prevent them from contaminating.

The spread of the practice of veiling among converts to Islam during the early days of the Arab conquest was in status emulation of the Prophet. It was more an urban than a rural phenomenon; in the cities the conquerors established domination of their new Islamic empire and in the cities man had to protect his women from the eyes of strangers. Veiling subsequently became a widespread custom respected by all believers. As Islam expanded, the segregation between the sexes became more marked. Seclusion and veiling acquired singular importance. As the number of slaves and concubines increased so did the use of the veil. Arabs were in position of conquerors and thus distinguished their respectable women from slaves by veiling them. A well known writer and poet of the period, Ibn El Muqafa'a, wrote, "Blind women's eyes by veiling them. Such rigid treatment is better for the men because it saves much doubt and anxiety. Their confinement at home is better than having them receive strange men that you cannot *trust*. If you can keep them from knowing anybody else beside you, then do so" (Zanati 1959, p. 77).

The Arabic word for veiling, *hidjab*, expresses a double meaning of protection and concealment: to protect the woman from danger by "covering up" and to prevent her from polluting man's honor and respectability by "seclusion." The term itself is not restricted to the veiling of women but pervades other aspects of Islamic society. For example, *hidjab* signifies the curtain behind which the Caliph and rulers concealed themselves from the household. It was introduced into Egypt, North Africa, and Andalusia during the conquest and its meaning grew more complicated under the Fatimids. The Fatimid caliphs were considered almost Divine and were practically objects of worship. Because of this the Caliph was expected to hide himself as far as possible from the eyes of his faithful followers to protect them from the radiance of his countenance. And as the Divine, he was protected from the polluting effects of others (*Encyclopedia of Islam* 1966, pp. 45–46). Ibn Hazm, one of the greatest Arabic poets of tenth century Umayyad Spain, states, "The gravest offence that a servant of God can commit is to violate the veil which God extends over His servants" (Arberry 1953, p. 258). The cultural meaning of veiling is protection. As man protects woman by veiling, God protects man from Satan.

In the eyes of the mystics, *hidjab* signified everything that conceals the true end, all that makes man insensitive to Divine Reality. And throughout the Middle East the amulets that people wear to protect themselves from the evil eye are called *hidjabs*. In a recent study on ritualistic symbols in contemporary Egypt, Mazloum and El Sayed (1972) discovered that there are two categories of hidjab—public and private and that both are associated with the notion of baraka (blessedness, purity).

Hidjabs are often created from the birth material. For example, many women from the lower classes take the child's umbilical after it drops off and make a hidjab that the child will wear around his neck until he loses it. This will ensure long life to the child. These same women take the placenta and bury it under the house "to get baraka to the child," or throw it in the Nile river to "ensure a good flow of milk for the baby," or in some cases, the placenta is thrown outside a jeweller's shop "to ensure luck." On the other hand, if nothing is done with the placenta, it is believed that it might get eaten by a dog or cat which would be bad for the child (Fahmy 1969). Given the association of hidjab with protection from the catastrophes that woman may unleash upon the world and the basic cultural premise that the honor of man is contained in the sexual purity of his woman, it is not hard to understand men's basic distrust of women's sexuality nor the elaborate institutional means by which women were kept a submerged "biologically inferior" group.

When we examine the Quran we see how the sacred book embodies the transcendental, expressive values of society uniting the real with the ideal, the world of the natural with that of the supernatural.

> The creation of woman from a rib taken from the left side of man, as stated in the traditions, suggests that the physical and animal side in woman is stronger than in man, and that the spiritual and angelic is greater in man than in woman, since the right side is the symbol of the spiritual and the left symbol of the physical nature (Yusuf 1965, p. 356).

The thirteenth century commentator, Baydawi, whose word is respected by Sunnites to the present day, sets out categorically different ways in which man is superior to woman and expresses the traditional Muslim view of women as creatures morally and ritually inferior to man.

> Allah has preferred the one sex over the other in the matter of mental ability, and good counsel, and in their power for the performance of duties and for the carrying out of divine commands. Hence, to men have been confined prophecy, religious leadership, saintship, pilgrimage rites, the giving of evidence in law courts, the duties of Holy War, worship in the Mosque on the day of assembly. They also have the privilege of electing chiefs, have a larger share of inheritance and discretion in the matter of divorce (Levy 1965, p. 99).

Traditional Islam envisages man's and woman's role as complementary, not competing. Each has certain privileges and duties in accordance with his or her nature and sphere of influence. The man has political authority and mobility within the larger society where he has to perform certain duties. He bears all economic responsibility for his wife and family despite the fact that his wife may be economically independent. In the extended family system the man often supports not only his wife, but his mother, sisters, aunts, and in-laws. Accordingly, the woman can claim considerate treatment by the husband, and a wife is entitled to be fed and clothed at her husband's expense (Anderson 1950–51). The woman does not have to worry about earning a living—there is always the larger family structure in which she can take refuge.

Women are allowed to inherit and to maintain complete control over their own property and to dispose of it without mediation of husbands or guardians. Discrimination against women as heiresses is not a consequence of Muslim law (despite the fact that males inherit twice as much as females), but of particular practices which have developed (Levy 1965, p. 98). Women's chief responsibilities are to provide homes for their families and to bring up their children properly. For the Muslim woman the home and the larger family structure are her world.

Traditionally, the Muslim woman had no right to get a divorce without her husband's consent except if at the time of marriage contract she asked "to have the *'isma* in her hand." This phrase refers to the introduction into the marriage contract of the right of the woman to divorce her husband if certain circumstances should arise that make life between them impossible. If the woman does not have the *'isma* and can prove her husband is either mad, impotent, unable to support her, or extremely cruel she has the right to go to a judge and divorce. On the other hand, a man can divorce his wife with no justification of his action simply by pronouncing the *talaq* (I divorce thee) three times. Such an unequal legal status created a fragile and insecure marital relationship for women. With the prevalence of polygamy, women often had to take a practical view of a second or third wife and accept their new status rather than divorce, which traditional society did not accept. In the provisions of the Quran, monogamy was the rule for a woman.

By way of summary we can say that the Shari'a (Muslim law) envisages the role of men and women as complementary and unequal. Islam watches carefully over the virtue of its respectable women and enforces strict public morality. It is not surprising, therefore, to see that conventions of public decency, or what Antoun has called the "modesty code," are highly developed in this region of the world (Antoun 1968; Dodd 1973).

Beginning in the late eighteenth century with the impact of Western colonialism on traditional Islamic societies, many of these basic premises were called into question. The movement against veiling and toward emancipation began in towns with the upper bourgeoisie.

THE COLONIAL ENCOUNTER: EDUCATION AND THE EMANCIPATION OF WOMEN

Beginning with the Napoleonic invasion of Egypt in 1791, the Egyptians have experienced social crises that have virtually ruptured their traditional medieval society (see Radwan 1951). From these crises has emerged a growing awareness of the ideas of freedom, self-determination, and the emancipation of women. The call to social freedom from colonial masters was paralleled by the call to personal freedom for the woman.

Educational change was the single greatest event influencing Egyptian identity in general and the consciousness of men and women towards women's emancipation in particular. The ultimate aim of Egypt's national policy at the beginning of the nineteenth century was to revolutionize a culture which was unaware of four hundred years of European development. It was with this in mind that Mohammad Ali designed his new educational system, using France as his model. He saw education as the principal tool to revolutionize society, to bring about social change, and to realize his aspirations of "raising a large army and conquering the world around him" (Radwan 1951, p. 113). The embryonic state school system under Mohammad Ali was military in character, organization, and purpose, and female education was unknown.

The legacy of the nineteenth century was a dichotomy between the cultural outlook produced by the introduction of a state school system modeled on European lines and the expansion of missionary and foreign community schools superimposed over the religious *kuttab* system (traditional religious schools). Despite creating this cultural ambivalence, the new system did lay the seeds for the movement towards the emancipation of women.

Following the revolutionary conception of education ushered in by Mohammad Ali was an increased awareness on the part of some men and women that women ought to have not only equal rights in education but also the same legal status as men, particularly with regard to personal status (divorce, custody of children, alimony, and polygamy).

Egyptian male writers such as Tahtawy and Qasim Amin advocated women's education to prepare them for "positive citizenship." Amin and others wrote a small book on the *Emancipation of Women* (1900) and raised the most violent controversy of the period, one which provoked no less than thirty books and pamphlets in answer. It roused the *culema* (Muslim religious leaders) to such anger that the Khedive—who constantly tried to please them—would no longer receive Amin at his levees. Amin's book advocated that women should receive a "modest degree of education, and that they should no longer be secluded from society." The uproar caused Amin to write a second one entitled *The New Woman* (1901) to refute the charges made against him. In the second book, he advocated stronger measures and claimed that a change in Egypt's mental attitude was necessary—a mental and intellectual revolution. He said that women were held in bondage by their ignorance, and could not fulfill the role they ought to play in society. Hence the moral basis of society had decayed and had caused the whole of Islam to decay. This bondage of women, he claimed, was not an Islamic trait, but one introduced to it from the outside, and therefore one that needed to be set aside. The heart of the social problem lay in the position of women in the society, a position which could be improved only by allowing them to become educated.

Although Amin's aspirations for the emancipation of women are, by modern standards, very modest, they were the first expression of such an attitude towards women; though they roused controversy, others picked up the same idea. Soon the emancipation of women became one of the tenets of nationalists such as Lutfi-al-Sayyid and, in the 1919 revolution, Saad Zaghlul (Lutfi-al-Sayyid 1968). Whereas in the 1890s and in the Great War the emancipation of women had been almost exclusively a male interest, after independence (1922–23) feminism became an active organizational concern of women themselves. In Qasim Amin's writings the question of woman's emancipation was first broached publicly. Yet, the changes in education, the influx of foreigners, and the opening of foreign schools since the reign of Khedive Ismail had also contributed to bringing this problem to national consciousness. Malak Hifni Nasif (Pseud. *Bahithat al Badiya*, The Desert Researcher) in her essays *al-Nisa'iyyat* (ca. 1910, 2 vols) argued the question of improving the conditions of women as wives and mothers both in education and marriage, but explicitly did not advocate emancipation in the sense of equality between the sexes. It was not until 1919 that a true feminist movement began in Egypt. Hoda Sha'rawi, wife of one of the three founders of the Wafd party and daughter of one of the richest landowners in Egypt, inspired it.

> On March 16, 1919, word spread over Cairo that a procession of veiled women planned to march through the streets in protest against the decision of the Occupying British forces to exile four of the Wafd nationalist leaders. One of the four men sentenced to exile was the husband of Hoda Sha'rawi and it was she who led the procession of women. This act was the first step on the road she was destined to travel as a pioneer leader for women's rights, not only in Egypt, but in all countries of the Arab world. When people began to get over their initial surprise of seeing this procession of veiled women, a number of gallant gentlemen, passers-by joined hands around the group of ladies and formed a cordon for their protection and dignity. Meanwhile, expressions of encouragement and cheers of admiration rose from the ever-increasing crowds. Soon, however, British soldiers of the Army of Occupation encircled the procession and brought it to a halt. They held up the advance of the women with pointed bayonets. Many of the women fainted from heat and exhaustion (Rasheed 1973, p. 8).

Four years later, following her return from an International Congress of Feminists in Rome, Hoda Sha'rawi threw off her veil as she disembarked from her ship in Alexandria, symbolically giving notice that the struggle for equal rights for women had begun. On March 16th of that year she founded the Egyptian Feminist Union.

By the mid-twentieth century the emancipation movement had not only expanded the possibilities for free education for women to middle and lower classes, but also changed the conception of the "educated woman." Today the goal of education in the schools and universities of Egypt is to train women (as well as men) for active participation in shaping the life of the country:

> Woman must be regarded equal to man and she must therefore shed the remaining shackles that impede her free movement so that she may play a constructive and profoundly important part in shaping the life of the country (Egyptian National Charter 1962).

> Women constitute one half of the society and to deny women the opportunity to participate in our comprehensive strategy aimed at achieving progress is to deprive the society of the capabilities of one half of its members. Education, labor and just human treatment are surely compatible with the tolerant Islamic Law (Sadat, October Paper 1974).

The important theme expressed in these statements is that education means education for work in a revolutionary and progressive society. This notion of a "working partner" would have seemed absurd to a traditional Islamic society which veiled and secluded its women. Education has meant a greater independence for women in directing their own lives. With a university education and jobs women are equipped to earn their own living and do not have to depend on men for material security. This has led to a greater demand on the part of women to choose their own husbands rather than having them chosen by parents who are concerned about their daughter's security. In Egypt where inherited wealth is no longer a potential source of financial security, working wives are becoming much more numerous, particularly among the middle classes.

Emancipation has brought the Egyptian woman equal rights to education and the right to vote but not the right to divorce, to receive alimony, or to have custody of her children. Herein lie some of the ambivalences regarding the equality of women. On the one hand, the woman is being actively encouraged to enter into the public world of university, industry, and government as a "constructive force"; on the other hand, her new status desires create anxiety for the man who is psychologically ill equipped to accept a woman as an equal. Having a working woman as a wife creates certain anxieties; interacting with a woman on the job creates others. Both situations reflect the degree to which the man, more than the woman, is committed to the traditional cultural conceptions of social self-identity.

CONTEMPORARY REALITIES: SOCIAL CHANGE AND SEXUAL IDENTITY

There are conflicting premises as to the quality and nature of the male-female relationship. For example, if a woman maintains one set of premises about her sexual identity and a man maintains another, there is bound to be more difficulty in psychological adjustment than if both man and woman accept the same defining premises for their relationship. The latter situation was most likely the case from the early days of the Arab Islamic conquest of Egypt until the beginnings of Western colonialization. The former situation is more characteristic today.

In what concrete ways has the trend toward the emancipation of woman affected sexual identity and the total pattern of relations between the sexes? The fact that woman's role has changed and is changing means that man's role must also be changing—or at least the traditional beliefs and values guiding the conduct between the sexes are being called into question, which in turn is creating different kinds of conflict for man and woman. The main difficulty facing the man is the loss of authority, which threatens his self-image of masculinity. The main difficulty facing the woman who aspires to emancipation is being accepted as a *person* subject to the same legal rights as men, rather than as a sexual object that threatens men's honor or as a source of pollution that society must debase and subordinate.

As we turn to specific illustrations from contemporary Egypt, it is instructive to consider the period between the two world wars as reflecting the beginning of rapid social change, a time in which the possibilities of taking on new definitions of social self-identity begin to expand and sexual identity conflicts become increasingly evident. We first turn to the novelists, for they are the most sensitive and articulate in describing how the Egyptian perceives and expresses the condition of the woman in society, as well as how conflicts emerge between the sexes as women attempt to struggle out of their social bondage.

Naguib Maḥfūẓ, Egypt's outstanding contemporary novelist, gives us the best account of the rapidity of social change. His best known works draw on the names of Cairo's neighborhoods for their titles, depicting a city where changes are undermining traditional patterns. In these novels the social protest theme is dominant. Maḥfūẓ is always aware that the Egyptian woman is a doubly-oppressed human being. Often women are the protagonists. The author is not tempted, as are many Egyptian novelists, to "borrow" women who are totally European in behavior in order to facilitate a love story. His love scenes are seldom romantic; his lovers are seldom carefree. All of the lovers have an obstacle course of social and psychological taboos to tackle before they can know or speak to each other.

Most of his characters are oppressed. In some cases the oppressed men are able to revolt by becoming selfish or antisocial, but the women have little, if any, outlet. They are subject to life-long imprisonment. The mothers suffer greatly, but quietly. As a rule the older women accept the order of things without much complaint. Of a different order is the plight of the younger women. They have matured in a rapidly changing world, but belonging as they do to the poorer lower-middle classes, they remain subject to severe restrictions. If they are lucky and attractive, they can hope to gain a relative freedom through marriage; otherwise, they face the prospect of becoming spinsters or of being married to old or illiterate men. They have no means of rebelling against their fate, and in the few cases in which they try to do so, end up as prostitutes or concubines.

In his celebrated trilogy Maḥfūẓ portrays the political scene of Egypt and the daily life of the middle class Cairene through a period of twenty-seven years (1917–1944). The change of social patterns is admirably recorded: the rapid rejection of time-honored social norms, the slow emancipation of women from medieval shackles, the spread of education and scientific thinking, the increasing influence of Western culture, the decline of religious adherence among the urban middle class.

The last two novels of his trilogy describe the changes taking place in Egypt between the two world wars and their effect on family relations. This is the period of the Egyptian feminist movement led by Huda Sha'rawi, and the novelist depicts the great gulf between the generations, particularly separating mother and daughter.

A new genre of writing appears in late 1950s and early 1960s in which the theme of the "emancipated woman" is carried to the extreme by male authors. Representative of this literature is the work of Ehasan Abdul Quddus. In his novel *La Taghrub Ash-Shams* (The Sun Does Not Set), he writes about the role of the older brother in a family following the father's death. The hero, after the 1956 Port Said attack, begins to appreciate his sisters' problems—one loves a man who is already married and the other wishes to divorce her arranged-marriage husband. The issue of personal freedom has become a central theme. The young man sees clearly that he has freedom that is not allowed his sisters. The writer argues that the one sister ought to be given her freedom to marry the man she wants and she ought to have the right to divorce. In another novel, *Ana Hurra* (I Am Free), Quddus argues that the woman's right to freedom is not an end in itself but something the woman must know what to do with. In this novel the heroine revolts against her father and the whole idea of an arranged marriage, enters the American University in Cairo, becomes "emancipated," gets an apartment by herself—but suffers in her freedom by becoming alienated from her family and society. Quddus finally creates a negative and stereotyped image of the post-revolutionary "new woman"—one who pursues sex as a symbol of new but alienating freedom.

In the 1950s and continuing through the 1970s, women writers emerged with serious concern about *la querelle féminine*. Through their work we gain a deeper understanding of what it means to be an Egyptian woman.

One of the most fascinating figures writing about the feelings and condition of women in contemporary Egypt is Nawal Sadawy—medical doctor turned novelist—who has earned the reputation over the past ten years as spokeswoman for radical feminists in Egypt today. Her first novel, *Memoirs of a Lady Doctor* (1954) is an autobiographical account of her experiences as a village doctor struggling to overcome the deep-seated patriarchal attitudes toward women in rural Egypt. In addition to a book of short stories, *A Thread on the Wall* (which won her a nomination for the State Merit Prize in 1974), she has written a series of novels, *The Absent* (1968), *The Searcher of Love* (1969), *The Female as Origin* (1973), and *The Woman at the Point of Zero* (1974).

Through her novels one gets a glimpse into the life of women in contemporary Egypt, their dilemmas, and their relationships with men. Central in her work are the themes of autonomy through love, of the search for a deep and authentic relationship between the sexes, of a society and religion which create social and political systems destructive to men and women. She emphasizes that the relation between the sexes is characterized by lies and deception as men and women conform to what they think society expects. Her woman is not the submissive and tender mother of Maḥfūẓ, but a young, strong, and vibrant seeker of self-fulfillment. The struggle for emancipation is expressed as the struggle of the one against the many, and though the heroine is ultimately crushed by the social norms and taboos, she is portrayed as having "acted freely" in terms of authentic selfhood.

Her most controversial book, *Women and Sex* (1972), sold out within the first few weeks of its publication, brought her nearly total condemnation from the pulpits of the mosques of Cairo, turned her into a folk heroine among most university students, and gained her the dubious reputation as the "Germaine Greer of Egypt."

The book is important not only because it is the first feminist tract ever to be written and published in the Arab world, but also because it contains actual case studies of particular women who have to cope wth the taboos and restrictions that continue to structure the relationships between the sexes.

Dr. Sadawy was originally inspired to write *Women and Sex* when a young man brought his bride in to her complaining that she was not a virgin because there had been no blood after their first intercourse. Upon examination, the doctor discovered that the girl's hymen was intact, but of a flexible type which did not rupture. The young man seemed to understand. Several days later, however, the girl returned; her husband had divorced her and she had scandalized her family. When she brought her father to hear the doctor's explanation, he blamed the doctor for knowing the facts but hiding them from the people. Sadawy hoped that by writing *Women and Sex*, such ignorance and its resultant suffering could be alleviated.

Dr. Sadawy and her husband began a health journal in 1970 to disseminate information on family planning and health issues. In this journal, she wrote frankly and openly about the sexual problems of men and women in Egypt. The newly appointed Minister of Health tried to stop its publication because he was disturbed by the frankness of the articles. Sadawy fought this decision and with the help of Aisha Rateb, the Minister of Social Affairs, and second female cabinet member, was allowed to continue it. However, she lost her job at the Ministry of Health, being told to "stay at home" while continuing to receive her salary. Obviously, her ideas are threatening to the more conservative, traditionally oriented male authority.

Another incident illustrates the controversiality of the chastity code in contemporary Egypt. In 1972, following student unrest at the national universities, hundreds of young, educated women started going back to the veil, as a kind of penance and out of frustration over the half war of the Middle East. The feminists were enraged. In an interview with a foreign correspondent Mrs. Amina el Said, another leading feminist writer stated,

> They started wearing costumes with a headpiece and pants with a long coat. It was a kind of relapse. After 50 years of emancipation, we found some women going back to Purdah (seclusion from observation). It was especially dangerous since they were educated women—from the universities! "We want to be good Muslims" they told me. They insisted that what has happened in Egypt and to them in losing the 1967 war and in this half war that we live in was an act of God because people forgot religion (*Chicago Daily News*, April 1973).

In her popular magazine, *Hawa*, el Said wrote a strong article ridiculing the new costume stating that the Quran only required that women wear dignified dress. She ran the ugliest picture she could find of a girl in the new costume. The largely conservative Muslim *culemas* reacted swiftly. In one day she was denounced in the pulpits of 10,000 mosques—Amina, said the *culemas*, is "not a good Muslim and is the Enemy of Chastity." El Said, who considers herself a very good Muslim, reacted by writing an even longer and more virulent article. "I was even more insolent in the second. Thousands of cables were sent to Sadat, but he was very nice—he only sent them to me saying, 'Maybe Amina would be interested in these.'"

A major theme emerging from the feminist writings is that the traditional conceptions of sexual identity are no longer applicable to the exigencies of the modern scene where the woman desires to be more independent in managing her own affairs and making her own decisions. Many women no longer accept the traditional notion that an "honorable woman is a secluded woman." They not only want to, but actually do, participate actively in the larger society (formerly only the man's world). However, as the feminist writers themselves are only too aware, the veil may have been removed, but the traditional values of purity and honor linger on in the minds of many women and men.

For example, in a study on self-images of husbands and wives among urban middle class Cairenes, a thirty-four-year-old woman with one child comments:

> After seeing how many so-called modern girls have suffered anxiety and depression, I feel that I should bring up my daughter the way I was raised. I want her to respect the norms of the society she lives in. A poignant example of such a woman is my brother's ex-fiancée. She was extremely *mutahurreya* (liberated), that's why she suffered a lot. When my brother wanted to marry her we all warned him that she was not our type, that she was too liberated for him. He was fascinated by the new image of the Egyptian girl, and he didn't listen to us. We all told him what we had heard about her behavior because the girl had a very bad reputation. There were many rumors about her. People said that she ran loose, smoked and drank excessively and talked freely with men; and that she was independent of her family. Because the girl had a strong personality, her influence on my brother was great and accordingly he would not stop the engagement. They stayed together for eight months after which my brother couldn't tolerate it. She used to drink a lot and did everything she felt like doing—dancing with other men, going out without asking brother's permission. My brother's main complaint was: "She did not make me feel like a man. And she never acted like a woman. She was independent and extremely emancipated. She never made me feel that she needed me" (Shahin 1974).

It is significant that the divorce rate has risen sharply since 1969. This increasing rate, coupled with the fact that men are making more multiple marriages but keeping the second one secret (something no one would have bothered about forty years ago), may indicate that women of the urban middle and lower classes are becoming less willing to tolerate unhappy marriages, despite the fact that divorce is difficult to obtain, often taking two to three years. One study on court divorce action offers this example of how a woman is subjected to humiliating and prejudicial treatment by the male judges:

> One judge claimed that if a woman failed to fix her husband some breakfast before he went to work or had herself left home for work before him, this would constitute negligence on her part. On another occasion when actual litigation was taking place, the judge turned to the male defendant and said, "Why don't you repudiate her yourself? Why would you want to keep this filthy woman anyway?" After the man agreed to repudiate his wife and left the courtroom, the judge turned to the court and said: "That is the second Man I have come across today" (Zaalouk and Azer 1972, pp. 61–64).

In another courtroom scene a husband fired his revolver at his divorced wife, her sister, and her lawyer during the hearing of the wife's plea for alimony. She was asking that her monthly alimony be raised from four and a half Egyptian pounds to seven (from approximately $10.00 to $17.50). He had attempted to dissuade her from going to court a few days earlier by inviting her out to tea and buying her a new pair of shoes (*The Egyptian Gazette*, May 1974).

Despite the persistent male and religious opposition to women's attempts to redefine their status according to values and behaviors that society has not yet deemed appropriate, the movement for the equality of women's status is gaining a quiet hold.

The movement is fostered by the increasing number of women who are employed outside the home and by the increasing number who pursue higher education. In 1947 2.3 percent of the adult female population over fifteen years of age were employed in jobs outside the home. By 1969 the percentage rose to 4.8 percent representing 618,196 out of a total female population of 12,848,753. This does not represent the great majority of women (nearly five million) who engage in agricultural work without wages within the peasant family system (A.R.E. Census, 1970). These figures are not high by American standards, but the trend to women's holding outside jobs has definitely gained a foothold in Egypt. The statistics of trends in women's participation in higher education are even more significant. In 1952 only ten percent of university students were women; by 1965 the figure had increased to twenty-two percent. Only five years later, in 1970 the figure was thirty percent.

Perhaps no events in recent history have done more to create a social acceptance of women's equal status in Egypt than the Arab-Israeli Wars of 1967 and 1973. The Six Day War of 1967 shocked Egyptians into an awareness of certain internal shortcomings, not least of which was the implication of the unequal status of women and the recognition of the need for radical internal reform. As one prestigious Islamic reformer stated:

> Many articles in our press have emphasized the fact that the causes of our defeat were not merely military weakness, but deep-rooted cultural, moral, and social diseases of which our military weakness was only the sum and final expression. On this particular subject of woman's emancipation, I have more than once heard the ordinary man-in-the-street declare that one of the reasons why the Israelis defeated us was that their women took part, not only in the preparation but even the execution of that war (Nowaihi 1968, p. 17).

Following the October 6th War, 1973, women have been much more visible in public life, particularly Mrs. Jehan Sadat, who has emerged in the past several months as Egypt's first "First Lady." Unlike Mrs. Nasser, who was rarely seen publicly at her husband's side, Mrs. Sadat has played an enormously important role in bringing into public consciousness the "woman's question." Along with the present Minister of Social Affairs, she has rekindled a movement begun fifty years ago by Hoda Sha'rawi to alter the Personal Status Law to equalize divorce for women. There are indications that it will be a difficult struggle, as the bastions of Muslim tradition have alleged that the government is waging a conspiracy against Islam. But for the first time the President of the Republic has made the women's struggle a central plank in his platform for reconstruction. Sadat stated this in his October Working Paper on April 19, 1974:

> The state ensures a compromise between the duties of women towards their families and their work in society. It also ensures equality between men and women in the political, social, cultural and economic aspects of life without violating the provisions of Islamic Law. I am keen to point to Women's Emancipation which has *made the woman a partner in national struggle.* She has shared in production, in services and she looked after the wounded soldiers and families of the war-dead with great honesty.

This public and male support at the highest level of government for woman's participation in the man's arena of military and political struggle suggests that there is a growing awareness of the true meaning of emancipation—just, human treatment coupled with equal rights and equal responsibilities as partners in the national struggle.

SUMMARY AND CONCLUSION

This chapter has attempted to offer some evidence that the traditional cultural conceptions of sexual identity, despite the changes these conceptions are undergoing in the contemporary period, still influence the pattern of interaction between men and women. As a basis of self-esteem, purity-honor is still crucially significant to most women. For a man to show timidity, blush, or attempt to maintain his own sexual purity is to make himself an object of ridicule. Other men show their contempt by referring to him as *da sitt* (*that* one is a woman). The most opprobrius insult a man can receive is to be called *khwal* (the passive "female" partner in a homosexual relationship). The woman who displays behavior designated as masculine, such as physical violence, sexual freedom, or political authority, is subjected to hostile insults. Nawal Sadawy described her own experience with this code in *Women and Sex*: "Very often, the epithet 'male' followed me whenever I excelled in my studies or work. If I kept my word and fulfilled my promise, they said, 'man'; if I walked fast in flat shoes, they said, 'man'; if I practiced sports and built up my muscles, they said 'man' " (1972, p. 14).

Nevertheless, the ideas of the twentieth century are bringing social freedom to greater numbers of women of the urban middle and upper classes. As they enter into the public world of men, they do not feel they are losing self-esteem, but on the contrary, through education and the experience that only emancipation can give, they are acquiring a new definition of their sexual identity. The problems of psychological adjustment that this process creates has been summarized by Berreman:

> What a person thinks of his status is primarily important in so far as it leads to behavioral manifestations. If a person acts in a way that is incompatible with his status as defined by the dominant society, he may be subjected (and usually is) to severe sanctions from within his group or without. Such instances are often the result of a disparity between subjective status on the one hand, and accorded status on the other, where the individual has attempted to objectify his subjective status and the attempt has not been validated by public approval—the new status has not been accorded to him. He may then retreat to behavior appropriate to his publicly defined status or he may continue to defy public opinion, in which case, he is likely to be brought sharply to account (Berreman 1967, p. 289).

The evidence suggests that the Egyptian woman shows every indication of wanting to and being capable of participating as a partner in this new era of reconstruction. With increasing numbers in higher education, in Parliament, in the government decision-making bodies, and as courageous and articulate spokeswomen and writers on the central issues of their society, it would seem that Amina el Said's statement, ". . . that women in public life can change the human condition," will have a chance to be proved true. It is too early to determine the ultimate psychological, social, or cultural effects of the changing status of women in Egypt, but there is every indication that their status is indeed changing.

REFERENCES

Abu-Lughod, J., and Amin, L. 1961. "Egyptian Marriage Advertisements: Microcosm of a Changing Society," *Marriage and Family Living*: 127–36.
Ahmed, Jamal M. 1960. *The Intellectual Origins of Egyptian Nationalism*. London: Oxford University Press.
Anderson, J. N. D. 1950–51. "Recent Developments in Sha'ria Law," *The Moslem World* 113–26; 271–88.
Antoun, Richard. 1968. "On the Modesty of Women in Arab Muslim Villages," *American Anthropologist* 70:671–97.
Arberry, A. J. 1953. *The Ring of the Dove* by Ibn Hazm. London: Luzacs and Company.
Berger, Morroe. 1964. *The Arab World Today*. New York: Doubleday (Anchor).
Berque, Jacques. 1964. *The Arabs: Their History and Future*. London: Faber and Faber.
Berreman, Gerald. 1967. "Structure and Function of Caste Systems," in *Japan's Invisible Race: Caste in Culture and Personality*, edited by George DeVos and H. Wagatsuma. Berkeley: University of California Press.
──────. 1972. "Race, Caste and Other Invidious Distinctions in Social Stratification," *Race* 13:4:385–414.
Dawood, N. J. 1959. *The Koran*. Translation and revised edition. Middlesex, N.J.: Penguin Classic.
DeVos, George. 1966. "Conflict, Dominance and Exploitation in Human Systems of Social Segregation: Some Theoretical Perspectives from the Study of Personality in Culture," in *Conflicts in Society*, edited by A. V. S. de Reuck and Julie Knight. London: Churchill.
──────. 1967. "Psychology of Purity and Pollution as Related to Social Self-Identity and Caste," in *Ciba Foundation Symposium on Caste and Race: Comparative Approaches*, edited by A. V. S. de Reuck and Julie Knight. London: Churchill.
Dodd, Peter. 1973. "Family, Honor and the Forces of Change," *International Journal of Middle East Studies* 4:40–54.
Fahmy, Aida I. 1969. "The Hakima: A Study of Professional Socialization in Egypt." Master's Thesis, The American University in Cairo.
Goode, W. J. 1963. *World Revolution and Family Patterns*. New York: Collier-Macmillan-Free Press.
Lerner, Daniel. 1958. *The Passing of Traditional Society*. Glencoe, Ill.: Free Press.
Levy, Reuben. 1965. *The Social Structure of Islam*. Cambridge: Cambridge University Press.

Lutfi-al-Sayyid, A. 1968. *Egypt and Cromer: Study of Anglo-Egyptian Relations*. London: Murray.
Mazloum, C., and El Sayed, H. 1972. "Hidjab, Amal and Bukhur: Study of Egyptian Symbols." Seminar paper, Department of Sociology-Anthropology-Psychology, American University in Cairo.
Nowaihi, M. 1968. "Problems of Modernization in Islam." Paper presented to a colloquium on Islam and Modernism, American University in Cairo.
Patai, R. 1969. *Golden River to Golden Road: Society, Culture and Change in the Middle East*, 3rd edition. Philadelphia: University of Pennsylvania Press.
_____. 1973. *The Arab Mind*. New York: Charles Scribner's Sons.
Polk, William R. 1965. "The Nature of Modernization," *Foreign Affairs* 44:100–111.
Radwan, A. A. 1951. *Old and New Forces of Education in Egypt*. New York: A. M. S. Press.
Rasheed, B. 1973. *The Egyptian Feminist Union*. Cairo: Anglo-Egyptian Books.
Saleh, Saneya. 1972. "Women in Islam: Their Status in Religious and Traditional Culture," *International Journal of Sociology of the Family* 2:1–8.
_____. 1972b. "Women in Islam: Their Role in Religious and Traditional Culture," *International Journal of Sociology of the Family* 2: 193–201.
Sasson, Somekh. 1973. *The Changing Rhythm: A Study of Naguib Maḥfūz's Novels*. Leiden: E.J. Brill.
Schutz, Alfred. 1953. "Common-Sense and Scientific Interpretation of Human Action," *Philosophy and Phenomenological Research* 14:1–37.
Sfeir, G. 1966. "The Contemporary Arabic Novel," *Daedalus*, Fall Issue, pp. 41–46.
Shahin, Zeinab. 1974. "Fieldnotes." Master's Thesis, American University in Cairo.
Vatikiotis, P.J. 1969. *History of Modern Egypt*. London: Weidenfeld and Nicolson.
Yusuf, Hajji Shaykh. 1965. "In Defense of the Veil," in *Contemporary Middle East: Tradition and Innovation*, edited by B. Rivlin and J. S. Szyliowics. New York: Random House.
Zaalouk, M., and Azer, A. 1972. *Taqliq: Divorce Through Court Action*. Seminar paper, Department of Sociology-Anthropology-Psychology, The American University in Cairo.
Zanati, M. S. 1959. *The Relations Between Men and Women Among the Arabs* [In Arabic]. Cairo: Dar el Gameat.

Conclusion

Responses To Change: Recurrent Patterns

In attempting to integrate and summarize the contributions to this volume, it may be helpful to state what we did not attempt as well as what we did. In so doing I can clarify the focus and limitations of our comparative examinations of responses to change in cultures throughout the world.

First, this volume was not intended, and does not intend, to formulate an abstract, systematic theory of culture change and psychocultural response. Instead, it seeks to discover some of the range and variations in the patterns of response that have emerged throughout a world which, in its modern history, has undergone drastic social and geographic interpenetration of previously isolated cultures. By 1850 massive culture contacts had occurred almost everywhere under conditions of political and technological dominance exerted by Europe and the United States. Second, the unit of consideration in this volume was not the individual as seen through a psychocultural analysis of particular life histories. Instead, we examined culture-specific patterns of internally adjustive and socially adaptive change.

Although not a focus of concern, one can note some underlying consensus among the contributors that, whatever the specific circumstances of change and whatever the cultural patterns governing response, the functioning of human beings occurs according to psychological processes common to all people. Nevertheless, within both large geographic areas and specific cultures, one can note patterns of response characterizing a number of unrelated cultures which retain communalities despite lack of contact. Such areal patterns occur in Africa, North America, Polynesia, and Melanesia, as well as in European cultures stemming from the Greco-Roman, Judeo-Christian heritage.

This volume hopes to contribute some middle-range theoretical conclusions to an examination of the psychological and cultural features of change as they occur in society, stimulated internally as well as externally.

Internally, societies are stimulated to change by a number of factors: (1) There may be shifts in the external, natural environment that necessitate shifts in technological, political, economic, or social patterns of survival. Change in climate, exhaustion of game or some natural resource, and invention allowing for some new exploitation of the natural environment are all examples of the stimulus for change. (2) Internal changes may be due to the force of population increase or, conversely, a pattern of endemic disease that lowers population. (3) Shifts in social patterns can change patterns of economic distribution; exceptional individuals and their political-social or their economic-technological innovations can be an initial stimulus for far-reaching changes within a society. Such events, while possible, are difficult to document, but in the history of change within given cultures they no doubt occur periodically.

While indigenous change within given cultures occurs, one could presume that, by and large, change is more frequently stimulated by external contact with other groups. The nature of such responses to contact is conditioned by a combination of several general determinants:

1. *The organization of the precontact culture* subject to intrusion—its characteristic modes of technological, political, and psychocultural adaptation and adjustment.
2. Degree of similarity in economic, religious, social, and political *conditions operative in the intrusive contacting culture.*
3. *The social, political, and economic conditions of contact,* especially relations of dominance under drastic asymmetries of technology, organization, and power. These conditions can range from trade and aid, through religious conversion to violent conquest.
4. *Types of resulting contact cultures* (for example, syncretic or plural societies emerge from prolonged, intensive contact) including:
    a. *Colonized societies* with degrees of control exercised by outsiders ranging from administration with minimum presence, to military occupation, to massive settlement and control by outsiders.
    b. *Modernizing societies* with foreign enclaves of technological specialists.
    c. *Composite immigrant societies* characterized by various degrees and rates of assimilation.
5. *The degree and immediacy of the effect of change on major social and economic institutions and on cultural ethos* (on general values, orientations, and preferred modes of interpersonal relations). The degree of culture continuity depends on:

a. *The degree of disruption or continuity* of the agencies of transmission and inculcation of ethos—family, religion, and other conservators of traditional symbols and values.
b. The conditions and manner under which contact takes place (point 3 above) *and* the extent to which these allow for the *adaptation of major new institutions* to the traditional ethos.
6. *The sequence of acculturative events*: the phases of contact. A phase is a period in which the conditions of change are relatively constant. A new phase occurs when the process of change itself changes due to some crisis or change of pace in contact. Observations on responses to change are relative to what historical phase is being observed at the time of contact.

A theory integrating these processes deserves extended analysis and study, but its development was not the subject of the present inquiry which focused more directly on culturally characteristic psychocultural processes of personal adaptation and adjustment in a variety of situations of contact.

It was our task to evaluate critically in a comparative framework psychological responses to the challenge of change characterizing particular groups. Some of the groups were similar in culture, but they differed in the situations encountered. Represented in the contributions of our authors are a wide variety of observed responses, ranging from defensive rigidification to facile adaptation. We attempted to bring some order out of the variety of situations by dividing the volume into four main topics. These topics were arrived at after the contributions were received.

By way of summary, therefore, I would like to suggest a different type of framework as a guide to a number of psychocultural processes that received recurrent attention in the individual chapters and in the discussions of the participants at the Hakone conference, but have not as yet been touched upon sufficiently in one of the introductions to the four parts of this volume. The processes of responding to change occur on three levels: level one is an intergroup area between cultures in contact; level two is an intragroup area in which change occurs selectively in given social segments within a culture; level three is the intrapersonal processes or personality variables selectively influenced by change. My major contention is that one can relate what occurs in each level to what I call "ethnic identity," a sense of social self shared by the members of a particular group that determines their selectivity to new experiences and how they ignore or assimilate past experiences in situations of change.

BETWEEN-GROUP PROCESSES

In the Introduction I discussed the reason for considering the concept of acculturation in its subjective, psychological dimension, limited to situations of conscious awareness by members of a culture who are adopting traits or characteristics from another culture group. The term diffusion, I suggested, can be considered a more encompassing term, including the adoption of traits over longer and less clearly delineated periods of time.

Since acculturation occurs when some awareness of outside influences arises in a contact situation, it is best analyzed in terms of what happens to the adaptive and adjustive patterns of members of a culture involved in this process. Let us illustrate some of these situations.

In the numerous situations of mutual exchange of material artifacts or social traits across well-defined territorial barriers, differences in the acceptance or rejection of traits relate to the individual's sense of threat to his ethnic identity. There is, for example, less threat when acceptance of a trait does not imply submission to the donor or loss of peer group respect.

There are situations of relative openness of personality, such as that described elsewhere for Polynesia by Robert Levy. Less threat to identity is implied in acculturative situations of geographic isolation. Where geographic barriers are arbitrary or weak, intrapsychic barriers are often used to supplement military ones to help maintain both group territory and group identity, in spite of acculturative contact.

Contact between cultures can produce occupational or subsistence specialization. Some cultural exchanges result in adaptive changes related to specialized methods of production which insure group continuity through technological specialization. These situations, however, often devolve into a blended cultural entity in which the groups concerned take on overall cultural similarities in those characteristics not related to their occupational specialization. A separate cultural persistence in such circumstances depends on the maintenance of a sense of separate ethnic identity.

There are a number of situations where cultures remain in overt conflict and competition with one another for ascendancy. Competition may be technological, economic, or religious. Political competition may continue with no permanent ascendancy accruing to either side.

The most frequent type of situation we explored is that of cultural systems of relative dominance and subordination. Some are of an economic-technological nature, as in the relationship of Western countries to China and Japan in the nineteenth century. Others involve political, religious, and economic acculturative experiences as in the case of Melanesia.

In the last section we explored minority or subordinate status and ethnicity. In these latter instances we note continuing psychological boundary maintenance—identity persistence without the benefit of territorial separation.

A number of motives act to stimulate acculturation. The most obvious are material ones. The material traits that enhance life or make it easier for the group are readily appreciated and quickly adopted when the knowledge of the necessary appropriate behavior becomes available. Such material borrowings themselves pose very little direct threat to social identity.

There are also whole series of interactions of a nonmaterial nature that are powerful motives for acculturation since they involve *status enhancement*. When a new trait can be used within a culture's existing definition of status to enhance the position of individuals, there will be a strong inducement for the members of the group to exhibit the new trait. Again, such situations may cause no internal disharmony, except when the influx of new traits disturbs the group's economic balance. Internal psychological conflicts can arise when a desired status can only be attained by a change in group identity. There are numerous situations where ethnic behavior is depreciated by a dominant group. These depreciations are often accepted by the weaker group and internalized. Under such circumstances individual status enhancement by means of acculturation or "passing" can be a highly demoralizing, disruptive force, seriously injuring the viability of the subordinate culture (DeVos and Romannuci-Ross 1975).

As Inkeles pointed out in one of the discussions held among the contributors, acculturation itself may be a neutral concept. The social, political, and psychological *contexts* in which it occurs are the sources of stress rather than change per se. One cannot simply assume that all change is stressful. One must examine the manner in which stress is induced or occurs within individuals undergoing change. For example, Schwartz's discussion of "pathomimetic behavior" warned us against too readily using the concept of stress to explain behavioral activities. It would, according to Schwartz, be erroneous to assume that the appearance of symptoms which *can* be associated with stress always are the result of stress. They may simply be modes of adaptive religious behavior.

THE TIME SEQUENCE IN ADAPTIVE ACCULTURATION

Robert Levy in a discussion at Hakone elaborated upon the sequences of relative adaptation and maladaptation to culture change in the Polynesian and Micronesian situations. Hawaiians exhibit greater stress signs today than in some previous periods since contact. The first reaction of Polynesians to culture contact and the consequent modifications of their culture were generally positive, despite the horrendous results of the introduction of Western diseases against which they had no defenses. Only in later stages of adaptation to modern life did psychological stress become apparent.

One has to go back to the previous precontact situation to see that some traditions—such as the taboos about commoners and women—were in themselves already chronically stressful. Thus, the Polynesians were relieved by the Christian missionaries' insistence that the taboos be abolished.

The greater incidence of stress among Hawaiians today is indicated by more signs of neurotic maladjustment, such as sleeplessness, psychosomatic reactions, and so forth. Only five percent of Hawaiians finish high school and only two percent finish college. More Hawaiians are on public welfare; the incidence of delinquency has recently risen.

On the other hand, Chinese and Japanese against whom discrimination was greater have survived the minority experience better than native Hawaiians. Inkeles raised the interesting point that one of the striking differences between the American Indian and Hawaiian situations is that the Indian situation was quickly and chronically characterized by alcoholism and other indices of maladjustment, as well as social maladaptation. Until recently, there has been very little similar evidence among Hawaiians. Community, family, and personality factors, including social self-identity specific to Hawaiians or Polynesians, must be taken into consideration to account for this difference and for the change in Hawaiian social adaptation. The new developments may be related to a shift in the status position of Hawaiians since statehood. They may be partially the result of the influx of mainland white population and the increasing pressures of a more competitive social environment. Whatever the case, increased internal conflict related to self-acceptance and self-derogation is evident.

As Levy made clear, the experience of the Hawaiians and others indicates that one cannot predict the stages at which characteristic modes of maladjustment will or will not appear in acculturation situations. The appearance of either adjustment or maladjustment can be temporary and not a stabilized reaction. It does seem clear, however, that the closer a subordinate group gets to assimilation, the greater the degree to which the images (whether positive or negative) of the dominant group may be internalized.

INTRAGROUP OR INTRASOCIETAL SEGMENTATIONS AND PROCESSES OF CHANGE

Only in simple societies do processes of acculturation affects the total society equally. More often acculturation selectively affects segments of societies. The educated elite of India, for example, were much more influenced by British colonization than were the people living in rural villages, while social change today may affect the Brahmans more than other segments.

Social change in a hierarchical society has a differential rate within various population and economic sub-groups. Some forms of disruption may be sufficient to bring about revolutionary upheavals, overturning previous status hierarchies and creating new ones. These revolutions can be conservative, as with the abolition of the Samurai class in Japan; or more radical and bloody, as in the Soviet Union where a managerial-intellectual elite was established, drawn from a mixture of previous elite groups and submerged social groups that had no previous voice. The complexities of such occurrences on a psychocultural level need much more examination than has been given to date.

Processes of change also differentially affect associational or kinship networks within a culture. In some circumstances, kinship networks can continue to function well, as they have for the Batak of Sumatra. The Chinese kinship network seems particularly strong and capable of maintaining itself, despite large scale geographic movement by overseas Chinese. Some groups, therefore, can maintain their cultural identity on a variety of unit levels, either as kin groups or through the maintenance of voluntary associational networks related to some point of origin. The group identity may be maintained simply by family units. Individual migration and individual shifts in reference groups which are characteristic in Amercian society may actually be a rare phenomena in other situations.

Social change may result in radical shifts in the manner of according status to individuals. With industrialization there is a characteristic shift from ascribed to achieved status. There may be a shift in some societies toward according youth greater status and the aged less status. There may also be a shift in the status positions of men and women, as in Egypt. There may be shifts in relative status of the individual within the nuclear family or the individual within the kin group.

In some circumstances of change the resultant stress is most apparent in the conflicts and tensions aroused between different social segments or classes. Modernization may not necessarily lead to individuation. Some modern societies remain group oriented. One must not succumb to a bias based on familiarity with the American emphasis on individualism. Other societies, such as the Japanese, have become modernized without necessarily becoming individualistic. Berreman points out, for example, how social mobility within present day India is not only an individual, but also a group movement.

INTRAPERSONAL PROCESSES INVOLVED IN ACCULTURATIVE SITUATIONS

It is appropriate here to reintroduce consideration of five psychocultural concepts of adaptation and adjustment that Wagatsuma and I have found helpful in discussing problems of minority status among Japanese outcastes. These five concepts help to summarize a number of issues raised in the chapters of this book: *differential socialization, selective permeability, reference group, differential role expectations,* and *social self identity.*

In the course of our discussions, the issue was raised whether a concept of personality dealing only with internal adjustment is as useful as a more interactional concept suggesting that individual behavior must be examined not only within the individual but in his relationship to others. The point is well taken that adjustment cannot be studied without some attention to social interaction. When we consider personality, we are concerned with internalizations which automatically guide behavior. Coping mechanisms or defense mechanisms are only structured in interaction. The modality of perception itself—what information is taken in, how it is cognitively processed and the nature of reactions to it—is to some degree a product of a culturally specific socialization experience which occurred in family and early peer group interaction, and continues to appear in other forms of interaction.

Differential Socialization

In comparing groups it is obvious that to explain the facility or difficulty in adopting new traits one has to refer to some form of *differential socialization*. The concept by itself does not explain what the differences are, but merely suggests that they have to be investigated systematically to learn why there are both individual differences within groups, and collective group differences in the adaptation of particular forms of modernization. For example, in a discussion at Hakone of the Hawaiians' difficulty in a formal school situation, Levy briefly referred to the fact that a long-range, ongoing study of learning behavior of Hawaiians, both preschool and grade school, has turned up some interesting differences in the use of verbal communication between the parents of Hawaiians and those of other groups. It became obvious to the investigators that the cognitive styles of those raised within a Hawaiian native culture are significantly different from those of other groups which must adapt to the middle-class-dominated elementary school system.

Caudill points out that cultural continuity occurs in Japan through the maintenance of basic socialization practices both within the family and in the face to face social groups that transmit the culture's ethos from one generation to the next; this process continues despite some radical shifts in parts of the social structure with modernization. Similarly, Spiro's studies of the Burmese suggest that despite surface behavioral shifts in functional equivalents, a direct continuity in the nature of aggression and hostility remains part of Burmese culture.

It is clear that one must start with some analysis of the particular socialization experiences of a group to be able to say how change will influence them. In our series of papers, this idea is supported. For example, Schwartz indicated why the Cargo cult was the peculiar type response of Melanesian personality structure. Abbott's empirical data suggests the striking similarities of structural patterns on a psychological test taken by the Cantonese Chinese in San Francisco and the Fukienese Chinese in Taiwan who have had no contact with one another for several hundred years. There seems to be good evidence that culture depends heavily on the continuity of the specific patterns of socialization characteristic of the group.

Selective Permeability

A second psychological concept that I have found useful in considering identity maintenance in situations of continual contact between members of different cultures is what I term *"selective permeability."* This concept cannot be separated from the concepts of *reference group allegiance, social role expectancies,* and *identity*, which I shall presently reexamine.

Selective permeability refers to a conception of ego boundaries as somewhat analogous to the boundaries of a functioning biological cell; the ego's boundary relationship with the environment resembles the processes of osmosis. Certain experiences are allowed to "penetrate," while others are selectively excluded as potentially damaging to life. The well-functioning, socially-oriented ego in the process of developing learns to accept experiences relating the individual to his cultural identity; at the same time, it protects him from the intake of experiences which would challenge his integrity. Barth's theory of ethnic boundaries is a very similar concept applied to group boundary maintenance. Barth and I agree that ethnicity is not a matter of overt language, religion, or other specific traits. Ethnicity is the *emblematic use* of such traits to differentiate between groups in order to keep them socially and psychologically separate from one another.

Psychologically, one cannot incorporate a given culture trait if it threatens one's identity integrity. To do so may create a sense of emotional dissonance within the individual. Festinger's (1956) theory of cognitive dissonance might help in explaining how internal psychological consistency is maintained in social identity. I would suggest, however, that the problem is one of "affective" dissonance (DeVos 1975c) and that Festinger's theory has to be related to some model of an ego that is capable of selective defensive maneuvers to exclude threatening perceptions related to affective states.

Dissonance reduction as a constant human goal was questioned by Schwartz. He pointed to the importance of inconsistency, ambiguity, and ambivalence of feeling and belief to the duration and momentum of cults and social movements. In this case, the inconsistencies must themselves be maintained, not reduced, if the impetus of these cultural forms as moving, self-excitatory systems is to be maintained. This takes us into the complexities of human nature—that indeed some individuals or groups welcome an internal sense of marginality while others find such an unresolved state intolerable.

The developmental theory of Jean Piaget (Flavell 1963) posits that the cognitive functions of the organism operate by a series of "schemata" that are built up at least partially in the processes of socialization. New experience is "assimilated" to the already operative schemata. This new experience can modify the schemata by a process of "accommodation." The digested experience causes some alteration of the previous structure. These processes of assimilation and accommodation are the mechanisms by which the organism maintains consistency yet allows itself to be modified by continuing new experiences.

If we take this conceptual model and consider how it operates in a situation of continuous culture contact between two groups in which each maintains its *own individual identity* (by a differential socialization of its members) we must at the same time consider how the individuals living in a similar external environment are socialized to respond to selective experiences. Indeed, change does occur, but the individual does not always sense any disruption. In the ethos shared by the Batak, cited by Bruner, there is no threat to identity, because there is no conscious sense that the *adat* or law is being changed by modernization. A secure identity depends on *sufficient continuity* rather than on total stability and lack of change in experience.

A most ready example of selective permeability to new experience is the American school room experience in the elementary grades for members of different ethnic minorities. What is imparted by the middle class teacher is differentially perceived, differentially integrated, and results in different responses depending upon the child's group identity. The black ghetto child or the Mexican-American child finds it difficult to assimilate to his own developing schemata elements of white culture that may threaten his sense of integrity.

The nature of this process deserves systematic examination. Fortunately it has become the recent focus of a great deal of attention by developmental psychologists. I would suggest that anthropologists and sociologists should also examine the permeability processes at work in pluralistic cultural settings or in societies with sharp segmental cleavages of occupation or hierarchical status.

Reference Group Theory and Processes of Acculturation

Some psychologically-oriented approaches to socialization have tended to neglect the crucial developmental period of peer group socialization. When one looks at situations of acculturation this becomes a particularly important consideration. The integrated school in a society of pluralistic ethnic groups is a powerful force for relative assimilation, although as Glazer points out, the melting-pot, to some extent, is a myth. Nevertheless, the socialization experience of the American school has tended to "Americanize" and unite the children of immigrants from highly diverse cultures. Although selective permeability does operate in the school situation, the peer group often breaks down previous culture differences. School children become more permeable to the experiences of the peer group as the dominant reference group. In most instances, peers become more powerful identification models than parents.

Language behavior in urban United States schools is a case in point. Most immigrant children entering New York schools at the turn of the century spoke only their native tongues, yet in the course of several years of elementary schooling, American speech patterns rather than their parents' speech became natural for them. Not only were they permeable to their teachers, but, more importantly, they found it emotionally and psychologically necessary to communicate with their peers. In other pluralist societies, and to some small extent in America, minority cultures have attempted to maintain themselves by keeping control over what is taught their children, either in religion or language classes. These classes succeed in their purpose only if the peer group atmosphere supports them. Japanese-American Nisei did well in the American schools because peer group pressures supported scholastic achievement. In Japanese-language schools, in contrast, peer groups were antagonistic and students resisted efforts of teachers to instruct in Japanese. As a consequence, few American-born Japanese acquired an active knowledge of spoken Japanese.

Reference group theory can help us understand acculturation. One difficulty involved in the application of reference group theory has been the fact that its exponents tend to take an antipsychoanalytic orientation, ignoring any consideration of how the psychodynamic processes of early socialization and internalization relate to the later forces shaping identity in peer group or reference group emulation. There is a dynamic continuity between the degree to which any individual internalizes early images and maintains them rigidly (by means of superego formation) and the degree to which he remains permeable to the later influences of the peer group or other reference groups for his sense of self.

A key to this issue is a concept of "status emulation" as related on a later social level to the earlier more specific psychoanalytic concept of "identification with the aggressor." There are a number of motives related to status emulation beside that of fear of attack or motives on this primitive level of development. It is obvious in hierarchical societies that behavior related to particular status positions helps enhance the individual's own sense of self. There is in societies permitting social mobility a need in individuals to make choices at certain crisis points in the life cycle whether to continue the behavior which identifies them with their group of origin or whether to modify behavior so as to gain the rewards of social mobility by taking on behavior patterns occupationally or socially committing the individual to seek inclusion in a group different from that of origin.

During the sequential course of socialization occurring in mobile societies one moves from earlier unselfconscious, more spontaneous levels at which emulation occurs automatically without deliberation, to later periods where there is a conscious awareness of behavioral change which makes the assumption of new modes of behavior "feel" relatively "unnatural" to the individual who attempts them. At these later stages, the element of conscious choice enters, bringing with it dilemmas of integrity.

The process of Sanskritization in Hindu society mentioned by Berreman is an excellent historical example of group social mobility as a means of status enhancement in a highly stratified social system. It may be said generally that one of the principle dynamics in reference group behavior is the internal motivational pressure toward status enhancement.

Differential Role Expectations and Acculturation

The concept of social status is central in understanding groups' reactions to problems in the assignment of role expectations—whether across cultural or even sex role boundaries. Within-group definitions are applied to the members of a given community; in situations of culture contact outsiders are defined in terms that relate to the already existing group definitions.

Lloyd Warner once described how when he entered an Australian aboriginal community he was to study he had to be defined by the members of this community within their kinship system, for they had no other way to relate to strangers. They could not relate to him until they could define his expected behavior. If a group cannot anticipate what to expect they are liable to be fearful; if the culture has established a schemata for bringing in strangers, there is a defined way to relate. It is thus inevitable that a culture develops prejudicial attitudes about the behavior of members of other groups. The strange individual must be first put into some total category. It is less likely that he will be reacted to more individually until more complex schemata have been developed to handle different members of his alien group. Within a culture, of course, the individual has intensive and complex experiences with those of his own group and quickly learns to treat individuals selectively. Nevertheless, even within cultures individuals are strongly defined by role expectations, not simply as highly individuated human beings. The less we know a person the more we treat him in terms either of role expectations or of some larger diffuse concept of ethnicity which defines him for us.

In pluralistic societies minority group members encounter highly stereotyped role definitions imposed upon them by the majority culture. It is thus very difficult for minorities to escape some degree of internalization of the expectation of the majority culture. Such internalization of definitions alters the internal psychic balance of the minority group members. For example, Japanese outcastes are thought by the majority of the population to be more innately aggressive than ordinary Japanese. It is difficult for outcastes, at times, not to succumb to the expectation that they will be violent by becoming aggressive when ordinary Japanese would display greater self-control. The outcaste's aggressive behavior confirms the expectation and creates a vicious circle. In situations of dominance and subordinance in cultural contact the dominant group tends to define how the members of the subordinate group will behave, and to a certain degree this definition influences individuals to fulfill subordinate role models.

This does not always happen. If the internal definitions enforced within groups are strongly supported by community and family sanctions, individuals can resist these role expectations imposed by an outside dominant majority. The Japanese-Americans and the Chinese are good cases in point. Despite horrendous discrimination they have been able to adjust to American society more in the terms of their own traditional cultural values than in terms imposed upon them by external concepts of the role of "Orientals."

IDENTITY

Throughout the discussions at Hakone it became apparent that some concept of identity, especially "ethnic identity" is crucial for an understanding of the processes of acculturation as they are subjectively experienced. This concept summarizes and integrates a psychological approach to the survival and continuity of culture as it is carried forth from one generation to the next within individuals. It subsumes the four variables already discussed—differential socialization, permeability, role expectations, and reference group orientations. The concept of identity is particularly pertinent in understanding the maintenance of a culture pattern in the face of social, political, and economic pressures for individuals to identify with a powerful alien culture.

The reasons for identity maintenance in a subordinate or minority role in society are complex and varied. They are not to be explained solely as a result of not being permitted to change identity. The approach to ethnic identity must be historical and sociological as well as psychological (DeVos and Romannucci-Ross 1975).

Historical Vicissitudes and the Formation of a Minority Identity

One cannot understand identity without some exploration of the historical circumstances creating the status positions and role expectations of given individuals which they internalize so as to become part of the self. In the various papers on change in this volume note how there are differences in the history of contact which are varied and diverse depending upon the area of the world examined. These differences in circumstance must be dynamically related to the cultural specific modes of response to acculturation that arise out of social structure and personality considerations within given cultures. In examining acculturation processes it is peculiarly those circumstances where the group is defeated or collectively reduced to a subordinate status that the greatest amount of adjustment problems seem to arise.

The disturbance of identity is one major manifestation of internal maladjustment and hence a critical one in understanding forms of maladaptation to change.

There are varying examples of political defeat where the defeated culture group has been placed in a special social position, as a caste or class, so as to be used, either instrumentally or expressively, by the dominant group (DeVos and Wagatsuma 1967). This usage of individuals often results in self-perpetuating patterns which cannot be explained other than by concluding that the dominated group has internalized an identity which helps to continue the rigid system of social stratification. Defeated ethnic or cultural minorities often adjust to their defeat by incorporating it as part of their ethnic identity. This sometimes results in maladaptive apathy; in other cases, it results in adaptive or maladaptive compensatory assertions of group solidarity through religious or political movements. The nature of these religious or political movements, as indicated in some of our chapters, is strongly influenced by personality factors common to the group and by external political or social circumstances.

Acculturation patterns in migratory situations, as we have discussed, may have a neutral effect on adjustment and adaptation. Definitions of status or the ability to find satisfactory occupations may be the crucial variables in positive patterns of adjustment or adaptation. The section on urbanization well illustrated the fact that the urbanization process itself is a neutral one. Difficulties lie rather in the problems of social self-identity and status security experienced subjectively.

Modes of Identity Maintenance or Cultural Persistence

Ethnic identity is symbolic; one's sense of cultural continuity is symbolized by a number of different characteristics. Among the most significant is *geographic territoriality*, or the relation of self to territory, that is, a section of geographic space with which the individual identifies. Identity may have an economic or *occupational sense of continuity*. Identity may be related to *religious beliefs* and a special type of relationship between the individual, his group, and the supernatural. Identity maintenance may be a question of *language* and modes of verbal communication which are maintained by specific groups. Identity maintenance may be a question of *esthetic cultural patterns*, such as art, modes of dress, or cosmetic enhancement of the body. A group may identify with stylistic devices in any of the arts—architecture, dance, graphic representations—to symbolize continuity.

Ethnic identities can serve different psychocultural "uses." Identity, for example, may distance someone from other persons or groups. The distancing may have instrumental or expressive dimensions. Identity can symbolize the "good," with the "bad" attributed to an out-group. In caste systems the dominant groups, for example, can attribute disavowed characteristics to the outcastes. Individuals in the outcaste group then have difficulty avoiding the incorporation of negative models when they remain part of a culture that systematically disparages members of their group. Out-groups are used by all cultures as scapegoats, as repositories of what is socially and intrapsychically disavowed within one's own group.

Identity Manipulation: Uses of Identity in Status Enhancement

In a complex society with many reference groups and social roles, it is possible to manipulate and move between identities according to instrumentally perceived self-interest. Some ethnic minority group members practice what Margaret Mead has aptly termed "identity prostitution," the manipulation of ethnic or cultural identity to gain economic advantage.

In some conflict situations between ethnic minorities, one or another exhibit what Theodore Schwartz has termed "conspicuous ethnicity." An individual may flaunt particular identity characteristics to identify himself overtly with a particular group; in such situations the individual consciously defends against any identification as part of the majority group, and against the, perhaps unconscious, temptation to be so identified.

Acculturation, Social Mobility, and Identity Betrayal

The group discussion at Hakone returned several times to the crucial issue of social self-identity and the symbolic meaning of taking on alien forms of behavior as a means of status enhancement in a host society.

Bruner distinguished the different types of adaptation he has witnessed in his own research work among American Indians and the Batak of Indonesia. In the one instance, maladaptive and maladjustive responses result from acculturation, while in the other case, modernization has been successful. The American Indian is usually very aware of processes of acculturation and is sensitive to the requirements of change, whereas the Batak have no self-consciousness that they are in any way Westernized. While they recognize social change, they have a subjective sense that the *adat* or law is being maintained. Modernization has not as yet substantially challenged their sense of social self-identity.

Bruner points out that for the Batak, new cultural traits have no symbolic implications related to identity. But the American Indian knows continually and painfully that anything new comes via the dominant white culture that has defeated him, taken his land, and relegated him to the position of a scarcely tolerated, despised minority.

In the American Indian case, movement in the direction of modernization is symbolically labeled as "capitulating" or taking advantage of the white man's culture. By changing behavior to become acceptable to the white group, the individual loses status within the Indian community. In the case of the Batak, in contrast, the individual can take on new modes of behavior without in any way alienating himself from his group.

Another very important distinction pointed out by Bruner is that so many of the changes made in the case of the American Indian were stimulated by some superordinate authority. In the case of the Batak, an external political or social power had nothing to do with motivation for change; the changes were taken on spontaneously without external pressure.

Another important consideration of contrast between the Batak and the American Indian groups is that the Batak do not label people who are unsuccessful in such a way as to emphasize their deviant position. In other words, there is no tendency to label unsuccessful or nonconforming individuals as deviants. There is no judgment of negative role expectations related to modernization.

Nathan Glazer commented that in the case of American Jews or Jews of other communities one finds two types of leaders, those who remain identified within the Jewish communities and those who are successful in terms of the majority community. Members of this latter group, nevertheless, retain their identity within the Jewish community and are even respected for the ability, not suspected as traitors. Glazer points out how this contrasts sharply with the situation among American blacks today: if a black is successful in terms acceptable to the majority culture he will be suspected of being an "Uncle Tom," who accommodates to the white society rather than remaining loyal to the needs and aspirations of his own group. This impasse has caused difficulty in the assumption of role models for some black Americans.

Theodore Graves responded that similar findings were emerging in the research of Mrs. Graves dealing with Ghanian modernization. Becoming a modern individual is quite acceptable and in no way a problem for the individual. This is in stark contrast with Mrs. Graves' previous experience with Spanish-Americans in the United States for whom social mobility or acculturation is equated with identity betrayal. The frequent use of the word "falso" attests to this attitude. This group attitude is self-perpetuating, since there is a continual loss of leadership through the exclusion of successful members.

This feature of Latin American attitudes has to be seen in its historical dimension, as a result of previous generations of class exploitation. Those who obtained power, either by economic or political means, have used the power for their own enhancement by exploitation of others. Those who live in subordinate social position have learned to defend themselves by becoming impermeable to the influence of individuals in authority. As already indicated, this is one reason many Mexican American children do not learn in American schools; their egos have been trained to be impermeable to Anglo teachers.

Many Indian groups are in the same kind of conflicted situation. As an example, there is the following incident which was told to me by an anthropologist in contact with the Mescalera Apache. An Indian youth was given a scholarship to attend college. In retaliation for his betrayal of Indian culture for white culture his peer group killed his dog and gave him a severe beating. The very act of accepting the scholarship was experienced as a terrible threat to the group's maintenance of its Indian image.

For many Mexican Americans, Indians, and black minority group members in America the dilemma of maintaining cultural identity or taking on white identity remains unresolved.

Forces Operating Toward Acculturation and Loss of Previous Identity

Adaptive and adjustive difficulties occur when there is a conflict between patterns of identity maintenance on the one hand, and strong inducements to change and give up one's previous cultural patterns on the other. The most obvious blandishment to change cultural frames of reference is, as we have stressed, some form of status enhancement by which an individual is promised higher status if he symbolically changes his behavior to present himself as a member of a dominant ethnic group.

Adjustment and adaptation problems occur at particular crisis situations in the life cycle of the individual. Eric Erickson's concepts of "identity diffusion" and "identity moratorium" are very applicable to an understanding of the individual's adjustive crises in complex modern societies. No modern man escapes the presence of a spectrum of alternative modes around which to structure his life commitment—some limited to ethnic background, some to occupational demands, others to a variety of ways to achieve self-actualization. Crises in the life cycle are particularly difficult in pluralistic societies where there are many social-structural inducements for the individual to change his identity.

•

This volume expects to have raised as many questions as it has sought to resolve by discussion and exposition. The combined hope of the various contributors is that their work is developing a continuity within social science, dedicated to the systematic exploration of psychocultural responses to change.

REFERENCES

Barth, Fredrik. 1969. *Ethnic Groups and Boundaries.* Boston: Little, Brown.
DeVos, George. 1975a. "Dangers of Pure Theory in Social Anthropology," *Ethos.*
―――. 1975b. "Affective Dissonance and Primary Socialization: Implications for a Theory of Incest Avoidance," *Ethos.*
DeVos, George, and Romannucci-Ross, Lola, eds. 1975. *Ethnic Identity.* Palo Alto: Mayfield Publishing Co.
DeVos, George, and Wagatsuma, Hiroshi 1967. *Japan's Invisible Race: Caste, Culture and Personality.* Berkeley: University of California Press.
Erickson, Eric. 1968. *Identity: Youth and Crisis.* New York: Norton.
Festinger, Leon. 1956. *When Prophesy Fails.* Minneapolis: University of Minnesota Press.
Flavell, John. 1963. *The Developmental Psychology of Jean Piaget.* New York: Van Nostrand.

Index

Abate, Mario, 30
Abbott, Kenneth A., 16, 74–100, 350
Abegg, Lily, 75
Abel, Theodora, 59
Abel, Theodore M., 88
Aberle, D., 178
Aborigines, Australian, 272–73
Abou-Zeid, A. M., 150
Acculturation:
    between-group processes, 344–46
    defined, 2
    differential role expectations and, 353–54
    ethnic identity and, 3–4
    in individual and society, 2–4
    intragroup or intrasocietal segmentations, 347–48
    intrapersonal processes involved in, 348–54
    political defeat and, 271–72
    reference group theory and, 352–53
    time sequence in adaptive, 346–47
Ackroyd, Joyce, 38–39
Adaptation:
    differential role expectations, 353–54
    differential socialization, 349–50
    differing patterns of, 283–85
    distinction between adjustment and, 4–8, 285–86
    effects of ethnicity on, 283–91
    reference group theory, 352–53
    selective permeability, 350–51
    social self-identity, 354–59
    See also Urbanization
Adjustment:
    differential role expectations, 353–54
    differential socialization, 349–50
    difficulties of studying, 286–91
    distinction between adaptation and, 4–8, 285–86
    effects of ethnicity on, 283–91
    reference group theory, 352–53
    selective permeability, 350–51
    social self-identity, 354–59
    urbanization and, 214–32
        conceptualization and measurement of, 217–22
        education, 222–23, 228
        factory experience, 224–26, 228–29
        geographical and occupational mobility, 227–28
        mass media, 226–27
Admiralty Islands, *see* Melanesia
Afghanistan, 320
Africa:
    agriculture in, 113
    change, adaptation to, 131–35
        economic incentives, 133–34
        intergenerational differences in acculturation, 134
        mobility, 132–33
        scarcity of resources, 135
    competition in, 122, 126, 133–34
    education in, 124, 133–34
    family in, 113–14
        age and sex hierarchy, 119–20
        material transactions and, 122–23
        mobility and, 132–33
        social distance between age and sex groups, 116–19
    kinship system in, 113–14, 132–33
    personality patterns in, 106–07, 112–35

362 Index

Africa (continued)
    age and sex hierarchy, 119–20
    functional diffuseness of authority relations, 123–25
    material transaction in interpersonal relations, 121–23
    reactions to disaster and difficulty, 125–27
    separation anxiety, absence of, 127–30
    social distance between age and sex groups, 116–19
    thought, concreteness of, 130–31
    uniformities and variations in, 115–31
    women in, 118, 120
Age segregation, 116–19
Age–sex hierarchies, 119–20
Agriculture:
    in Africa, 113
    in India, 316
    in Japan, 37, 253–54
Ainsworth, Mary D. S., 128–29
Aitutake Island, 108–09
Alcoholism, 271
Algeria:
    urbanization in, 146–47
    women in, 149–50
Amearu, concept of, 33–34
American Indians, 234, 280–81, 284, 347, 357, 358
    acculturation and, 270–71
    effects of modernization on, 212, 243–45
Amin, Qasim, 329–30
Ammar, Hamed, 143
Anderson, J. N. D., 327
Antoun, Richard T., 150, 328
Arab world, 107, 108, 109
    child rearing, 145, 149, 153
    divisiveness, 140–47
    effects of personality on culture change, 147–54
    family in, 108, 109, 143–49
    kinship system, 108, 109, 143–47
    urbanization, 146–47
    women in, 143–45, 148–53, 276, 323–40
        colonial encounter, 328–31
        contemporary realities, 332–38
        divorce, 328, 336–37, 338
        education, 329, 331, 337
        emancipation movement, 329–31
        heritage from past, 325–28
        literature, 332–36
Arberry, A. J., 326
Argentina, individual modernization in, 216–32
Arkoff, Abe, 98
Asiatic Mode of Production, 48
Atomization, 28
Australian aborigines, 272–73
Authority relationships, functional diffuseness of, 123–25
Ayoub, Millicent, 145
Azer, A., 337

Balazs, Etienne, 48, 49
Bangladesh, 320
Barnett, Milton L., 95
Barry, Herbert H., 113
Barth, Fredrik, 350
Batak society, 234–51, 357
    approaches to culture change, 238–43
    effects of modernization on, 212, 243–45
    history and culture, 235–38
    theory of change, 246–51
Bateson, Gregory, 9, 105
Bauer, Raymond, 274
Beggars' democracy, concept of, 49
Bellah, Robert N., 32
Bendix, Reinhard, 22
Benedict, Burton, 149
Benedict, Ruth, 137, 138, 261
Bennett, John, 32
Berger, Morroe, 323
Bermann, Gregoris, 70
Berndt, Ronald M., 163
Berque, Jacques, 323
Berreman, Gerald D., 243, 277, 294–320, 324, 339, 348, 353
Berrien, F. K., 30
Between-group processes of response to change, 344–46
Bill, James, 140
Bismarck Archipelago, *see* Melanesia
Blacks, American, 281–82, 284, 287, 288, 290, 301
Blumer, Herbert, 234
Bodde, Derk, 47, 48, 80, 81
Bourdieu, Pierre, 144, 149–50
Bowman, Karl M., 69

Bradburn, Norman, 220
Brazil, 153
Breastfeeding, 6, 53
Bride price, 114, 122
Bruner, Edward M., 211–12, 213, 234–51, 351, 357
Buddhism, 57, 94
Burch, Thomas K., 24–25
Burma, 349
   child rearing, 198
   colonialism, effect of, 107–08

California Psychological Inventory (CPI), 74–80, 84–85, 89–90, 97, 99
Cameron, Richard M., 93
Cargo cult, 157–203, 350
   character of European contact, 162–67, 180–81
   general characteristics, 160–72
   paranoid ethos and, 191–201
   pathomimetic behavior, 184–91
      cognitive dissonance, 187–91
      metastable state, 186–91
   psychocultural factors, 191–97
      cultural features and adaptive practices, 193–95
      networks and wealth assemblage, 195–97
   theoretical explanations of, 168–83
      cognitive inconsistency and stress, 181–83
      deprivation theory, 178–79
      oppression theory, 172–79
      psychological stress, theories of, 179–81
      sociohistorical explanations, 168–72
   as "type-response," 157, 159–60
Caste system, *see* India, social mobility and change in
Caudill, William, 6, 9–10, 13–15, 18–41, 208, 259, 285, 349
Cawte, J. E., 272–73
Chance, Norman A., 243
Chaney, David, 96
Chang Shiao-chun, 96
Chen, Theodore Hsi-en, 95
Ch'en Li-fu, 94, 95
Chi Ch'ao-ting, 49
Chiang Kai-shek, 81, 84
Chien-hou Hwang, 88

Child rearing:
   in Arab world, 145, 149, 153
   in Burma, 198
   in China, 53–55, 59, 74, 83–86, 96
   in Japan, 39–40, 260–61
Chile, individual modernization in, 216–32
Chin, Ai-li S., 52, 97
China, 45–71, 74–100, 320
   child rearing in, 53–55, 59, 74, 83–86, 96
   cultural continuity and change, 16, 60–71
   class and status, 16, 65–67
   family, 64–65, 66–67
   mental health, 69–70, 73
   People's Republic of China and, 60, 62–70
   political changes, 63–64
   Republic of China and, 60–62
   youth, 67–69
Cultural Revolution, 48, 54, 65, 69
   culture and society, basic generalizations of, 46–50
   divorce in, 84
   drug addiction in, 53
   education in, 48, 89–90
   environment, alteration of, 47–48
   family in, 48, 64–65, 66–67, 95–98
   intellectuals in, 66
   kinship system in, 48, 49, 348
   mental health in, 69–70, 93
   personality, 15, 16–17, 47, 50–60, 74–100
      adaptation and adjustment in, conclusions about, 94–100
      Chinese Family Life Study, 74–80, 84–85, 87, 89–90, 97, 99
      dependency and orality, 51–55, 86, 88
      dependency and sociocultural behavior, 58–60
      family and, 81, 95–98
      holistic perception, 16, 89–91
      intragroup dependency and self-restraint, 16, 86–89
      projection, 91, 92–94
      sexuality and orality, 55–58
      socialization of children, 74, 83–86
      somatization, 91, 92
      value system, 80–86
   private property in, 63–64

Cultural Revolution (continued)
    social structure, 49–50, 65–67
    suicide in, 93
    women in, 50, 51, 54–55, 56–57, 66–67, 84, 85, 93
    youth in, 66, 67–69, 84–85, 96
Chinese Americans, 74–80, 84–85, 87, 89–90, 97, 99
Chinese Family Life Study, 74–80, 84–85, 87, 89–90, 97, 99
Chu, Godwin C., 51–52
Chu, Solomon S., 97
Chu Hsi, 82, 94
Cities, *see* Urbanization
Civil Code of Japan, 38
Clignet, Remi, 131
Cognitive dissonance, 182, 187–191
Cognitive inconsistency, 181–183
Cohn, Bernard S., 308
Cole, Allen B., 94
Cole, Michael, 130
Collectivity vs. individuality, 95–98
Communism, in India, 314, 318
Competition, in Africa, 122, 126, 133–34
Confucianism, 57, 81–82, 94, 265
Crime, in Japan, 261–63
Cultural continuity:
    in China, 16, 60–71
        class and status, 16, 65–67
        family, 64–65
        mental health, 69–70
        political changes, 63–64
        youth, 67–69
    in Japan, 18–41
        national characteristics, 26–30
        overview, 19–26
        psychological and behavioral characteristics, 14, 26–30
        psychological implications of, 31–40
Cultural relativism, 137–39
Cultural Revolution, 48, 54, 65, 69
Culture:
    ethos of, 9, 10, 13, 105
    thematic approach to, 49–50
    See also names of countries

Dai, Bingham, 82, 88, 93
Dalit Panthers, 301, 313–14, 318
Damle, Y. B., 297

Daniels, Robert E., 131
Dawson, Raymond, 75
Delinquency, in Japan, 261–63
Dependency, in Chinese personality, 52–55, 58–60
Deprivation theory of cargo cults, 178–79
Des Villettes, Jacqueline, 150
Deshmukh, M. B., 215–16
DeVos, George, 1–11, 23, 34–35, 54, 144, 150, 243, 250, 263, 264, 277, 285, 324, 325, 346, 350, 355
Differential role expectations, 353–54
Differential socialization, 274, 349–50
Dissonance reduction, 351
Divisiveness, Arab, 140–47
Divorce:
    in Arab world, 328, 336–37, 338
    in China, 84
    in Egypt, 336–37, 338
    in Japan, 259–60
Dobuan people, 137
Dodd, Peter C., 145, 153, 328
Dohrenwend, Barbara S., 287
Dohrenwend, Bruce P., 287–88
Doi, L. Takeo, 33–34, 261, 265
Doob, Leonard, 131
Dore, R. P., 37
Dozier, E. P., 245
Drug addiction, in China, 53
Dubetsky, Allen, 145
Durkheim, Emile, 222, 228
Dushkin, Lelah, 309
Dysfunction, concept of, 138, 139

East Pakistan, individual modernization in, 216–32
Eberhard, Wolfram, 53, 55, 58, 88
Economic development:
    in India, 275, 316, 318
    in Melanesia, 167
Economism, 64
Edgerton, Robert B., 131
Education:
    in Africa, 124, 133–34
    in Batak society, 236
    in China, 48, 89–90
    in Egypt, 329, 331, 337
    in India, 317
    in Japan, 35, 265
Egypt, 107

Index 365

divorce in, 336–37, 338
family in, 144
welfare services, 146
women in, *see* Arab world, women in
Eisenstadt, S. N., 22
El Said, Mrs. Amina, 335–36, 340
El Sayed, H., 326
Elvin, Mark, 47
Emancipation movements, in India, 313–15
Emulation, 275, 297–98
Environment, alteration of, in China, 47–48
Erickson, Eric, 359
Ethnic groups, American, 269, 270, 278–91
adaptation and adjustment, 283–91
diversity of, 278–83
Ethnic identity, 271, 344, 345, 354–56
acculturation and, 3–4
historical vicissitudes and, 355–56
identity betrayal, 358–59
manipulation of, 356–57
modes of maintenance, 356
See also names of countries
Ethnocentrism, 138
Evans-Pritchard, E. E., 132

Factory experience, psychosomatic symptoms and, 224–26, 228–29
Fahmy, Aida I., 327
Fallers, Lloyd, 238, 239
Family:
in Africa, 113–114
age and sex hierarchy, 119–20
material transactions and, 122–23
mobility and, 132–33
social distance between age and sex groups, 116–19
in Arab world, 108, 109, 143–49
basic structures of, 23–25, 37
in Batak society, 236, 248
in China, 48, 64–65, 66–67, 95–98
Chinese Family Life Study, 74–80, 84–85, 87, 89–90, 97, 99
in Egypt, 144
in India, 305
in Japan, 7, 25, 29, 36, 37–40, 257, 259–61
in Lebanon, 148–49
in Melanesia, 197–99
Farsoun, Samih K., 148–49

Feld, Sheila, 218
Fenz, Walter D., 98
Festinger, Leon, 171, 179, 182, 189, 190, 350
Finney, Joseph C., 91–92
Firth, R., 200
Fisher, J. L., 30
Fiske, Adele, 313
Flavell, John, 351
Fong, Stanley L. M., 100
Forget, Nelly, 151–52
Fortune, R., 198, 200
Fox, Lorene K., 118, 120, 122
French, J. P. R., Jr., 220, 228
Freud, Anna, 127
Freud, Sigmund, 20
Fried, Morton H., 15–16, 45–71, 58, 84
Friedl, Ernestine, 245
Fuller, Anne H., 143
Functional diffuseness of authority relations, 123–25

Galanter, Marc, 309
Gallin, Bernard, 96
Gamō, M., 254
Ganda people, 128–29
Gardner, R., 163
Geiger, H. Jack, 218, 223
Gestalt school, 14
Glazer, Nathan, 270, 275, 278–91, 352, 357–58
Goode, William J., 23–24, 323
Goodnow, Robert E., 89
Gough, Harrison G., 76
Gough, Kathleen, 295, 314
Gould, Harold, 303
Graves, Theodore, 270–74, 358
Greeley, Andrew, 290
Group mobility-striving, in India, 306–10
Gulick, John, 8, 107–09, 137–54
Gulick, Margaret E., 153
Gurin, Gerald, 218
Gusfield, Joseph R., 22
Gutkind, P. C. W., 250

Hadar, Josef, 22
Hall, Edward T., 19
Han Yu-shan, 47, 48
Hansen, Henry Harold, 150
Harkabi, Y., 142

Harvard Project on the Social and Cultural Aspects of Development, 216
Hausa people, 106, 117
Hawaiians, 346–47, 349
Hearn, Lafcadio, 27–28
Heider, H., 163
Hellersberg, Elizabeth F., 89
Herberg, Will, 280
Heyer, Virginia, 56
Hibbett, Howard, 30
Hodge, Robert W., 21
Hoebel, E. A., 49
Holistic perception, 16, 89–91
Hollingshead, A. B., 286
Hong-min Chu, 92
Hsien Rin, 52, 55, 87, 92
Hsu, Francis L. K., 15, 49–50, 53, 58–59, 81, 83–84
Hsu Jing, 94
Hsun-tzu, 82
Hu Hsien-chin, 98
Huang, Lucy, 98
Hughes, Charles C., 243

Iatmul culture, 105
Ibo people, 106
India, 270, 274–75
  agriculture in, 316
  communism in, 314, 318
  economic development in, 275, 316, 318
  education in, 317
  family in, 305
  individual modernization in, 216–32
  industrialization in, 303, 315
  reform in, 312
  religion in, 299–300
  secularization in, 315
  social mobility and change in, 294–320, 348
    consensus and conflict, 310–15
    contemporary traditional India, 295–302
    emulation and, 275, 297–98
    group mobility striving, 306–10
    power and, 298–301
    rural/urban continuity and change, 302–06
    Sanskritization, 275, 295, 297–98, 317, 353
    solidarity, 301–02
  urbanization in, 302, 315
Industrialization, 13, 207–10
  in India, 303, 315
  in Japan, 36, 208
  socialization and, 209–10
  See also Urbanization
Inglis, J., 168
Inkeles, Alex, 21, 211, 213, 214–32, 274, 346, 347
Intellectuals, in China, 66
Intragroup dependency, 16, 86–89
Iran, 153, 320
  political elite of, 139–40
Iraq, women in, 150
Isaacs, Harold, 303
Israel, 140, 142
  individual modernization in, 216–32
Italian Americans, 279, 280, 289–90

Japan, 22, 349
  agriculture in, 37, 253–54
  child rearing in, 39–40, 260–61
  crime and delinquency in, 261–63
  divorce in, 259–60
  ecology, 32–33
  education in, 35, 265
  family in, 7, 25, 29, 36, 37–40, 257, 259–61
  historical trends, 31–32
  industrialization in, 36, 208
  marriage in, 14, 38, 265
  mass media in, 255
  personality, 14, 26–30
  retirement in, 40
  social change and cultural continuity, 18–41
    national characteristics, 26–30
    overview, 19–26
    psychological and behavioral characteristics, 14, 26–30
    psychological implications of, 31–40
  social structure, 33–36
  suicide in, 254, 257, 263
  unions in, 35
  urbanization in, 33, 37, 212, 213, 253–67
    crime and delinquency, 261–63
    divorce, 259–60
    family and, 257, 259–61

generational rift, 263–67
overpopulation and congestion, 257–58
rural life, changes in, 253–57
social change, 259–63
women in, 38–39, 257, 259–60, 264
youth in, 254, 255, 261–62, 263–67
Japanese Americans, 285, 287, 352, 354
Jews, American, 279–80, 286–89, 357–58
Jordan, women in, 150

Kan Yu-Wei, 81
Kardiner, Abram, 243
Kast, Stanislas V., 218
Kennedy, John G., 147
Kennedy, Ruby Jo Reeves, 280
Kenya, 117, 120
Khalaf, Samir, 149
Khatchadourian, Haig, 145
Khuri, Fuad I., 152
Kiev, Ari, 70
Kinship system, 109–10
  in Africa, 113–14, 132–33
  in Arab world, 108, 109, 143–47
  in Batak society, 236, 248, 348
  in China, 48, 49, 348
  in Melanesia, 197–99
Kishner, Ira, 133
Klein, Nancy, 131
Kluckhohn, Clyde, 5, 91
Kohn, Melvin L., 22
Kornhauser, Arthur, 218, 219
Koyama, Takashi, 37–38
Kuhlen, Raymond G., 98–99
Kurokawa, Minako, 287
Kuwata, Y., 259, 260

La Barre, Weston, 159
Lanternari, V., 159, 172
Lattimore, Owen, 49
Law of diminishing administrative returns, concept of, 49
Lawrence, P., 159
Lebanon, 146
  family in, 148–49
  women in, 150, 151, 152
Lee, C. J., 271
Lee, E. S., 286
Leighton, Alexander, 218, 219, 223
Lenski, Gerhard, 290

Lerner, Daniel, 208, 323
Lesser, Gerald, 290
LeVine, Robert A., 106–07, 112–35
Levy, Howard S., 57
Levy, Marion J., 24
Levy, Robert, 107–10, 345, 346, 347, 349
Levy, Reuben, 327, 328
Lewis, Oscar, 215, 250
Li, Anita King-fun, 98
Liang Shu-ming, 94
Lifton, Robert, 69
Light, Ivan, 284
Lin Piao, 70
Lin Tsung-yi, 70, 82, 93
Liu, William T., 82, 96
Liu Shao-ch'i, 70
Lo, Irene, 85–86, 96
Lorenz, Konrad, 20
Lung Kuan-hai, 96
Lung Kuan-hai, 96
Lutfi-al-Sayyid, A., 330

Maḥfūẓ, Naguib, 332–33
Male-female relationship, *see* Women
Malik, Harji, 313, 314
Malzberg, B., 286
Manus, *see* Cargo cults
Mao Tse-tung, 45–46, 52, 54–55, 57, 62–63, 66, 68, 81, 85
Marriage, 132
  in Japan, 14, 38, 265
  in Melanesia, 167
Marsella, A. J., 94
Maruyama, Masao, 28
Masai, 117
Mass media, 226–27, 255
Materialism, 346
  in Africa, 121–23
  in Melanesia, 193–94
Matsubara, J., 257
Matsumoto, Misao, 40
McClelland, David C., 97, 194
Mead, Margaret, 108, 158, 356
Mehnert, Klaus, 29
Melanesia:
  conversion, 164–65
  defined, 157
  economic change in, 167
  family in, 197–99
  kinship system in, 197–99

Melanesia (continued)
  marriage in, 167
  materialism in, 193–94
  multiethnicity in, 194–95
  occupational change in, 167, 173
  pacification, 164–66
  Paliau Movement, 159, 168, 169, 177, 182, 190
  paranoid ethos in, 191–201
  race relations in, 173–74
  religion in, 164–65, 166–67, 186, 188, 199–201
  socialization in, 197–98, 201
  wealth and consumption, concepts of, 196
  women in, 167, 198–99
  See also Cargo cults
Mencius, 82, 94
Mental health, 286
  in China, 69–70, 93
  definition of, 6
  See also Adjustment
Merit examination system, Chinese, 48
Merton, Robert K., 178
Metastable state, cargo cults and, 186–91
Metzger, Thomas, 54
Mexican Americans, 280, 284, 285
Micronesia, 107, 110, 159
Middle East, *see* Arab world
Mien-tzu (face), concept of, 98
Migration, urban, *see* Urbanization
Miner, Horace, 144, 147, 150, 277
Mitchell, Robert E., 83, 85–86, 96
Mitsukawa, T., 257, 259, 260
Modernization, 20–22, 207–10
  American Indians and, 243–45
  in Batak society, 234–51
  See also Urbanization
Moore, Wilbert E., 8
Morioka, Kiyomi, 39
Morocco, 107
  dyadic relationships in, 145–46
  political elite of, 147
  women in, 151–52
Mother-child relationship, *see* Child rearing
Moynihan, Daniel P., 281, 284, 290
M'rabet, Fadela, 150
Muensterberger, Warner, 52, 53, 86, 88, 133
Muhyi, Ibrahim A., 152
Multiethnicity, in Melanesia, 194–95

Munroe, Robert L., 131
Murdock, George P., 113

Naka, H., 263
Nakamura, Hajime, 29
Nakane, Chie, 33, 264, 265
Nasif, Malak Hifni, 330
Nassiakou, Maria, 30
National character, *see* Personality
Nazi Germany, 138
Nelson, Cynthia, 8, 108, 276, 323–40
Neo-Confucianism, 57
Nerlove, Sara B., 131
New Caledonia, *see* Melanesia
New Guinea, 105, 137, 157
  See also Melanesia
New Hebrides, *see* Melanesia
Nigeria, 106–07, 120
  individual modernization in, 216–32
Nishihira, Shigeki, 34
Nitobe, Inazo, 28
Niyekawa, Agnes M., 29
Norbeck, Edward, 20
Nouacer, Khadidja, 152
Nuer people, 132
Nyakyusa people, 117

Occupational change, in Melanesia, 167, 173
Odaka, Kunio, 34, 35
O'Hara, Albert, 83
Ōhara, K., 257
Okuda, M., 254, 258
Ōmura, R., 256
Omvedt, Gail, 313
Oppression theory of cargo cults, 172–79
Orality, Chinese, 52–58
Ovesey, Lionel, 243
Owen, Constance, 131

Padgaonkar, Dileep, 313
Pakistan, 320
Paliau Movement, 159, 168, 169, 177, 182, 190
Papanek, Hanna, 150–51
Paranoia, 92–93
Paranoid ethos, 158
  in Melanesia, 191–201
Park, Robert, 215
Passin, Herbert, 31, 33
Patai, R., 323

Pathomimetic behavior, 7–8, 346
  in cargo cults, 184–91
Peacock, James L., 244
Pearlin, Leonard I., 22
Peer group socialization, 352–53
People's Republic of China, *see* China
Permeability, selective, 350–51, 352
Personality, 2, 3
  in Africa, 106–07, 112–35
    age and sex hierarchy, 119–20
    functional diffuseness of authority relations, 123–25
    material transaction in interpersonal relations, 121–23
    reactions to disaster and difficulty, 125–27
    separation anxiety, absence of, 127–30
    social distance between age and sex groups, 116–19
    thought, concreteness of, 130–31
    uniformities and variations in, 115–31
  approaches to, 14
  in Arab world, 147–54
  in China, 15, 16–17, 47, 50–60, 74–100
    adaptation and adjustment in, conclusions about, 94–100
    Chinese Family Life Study, 74–80, 84–85, 87
    dependency and orality, 51–55, 86, 88
    dependency and sociocultural behavior, 58–60
    family and, 81, 95–98
    holistic perception, 16, 89–91
    intragroup dependency and self-restraint, 16, 86–89
    projection, 91, 92–94
    sexuality and orality, 55–58
    socialization of children, 74, 83–86
    somatization, 91, 92
    value system, 80–86
  in Japan, 14, 26–30
Peskin, Harvey, 100
Petersen, Karen K., 144, 146, 148, 149
Petersen, William, 284
Philosophical concepts, Chinese, 80–86
Piaget, Jean, 351
Plath, David W., 30, 39, 40

Podmore, David, 96
Political changes, in China 63–64
Political leadership, 210
Polk, William R., 323
Polygamy, 109
Polygyny, 113, 114
Polynesia, 107–10, 159, 194, 345, 346–47
Power, social mobility and, 298–301
Price-Williams, Douglas, 20
Primogeniture, 38
Private property, in China, 63–64
Privatization, 28
Projection, 91, 92–94
Prothro, E. Terry, 153
Psychological stress, cargo cults and, 179–81
Psychosomatic symptoms:
  education and, 222–23, 228
  effect of geographical and occupational mobility on, 227–28
  factory experience and, 224–26, 228–29
  urbanization and, 223–24
Puerto Ricans, 280, 284, 285, 287

Quddus, Ehasan Abdul, 333–34
Quigley, Carroll, 142–43

Race relations, in Melanesia, 173–74
Radwan, A. A., 328, 329
Rainwater, Lee, 290
Ram, Mohan, 314
Ramsey, Charles E., 21
Raratonga Island, 108–09
Rasheed, B., 330
Ratnavale, David M., 94
Redlich, F. C., 286
Reference group theory, 270, 271, 352–53
Reich, Charles A., 266
Reischauer, Edwin, 31
Relative deprivation, cargo cults and, 178–79
Religion:
  in India, 299–300
  in Melanesia, 164–65, 166–67, 186, 188, 199–201
Republic of China, *see* China
Retirement, in Japan, 40
Richards, Audrey, 121
Rinder, Irwin D., 286

Romanucci-Ross, Lola, 3, 166, 346, 355
Roos, Leslie L., 22
Rosen, Bernard, 153
Rosen, Lawrence, 145–46
Rosenfeld, Henry, 144, 149
Ross, Alan Q., 242
Rossi, Peter, 21
Rowe, William L., 300, 303, 308
Ruey, Yih-fu, 82
Rural life, in Japan, 33, 36–37, 253–57

Sadat, Anwar el, 338
Sadat, Mrs. Jehan, 338
Sadawy, Nawal, 334–35, 339
Sadomasochism, 127–29
Sahlins, M., 199
Sakamoto, J., 255
Salaff, Janet W., 84
Saleh, Saneya, 325
Samoa, 108
Sanskritization, 275, 295, 297–98, 317, 353
Sargeant, W., 179
Saunders, Lucie Wood, 149
Sawyer, Jack, 113
Scarr, Harry A., 23, 27
Schneider, Jane, 143
Schram, Stuart, 46, 52
Schutz, Alfred, 324
Schwartz, Theodore, 7–8, 13–14, 107, 109–11, 157–203, 346, 350, 351, 356
Scofield, Robert W., 59, 93
Scotch, Norman A., 218, 223
Scott, William, 217
Seclusion of women, 325–26, 331, 335
Secularization, 209, 315
Seidensticker, Edward, 28
Selective permeability, 350–51, 352
Self-restraint, 16, 86–89
Sentimentality, 127–30
Separation anxiety, 127–30
Sex segregation, 116–19
Sexuality, Chinese, 55–58
Shaman, 7, 8
Sha'rawi, Hoda, 330–31, 333
Sharma, H. P., 315
Sharma, K. N., 305
Shikata, T., 260
Sidel, Ruth, 51
Singh, Paras Nath, 95
Slotkin, James S., 215

Smith, David H., 211, 213, 214–32
Smith, Henrietta T., 40
Smith, Robert J., 21, 25, 37
Snow, Edgar, 55, 68
Social change, defined, 8
Social mobility in India, 294–320, 348
    consensus and conflict, 310–15
    contemporary traditional India, 295–302
    emulation and, 275, 297–98
    group mobility striving, 306–10
    power and, 298–301
    rural urban continuity and change, 302–06
    Sanskritization, 295, 297–98, 317
    solidarity, 301–02
Social self-identity, see Ethnic identity
Social structure, 13, 14, 18, 20–26
    in China, 49–50, 65–67
    in Japan, 33–36
Socialization:
    in Chinese children, 74, 83–86
    industrialization and, 209–10
    kinship organization and, 109–10
    in Melanesia, 197–98, 201
    peer group, 352–53
Sofue, Takao, 209, 212, 253–67
Solidarity, social mobility and, 301–02
Solomon, Richard, 54, 86
Solomon Islands, see Melanesia
Somatization, 91, 92
Sorcery, 126, 135, 199, 272, 273
Sorokin, Pitirim, 215
Specialization, 208
Spindler, George D., 243
Spiro, Melford, 107, 198
Sri Lanka, 320
Srinivas, M. N., 295, 298
Srole, Leo, 218, 284, 286, 287
Stanner, W., 168, 179
Status emulation, 297–98, 352–53
Status enhancement, 4, 356–57
Stodolsky, Susan Silverman, 290
Stone, I. F., 140
Stoodley, Bartlett H., 94, 96
Stouffer, Samuel A., 178, 218
Stover, Leon, 58
Stress, 125–27
    cognitive inconsistency and, 182–83
    rational or irrational responses, 179–81
Strodtbeck, Fred L., 284, 289, 290

Structural-functionalism, 138, 139
Sudan, 117, 132
Suicide:
  in China, 93
  in Japan, 254, 257, 263
Sumatra, see Batak society
Sun Chin-wan, 59
Swaddling, 6, 86
Syria, 107

Taira, Koji, 35
Tanaka, Yusumasa, 30
Tannous, Afif I., 144
Taoism, 57, 94
Technology, 81, 208
Tepoztecan peasants, 215
"Thanatosis," phenomenon of, 273
Thought, concreteness of, 130–31
Tillion, Germaine, 150
Toba Batak, see Batak society
Tominaga, Ken'ichi, 35
Torgerson, Fernando G., 93
Traiman, Donald J., 21
Triandis, Harry C., 30
Tsang, Annie, 83
Tseng, Wen-shing, 82, 94
Tsung-yi Lin, 92
Tung Pien, 66
Turkey, 145
Turner, Ralph H., 240, 297

Uganda, 128–29
Unions, in Japan, 35
Urbanization, 207–67
  adjustment, 214–32
    conceptualization and measurement of, 217–22
    education, 222–23, 228
    factory experience, 224–26, 228–29
    geographical and occupational mobility, 227–28
    mass media, 226–27
  in Arab world, 146–47
  as influence on adjustment and adaptation, 211–13
  in Japan, 33, 37, 212, 213, 253–67
    crime and delinquency, 261–63
    divorce, 259–60
    family and, 257, 259–61
    generational rift, 263–67
    overpopulation and congestion, 257–58
    rural life, changes in, 253–57
    social change, 259–63
    suicide, 254, 257, 263
  See also Modernization

Vailala Madness, 188
Valentine, C., 173
Value dominance, 174, 175, 201
Value system, Chinese, 80–86
van Gulik, R. H., 57–58
Vassiliou, Vasso, 30
Vatuk, Sylvia, 303
Veiling of women, 325–26, 328, 330, 331, 335
Veroff, J., 218
Vinacke, W. Edgar, 95
Vogel, Eyra F., 35, 37

Wagatsuma, Hiroshi, 34–35, 277, 348, 355
Wallace, Anthony F. C., 50–51, 179, 182, 183, 184, 187, 310
Wallis, Wilson D., 186
Warner, W. Lloyd, 284, 285, 353
Waterbury, John, 147
Watsuji, Tetsuro, 28–29
Weakland, John H., 52, 55, 58, 88, 91
Weber, Max, 49
Weinstein, Helen, 26, 39
White, Lucia, 214–15
White, Morton, 214–15
Williams, F. E., 179, 188
Williams, Herbert H., 144–45, 146, 149
Williams, Judith R., 146, 149, 151
Wilson, Richard, 85, 86
Witchcraft, 5, 126, 135
Witt, Shirley Hill, 243
Wittfogel, Karl A., 48, 49, 64
Wolf, Margery, 51, 54, 86
Women:
  in Africa, 118, 120
  in Arab world, 108, 143–45, 148–53, 276, 323–40, 348
    colonial encounter, 328–31
    contemporary realities, 332–38
    divorce, 328, 336–37, 338
    education, 329, 331, 337
    emancipation movement, 329–31
    heritage from past, 325–28
    literature, 332–36

Women (continued)
  in China, 50, 51, 54–55, 56–57, 66–67, 84, 85, 93
  in Japan, 38–39, 257, 259–60, 264
  in Melanesia, 167, 198–99
  Zulu, 272
Worsley, Peter, 194

Yancey, William, 290
Yang, 56
Yang, K. C., 81
Yang, Martin, 83
Yang Kuo-shu, 59, 60, 87
Yeh Eng-kung, 93
Yin, 56
Yokoyama, S., 264

Yoruba people, 106, 119, 218
Yoshida, Teigo, 30
Young, Marilyn, 51
Youssef, Nadia, 151, 153
Youth:
  in China, 66, 67–69, 84, 96
  in Japan, 254, 255, 261–62, 263–67
Yusuf, Hajji Shaykh, 327

Zaalouk, M., 337
Zaghlul, Saad, 330
Zanati, M. S., 326
Zelliot, Eleanor, 313
Zonis, Marvin, 139–40
Zulu people, 117, 218, 271–72

Contributors

Kenneth A. Abbott (D.S.W., University of California, Berkeley) is Associate Professor and Coordinator of Master's Research at the Smith College School for Social Work. He served as Project Head of the Chinese Family Life Study. He is the author of *Harmony and Individualism: Changing Chinese Psychosocial Functioning in Taipei and San Francisco.* In addition, he has contributed chapters to *Youth, Socialization, and Mental Health* (ed. Lebra) and to *Asian American Psychological Perspectives* (eds. Sue and Wagner).

Gerald D. Berreman (Ph.D., Cornell University) is Professor of Anthropology at the University of California, Berkeley. He has done field research in the Aleutian Islands, Himalayan villages, and urban areas of India. A former president of the Southwestern Anthropological Association and former member of the American Anthropological Association's Executive Board, he is the author of *Hindus of the Himalayas: Ethnography and Change* and of *Caste in the Modern World* (a module).

Edward M. Bruner (Ph.D., University of Chicago) is Professor of Anthropology at the University of Illinois, Urbana. He has contributed articles to the *American Anthropologist, Ethos, Southwestern Journal of Anthropology, Man,* and others. He has contributed chapters to *Urban Ethnicity* and to *Urban Anthropology.* In addition, he is a former Chairman of the Committee on Advanced Testing in Anthropology of the Educational Testing Service.

William A. Caudill (Ph.D., University of Chicago) was the director of the Socioenvironmental Laboratory of the National Institute of Mental Health at the time of his death in 1972. He was the author of *The Psychiatric Hospital as a Small Society* and coeditor of *Mental Health Research in Asia and the Pacific,* with Tsung-Yi Lin. He also contributed articles to numerous journals related to culture and personality research and theory.

Contributors

George A. DeVos (Ph.D., University of Chicago) is Professor of Anthropology at the University of California, Berkeley. A Ph.D. in psychology, he specializes in culture and personality, problems in mental health, and problems related to social change. He is the author of *Oasis and Casbah: Algerian Culture and Personality in Change*, with Horace Miner; *Japan's Invisible Race*, with Hīroshi Wagatsuma; *Socialization for Achievement;* and *Ethnic Identity*, with Lola Romannucci-Ross.

Morton H. Fried (Ph.D., Columbia University) is Professor of Anthropology at the University of California, Santa Barbara. He has contributed to numerous journals and is the author of *The Notion of Tribe, The Study of Anthropology,* and *The Evolution of Political Society.*

Nathan Glazer (Ph.D., Columbia University) is Professor of Education and Social Structure at Harvard University. He writes regularly for *Commentary Magazine, The Public Interest* and the *New York Times Sunday Magazine.* Among his publications are *The Lonely Crowd*, with David Riesman and Reuel Denney; *Faces in the Crowd*, with David Riesman; *The Social Basis of American Communism; Beyond the Melting Pot*, with Daniel P. Moynihan; and *Ethnicity: Theory and Experience*, with Daniel P. Moynihan (forthcoming).

John Gulick (Ph.D., Harvard University) is Professor of Anthropology at the University of North Carolina, Chapel Hill. In addition to his journal contributions, he is the author of *Social Structure and Culture Change in a Lebanese Village, Cherokees at the Crossroads, Tripoli: A Modern Arab City,* and *The Middle East: An Anthropological Perspective* (forthcoming). He is a former president of the Southern Anthropological Society.

Alex Inkeles (Ph.D., Columbia University) is Margaret Jacks Professor of Sociology and Education at Stanford University. He has authored numerous journal articles and has authored or coauthored several books including, *What Is Sociology, Social Change in Soviet Russia, The Soviet Citizen,* and *Becoming Modern,* with David Smith. He is vice-president of the American Sociological Society.

Robert A. LeVine (Ph.D., Harvard University) is Professor of Anthropology, Psychiatry, and Human Development at the University of Chicago. He has contributed articles to numerous journals and chapters to several books. He is the author of *Culture, Behavior and Personality;* and coauthor of *Nyansongo: A Gusii Community in Kenya,* with B.B. LeVine; and *Ethnocentrism: Theories of Conflict, Ethnic Attitudes and Group Behavior,* with Donald T. Campbell.

Cynthia Nelson (Ph.D., University of California, Berkeley) is Professor of Anthropology and Chairperson of the Department of Sociology, Anthropology, and Psychology at American University in Cairo. She has contributed to several journals and is the author of *The Waiting Village: Social Change in Rural Mexico* and editor of *The Desert and the Sown: Nomads in the Greater Society.*

David H. Smith (Ph.D., Harvard University) is Associate Professor of Sociology at Boston College. He is coauthor of *Becoming Modern,* with Alex Inkeles, author of *Latin American Student Activism,* and editor of *Voluntary Action Research.* He is president and current executive officer of the Association of Voluntary Action Scholars and the editor of the *Journal of Voluntary Action Research.*

Takao Sofue is Professor and Director of East Asian Studies at the National Museum of Ethnology in Ōsaka. He has done field work in Japanese villages, among Alaskan Eskimos, and among Navajo Indians in Arizona. He is the editor of *Nihonjin wa dō Kawattaka?* [How Have the Japanese Been Changed?] and of *Nihonjin: Bunkato to Seikaku* [The Japanese: Readings in Culture and Personality].